Alcohol and Drug Counselor (ADC) Exam Review

Christine Tina Chasek, PhD, LIMHP, LPC, LADC, MAC, has been a licensed addiction and mental health counselor for over 30 years and is currently a professor and chair of the Counseling Department at the University of Nebraska at Omaha. Dr. Chasek holds a doctorate in Counselor Education from the University of South Dakota with an emphasis in addiction counseling. She has worked in the addiction counseling field as a practitioner for 30 years and a supervisor for 20 years. Dr. Chasek was an International Certification and Reciprocity Consortium (IC&RC) delegate for the State of Nebraska for 5 years and served a 3-year term as the president of the International Association of Addiction and Offender Counselors. Dr. Chasek has published numerous articles and book chapters on addiction counseling and teaches addiction and mental health counseling courses at the graduate level. In 2019, Dr. Chasek was awarded the Oustanding Educator of the Year for her work in addiction counseling teaching and curriculum development. These experiences have prepared her well for understanding the academic and licensure requirements for addiction counselors.

Thomas Z. Maxson, MS, LIMHP, LADC, MAC, SAP, has been a licensed addiction and mental health counselor for 25 years. Mr. Maxson began his career working at a community mental health center providing outpatient, intensive outpatient, and halfway house counseling. He is currently co-owner of and counselor at Insight Counseling and Recovery, LLC. His specialty areas include evaluations and counseling of individuals with co-occurring disorders, personality disorders, and those involved in the criminal justice system. Mr. Maxson served on the Nebraska licensure board of Mental Health Practice for 10 years and currently serves on the Nebraska licensure board for Alcohol and Drug Counselors. In 2019, he was awarded the 2019 Nebraska Behavioral Health Professional of the Year for his work in providing counseling services. He is an adjunct faculty member at the University of Nebraska at Kearney where he developed and teaches addiction counseling classes in the Clinical Mental Health Counseling graduate program.

Contributor

Becca Moore, LIMHP, LADC, NCC, CCMHC, is a clinical supervisor at University of Nebraska Omaha, Omaha, Nebraska.

Alcohol and Drug Counselor (ADC) Exam Review

Christine Tina Chasek, PhD, LIMHP, LPC, LADC, MAC

Thomas Z. Maxson, MS, LIMHP, LADC, MAC, SAP

 SPRINGER PUBLISHING

Springer Publishing Company, LLC
902 Carnegie Center, Suite 140
Princeton, NJ 08540
www.springerpub.com

Acquisitions Editor: Jaclyn Koshofer
Content Development Editor: Julia Curcio
Compositor: Transforma
Production Editor: Dennis Troutman

ISBN: 978-0-8261-5315-9
e-book ISBN: 978-0-8261-5316-6
DOI: 10.1891/9780826153166

24 25 26 27 / 5 4 3 2 1

The author and the publisher of this Work have made every effort to use sources believed to be reliable to provide information that is accurate and compatible with the standards generally accepted at the time of publication. Because medical science is continually advancing, our knowledge base continues to expand. Therefore, as new information becomes available, changes in procedures become necessary. We recommend that the reader always consult current research and specific institutional policies before performing any clinical procedure or delivering any medication. The author and publisher shall not be liable for any special, consequential, or exemplary damages resulting, in whole or in part, from the readers' use of, or reliance on, the information contained in this book. The publisher has no responsibility for the persistence or accuracy of URLs for external or third-party Internet websites referred to in this publication and does not guarantee that any content on such websites is, or will remain, accurate or appropriate.

Library of Congress Cataloging-in-Publication Data

Names: Chasek, Christine Tina, author. | Maxson, Thomas Z., author.
Title: Alcohol and drug counselor (ADC) exam review / Christine Tina
   Chasek, Thomas Z. Maxson.
Description: New York : Springer Publishing Company, LLC, [2025] | Includes
   bibliographical references and index. | Summary: "While there are many
   educational paths to pick from when pursuing a career in addiction
   counseling, they all follow the most important first step on the career
   path: passing the national examination. Passing the national examination
   demonstrates that you have the requisite knowledge, skills, and
   competency needed to provide ethical care. While it can seem
   overwhelming and daunting, the key to passing the exam is to prepare.
   This book is designed to help you prepare for the International
   Certification and Reciprocity Consortium's (IC&RC) Alcohol and Drug
   Counselor (ADC) exam. The ADC exam is the final step in the
   credentialing process for candidates who desire to become licensed or
   certified as an addiction counselor in the states and/or jurisdictions
   that require this exam"-- Provided by publisher.
Identifiers: LCCN 2024013458 | ISBN 9780826153159 (paperback) | ISBN
   9780826153166 (e-book)
Subjects: MESH: Alcohol-Related Disorders | Substance-Related Disorders |
   Counseling | Examination Questions
Classification: LCC HV5125 | NLM WM 18.2 | DDC
   616.86/10076--dc23/eng/20240506
LC record available at https://lccn.loc.gov/2024013458

Contact sales@springerpub.com to receive discount rates on bulk purchases.

Publisher's Note: **New and used products purchased from third-party sellers are not guaranteed for quality, authenticity, or access to any included digital components.**

Printed in the United States of America by Gasch Printing.

The Alcohol and Drug Counselor (ADC) examination is developed by the International Certification and Reciprocity Consortium (IC&RC). The IC&RC does not endorse this resource, nor does it have a proprietary relationship with Springer Publishing Company.

Contents

Foreword   *ix*
Preface   *xi*
Acknowledgments   *xiii*
Pass Guarantee   *xv*

PART I.   ALCOHOL AND DRUG COUNSELOR EXAM OVERVIEW

Chapter 1.   Introduction to Addiction Counseling and the Alcohol and Drug Counselor   *1*

Chapter 2.   Test-Taking Strategies and Tips   *13*

PART II.   ALCOHOL AND DRUG COUNSELOR EXAM CORE CONTENT

Chapter 3.   Physiology and Psychopharmacology   *23*

Chapter 4.   Engaging the Client   *71*

Chapter 5.   Assessing the Client   *89*

Chapter 6.   Planning Treatment With the Client   *123*

Chapter 7.   Counseling With the Client   *153*

Chapter 8.   Legal, Ethical, and Professional Issues   *209*

PART III.   PRACTICE TEST

Chapter 9.   Practice Exam   *245*

Chapter 10.   Practice Exam: Answers   *269*

Index   *287*

Foreword

We are honored to have been asked to write a foreword for the first edition of the *Alcohol and Drug Counselor (ADC) Exam Review* by Christine Tina Chasek, PhD, LIMHP, LPC, LADC, MAC, and Thomas Z. Maxson, MS, LIMHP, LADC, MAC, SAP. We became aware of how gifted Dr. Chasek and Mr. Maxson are as counselor educators, supervisors, and alcohol and drug clinicians 15 years ago through our shared pursuits of training quality professional counselors. Dr. Chasek and Mr. Maxson consistently exceed the standards of excellence for client welfare and clinical training. They have provided course instruction, supervision, and mentoring for hundreds of counseling students and provisionally licensed alcohol and drug counselor supervisees. Comments from students have always mentioned their passion for addiction counseling, their pride in serving this population, their expert knowledge of the topic, and their ability to help students understand the material to effectively work with clients who struggle with an addiction.

Both Dr. Chasek and Mr. Maxson are well known and respected clinicians in the addiction counseling field. It is evident that this is their true passion. Dr. Chasek is a strong advocate on the state and national level for integrated substance use treatment, even training medical professionals about appropriate screening practices. They both have been members and leaders of state counseling boards (mental health and addiction) as well as actively engaged in workforce development efforts to improve and advocate for the addiction counseling profession.

Dr. Chasek was appointed to the Nebraska State Board of Alcohol and Drug Counseling Licensure (LADC Board) in 2012, elected as the vice chair in 2013 and chair in 2019. As the educational reviewer for the State of Nebraska, she also evaluated all applications for the required alcohol and drug counseling educational training and the clinical training requirements. Through her association with the Nebraska Alcohol and Drug Counseling Board, she became the Nebraska delegate for the International Certification and Reciprocity Consortium, the group responsible for developing and monitoring the credentialing and licensing processes for counselors in this field at the state, national, and international levels. Dr. Chasek advocates for Nebraska's interests while also advancing the field through clinical competency standards. For these efforts she was awarded the Robert Rencken Emerging Professional Leader Award by the American Counseling Association and the Addictions/Offender Educator Excellent Award from the International Association of Addictions and Offender Counselors (IAAOC).

Dr. Chasek is a prominent state leader for the Behavioral Health Education Center of Nebraska whose mission is to grow and enhance the mental and behavioral health workforce. She is the only addiction counseling member overseeing this important work, making sure the needs of the profession are addressed. As a member of the American Counseling Association (ACA), the IAAOC, and the Nebraska Division of Addiction and Offender Counselors which she helped start, Dr. Chasek is active in contributing to the research on practice and professional issues in addiction counseling through peer reviewed presentations and research collaboration with colleagues in the field. She is a sought-after presenter on addiction-related topics locally and on the state, regional, and national levels. She also regularly teams up with other faculty and professionals to present on issues related to offenders, substance use, and criminogenic needs nationwide.

Mr. Maxson has a unique clinical lens from his training as a psychology assistant and licensed professional counselor. He has been in clinical practice for 25 years with a specialty in substance use and justice-involved clients. He has mentored and supervised countless providers in the field and has a thriving outpatient practice where he serves a diverse client population. Mr. Maxson currently serves on the Nebraska State Board of Alcohol and Drug Counseling Licensure (LADC Board) and has been a member delegate for the International Certification and Reciprocity Consortium.

Mr. Maxson presents on addiction-related topics locally and on the state, regional, and national levels. He is well known for his expertise in issues related to substance use, the criminal justice system, and criminogenic needs. His expertise in the treatment of individuals with substance use disorders and his daily use of the 12 core functions lend rich content to the clinical practice and application parts of the book.

According to the Association for Addiction Professionals our country faces a dramatic treatment gap, an ever-increasing demand for services, and an addiction counseling professional shortage that will only worsen. This book by Dr. Chasek and Mr. Maxson augments learners' education and clinical training with a detailed blueprint of content to be mastered to pass the addiction exam. The book builds a strong addiction knowledge base as well as helping learners gain strategies and tips for test taking, an understanding of the addiction counseling specialization, a comprehensive examination of the four alcohol and drug counselor performance domains and the 12 core functions, and a practice test with answers that encourages learners to assess their own level of mastery and create a plan of study to address areas of further study. Through their continued commitment to the profession and their expertise with decades of experience as addiction counselors, educators, and supervisors, the authors provide a study guide that stands out from all the other resources and will contribute to enhancing the addiction counseling workforce. Dr. Chasek and Mr. Maxson bring a systemic perspective, integrative, and insightful approach to their book. They utilize effective and creative learning principles throughout the text to help the reader gain in-depth knowledge of scientific principles, evidence-based screening, assessment, treatment planning, therapeutic interventions, and referral processes necessary to pass this exam.

Thank you, Dr. Chasek and Mr. Maxson, for your extraordinary work in the addiction counseling field and best of luck to the exam readers.

Grace A. Mims, PhD, LIMHP
Counselor Educator and Supervisor
University of Nebraska at Kearney
Kearney, Nebraska

Marissa A. Davala, PhD, LIMHP, BC-TMH
Counselor Educator and Supervisor
University of Rochester
Rochester, New York

Preface

While there are many educational paths to pick from when pursuing a career in addiction counseling, they all follow the most important first step on the career path: passing the national examination which demonstrates that you have the requisite knowledge, skills, and competency needed to provide ethical care. While it can seem overwhelming and daunting, the key to passing the exam is to prepare. This book is designed to help you prepare for the International Certification and Reciprocity Consortium's (IC&RC) Alcohol and Drug Counselor (ADC) exam. The ADC exam is the final step in the credentialing process for candidates who desire to become licensed or certified as an addiction counselor in the states and/or jurisdictions that require this exam.

This book covers the IC&RC's performance domains and the core functions of an addiction counselor—the material needed to pass the ADC exam. Each chapter is organized around an identified performance domain and the core functions performed in that domain. Within each core function the global criteria are explored, further enhancing your understanding of the responsibilities of addiction counseling. The material is designed to help you remember the content by connecting it to real-world scenarios. It also helps you link your existing knowledge and educational training to the exam. Each chapter uses case studies, key concepts, and tips from the field to help you prepare and recall the information you have learned in your journey to become an addiction counselor. At the end of each chapter there are knowledge check questions with answers that will reinforce the key concepts in the chapter. These questions also help familiarize you with recalling information in the multiple-choice format that is used in the exam. To further prepare you, there is a full practice exam at the end of the book that closely aligns with the test you will encounter on testing day. Challenge yourself to take the full practice exam in the manner outlined in Chapter 1 to simulate what you will experience on testing day.

The book is arranged into eight chapters and the practice exam. Chapter 1, "Introduction to Addiction Counseling and the Alcohol and Drug Counselor" provides a brief history of the addiction counseling field, credentialing basics, the IC&RC, overview of the ADC exam, test scoring guidelines, and test-day logistics. Historical and conceptual foundations of addiction counseling and exams are covered as well as the licensing and credentialing process. The four performance domains and the 12 core functions are introduced and defined in this chapter. Chapter 2, "Test-Taking Strategies and Tips," covers testing anxiety, tips for studying, test-day logistics, and self-care plans. This is an important chapter to review and come back to when it's close to test day.

Chapter 3, "Physiology and Psychopharmacology," begins coverage of the core knowledge content needed for the exam in the performance domains and the core functions. This chapter covers Domain 1: Scientific Principles of Substance Use and Co-Occurring Disorders and the Screening and Assessment Core Functions. The models of addiction, neurobiology of substance use disorders, risk and protective factors, substances of misuse and their withdrawal effects, postacute withdrawal, and co-occurring mental health and medical disorders are included in this chapter. Medication-assisted treatment and other psychopharmacology topics related to addiction medicine are also included. This is an important chapter that builds the foundation and knowledge needed to work with clients and pass the exam.

Chapter 4, "Engaging the Client," begins the process of working with clients and covers Domain 2: Evidence-Based Screening and Assessment and the Screening, Intake, and Orientation Core Functions. In this chapter, you are introduced to Jim, a client you will follow throughout the book to help you understand and apply the concepts to the clinical work you will be doing in your practice. This approach reinforces the key concepts and helps you remember them for the exam.

Chapter 5, "Assessing the Client," continues with Domain 2: Evidence-Based Screening and Assessment and the Assessment Core Function. The ADC core content in assessing the client for services and level of care is covered.

Chapter 6, "Planning Treatment With the Client," continues to build the clinical treatment process by covering Domain 3: Evidence-Based Treatment, Counseling, and Referral and the Treatment Planning, Case Management, and Referral Core Functions. The process of screening, orienting, and admitting a client to treatment are included in this chapter. Jim's story continues with a full assessment in Chapter 5 and treatment planning in Chapter 6.

Chapter 7, "Counseling With the Client," is an important chapter covering counseling treatment theory and technique; individual, group, and family counseling; co-occurring disorders; special populations; relapse prevention and other topics covering Domain 3: Evidence-Based Treatment, Counseling, and Referral and the Counseling, Crisis Intervention, and Client Education Core Functions. Chapters 6 and 7 are especially important to review and come back to as the highest percentage of questions on the exam are in this content area. Further study resources are recommended in Chapter 7 to help ensure you are confident in your preparation in this area.

Chapter 8, "Legal, Ethical, and Professional Issues," examines the important areas of ethical and legal practice which are included in Domain 4: Professional, Ethical, and Legal Responsibilities and the Report and Record Keeping and the Consultation Core Functions. The ethical codes of addiction counseling and examples of ethical and legal conceptualization cases are presented in this chapter as well as the process of documenting a client's treatment from intake to discharge. This chapter encourages you to think about ethical decision-making and provides a model to help you understand the challenges you may face in the field and on the exam.

The practice exam in the book is critically important in your preparation as are all the knowledge check questions you will encounter in each chapter. These practice multiple-choice questions will build your confidence in your ability to select the correct answer among lots of information. The answers are given as well as why something is not correct. This learning process from both the correct and incorrect answers expands your ability to evaluate and critically examine each question to arrive at the best correct answer. It is our hope that by using this book and preparing for the exam through the resources and activities provided, you will walk into test day confident and ready to tackle the last step on your journey to becoming an addiction counselor: passing the national exam. Prepare, believe in yourself, and trust your training. You got this!

Christine Tina Chasek
Thomas Z. Maxson

Acknowledgments

With sincere gratitude, we would like to acknowledge Becca Moore, LIMHP, LADC, NCC, CCMHC, for her significant contributions to this book. Becca's years of experience and dedication to education are evident in the chapters she wrote and in all academic pursuits. Her vast knowledge of the counseling world and her ability to share her experiences and expertise with students is evident in all she does. Without her help this book would not be in your hands.

A book such as this does not arise from just two authors, but rather from collective years of interactions with students and clients. From hours of studying in school, reading test study guides to prepare for a licensing test, late night crisis calls while working as an on-call counselor, to sitting with a mother relieved that her son is in jail because at least she knows he is alive and not on the street getting high; the counseling profession requires a great deal from the counselor. The work a counselor does changes them as much as it changes a client.

We acknowledge the clients, the students, the mentors, and supervisors and most of all our families who have traveled with us on this journey these many years. A thank you goes out to the clients that have trusted us with their stories as they continue their journey; the supervisors and mentors who have guided us during the difficult times; and our families who have experienced the evenings when the day has been heavy and you just don't want to talk anymore.

So, to all that read this book, your journey is just beginning. Embrace the beginning but in the middle or toward the end, never stop learning, sharing, and growing!

Pass Guarantee

If you use this resource to prepare for your exam and do not pass, you may return it for a refund of your full purchase price, excluding tax, shipping, and handling. To receive a refund, return your product along with a copy of your exam score report and original receipt showing purchase of new product (not used). Product must be returned and received within 180 days of the original purchase date. Refunds will be issued within 8 weeks from acceptance and approval. One offer per person and address. This offer is valid for U.S. residents only. Void where prohibited. To initiate a refund, please contact Customer Service at csexamprep@springerpub.com.

PART I: ALCOHOL AND DRUG COUNSELOR EXAM OVERVIEW

Introduction to Addiction Counseling and the Alcohol and Drug Counselor

Christine Tina Chasek

Addiction counseling is a growing field that is projected to continue growing at a much faster rate than all other occupations (Occupational Outlook Handbook, 2022). Society's increasing understanding of substance use, addiction, and treatment, along with the large number of people who need services, has made this a profession attractive to many. While there are many educational paths to a career in addiction counseling, the correct credentials are required to practice in the field. This not only involves advanced education but the ability to pass a national examination demonstrating that the requisite knowledge, skills, and competency to provide ethical care have been gained. To help those who wish to enter the field, this book outlines the information needed to prepare for and pass the **International Certification and Reciprocity Consortium's (IC&RC)** alcohol and drug counselor (ADC) examination. This chapter provides a brief history of the addiction counseling field, credentialing basics, the IC&RC, an overview of the ADC exam, test scoring guidelines, and test day logistics.

▶ HISTORY OF THE ADDICTION COUNSELING FIELD

The first professional in the United States to articulate the modern concept of addiction as a disease state to be treated was Dr. Benjamin Rush (1746–1813; Thombs & Osborn, 2019). Dr. Rush, a Philadelphia physician and signer of the Declaration of Independence, conceptualized alcohol as an addictive substance and frequent drunkenness as a disease (Sarkar, 2021). His writings laid the foundation for early ideas regarding treatment and the need for treatment providers while simultaneously setting the stage for the temperance movement that evolved in the early 1800s. The temperance movement made way for the Harrison Narcotic Act of 1914, criminalizing the nonmedical use of drugs, and the 18th Amendment, which was added to the U.S. Constitution in 1919, prohibiting the sale, manufacture, and transportation of alcoholic beverages. These public policies and regulations along with the temperance movement set into place the different, conflicting beliefs that substance use was an immoral sin and a disease (Center for Substance Abuse Treatment [CSAT], 2017; Thombs & Osborn, 2019).

The development of the modern system of care in substance use treatment dates to the late 1960s when public drunkenness was decriminalized (CSAT, 2017). Since that time, the view of addiction and addiction treatment has changed dramatically. Addiction is now seen as a treatable illness based on a multidetermined perspective of addiction and addiction treatment. Research has shown that addiction treatment works when conducted from a biopsychosocial-spiritual model (Miller et al., 2019; Project MATCH Research Group, 1998). The understanding of addiction as a multidetermined disease state has changed the way treatment is provided and the way treatment providers are trained. As society has become more knowledgeable about addiction and treatment, a need has been created for highly trained and competent addiction counselors to provide treatment. Addiction counselors must have the necessary knowledge, skill, attitudes, and self-awareness to treat a client's addiction effectively (CSAT, 2017). These competencies are measured through the credentialing process which includes passing a national examination.

To practice in the field of counseling, a professional must hold the correct credentials. Addiction counseling preparation, certification, credentialing, and licensure has developed along several different paths simultaneously since the passage of the Comprehensive Alcohol Abuse and Alcohol Prevention, Treatment, and Rehabilitation Act in 1970 (West et al., 1999). Professional counseling **credentialing** and licensure indicates that the counselor has met the minimum requirement of educational and practical competence in the field and has passed a national addiction counseling exam (Miller et al., 2010).

▶ CREDENTIALING BASICS

Quality care in any profession requires a competent workforce certified through a credentialing process. Credentialing in the helping profession ensures that the workforce is educated, well-trained, and highly skilled in providing appropriate ethical care. Credentialing also ensures the protection of the public. Addiction counseling credentialing standardizes practice across a wide variety of settings and regulatory jurisdictions and acts as the gate through which professionals must pass for the privilege to practice.

PURPOSE OF ADDICTION COUNSELING EXAMS

The foundation of any credential is the **job analysis**, a methodical process that analyzes what elements of practice and knowledge are important to assess as a part of the certification exam. Subject matter experts (SMEs) who work in the field are gathered from across the country to contribute and define what tasks, knowledge, skills, and abilities they use in their jobs. This information is used to create a public survey that is administered to professionals to determine if they do indeed use these tasks and how important they would rate them. A psychometrician then works with a second group of SMEs who review the results of the survey, adjusting the original tasks, knowledge, skills, and abilities to arrive at the final job analysis which becomes the blueprint for the credentialing exam. Passing the credentialing exam is the last step in the process of earning the addiction counseling credential.

For the addiction counseling field, there is no single national unifying credentialing process. Instead, each state or regulatory body sets the standards for which certifying or credentialing process to be used to credential addiction counselors. In the United States, there are two main national credentialing exams that regulatory bodies can choose from: the IC&RC or the Association for Addiction Professionals (National Association for Alcoholism and Drug Abuse Counselors [NAADAC]). This book prepares candidates for the IC&RC's national ADC examination, the most widely used exam for certifying and licensing addiction counselors.

The International Certification and Reciprocity Consortium

The IC&RC is a nonprofit, voluntary membership organization whose members comprise the alcohol and drug counseling certification boards. Boards are currently located in 47 states, the District of Columbia and include the Indian Health Service; the U.S. Air Force, Army, Navy, and Marines; and 24 additional countries. The IC&RC was incorporated in 1981 with the mission of providing public protection through the credentialing of professionals who engage in prevention and treatment of substance use disorders. The purpose of the IC&RC is to provide international certification for substance use disorder professionals through member boards, promote uniform professional standards, provide reciprocity for counselors when they relocate, and provide information and training on the certification process for member boards.

It is the policy of the IC&RC to administer valid, reliable, and legally defensible examinations for the addiction counseling field. To this end, the IC&RC regularly updates the exam through the job analysis process. The most recent job analysis completed by the IC&RC was in 2022 with the first administration for the updated examinations beginning in February 2023 (IC&RC, 2020).

> **Tips From the Field**
>
> To prepare for the ADC exam, start by researching the IC&RC member board in your state or jurisdiction. Review the eligibility requirements and how to register for the exam. Talk to others in the field about the logistics of the exam and what to expect on the day of the test.

▶ OVERVIEW OF THE ALCOHOL AND DRUG COUNSELOR EXAM

The IC&RC Alcohol and Drug Counselor credential is the most widely recognized credential for ADCs. It is designed as an entry-level credential covering the basics of addiction counseling. It is the basis of the mandated credential or license for many jurisdictions and is earned only after passing the ADC exam.

ALCOHOL AND DRUG COUNSELOR EXAM CONSTRUCTION

Performance Domains

The ADC exam is constructed from the job analysis process. The 2022 IC&RC ADC job analysis identified four performance domains for an ADC with several tasks identified within each domain (IC&RC, 2022). Table 1.1 outlines the four performance domains and the percentage of questions from each domain that are on the ADC exam.

Table 1.1 Four Performance Domains and Percentage of Questions From Each Domain on the ADC Exam

Performance Domain	Percent of Test Questions
I. Scientific principles of substance use and co-occurring disorders	25%
II. Evidence-based screening and assessment	20%
III. Evidence-based treatment, counseling, and referral	30%
IV. Professional, ethical, and legal responsibilities	25%

ADC, alcohol and drug counselor.

To clearly understand each of the performance domains, a complete listing of the domains and the corresponding tasks, knowledge, and skills that are included in each domain is provided in Appendix 1.1.

The tasks in the performance domains provide the basis for questions in the exam based on the knowledge and skills needed as an addiction counselor. The tasks of a counselor are also set out in the 12 core functions of an addiction counselor, which contains 46 global criteria across all functions.

12 Core Functions

In addition to the four domains and the tasks associated with each of them, the ADC exam also includes the 12 core functions of an addiction counselor. These 12 core functions are the empirically determined tasks that an addiction counselor uses in the process of helping clients (Kulewicz, 2000). The 12 core functions and their definitions are found in Table 1.2 (Herdman, 2021).

Each core function of the addiction counselor is based on a set of global criteria that further defines the function and the tasks that are involved. The 12 core functions with the definitions and full set of global criteria under each function can be found in Appendix 1.2. These core functions and the global criteria that define the tasks of the addiction counselor are included in the ADC exam. Because of the importance of the 12 core functions and the four performance domains, each chapter of this book provides in-depth information covering the performance domain and the core functions included in that domain.

Table 1.2 12 Core Functions

Core Function	Definition
1. Screening	The process by which the client is determined appropriate and eligible for admission to a particular program.
2. Intake	The administrative and initial procedures for admission to a program.
3. Orientation	Describing to the client the following: General nature and goals of the program; rules governing client conduct and infractions that can lead to disciplinary action or discharge from the program; in a nonresidential program, the hours during which services are available; treatment costs to be borne by the client, if any; and client rights.
4. Assessment	Those procedures by which a counselor/program identify and evaluate an individual's strengths, weaknesses, problems, and needs for the development of the treatment plan.
5. Treatment Planning	Process by which the counselor and the client identify and rank problems needing resolution; establish agreed upon immediate and long-term goals; and decide upon a treatment process and the resources to be utilized.
6. Counseling	The utilization of special skills to assist individuals, families, or groups in achieving objectives through exploration of a problem and its ramifications; examination of attitudes and feelings; consideration of alternative solutions; and decision-making.
7. Case Management	Activities that bring services, agencies, resources, or people together within a planned framework of action toward the achievement of established goals. It may involve liaison activities and collateral contacts.
8. Crisis Intervention	Those services in response to an alcohol and/or drug user's needs during acute emotional and/or physical distress.
9. Client Education	The provision of information to individuals and groups concerning alcohol and other drug use and the available services and resources.
10. Referral	Identifying the needs of a client that cannot be met by the counselor or agency and assisting the client to utilize the support systems and community resources available.
11. Report and Record Keeping	Charting the results of the assessment and treatment plan, writing reports, progress notes, discharge summaries, and other client-related data.
12. Consultation	Relating with in-house staff or outside professionals to assure comprehensive, quality care for the client; involves meetings for discussion, decision-making, and planning.

Tips From the Field

During your clinical experiences, ask your supervisor to help you organize your clinical practice tasks into the 12 core functions. This will help you attach knowledge of the core functions to your daily activities, making it more likely you will remember them when it comes time for the exam.

SCORING GUIDELINES FOR THE ALCOHOL AND DRUG COUNSELOR

To ensure valid and reliable testing, the IC&RC contracts with Prometric, a full-service testing company that administers and scores all examinations. The ADC examination contains 150 multiple-choice questions administered within a 3-hour time limit. The exam includes 125 scored questions and 25 pretest or development questions that are not included in the candidate's final score. Each multiple-choice question is presented with three or four options with only one correct or best answer. Test takers should answer every question since the number of correctly answered questions determines the final score; there is no penalty for guessing on a question. The exam is taken via computer-based testing at a designated Prometric testing site or at home via Prometric's "remote proctoring" if allowed by the member board.

There are multiple forms of the same examination for every IC&RC examination. Each form uses different questions but tests the same content. These exams are updated frequently to ensure test security. Statistical analysis is completed on each question and the passing score is adjusted accordingly for any differences in the test form. This systematic and documented approach to test construct and scoring establishes an accurate, reliable, and legally defensible pass/fail score on the exam.

Passing scores for the ADC exam are **NOT** determined based on a percentage of questions answered correctly as one might expect. The IC&RC uses **scaled scores** from 200 to 800 with a 500 score as a minimum passing scaled score. The process of determining the scaled scores is done using a Modified Angoff Study to determine a cut score for each examination. SMEs working with the testing company and a psychometrician determine the specific knowledge, skills, and abilities needed to demonstrate minimum competence by rating the difficulty of each question on the exam. The ratings are then combined to determine the final cut score for each exam. The final cut score is transformed to an equivalent scaled score with all exam questions weighted equally.

Candidates are provided with an official score letter that reports the scaled score and the percentage of items answered correctly in each domain. Candidates who DO NOT pass the exam are able to use the report to study content in the performance domains where they scored low to increase the likelihood of passing on the next try. Candidates are allowed to retake the exam after a minimum waiting period of 90 days after the previous examination. The test taker must register and pay for each administration of the exam. The exam can be taken up to four times per IC&RC policy. After four failed attempts, the candidate must work with the member board to determine next steps.

TESTING LOGISTICS FOR THE ALCOHOL AND DRUG COUNSELOR EXAM

IC&RC credentialing exams are administered exclusively by the IC&RC member boards who determine eligibility for the exams. Candidates can register for the exam once they meet the eligibility requirements of the member board. After registering successfully for the exam, candidates will receive instructions on scheduling the exam date, time, and location. If a test taker requires special accommodations, they must be requested prior to the examination through written request to the IC&RC member board who will facilitate any modifications to the standard testing protocols. Canceling or rescheduling the exam must be done 5 days or more prior to the scheduled exam date through the website that is provided when registering for the exam.

On the day of testing, the candidate must bring a valid government-issued photo ID as well as the candidate admission letter that was generated after registering for the exam. The candidate admission letter contains all the testing policies and procedures the test taker will need to know. This letter should be carefully read and understood before coming to the exam. At the beginning of the exam, a brief tutorial will be given on the computer-based testing process and, following the exam, a short survey will be given. Extra time is allotted for the tutorial and the survey so the total testing time for the exam will not be impacted. Candidates are not allowed to bring any materials into the testing room and no questions may be asked during the exam. Any misconduct on the part of the test taker may result in dismissal from the exam, voided exam scores, and/or forfeiture of the exam fees.

All exam scores are final and cannot be appealed; however, if a test taker believes that something occurred which caused a significant negative effect on their exam performance, they can submit a grievance in writing to the IC&RC for review. The grievance must be submitted on the appropriate forms within 14 calendar days of the exam. These forms can be found on the IC&RC's website. There is a fee for filing a grievance. If the grievance is verified, the fee will be returned and the test taker will be offered a free retake of the exam.

Preparation is crucial for passing the ADC exam. Knowing the test day logistics as well as how the ADC exam is developed, administered, and scored can help a test taker feel prepared and confident going into the exam. Strategic studying in the basics of the exam as well as the four performance domains and the 12 core functions of an addiction counselor as outlined in the chapter will help the test taker prepare for the exam. There are also other ways that a test taker can prepare for the exam which will be explored in depth in the next chapter.

▶ KEY POINTS

- An addiction counselor must hold the proper credentials required in the counseling field which include advanced education and passing a national examination.
- Passing the ADC exam ensures that the counselor has the knowledge, skills, and competency to provide ethical care.

- The most common examination in the addiction counseling field is the ADC exam which is administered by the IC&RC.
- The ADC exam is based on four performance domains and the 12 core functions of an addiction counselor.
- Good preparation and knowing the exam process can help test takers feel confident going into the exam.

Appendix 1.1 Performance Domains, Tasks, Knowledge, and Skills for the ADC Exam

DOMAIN 1: Scientific Principles of Substance Use and Co-Occurring Disorders
A. Recognize how addiction affects the brain (e.g., disease model, reward pathways, tolerance, cravings)
B. Identify risk factors for developing substance use disorders (e.g., trauma, family history)
C. Identify behavior, patterns, and progressive stages of substance use disorders
D. Differentiate among common substances of abuse and their characteristics
    1. Pharmacology (e.g., drug classifications, interactions, cross-tolerance)
    2. Signs and symptoms of intoxication and overdose
    3. Stages and symptoms of withdrawal
    4. Physiological, psychological, and social effects
E. Identify signs and symptoms of co-occurring mental health conditions
F. Identify signs and symptoms of co-occurring medical conditions (e.g., cirrhosis, respiratory deficits, sexually transmitted infections)

DOMAIN 2: Evidence-Based Screening and Assessment
A. Utilize established interviewing techniques (e.g., motivational interviewing, probing, and questioning)
B. Utilize established screening and assessment methods and instruments (e.g., Addiction Severity Index [ASI], adverse childhood experiences [ACE], Substance Abuse Subtle Screening Inventory [SASSI]
C. Identify methods and interpret results from drug and alcohol testing
D. Utilize established diagnostic criteria for evaluating substance use (i.e., *Diagnostic and Statistical Manual of Mental Disorders* [DSM])
E. Assemble a comprehensive client biopsychosocial history (e.g., health, family, employment, collateral sources)
F. Determine the course of action to meet the individual's immediate and ongoing needs
G. Determine level of care based on placement criteria

DOMAIN 3: Evidence-Based Treatment, Counseling, and Referral
A. Demonstrate practicing and responding to verbal and nonverbal communication skills
    1. Learning styles
    2. Communication styles (e.g., person-centered language)
B. Recognize methods and opportunities to build rapport with clients
C. Review client's patterns and methods of use
D. Recognize and respond to emergency/crisis events (e.g., de-escalation)
E. Recognize when to utilize and how to facilitate referrals for clients (e.g., case management, follow-up)
F. Identify and respond to concerns related to specific populations (e.g., LGBTQ+, pregnancy, youth, justice-involved, housing insecure)
G. Collaborate with multidisciplinary team, other professionals, and client supports (e.g., family) to determine and provide care
H. Recognize the relationship between substance use and trauma
    1. Effect on client (e.g., adverse childhood experiences, domestic violence)
    2. Effect on counselor (e.g., vicarious trauma, burnout)
I. Utilize methods to address client ambivalence or resistance to change

(continued)

Appendix 1.1 Performance Domains, Tasks, Knowledge, and Skills for the ADC Exam (*continued*)

J. Utilize best practices in developing and updating a treatment plan
   1. Goals and objectives
   2. Strategies and interventions (e.g., relapse prevention, coping skills)
K. Identify available resources to meet client needs
L. Utilize counseling approaches specific to group sessions
   1. Structured curriculum and process
   2. Group dynamics and cohesiveness
M. Recognize elements of discharge planning
N. Explore multiple pathways of recovery (e.g., medication-assisted treatment [MAT], holistic health, support groups)
O. Utilize methods and techniques for providing feedback (e.g., reflection, reframing, clarification)
P. Recognize when to terminate the counseling process

DOMAIN 4: Professional, Ethical, and Legal Responsibilities
A. Demonstrate professional boundaries and practice self-awareness regarding:
   1. Dual relationships
   2. Self-disclosure
B. Develop and utilize multicultural perspectives throughout the counseling process
C. Recognize and respond to issues that are outside the practitioner's scope of practice
D. Demonstrate best practices in documentation
   1. Record keeping
   2. Storage
E. Demonstrate compliance with confidentiality and privacy laws
F. Identify and address potential conflicts of interest
G. Demonstrate compliance with informed consent guidelines
H. Identify and utilize sources of supervision and consultation
I. Recognize the grievance process and respond to client grievances
J. Identify, respond, and advocate for diversity, inclusion, and equity in care
K. Demonstrate adherence to established client rights

Appendix 1.2 12 Core Functions and Global Criteria

I. **SCREENING:** The process by which the client is determined appropriate and eligible for admission to a particular program.
   Global Criteria
   1. Evaluate psychological, social, and physiological signs and symptoms of alcohol and other drug use and abuse.
   2. Determine the client's appropriateness for admission or referral.
   3. Determine the client's eligibility for admission or referral.
   4. Identify any coexisting conditions (medical, psychiatric, physical, etc.) that indicate the need for additional professional assessment and/or services.
   5. Adhere to applicable laws, regulations, and agency policies governing alcohol and other substance use services.
II. **INTAKE:** The administrative and initial assessment procedures for admission to a program.
   Global Criteria
   6. Complete required documents for admission to the program.
   7. Complete required documents for program eligibility and appropriateness.
   8. Obtain appropriately signed consents when soliciting from or providing information to outside sources to protect client confidentiality and rights.

(*continued*)

Appendix 1.2 12 Core Functions and Global Criteria (*continued*)

III. **ORIENTATION:** Describe to the client the following: General nature and goals of the program; rules governing client conduct and infractions that can lead to disciplinary action or discharge from the program; in a nonresidential program, the hours during which services are available; treatment costs to be borne by the client, if any; and client rights.

Global Criteria

9. Provide an overview to the client by describing program goals and objectives for client care.
10. Provide an overview to the client by describing program rules, and client obligations and rights.
11. Provide an overview to the client of program operations.

IV. **ASSESSMENT:** The procedures by which a counselor/program identifies and evaluates an individual's strengths, weaknesses, problems, and needs for the development of a treatment plan.

Global Criteria

12. Gather relevant history from the client including but not limited to alcohol and other substance use using appropriate interview techniques.
13. Identify methods and procedures for obtaining corroborative information from significant secondary sources regarding the client's alcohol and other substance use and psychosocial history.
14. Identify appropriate assessment tools.
15. Explain to the client the rationale for the use of assessment techniques in order to facilitate understanding.
16. Develop a diagnostic evaluation of the client's substance use and any coexisting conditions based on the results of all assessments in order to provide an integrated approach to treatment planning based on the client's strengths, weaknesses, identified problems and needs.

V. **TREATMENT PLANNING:** Process by which the counselor and the client identify and rank problems needing resolution; establish agreed upon immediate and long-term goals; and decide upon a treatment process and the resources to be utilized.

Global Criteria

17. Explain assessment results to the client in an understandable manner.
18. Identify and rank problems based on individual client needs in the written treatment plan.
19. Formulate agreed upon immediate and long-term goals using behavioral terms in the written treatment plan.
20. Identify the treatment methods and resources to be utilized as appropriate for the individual client.

VI. **COUNSELING** (Individual, Group and Significant Others): The utilization of special skills to assist individuals, families, or groups in achieving objectives through exploration of a problem and its ramifications; examination of attitudes and feelings; consideration of alternative solutions; and decision-making.

Global Criteria

21. Select the counseling theory(ies) that applies(y).
22. Apply technique(s) to assist the client, group, and/or family in exploring problems and ramifications.
23. Apply technique(s) to assist the client, group, and/or family in examining the client's behavior, attitudes, and/or feelings if appropriate in the treatment setting.
24. Individualize counseling in accordance with culture, gender, and lifestyle differences.
25. Interact with the client in an appropriate therapeutic manner.
26. Elicit solutions and decisions from the client.
27. Implement the treatment plan.

(*continued*)

Appendix 1.2 12 Core Functions and Global Criteria (*continued*)

VII. CASE MANAGEMENT: Activities that bring services, agencies, resources, or people together within a planned framework of action toward the achievement of established goals. It may involve liaison activities and collateral contacts.

Global Criteria

28. Coordinate services for client care.

29. Explain the rationale of case management activities to the client.

VIII. CRISIS INTERVENTION: Those services that respond to an alcohol and/or other substance user's needs during acute emotional and/or physical distress.

Global Criteria

30. Recognize the elements of the client crisis.

31. Implement an immediate course of action appropriate to the crisis.

32. Enhance overall treatment by utilizing crisis events.

IX. CLIENT EDUCATION: Provision of information to individuals and groups concerning alcohol and other substance use and the available services and resources.

Global Criteria

33. Present relevant alcohol and other substance use/abuse information to the client through formal and/or informal processes.

34. Present information about available alcohol and other drug services and resources.

X. REFERRAL: Identify the needs of a client that cannot be met by the counselor or agency and assist the client to utilize the support systems and available community resources.

Global Criteria

35. Identify need(s) and/or problem(s) that the agency and/or counselor cannot meet.

36. Explain the rationale for the referral to the client.

37. Match client needs and/or problems to appropriate resources.

38. Adhere to applicable laws, regulations, and agency policies governing procedures related to the protection of the client's confidentiality.

39. Assist the client in utilizing the support systems and available community resources.

XI. REPORT AND RECORD KEEPING: Charting the results of the assessment and treatment plan and writing reports, progress notes, discharge summaries, and other client-related data.

Global Criteria

40. Prepare reports and relevant records integrating available information to facilitate the continuum of care.

41. Chart pertinent ongoing information pertaining to the client.

42. Utilize relevant information from written documents for client care.

XII. CONSULTATION WITH OTHER PROFESSIONALS REGARDING THE CLIENT'S TREATMENT/SERVICES: Relate with in-house staff or outside professionals to ensure comprehensive, quality care for the client.

Global Criteria

43. Recognize issues that are beyond the counselor's base of knowledge and/or skill.

44. Consult with appropriate resources to ensure the provision of effective treatment services.

45. Adhere to applicable laws, regulations, and agency policies governing the disclosure of client-identifying data.

46. Explain the rationale for the consultation to the client, if appropriate.

▶ **REFERENCES**

Center for Substance Abuse Treatment. (2017). *Addiction counseling competencies: The knowledge, skills, and attitudes of professional practice.* Technical Assistance Publication (TAP) Series 21. DHHS Publication No. (SMA) 06-4171. Substance Abuse and Mental Health Services Administration.

Herdman, J. W. (2021). *Global criteria: The 12 core functions of the substance abuse counselor* (8th ed.).

International Certification and Reciprocity Consortium. (2020). *Alcohol and drug counselor (ADC)*. https://www.internationalcredentialing.org/creds/adc

International Certification and Reciprocity Consortium. (2022). *Candidate guide for the IC&RC alcohol and drug counselor examination*. https://internationalcredentialing.org/wp-content/uploads/2024/01/ADC-Candidate-Guide-09.2022_Final-Edit_10.31.22.pdf

Kulewicz, S. F. (2000). *The twelve core functions of a counselor* (4th ed.). Stanley Kulewicz.

Miller, G., Scarborough, J., Clark, C., Leonard, J. C., & Keziah, T. B. (2010). The need for national credentialing standards for addiction counselors. *Journal of Addictions & Offender Counseling, 30*, 50–57.

Miller, W. R., Forcehimes, A. A., & Zweben, A. (2019). *Treatment addiction: A guide for professionals* (2nd ed.). The Guilford Press.

Occupational Outlook Handbook. (2022). *Substance abuse, behavioral disorder, and mental health counselors*. https://www.bls.gov/ooh/community-and-social-service/substance-abuse-behavioral-disorder-and-mental-health-counselors.htm

Project MATCH Research Group. (1998). Matching patients with alcohol disorders to treatments: Clinical implications from project MATCH. *Journal of Mental Health, 7*(6), 589–602.

Sarkar, P. R. (2021). Spirits from the past: Stigma in historical medical literature on alcohol addiction and implications for modern practice. *The American Journal of Psychiatry, 16*(4), 8–10. https://doi.org/10.1176/appi.ajp-rj.2021.160405

Thombs, D. L., & Osborn, C. J. (2019). *Introduction to addictive behaviors* (5th ed.). The Guilford Press.

West, P. L., Mustaine, B. L., & Wyrick, B. (1999). State regulations and the ACA code of ethics and standards of practice: Oil and water for the substance abuse counselor. *Journal of Addictions and Offender Counseling, 20*(1), 35–47.

CASE STUDY 1.1

John has completed his course work to become an addiction counselor and is currently working on his clinical practice hours to meet the requirements for certification and licensure in his state. He knows he needs to take an exam before he can be licensed but does not know anything about it or where to find any further information. After some thought, he decided to talk to his supervisor because he knew that the supervisor had recently been licensed and must have gone through the same process. During one of his supervision sessions, John asked his supervisor about the exam and if she could help him figure out how to register and how to study. The supervisor was very agreeable to this request, and she immediately set up a plan to help John with the exam.

1. What should be the first steps for John and his supervisor in crafting his exam plan?

2. What things should John consider in preparing for his exam? What should he do first?

3. What things should the supervisor and John do in the supervision sessions to help him pass the exam?

(See answers on the next page.)

CASE STUDY 1.1 ANSWERS

1. John and his supervisor should work together to craft a timeline of important milestones working backward from the date of his exam. The plan should outline the details and logistics of the testing process, test materials, and dedicated time for studying. It also should identify the resources available to John and how to access them, such as study materials, study groups, and mentors who would be willing to help him prepare.

2. John should first consider setting aside dedicated time to study for the exam. This is critical as things that are not planned often don't get done. After setting aside the time to study, John should gather the materials he needs to study such as the 12 core functions, the performance domains, test prep materials, course notes, materials from his classes, and any other resources that would help him in his study process such as videos, online lectures, and any helpful resources like ExamPrepConnect that goes with this book. John should also consider connecting his clinical work to his studying, identifying the skills, knowledge, and competencies he is using in his daily clinical work.

3. In the supervisory sessions, it is important for the supervisor to help John understand the process and logistics for obtaining the addiction counseling credential as well as the clinical work being done. The supervisor can set aside time in each supervisory meeting to review a component of the exam, connecting the work that John is doing to the exam content. For example, when John is sharing his experience with a new client and how he is making decisions about diagnosis and treatment, the supervisor can help him identify which core function he is using and which of the global criteria pertain to that example. The supervisor can also help John understand the performance domain materials by connecting the best practices from his courses and the content he is studying to the client experience. Reviewing the material in the supervisory sessions and using the language of the exam in the work will help John encode the material into his long-term and working memory. Taking the exam is more than just memorizing the material; it should guide the counselor's work as an addiction professional.

Test-Taking Strategies and Tips

Becca Moore

2

▶ INTRODUCTION

The road to becoming an alcohol and drug counselor is a long one full of hard work, extreme effort, and many hours spent in the classroom and working with clients. Perhaps the most frightening step of becoming a drug and alcohol counselor is the final competency exam that verifies entry to the field. The exam is the last step in the process toward the coveted credential or license. Passing the exam certifies that the counselor has the required knowledge and skill to practice and treat clients. But what if you are an excellent student and fantastic clinician when working with clients, but are terrible at taking tests? Is there any hope? This chapter gives you many strategies and tips to help you pass the exam and become the counselor you've always dreamed of being!

▶ UNDERSTANDING THE BRAIN'S ROLE IN TESTING ANXIETY

In the mental health world, we are familiar with the flight, fight, freeze, and fawn reaction to a fear stimulus. What you may not know is that this reaction can be activated even when taking a test. Our amygdala is designed to keep us safe and to act as a "smoke detector" of sorts. It alerts us to danger and, in doing so, "hijacks" our prefrontal cortex, which is where our logical, decision-making brain resides.

Our amygdala can't determine whether a fear is real or perceived. So although you may think, "Taking a test should not trigger this kind of a response; it's only a test," it's quite possible that, especially given previous experiences, your amygdala feels that taking a test is in fact a very threatening situation.

Ordinarily, under low-pressure circumstances, we have access to our prefrontal cortex. And that's great when we are taking in information. However, when we experience a fear stimulus, such as thinking "What if I fail this test?," our amygdala can override our prefrontal cortex. For many with test anxiety, this is where their fear response comes in, often in the form of a freeze response. If you were answering the same questions as those that appear on the test in a casual conversation, you would likely answer them quickly and intelligently. But when you're sitting in front of a computer screen with a timer counting down the time you have left (in case the pressure of the exam isn't enough on its own), your brain goes completely blank.

The good news is that if you're like the 25% to 40% of the population who struggle with test anxiety, there are great strategies you can utilize to help calm down your amygdala and help you regain access to your prefrontal cortex, so that you get the score based on your actual knowledge rather than your shut-down brain response. Utilizing the following tips and tricks will help you prepare for and take the exam.

▶ BEFORE THE TEST

DO YOUR WORK

Odds are, by the time you are reading this book, you are coming to the end of your formal studies. Nonetheless, the work you are doing in school is designed to help you pass this test.

Sometimes it is easy to skip an assignment or two when they aren't necessary for a grade. While you might be able to get by grade-wise without completing every assignment, passing the licensure exam may depend on whether or not you've retained that assignment's material. Make sure to complete all your assignments and ask questions if there's anything you don't understand.

USE YOUR RESOURCES

Your instructors, professors, and supervisors have all been through this. Don't be afraid to reach out to them and ask them questions. While no one can tell you for sure what is on the test, they can give you ideas about what sections have caused trouble for other students in the past and where to place emphasis when studying. They can even share study habits that helped them or other students.

SCHEDULE YOUR EXAM

Try to schedule your exam at a time when you don't have a lot of other "stuff" on your plate. You want to be sure that you don't have anything else going on the day of the test, of course, but you also want to ensure that nothing in the days before the test will take away from your opportunities to study. You want to be able to dedicate as much time as possible to focusing on your exam. By being intentional about when you schedule, you are setting yourself up for success.

DON'T CRAM

One of the mistakes that people often make when they're getting ready to prepare for a test is cramming the night before. Unfortunately, this can also overload your brain and make it harder to retain information. Think about this: You are reading through all the information that might be on your test the night before. During the test the following day, you come across a challenging question and your brain tries to recall information. The trouble is that your brain has seen so many things the night before, it starts to be overwhelmed and can't accurately recall the information. *Was it this? Or was it that?*

Rather than cramming, a better approach to studying is to take it slow and steady. Besides overwhelming your brain the day of the test, cramming is ineffective if you want to learn the material and store it in your long-term memory. When you study slowly over time, you can take in a little bit of information, process it, and allow your brain to digest it before moving onto the next concept. Then when you take the test, your brain is better able to process the question because it isn't as likely to mix up information and can recall the information from long-term memory.

USE PRACTICE TESTS

While standardized tests are locked down in secrecy, there are multiple practice tests available (including at the end of this book). No one can predict exactly what will be on the test but utilizing practice tests is still a great idea for a couple of reasons.

First, a practice test gives you the opportunity to see what information you feel confident about and what information you might need to brush up on a little more. It also gives you an idea of what content might be asked on the actual test. Second, and equally importantly, practice tests help you understand the format of the test. Getting used to the format can be helpful so that when you take the test, you will know what kind of content will be asked and how that content will be presented. And, finally, you will practice answering questions under the same time pressure alotted for the actual test. You can use the techniques suggested in the following to help answer the questions with more confidence.

FORM A STUDY GROUP

Studying can be extremely daunting—especially for a licensure test. There is so much information that can be on the exam, it's hard to know what to cover and, even more challenging, to retain that information. Having a study group can make a tremendous difference. Studying with others gives you the opportunity to hear their points of view and learn from them. It also gives you the chance to see the material in a different way—if you are just reading the material to yourself, you're less engaged with it.

Studying in a group can also help you stay accountable to studying. We are all busy and have a million irons in the fire. Having a study group helps ensure that you are staying up to date with your study materials. As you work in your study group, you might set goals for which materials you want to cover and the date to achieve this. Start this technique early so that you have plenty of time to go over the material well in advance of the test.

FUEL UP

The day before the test and the day of the test, eat foods that will not upset your stomach and are easy to digest. The last thing you want is to go into a test with a stomachache or indigestion. You'll also want to avoid foods that are high in sugar as they give you quick energy but can lead to a "crash." But you will also want to avoid sitting for the test with an empty stomach. We need fuel to be able to focus. Eat a well-balanced breakfast and stick with foods that are good for you. Make sure that you stay hydrated but avoid drinking too much. Most testing centers will allow you to use the restroom if need be, but some do not, and you don't want to lose valuable test-taking time.

If you like a boost of caffeine in the morning, follow your usual routine but don't overdo. Too much caffeine can increase your anxiety level and make you jittery. Similarly, don't skip on the caffeine if you are accustomed to having some as the last thing you need on your test day is a withdrawal headache!

EXERCISE

Exercise can help you reduce stress. As you study and prepare, go for a walk, run, bike ride, lift weights, have a dance party—whatever is your pleasure. Physical movement is a great way to combat anxiety. Even if exercise isn't your norm, do some kind of movement to help your body adjust to the physical response of anxiety. If you get to the test center a little early, go for a walk around the building or walk the halls to help calm your nerves.

SLEEP

Getting enough rest is helpful for getting through a test. But that doesn't just mean the night before. In the weeks leading up to your exam, try to stay on rhythm and keep your body and brain in a consistent routine. Experts recommend at least 7 hours of sleep a night for optimal functioning during the day. If you aren't getting that much a night, work on a routine that allows for at least that much sleep time.

Unfortunately, if you are someone who struggles with test anxiety, sleeping, especially the night before a big exam, can be difficult. Fortunately, even if sleep is evasive, there are some things you can do to help you get some rest before your exam.

First, even if you aren't sleeping, allow your body to rest. One mistake we sometimes make when we are not sleeping is to try to force ourselves to sleep. The more we try to force it, the more frustrated we become when sleep doesn't arrive. And the more frustrated we become, the more we stay awake because now our heart rate is elevated. So even if you aren't sleeping, remind yourself that you are resting, and that's okay.

We can also sometimes have a tendency to push our anxious thoughts out of our brain. However, typically, when we try to push anxiety away, it pushes back harder. So instead, when anxiety about the test creeps in, allow yourself to notice it and utilize some positive self-talk about it. For example, "I'm anxious about this test tomorrow, and that's okay" or "I don't know how this test will go, but I will cross that bridge when I get there." Sometimes our brain doesn't need a solution; it just wants to know that we are aware of the stressor. Once it knows we are aware and we acknowledge it, our brain allows us to rest.

Tips From the Field

Anxiety Can Be Good!
Remember that not all anxiety is bad! It is worth noting that some anxiety is good! Anxiety can help us focus on the task at hand. So, when you are at the test center and you feel your anxiety rising; remember that anxiety can be your friend!

WHAT IF I NEED ACCOMMODATIONS?

When you sign up for the test, often you will be asked what, if any, accommodations are needed. You will need to have a note from a doctor, counselor, or other professional to show that you do qualify for accommodations. You can call the testing center prior to the exam and verify that they have received notice of your accommodations. When you get to the testing center, you can also verify that your accommodations are in place.

SEE A COUNSELOR

Taking a licensure exam can be extremely stressful. If you are someone who already wrestles with anxiety, this added stress can be too much to deal with on your own. It's perfectly acceptable to go see a counselor. Sometimes, as new professionals, we might feel stigma that others might judge us for seeing a counselor, but the truth is, many of us have been there. It's acceptable to reach out for help and counseling can give you an added boost of confidence. Whereas this chapter is focused on general advice, a counselor can work with you to help you find specific coping skills that are designed just for you to help you as you prepare for your test.

THE NIGHT BEFORE

Rest. You've studied. You've prepared. You know everything that you are going to know for the test. If you want to look over a few things as a review, go for it. But don't spend a lot of time trying to take in new information. Instead, do something relaxing. Get a massage, go for a walk, and binge watch a favorite TV show. Rest.

▶ DAY OF THE TEST

WEAR COMFORTABLE CLOTHING

There are no awards for cuteness at the test: Dress for comfort. You don't want to be fidgeting because you're uncomfortable during the test. Everyone feels comfortable in something different, so if sweats and a t-shirt are comfortable for you, wear them. If it's jeans, wear them. If it's dress clothes, wear them. You might also consider wearing layers as testing centers could run either hot or cold. Being comfortable is important, especially when you have a test that is several hours long.

Beyond comfort, most testing centers will have protocols about what you can and cannot wear. The instructions for test day will include information for what is allowed and what isn't. Read through that carefully prior to getting dressed on test day. For example, you might not be able to wear bobby pins, shirts with rhinestones, and so forth. Anything that could have a small hidden camera is banned. You may go through a security check much like at the airport, so avoid anything that can't easily go through a security check.

GET TO THE TESTING CENTER EARLY

You never know what traffic will be like or what you will encounter on your way to the test center. In addition, test centers have procedures similar to airport security that you must pass through upon arrival to ensure that you are who you say you are and that you don't have any hidden cameras to copy the test information. Most testing centers will also require you to empty your pockets (even of common items such as tissues or lip balm) and put your purse or wallet, cell phone, keys, and any other materials in a locker. Any materials you will need such as scratch paper are provided at the testing center. By getting to the testing center early, you can take time to use the restroom, get settled, and have plenty of time to acclimate to your testing environment in a way that isn't rushed so you feel more comfortable.

WHAT IF I'M SICK?

If need be, you can reach out to the test center and reschedule. If it's a couple of days before the test and you aren't sure if you'll be okay, err on the side of caution and reach out to the test center and ask what they advise.

▶ THE EXAM

FOLLOW THE INSTRUCTIONS

Make sure to take a moment to thoroughly read the instructions that appear at the beginning of the exam. If there are multiple sections to the exam, there will likely be instructions of some sort at the beginning of each section. Don't assume that the instructions will always be the same for each section. Take a moment to read and make sure you comprehend the instructions.

READ CAREFULLY

Test questions can be deliberately challenging. Make sure you read each question carefully and even read it several times to ensure that you understand what the question is asking. Often, tests will ask test takers to select the *best* or *most correct* answer, which can be frustrating because there are multiple answers that can be correct and it's up to you to determine which one is best. Reading the question carefully can help you make that determination.

Most, if not all, standardized tests have something called "field questions" or "test construction questions." These test questions are designed to see how test takers perform on the questions and if they will be appropriate to use on a later version of the test. Field questions are thrown out of your final score, so they don't hurt your grade if you don't know the answer. A good reframe if you find some particularly hard questions on your test is "This might be a field question."

Test takers aren't expected to score perfectly. Tests have "cut scores" which determine what level is acceptable to show proficiency in the content. No test requires 100% correct answers; every test has a different standard for what it means to "pass" and most are fairly generous based on the cut score. Testing banks have thousands of questions. If you find that you are struggling with some test questions or that you simply don't know the answer, remind yourself, it's fine to not know. You don't need to have all the answers.

RULE OUT

If you don't know an answer, rule out any possible answer selections you are able to and then make your best guess. While you still may not be sure which answer is correct, you are increasing your odds at getting a correct answer by narrowing the field of possibilities.

WATCH THE TIME

Licensure exams are timed, so it's important to keep your eye on the clock. Often there will be a timer on the screen to let you know how much time remains. If you get to a question that you just don't know the answer to or feel like it's on the tip of your awareness, use the markup feature and come back to it later. While there is plenty of time to take the test, time is of the essence. Don't spend all your time on questions you aren't sure of. Answer the ones you know and then go back to the ones you don't. If you still don't know the answer, give it your best guess and move on.

DOUBLE CHECK YOUR WORK

Tests usually have a highlight option where you can mark a question that you are unsure of. Mark the best answer and then highlight the question. As time allows, check your work after you get to the end of the test, paying specific attention to the questions you highlighted. But be cautious not to overthink and change all your answers. When in doubt, go with your original answer.

IGNORE DISTRACTIONS

There will likely be others taking the test with you. Thankfully, testing centers run a tight ship, so things like talking, gum chewing, and other distractions are usually not tolerated. But it can be easy to get caught up with what the people around you are doing, especially if you see them finishing a test and you're not even close to being done. Test centers hold many kinds of tests, so it's important to remember that although everyone there is taking a test, not everyone (and maybe not anyone) is taking *your* test. But even if they are, not everyone takes tests the same way and faster doesn't mean better. Take your time and focus on your test.

DON'T PANIC

Imagine you are sitting in a test and suddenly you start to realize you don't know the answers to the questions. Internally you start to have doubts and question your ability to pass this test. Some exams may even tell you "Response not indicated" as you skip past questions. Either way, it can be very daunting. You may say things to yourself like "I'm going to fail," "I can't do this," "I won't accomplish my goals." These messages are not helpful because they activate the amygdala and the stress response.

This can become something of a self-fulfilling prophecy as once you are dysregulated, it becomes harder to focus. With this frame of mind, you are more likely to become dysregulated and have a harder time focusing. Remind yourself not to panic and use the other skills we discuss here to stay regulated.

Breathe

Taking a test can be overwhelming, especially when encountering questions that you don't know the answer to. While tests are timed, the amount of time allotted is usually ample for the average test taker to complete the test. If you do start to panic, stop for as long as you need and just breathe. When we panic, our amygdala is in action. Breathing can help regulate our nervous system and calm down the amygdala so that we are able to access our prefrontal cortex again. Once you have given yourself time to breathe and self-regulate, you will be better able to focus on the task at hand.

Positive Self-Talk

Utilizing positive self-talk can be critically important as you regulate your amygdala. Positive self-talk might look something like this, "I've studied and I'm as prepared as I can be. I'm going to do my best and see what happens." Even if you truly think you are failing, a good reframe would be, "It will suck if I fail this test, but I can try again" or "Even if this test doesn't go as planned, it doesn't change who I am."

WHAT IF I'VE FAILED BEFORE?

Unfortunately, sometimes we give our best effort and still fail. But failure is part of how we grow and learn. It's just information. If you have failed the test in the past, don't assume that this isn't meant to be or that you can't do it. Figure out what you need to do to get to the finish line and start again. Every test is different, and every test environment is different. How you feel on each test day is different. Just because you failed once doesn't mean you will fail again.

KEEP THINGS IN PERSPECTIVE

This might seem intuitive, but sometimes we get so caught up in the exam and the implications of passing or failing, that we forget that all we can ever do is give it our best. Regardless of whether you pass or fail, you are still the same person you were before you took the test and your worth isn't dependent on how well you do.

▶ AFTER THE TEST

Some tests will let you know right away how you did. Others may require you to wait for your scores. Right after the test, whether you pass or fail, or whether you know how you did or not, do something to take care of you. This test was likely hard, and you did your best. Have a nice meal, treat yourself to a massage, or schedule a nap. Celebrate that you did it!

▶ REFERENCES

Estevan, I., Sardi, R., Tejera, A. C., Silva, A., & Tassino, B. (2021, March 10). Should I study or should I go (to sleep)? The influence of test schedule on the sleep behavior of undergraduates and its association with performance. *PLoS One*, 16(3), e0247104. https://doi.org/10.1371/journal.pone.0247104

Hamilton, N., Freche, R., Zhang, Y., Zeller, G., & Carroll, I. (2021, April). Test anxiety and poor sleep: A vicious cycle. *International Journal of Behavioral Medicine*, 28(2), 250–258. https://doi.org/10.1007/s12529-021-09973-1

Hanfesa, S., Tilahun, T., Dessie, N., Shumet, S., & Salelew, E. (2020, November 2). Test anxiety and associated factors among first-year health science students of University of Gondar, Northwest Ethiopia: A cross-sectional study. *Advances in Medical Education and Practice*, 11, 817–824. https://doi.org/10.2147/AMEP.S275490

The Hawn Foundation. (2018). *The MindUP curriculum: Grades 6–8: Brain-focused strategies for learning—and living.* Scholastic.

Kristo, A. S., Gültekin, B., Öztağ, M., & Sikalidis, A. K. (2020, January 10). The effect of eating habits' quality on scholastic performance in Turkish adolescents. *Behavioral Sciences (Basel)*, *10*(1), 31. https://doi.org/10.3390/bs10010031

Šimić, G., Tkalčić, M., Vukić, V., Mulc, D., Španić, E., Šagud, M., Olucha-Bordonau, F. E., Vukšić, M., & Hof, P. R. (2021, May 31). Understanding emotions: Origins and roles of the amygdala. *Biomolecules*, *11*(6), 823. https://doi.org/10.3390/biom11060823

Yusefzadeh, H., Amirzadeh Iranagh, J., & Nabilou, B. (2019, May 3). The effect of study preparation on test anxiety and performance: A quasi-experimental study. *Advances in Medical Education and Practice*, *10*, 245–251. https://doi.org/10.2147/AMEP.S192053

CASE STUDY 2.1

Elizabeth, a 41-year-old woman preparing for the alcohol and drug counselor exam, has a history of test anxiety. Often, the night before a test, she does not sleep or wakes up soon after falling asleep due to her anxiety, even if she's confident she has the knowledge to pass the exam. Knowing her test anxiety and how important it is to get a good night's sleep, Elizabeth has decided to have her sister schedule her exam for her so that she doesn't know the date ahead of time. For this to be effective, her sister filtered all her e-mails into a folder and used her own phone number for a reminder system from the testing center. Elizabeth also worked with her employer so that they would be flexible for time off when the test day arrived even though she wouldn't be able to give prior notice for the absence. She also had all details of the exam testing protocol reviewed ahead of time and was prepared with what to wear, what to eat, and how to get to the test center.

On the day of the exam, Elizabeth's sister called her and told her the details of where the exam would be and what time she would need to be there. She also told her to check her filtered e-mail to print off her test ticket. Although her strategy was unconventional, Elizabeth felt rested for the exam. When others questioned whether she felt not studying the night before was detrimental, Elizabeth shared that she knew everything she was going to know before the test, so she didn't feel that studying further the night before would have been effective for her.

During the test, Elizabeth encountered multiple questions she was not sure of. She utilized deep breaths and positive self-talk with comments such as "I don't have to know everything" to help her when she felt overwhelmed. She also utilized deep breathing when she felt unsure. She paused, took deep breaths, and waited until she felt calm enough to resume. By using her test-taking strategies, and with the help of her sister, Elizabeth was able to pass her test.

PART II: ALCOHOL AND DRUG COUNSELOR EXAM CORE CONTENT

Physiology and Psychopharmacology

Christine Tina Chasek

This chapter covers Domain 1 of the International Certification and Reciprocity Consortium (IC&RC) exam as well as the global criteria in the screening and assessment core function connected to the physiological signs and symptoms of substance use and the identification of co-occurring disorders that may require additional professional evaluation.

▶ SUBSTANCE USE MODELS AND SCIENTIFIC PRINCIPLES

Addiction is a serious problem that has been conceptualized in various ways over many years with two predominating, overarching models: the moral model and the disease model (Cavaiola et al., 2022; Lassiter & Spivey, 2018). Historically, the understanding of addiction has been based on the moral model, a perspective that theorized substance use problems as a moral failing to be met with punitive treatment methods to correct the maladaptive and negative behavior. In the moral model, abstinence is the only goal. The moral model guided the addiction counseling field for many years, and still operates today as evidenced by punitive public policy and legal sanctions for those with substance use disorders and the prevalence of abstinence being seen as the only acceptable outcome for those who misuse substances. However, in more recent years, research has supported the disease model of addiction. The **disease model** conceptualizes addiction as a chronic medical disease that is biologically based (Brown-Rice & Moro, 2018; Cavaiola et al., 2022; Erickson, 2018; U.S. Department of Health and Human Services [DHHS], 2016). Similarly, the **biological model** of addiction considers the influences of genetics, brain structures, and neurotransmitter imbalances in the disease process. The **psychological model** focuses on the role of personality traits, view of self, cognitions, attachment, and the impact of trauma in the formation of a substance use disorder (Cavaiola et al., 2022). Finally, the **sociocultural model** heavily emphasizes the role of the environment, culture, race/ethnicity, poverty, family, friends, peers, and other social influences in the misuse of substances (Cavaiola et al., 2022). The most comprehensive model of substance use is the **biopsychosocial model** of addiction which combines the disease model with the psychological and social/cultural models of substance use disorders to arrive at a comprehensive conceptualization of addiction—it is the most well accepted in the treatment field (Brown-Rice & Moro, 2018; Cavaiola et al., 2022; DHHS, 2016) This is evident in the **definition of addiction** as put forth by the American Society of Addiction Medicine (ASAM; 2019):

> **Addiction** is a treatable, chronic medical disease involving complex interactions among brain circuits, genetics, the environment, and an individual's life experiences. People with addiction use substances or engage in behaviors that become compulsive and often continue despite harmful consequences. Prevention efforts and treatment approaches for addiction are generally as successful as those for other chronic diseases (para. 1).

This definition clearly delineates addiction as a neurobiological disease within a biological, psychological, and social framework. It is critical to understand this model as a foundational part of working in the addiction counseling field.

▶ THE NEUROBIOLOGY OF SUBSTANCE USE DISORDERS

The Surgeon General's Report on Alcohol, Drugs, and Health (DHHS, 2016) is an important resource for understanding the neurobiology of addiction and the scientific principles of substance use. Years of research have demonstrated that chronic substance misuse profoundly disrupts the brain circuitry involved in the experience of pleasure, reward, habit formation, stress, and decision-making. Scientific evidence has also shown that substance use disorders are chronic brain diseases that have the potential for recovery and relapse that occur in a cyclical fashion (Brown-Rice & Moro, 2018; Cavaiola et al., 2022; DHHS, 2016; Erickson, 2018; Veach & Moro, 2018). There are many complicated processes that are involved in the brain in relation to the development of a substance use disorder. Breaking them down into three main concepts makes it much easier to understand:

1. Brain structures involved in substance use disorders.
2. The brain's neurotransmitter communication system.
3. The addiction cycle that fuels substance use disorders.

▶ BRAIN STRUCTURES INVOLVED IN SUBSTANCE USE DISORDERS

The brain is organized into two hemispheres, the right and left. They are connected by the corpus callosum, a thick band of nerve fibers that allows the two hemispheres to communicate. These brain structures and subcortical systems communicate through neural activity and chemical messengers called neurotransmitters.

The brain is divided into four sets of lobes. In relation to substance use disorders, the most important one to understand is the frontal lobe where the **prefrontal cortex (PFC)** resides; it is the executive command center of the brain, critical in problem solving, decision-making, moral reasoning, and emotional regulation—all important activities relative to substance use and misuse.

Deep inside the brain are many subcortical structures that connect into systems that affect healthy brain functioning, mental health, and substance use. The most important functional brain system in relation to addiction is the **limbic system** which helps people respond to emotional cues and threats and plays a role in motivation, addiction, and sexual behavior. While there are several subcortical structures in in the limbic system, the two most important ones for understanding the addiction cycle are the **basal ganglia** and the **amygdala**.

The **basal ganglia** functions as a person's reward and motivation system as it has a high concentration of dopamine projections. **Dopamine** is a neurotransmitter that is known as the "feel good neurotransmitter." It is associated with feelings of pleasure and reinforcement, motivating us to perform certain activities repeatedly. The basal ganglia controls the rewarding or pleasurable effects of substances and is responsible for the formation of the habitual use of substances.

The **amygdala** is involved in processing emotions and responding to threats and stress. The feelings of unease, anxiety, and irritability that occur with withdrawal from substances reside here.

HOW THE BRAIN COMMUNICATES

Communication in the brain is carried out via neurotransmission. **Neurotransmitters** are chemical messengers that carry messages across the millions of neurons located in the brain, either exciting or inhibiting the neurons. Dopamine and the brain's naturally occurring **opioid neurotransmitters** are key communicators in the brain's reward system. Drugs that are misused often increase dopamine levels, contributing to the rewarding effects of substance use. The naturally occurring opioid neurotransmitters play a role in pain relief, pleasure, and reward and are triggered due to various physiological and psychological stimuli such as during times of high stress, injury, or when engaging in pleasurable activities.

The brain's **reward pathway** is a complex neural process that is involved in regulating feelings of pleasure, motivation, learning, and in the formation of habits and behaviors. The pathway responds to pleasurable or rewarding stimuli by releasing dopamine into the limbic system, also known as the mesolimbic dopamine system. The release of dopamine reinforces the behavior or action that led to the reward. This system is said to be **hijacked** when highly rewarding drugs are misused. The exaggerated dopamine release and alterations in the brain's reward system when substances are misused can contribute to the development of addictive behaviors and substance use disorders.

▶ THE ADDICTION CYCLE

According to the Surgeon General's Report (DHHS, 2016) the addiction process involves a three-stage repeating cycle: **binge/intoxication**, **withdrawal/negative affect**, and **preoccupation/ anticipation** (Figure 3.1). These processes become more entrenched as a person continues to use substances that hijack the brain's reward pathway. This cycle produces dramatic changes in brain functioning, reducing a person's ability to control the use of substances. Each stage of the cycle with the corresponding brain structure involved is described in the following.

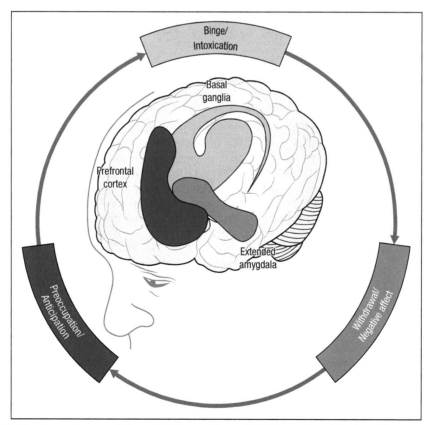

Figure 3.1 The three stages of the addiction cycle and their associated brain regions.

Source: From U.S. Department of Health and Human Services, Office of the Surgeon General. (2016, November). *Facing addiction in America: The Surgeon General's Report on alcohol, drugs, and health.* https://www.ncbi.nlm.nih.gov/books/NBK424849/figure/ch2.f3

1. **Binge/Intoxication Stage: Basal Ganglia**

   ■ Intoxicating substances are consumed and the brain's reward pathway in the brain is activated. The person experiences pleasurable effects and rewards.

   ■ Dopamine is released and the opioid signaling system is activated. The stimuli associated with the use of the substances is paired with the reward and over time the stimuli alone can trigger the dopamine and opioid signaling system.

   ■ The habit circuitry of the basal ganglia is engaged, contributing to compulsive substance seeking.

   ■ The reward pathway activation and habit neurocircuits explain **craving**, the intense desire for the substance and compulsive substance seeking.

2. **Withdrawal/Negative Affect Stage: Amygdala**

   ■ Following the binge/intoxication stage is the withdrawal state. This state activates future binges.

   ■ As withdrawal symptoms are experienced, negative emotions are triggered from the diminished activity in the reward circuitry, the diminished release of dopamine, and the activation of the brain's stress system in the amygdala.

   ■ The combination of decreased dopamine and increased stress neurochemicals reinforces the neurochemical process that drives compulsive substance use. Over time, the naturally occurring dopamine and opioid neurotransmitters slow down "production" due to the use of substances.

   ■ Decreases in the dopamine system account for the loss of pleasure in the use of substances and other pleasurable activities. People use more of the substance to try to regain pleasurable feelings. This is the definition of **tolerance**, using more of the substance to feel the same effects.

3. **Preoccupation/Anticipation Stage: Prefrontal Cortex**

   ■ This occurs when a person seeks substances after a period of abstinence. The period of abstinence can be long or short (i.e., hours, days, or months). Preoccupation with substances occurs throughout this time.

   ■ In individuals with substance use disorders, the prefrontal cortex *"go system"* is overactivated, driving substance-seeking behavior and the *"stop system"* is underactivated, promoting impulsive and compulsive substance seeking. This combination creates substance seeking behavior and a loss of impulse control.

The entire three-stage addiction cycle is repeated throughout the duration of substance use; changing the brain's reward pathway and leading to a loss of control over substance use. The addiction cycle is scientifically supported evidence of the biological disease model of addiction (Brown-Rice & Moro, 2018; Cavaiola et al., 2022; Erickson, 2018; DHHS, 2016; Herron & Brennan, 2015; Veach & Moro, 2018). Supported scientific evidence as outlined in the Surgeon General's Report (DHHS, 2016) shows that these changes in the brain persist long after substance use stops. It is not yet known how these changes can be reversed or how long that process may take. Treatment must consider the addiction cycle and leverage treatment modalities including medications, counseling, and social support to help heal the brain.

▶ RISK AND PROTECTIVE FACTORS FOR SUBSTANCE USE DISORDERS

The Surgeon General's Report on substance use disorders identifies important risk and protective factors that influence the likelihood of a person developing a substance use disorder (DHHS, 2016).

Risk factors increase the likelihood of beginning substance use, of regular and harmful use, and of other behavioral health problems associated with substance use. They can include a person's genetics; developmental, environmental, and social issues; as well as co-occurring mental health disorders. Biological, psychological, social characteristics, and experiencing trauma can also create vulnerabilities to develop a substance use disorder (Doweiko & Evans, 2024; DHHS, 2016; Veach & Moro, 2018).

Protective factors are the aspects in a person's life that directly decrease the likelihood of developing substance use problems or reduce the impact of the risk factors for developing a substance use disorder. They can be community-based and universal, as well as individually based and personal. Some examples of protective factors are a person's self-image, self-control, social competence, resiliency, parental involvement, positive mentoring and support relationships, and opportunities for positive community involvement (DHHS, 2016; Doweiko & Evans, 2024; Veach & Moro, 2018; Table 3.1).

Table 3.1 Risk and Protective Factors for Substance Use Disorders

Risk Factors	Protective Factors
Family history of substance use	Opportunities for positive social involvement
Genetics	Recognition for positive behavior
Early initiation of substances	Bonding and secure attachments
Rebelliousness	Committed personal relationships
Favorable attitudes toward substance use	Healthy beliefs and standards for behaviors
Peer and social group substance use	Emotional stability, good coping skills
Poor social skills	Behavioral and cognitive competence
Lack of commitment to school or work	Self-efficacy and self-control
Low cost and high availability of substances	Spiritual beliefs
Family conflict	Resiliency
Low economic status/poverty	Adequate financial resources
Community disorganization	Neighborhood pride

Risk and protective factors become influential at different times during a person's development and often correlate to physiological changes (e.g., puberty, aging, or health concerns) or to factors in a person's environment (e.g., moving, attending a new school, or divorce). Some risk and protective factors have influential effects across cultural groups and other sociocultural factors. Low-income and disadvantaged populations are generally exposed to more risk factors and to fewer protective factors (DHHS, 2016; Doweiko & Evans, 2024; Herron & Brennan, 2015; Veach & Moro, 2018).

There are a few important considerations to remember regarding risk and protective factors for substance use problems. First, no single individual or community level factor determines whether a person will develop a substance use disorder. Second, even though a substance use disorder can occur at any time and at any age, adolescence and young adulthood are critically important risk periods for substance use. Research indicates that most people who meet criteria for a substance use disorder started using substances before the ages of 20 to 25 (DHHS, 2016). This is likely because of the effects substances have on the developing brain, especially the prefrontal cortex which is not fully developed until somewhere between the ages of 21 to 25. The prefrontal cortex is the last brain region to develop and is primarily responsible for "adult" abilities (e.g., delay of reward, extended reasoning, and impulse control) and is the area of the brain most affected by a substance use disorder.

▶ PROGRESSIVE STAGES OF SUBSTANCE USE DISORDERS

As defined by the ASAM (2019), addiction is a treatable medical disease that involves complex interactions among the brain, genetics, the environment, and an individual's life experiences. Once a person starts to use substances, there is the likelihood that the use will progress along a pattern that can become problematic and continue despite harmful and negative consequences. The substance use, and the behavior patterns that surround the use, can become compulsive and impact many areas of a person's life (Waller, 2023).

The progression of substance use is classified on a continuum from abstinence to substance use disorder in a series of stages (DHHS, 2016; Fluyau & Charlton, 2022; Volkow & Blanco, 2023; Table 3.2). It is important to note that these stages are not linear and not everyone who uses substances progresses through the stages to a substance use disorder. Many factors converge to influence the progression of substance use including the person's genetics, environment, mental and physical health, and the individual's vulnerabilities and risk factors.

Table 3.2 Progression of Substance Use

Stage	Description
Nonuse or abstinence	No use of substances; may be due to personal choice, lack of access, cultural factors, or health considerations
Initiation or experimental use	First use; experiments out of curiosity, peer pressure, or other social influences, or an attempt to alleviate stress or discomfort
Regular and continued use	Uses substances more frequently and on a regular basis; substances are incorporated into routines and activities, increased frequency, and quantity of substance use
Harmful use and tolerance	Use starts to cause negative consequences; impacts areas of life such as work, relationships, physical or mental health, legal issues; struggles to control use; needs more of the substance to feel the effects; neurobiological changes occur as the brain attempts to maintain equilibrium
	Physical dependence: The body becomes dependent on the substance to function normally; leads to withdrawal symptoms if the substance is reduced or stopped
	Psychological dependence: Strong emotional and psychological cravings occur; reliance on the substance to cope with stress, regulate emotions, or feel pleasure
Addiction or substance use disorder	The clinical stage where individuals meet the criteria outlined in the *DSM*; can range from mild, moderate, to severe. Symptoms include craving, tolerance, withdrawal, impaired control over substance use despite negative consequences, changes in brain function in areas related to reward, motivation, and decision-making

DSM, Diagnostic and Statistical Manual of Mental Disorders.

If the use of substances continues to become a diagnosed substance use disorder, it is assessed using the *Diagnostic and Statistical Manual of Mental Disorders* **(DSM)** on a continuum from mild, moderate, and severe according to criteria outlined in the manual (American Psychiatric Association [APA], 2022). The *DSM* is the standard guide for classifying and diagnosing mental health disorders and substance use disorders. It provides the common language and criteria for practitioners to use to make a diagnosis. The *DSM* criteria for substance use disorders (Box 3.1) includes the presence of cravings, tolerance, withdrawal symptoms, unsuccessful attempts to quit or cut down, and continued use despite negative consequences. The criteria are broken down as follows:

- **Mild substance use disorder:** Diagnosed if person meets two or three criteria (Table 3.3). Involves a lower level of impairment due to substance use. The person might experience some negative consequences, but they generally retain some control over their substance use and the impact on their life.
- **Moderate substance use disorder:** Diagnosed if a person meets four or five criteria. The impact on the client's life is more pronounced and control over substance use diminishes. More significant impairment occurs in areas of life such as work, relationships, and health.
- **Severe substance use disorder:** Diagnosed if a person meets six or more criteria. Complete loss of control occurs in the client's life and there is significant impairment in multiple areas of life. Severe health, psychological, and or legal problems often occur in this stage (APA, 2022; Cavaiola et al., 2022; Veach & Moro, 2018; Volkow & Blanco, 2023).

Box 3.1 *DSM* Substance Use Disorder Criteria

The diagnosis of substance use disorder can be classified as mild, moderate, or severe based on the severity and number of symptoms observed out of an available 11. The exception is caffeine—which is diagnosed as either caffeine intoxication or withdrawal.

Presence of two or three symptoms indicates mild substance use disorder. Presence of four or five symptoms indicates moderate substance use disorder. Presence of six or more symptoms indicates severe substance use disorder.

Criteria/Symptoms

1. Strong urge to use substances.
2. Continual unsuccessful attempts to decrease or moderate substance use.
3. Substance is used over longer periods of time or in larger amounts than originally intended.
4. Use of the substance is repeatedly causing inability to fulfill obligations in work, school, or home.
5. Spending a significant amount of time and effort in obtaining substance, using substance, or recovering from its effects.
6. Continuing to use substance in spite of it repeatedly causing interpersonal problems.
7. Important social, occupational, or recreational activities are given up or reduced because of substance use.
8. Substance used recurrently in physically dangerous circumstances.
9. Substance use is continued despite causing persistent physical or psychological problems.
10. Tolerance shown by the need for increased amounts of the substance to achieve intoxication or desired effect or a weakened effect with continued use of the same amount of the substance.
11. Withdrawal as shown by the characteristic withdrawal syndrome for that substance or the substance being taken to relieve or avoid withdrawal symptoms. Not all substances result in withdrawal.

DSM, Diagnostic and Statistical Manual of Mental Disorders.

Source: American Psychiatric Association. (2022). *Diagnostic and statistical manual of mental disorders* (5th ed., text rev.). https://doi.org/10.1176/appi.books.9780890425787

Table 3.3 *DSM* Diagnosis Continuum by Symptom

Mild Use Disorder	Moderate Use Disorder	Severe Use Disorder
2 to 3 *DSM* Symptoms/Criteria	**4 to 5 *DSM* Symptoms/Criteria**	**6+ *DSM* Symptoms/Criteria**
• Intoxicating effects of the substance increase	• Tolerance begins	• Tolerance continues
• Reward process becomes established	• Give up activities that are not tied to substance use more frequently	• Wanting to cut down but unable to do so
• Primary peers begin to change to peers who share substance use	• Change of focus from future to right now	• Craving with compulsion to use occurs frequently
• Focus of energy, time, and resources begin to change (giving up activities due to substance use)	• Isolating occurs	• Frequently and predictably sacrifice activities to use substances
• Engaging in hazardous activities and desensitizing to them	• Lies, excuses, blame, hiding use and denial	• Failure at role fulfillment due to substance use
• Consequences increase and repeat (denial of problems increases)	• Loss of control accelerates	• Withdrawal symptoms
• Social and interpersonal difficulties begin due to substance use	• Consequences become more frequent and in more areas of life; i.e., job, family, friends, and financial	• Physical consequences (continued use despite recurrent physical or psychological problems)
	• Significant chaos in person's life	• Recovery can very difficult
	• Critical stage to begin recovery	• Death can occur if use continues

DSM, Diagnostic and Statistical Manual of Mental Disorders.

Source: American Psychiatric Association. (2022). *Diagnostic and statistical manual of mental disorders* (5th ed., text rev.). https://doi.org/10.1176/appi.books.9780890425787

▶ COMMON SUBSTANCES OF MISUSE AND THEIR CHARACTERISTICS

According to the *DSM-5-TR* (APA, 2022), substance-related disorders are categorized by the substance into 10 different drug categories. These categories are alcohol, caffeine, cannabis, hallucinogens, inhalants, opioids, sedatives, hypnotics and anxiolytics, stimulants, tobacco, and other (or unknown) substances. Each substance category correlates with the categories of substances that can be diagnosed as a substance use disorder in the *DSM-5-TR*, except for caffeine which can only be diagnosed as caffeine intoxication or caffeine withdrawal (APA, 2022). Each category of substances is described in the next section with the corresponding pharmacology, the psychological and social effects, drug interactions and cross-tolerance, short- and long-term effects, and withdrawal effects (Brown-Rice & Moro, 2018; Cavaiola et al., 2022; Center for Substance Abuse Treatment [CSAT], 2015; Doweiko & Evans, 2024; Herron & Brennan, 2015; Veach & Moro, 2018).

- **Cross tolerance:** The tolerance of one substance leading to reduced sensitivity or tolerance to another substance that shares similar effects on the same receptors or pathways in the body.
- **Withdrawal:** Predictable signs and symptoms that follow the abrupt discontinuation or rapid reduction in use of a psychoactive substance. It is critical to know to ensure clients receive the care they need and to avoid serious medical problems from discontinuing the use of a psychoactive substance. *The Detoxification and Substance Abuse Treatment Improvement Protocol (TIP 45)* published by the CSAT (2015) and *Concepts of Chemical Dependency*, 11th Edition, by Doweiko and Evans (2024) are good resources to study for in-depth information about the effects of psychoactive substances.

ALCOHOL
Pharmacology
The pharmacological actions of alcohol are complex and can vary based on many factors including genetics, body size, biological sex, tolerance, and overall health. Alcohol is a central nervous system (CNS) depressant that effects several systems in the body. Predominantly, it is taken orally where it is quickly absorbed into the bloodstream from the stomach, small intestines, and colon. The rate of absorption depends on how quickly the gastric system empties, mainly determined by the presence of food in the small intestines. If food is present, absorption is slowed, delaying the effects of the substance. Alcohol gains access to all body tissue as it is rapidly distributed through the body via the bloodstream. In pregnant women, alcohol affects the developing fetus as well as the mother.

Alcohol is broken down and metabolized by the liver. The rate at which the liver can metabolize alcohol can vary based on individual factors; however, as a general guideline, the liver processes one **standard drink** (Figure 3.2) per hour. Drinking more alcohol than the liver can metabolize leads to a rise in the blood alcohol concentration (BAC), which leads to the intoxicating effects of alcohol (Table 3.4). The effects of BAC are important to know when working with clients, and for the ADC exam.

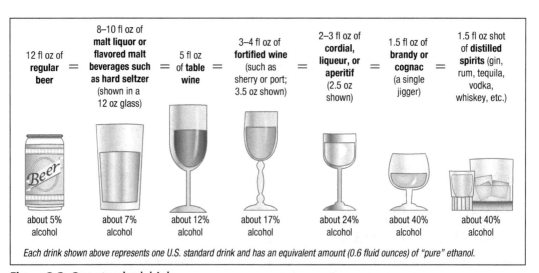

12 fl oz of regular beer	8–10 fl oz of malt liquor or flavored malt beverages such as hard seltzer (shown in a 12 oz glass)	5 fl oz of table wine	3–4 fl oz of fortified wine (such as sherry or port; 3.5 oz shown)	2–3 fl oz of cordial, liqueur, or aperitif (2.5 oz shown)	1.5 fl oz of brandy or cognac (a single jigger)	1.5 fl oz shot of distilled spirits (gin, rum, tequila, vodka, whiskey, etc.)
about 5% alcohol	about 7% alcohol	about 12% alcohol	about 17% alcohol	about 24% alcohol	about 40% alcohol	about 40% alcohol

Each drink shown above represents one U.S. standard drink and has an equivalent amount (0.6 fluid ounces) of "pure" ethanol.

Figure 3.2 One standard drink.
Source: From National Institute on Alcohol Abuse and Alcoholism. (n.d.). *What is a standard drink?* https://www.niaaa.nih.gov/alcohols-effects-health/overview-alcohol-consumption/what-standard-drink

Table 3.4 Levels of BAC and Effects

BAC	Effects
.02% to .03%	Mild relaxation, minor elevation of mood
.04% to .06%	Heightened relaxation, lowering of inhibition
.06% to .08%	Discoordination, impairment of judgment
.08% to .10%	Balance, speech, and reaction time impaired. Legal intoxication (in many regions)
.10% to .12%	Slurred speech, significant motor coordination impairment
.14% to .17%	Emotional instability, general severe impairment, potential for blackouts in memory
.18% to .20%	Profoundly intoxicated; potential for loss of consciousness
.25% to .30%	Severely intoxicated; risk of unconsciousness and alcohol poisoning
≥.35%	Severe risk of respiratory depression, coma, and death

BAC, blood alcohol concentration.

As a CNS depressant, alcohol's most obvious and observable effects occur in the CNS. Alcohol slowly puts the brain to "sleep" as the BAC increases. The prefrontal cortex, the part of the brain that is responsible for critical thinking and decision-making, is the first part of the brain impacted. As that part of the brain shuts down, people often make bad decisions and may behave inappropriately. When the prefrontal cortex is "asleep," the emotional part of the brain is in charge, meaning people are often unpredictable in their emotional responses. The next part of the brain to "fall asleep" if blood alcohol levels continue to rise is the cerebellum, which controls important motor movements such as walking and talking. This is why it is hard for people to "walk a straight line" at higher BAC levels and why speech is slurred. If the blood alcohol level continues to rise, the brainstem goes to "sleep." This is very concerning and dangerous because the brainstem controls the body's involuntary systems such as breathing, heart rate, blood pressure, and digestion. Death or coma can occur if this point is reached.

It is also important to understand that in addition to the liver and brain, alcohol affects many other organs in the body. The heart, pancreas, kidneys, and the gastrointestinal system are also impacted by heavy alcohol use. The gastrointestinal system includes the stomach and esophagus which can be damaged by heavy drinking. In addition to the organs, neurotransmitter activity is changed when alcohol is used. Gamma-aminobutyric acid (GABA), the inhibitory neurotransmitter, is enhanced leading to the calming and relaxing effect that is characteristic of alcohol intoxication. Alcohol also inhibits glutamate, which impairs cognitive and motor function as well as releasing the "feel good" neurotransmitters dopamine, endorphins, and serotonin. These neurotransmitters trigger the reward center of the brain leading to feelings of pleasure, relaxation, and well-being that reinforce substance use.

Psychological and Social Effects

Alcohol is the most commonly misused substance and while the pharmacological effects of alcohol are well known, they are complex and are rarely taken into consideration by those who misuse the substance or even by those who treat substance use disorders. This is largely due to alcohol being the most accepted drug to use; in fact, many do not consider it a "drug." Alcohol use has a long history and as such, both its positive and negative effects are a part of social and cultural life. Alcohol is used in ceremonies and religious practices, in cultural customs and traditions, as a symbol and status, as well as having economic significance. Many social gatherings and celebrations include alcohol, making it a challenge for some people to attend important events if they struggle with an alcohol use disorder.

Alcohol has many psychological effects. These include mood alterations, cognitive impairment, risk of dependence, and mental health consequences. Alcohol misuse can worsen existing mental health conditions and increase the risk of developing anxiety disorders, depression and, in some severe cases, psychosis. The social effects of alcohol are important to understand for diagnostic purposes. Excessive alcohol use can strain relationships with family, friends, and coworkers due to behaviors, conflicts, and communication problems. Alcohol use can lead to aggressive or risky behaviors, impaired decision-making in social situations, and social isolation and withdrawal. There are also legal consequences that can occur such as public intoxication charges, driving under the influence, or assault due to aggressive behavior while under the influence. Work and productivity can suffer leading to job loss. These all have a financial impact, causing more social problems.

Drug Interactions and Cross Tolerance

Alcohol can, and often does, interact with many different drugs. When combined with other CNS depressants, such as benzodiazepines or barbiturates, the sedative effects of both substances increase, leading to drowsiness, dizziness, impaired coordination, confusion, slowed breathing, and even loss of consciousness. Some medications mixed with alcohol can irritate the lining of the stomach leading to more severe gastritis, ulcers, or bleeding. Because alcohol and other medications are metabolized by the liver, mixing them can lead to potential liver damage or can interfere with the effectiveness of the medications.

Cross tolerance can occur with alcohol and other substances that act on similar neurotransmitters as alcohol does. Chronic alcohol use leads to increased tolerance to benzodiazepines, barbiturates, and other CNS sedatives.

Short- and Long-Term Effects

The short-term effects of alcohol use include slurred speech, drowsiness, vomiting, diarrhea, headaches, disturbed vision, impaired judgment, decreased coordination, altered perceptions, loss of consciousness, mood changes, disturbed sleep patterns, anemia, coma, and blackouts. Long-term effects include kidney and liver damage such as hepatitis and cirrhosis of the liver, malnutrition, stomach ulcers, gastritis, esophageal bleeding, high blood pressure, strokes, ulcers, sexual dysfunction, heart disease, dementia, and **Wernicke–Korsakoff's disease**, a neurological disorder that is the result of a severe deficiency in thiamine which occurs in chronic long-term alcohol consumption. It is characterized by confusion, problems with muscle coordination, involuntary eye movements, and severe cognitive deficits.

People who have alcohol use disorders can experience pancreatitis, an inflammation of the pancreas that causes severe abdominal pain, nausea, and vomiting. In severe cases, pancreatitis can be life-threatening. Alcohol use can also be life-threatening in other ways through alcohol poisoning, serious injury or accidents while under the influence, organ failure, suicide, chronic health conditions leading to death, drug interactions, and sudden withdrawal if the person has developed alcohol dependency.

Withdrawal Effects

Alcohol withdrawal occurs when someone who has been drinking heavily suddenly stops or reduces their alcohol use. **Alcohol withdrawal syndrome** is divided into two phases, **the acute** and **the extended phase**. The acute phase of alcohol withdrawal begins only hours after the last drink. Symptoms can be mild to severe depending on the duration and severity of the person's alcohol use, their overall health, and any other substance use disorders. The severity of the withdrawal can be assessed using formal assessment tools such as the Clinical Institute Withdrawal Assessment-Alcohol Revised (CIWA-AR), which will be discussed later. In mild alcohol withdrawal, agitation, anxiety, tremors, diarrhea, abdominal discomfort, exaggerated reflexes, insomnia, vivid dreams or nightmares, heart racing, headache, nausea, vomiting, memory problems, concentration issues, and possible seizures could occur and continue for about 48 to 72 hours after the last drink. In more severe cases of withdrawal, the symptoms can include hallucinations, hypothermia, sepsis, seizures, delirium tremens, and cardiac arrest. These symptoms can persist for up to 10 days after the last drink. In the most severe cases when the brain is dependent on alcohol, death can occur due to the neurons working erratically to correct the disruption in the delicate balance between the excitatory and inhibitory neurotransmission process that happens when alcohol is suddenly absent from the dependent brain.

Withdrawal from alcohol, in the acute phase, must be undertaken with care. A health assessment is important in determining the level of intervention needed to ensure withdrawal is safe and the most effective for long-term recovery. For high-risk clients, detoxification should be done in a medical setting to ensure health safety. Medications are very effective in easing alcohol withdrawal and facilitating detoxification (Table 3.5). In addition to medication, psychological support and counseling should be available to clients to address cravings, psychosocial issues, and to develop a recovery plan.

Table 3.5 Medications Used to Treat Alcohol and Opioid Use Disorders

Medication Name	Used for Substance	Application
Acamprosate	Alcohol	Reduces cravings by affecting neurotransmitters
Disulfiram	Alcohol	Discourages drinking by creating an unpleasant reaction in the body when alcohol is consumed
Naltrexone	Alcohol and opioids	Alcohol: Diminishes cravings Opioids: Reduces cravings by blocking opioid receptors and reducing euphoric effects of opioids
Buprenorphine	Opioids	Partially activates opioid receptiors to ease withdrawal and reduce cravings
Methadone	Opioids	Activates opioid receptors to reduce withdrawal and cravings. Often administered in specialty clinics under strict regulation

Many clients undergo withdrawal and detoxification without medical intervention, either due to being low risk for serious health problems or for lack of services. **Social detoxification** programs have been developed to help clients who might go through a more mild or intermediate withdrawal process. Social detoxification can vary by program; however, critical components should include an assessment by a qualified medical professional to determine level of care, access to life-saving services and support, qualified personnel familiar with the symptoms of withdrawal, social support, and basic life needs such as shelter and food.

Extended Withdrawal

The extended withdrawal phase, also known as postacute withdrawal, might last for 3 to 12 months after the last alcohol use. Some people experience anxiety, sleep problems, depression, emotional excitability and volatility, and fatigue. Recovery can be very difficult during this time as craving and sensitivity to triggers of alcohol use can lead to relapse.

CAFFEINE

Pharmacology

Caffeine is the most widely used mood altering substance in the world. It is estimated that 87% of the U.S. population uses caffeine regularly, from the morning cup of coffee, to a piece of chocolate to over-the-counter high dose caffeine drinks. Caffeine occurs naturally in many foods and beverages such as chocolate, coffee, and tea. It is also added into many things such as drinks, foods, and over-the counter medications and supplements where it can be found in high doses.

Caffeine is a fast-acting CNS stimulant that is rapidly and completely absorbed by the body after consumption. It is distributed throughout the body and reaches peak levels in about 30 to 45 minutes. It is metabolized by the liver with rates of elimination from the body varying widely as determined by variations in the individual consuming it. At moderate dose levels, caffeine increases blood pressure and has a minor effect on heart rate. It also stimulates gastric secretions and is a diuretic, meaning there is increased urination when caffeine is consumed. Caffeine also increases insulin, epinephrine, norepinephrine, cortisol, and activates dopamine. These physiological effects are directly tied to the psychological effects of caffeine.

Caffeine produces tolerance and withdrawal effect. Avoiding caffeine withdrawal is the most central reinforcing aspect of caffeine use. In the *DSM*, caffeine use is assessed and diagnosed as an intoxication and withdrawal issue but not as a substance use disorder problem. There is no formal recognition of caffeine use as a substance use disorder in the *DSM* due to more research being needed to determine the potential addictive or problematic aspects of caffeine use (APA, 2022).

Psychological and Social Effects

Caffeine is used to increase energy and prevent sleepiness but is also used for its pain relieving, or analgesic, effects. Caffeine has also been shown to improve cognitive and psychomotor performance. It also has some weight loss benefits; however, they are very minor. At low to moderate use, caffeine produces positive subjective effects such as an increased sense of well-being, happiness, energy, alertness, and sociability. There is a reason coffee is served at most social functions! At higher levels, though, caffeine can induce anxiety, nervousness, jitters, negative mood, upset stomach, and sleeplessness. This is why many people cease caffeine consumption later in the day. It's common to hear someone say, "I can't drink coffee in the afternoon, I won't be able to sleep!" The wide use and the reinforcing effects of caffeine make it a difficult substance to restrict on a large-scale social level and efforts to do so in the past have been unsuccessful.

Drug Interactions and Cross Tolerance

There are many drug interactions with caffeine as it is a widely used stimulant and is often combined with other substances producing known interactions. The most frequent substance combined with caffeine is nicotine. Cigarette smokers consume more caffeine than nonsmokers. Both caffeine and nicotine are stimulants and consuming them together increases their stimulating effects such as increased heart rate, blood pressure, and alertness. It also increases the individual's tolerance to both substances, meaning it will take more of both substances to reach the desired effect. When combined with other stimulants, such as amphetamines, methamphetamine, and some attention deficit hyperactivity disorder (ADHD) medications, an increase in heart rate, nervousness, and agitation can occur. Combining caffeine with benzodiazepines and other sedatives can reduce the sedative effects of the drugs. When combined with alcohol, a depressant, caffeine can mask or partially counteract the depressant effect of the alcohol. This leads to people feeling more awake and less impaired than they really are. This can increase the risk of overconsuming alcohol or engaging in more risky behaviors while drinking, leading to serious injury.

Short- and Long-Term Effects

Many perceive the short-term effects of caffeine as positive. These effects include increased alertness, increased physical performance, enhanced mood, reduced fatigue, and better cognitive functioning. Other effects that are less overtly positive are increases in heart rate, blood pressure, and urination. Excessive amounts of caffeine in the short term can cause headaches, digestive issues, anxiousness, and jitteriness.

There is a great deal of variation in the long-term effects of caffeine among individuals based on genetics, overall health, tolerance, and sensitivity to caffeine's effects. If used in moderation, the long-term effects of caffeine are considered safe for most individuals. However, excessive use of caffeine over time can lead to dependency and tolerance, sleep disturbances, increased anxiety and restlessness, digestive issues, cardiovascular problems, and poor bone health.

Withdrawal Effects

There are withdrawal effects associated with long-term caffeine use if the caffeine is abruptly stopped. This can include severe headaches, irritability, fatigue, and difficulty concentrating. There is a great deal of variation in the long-term effects of caffeine among individuals based on their genetics, overall health, tolerance, and sensitivity to caffeine's effects.

CANNABIS

Pharmacology

Marijuana, a member of the cannabis family of plants, interacts with the body's endocannabinoid system and is consider a depressant. Marijuana interacts with a complex network of receptors in the brain and CNS, enzymes that regulate various physiological processes, and naturally occurring cannabinoids in the body. The active ingredient in marijuana is delta-9-tetrahydrocannabinol (THC), a cannabidiol (CBD). THC is the primary psychoactive compound found throughout the marijuana plant with its highest concentration being in the small upper leaves and the flowering top of the plant, as well as hashish and hashish oil which are extracted from the marijuana plant. THC blocks neurotransmitters that inhibit dopamine release, allowing excess dopamine to be released into the body, creating a sense of relaxation. THC also interacts with cannabinoid receptors leading to euphoria, altered perception, increased appetite, and impaired memory and coordination. CBD interacts with the endocannabinoid system differently than THC. CBD influences the receptors indirectly which leads to more therapeutic effects in the body acting as an antiinflammatory and analgesic.

In addition to marijuana, there are also synthetic cannabinoid-like drugs that are important to know. Synthetic cannabinoids are created in a lab and designed to mimic the effects of THC. They are known as "Spice," "K2," "Black Mamba," and "Scooby Snax" and can be of varying potency producing unpredictable and sometimes severe intoxicating effects.

Even though marijuana is classified as a depressant drug, it does have psychedelic effects at high doses. The route of administration and the potency of the marijuana determine the intoxicating effects. Marijuana can be smoked, vaped, ingested as edibles, and used orally such via oils placed under the tongue. The most effective route of administration is inhalation. When smoked, THC quickly goes into the circulation system through the lungs and into blood-rich organs and tissues. Over time and with heavy use, THC builds up in fatty tissue and is slowly released back into the bloodstream. In these instances, THC can be detected in the body up to 30 days after the last use while more sporadic marijuana use can only be detected up to 4 days after the last use. Drug testing for marijuana use typically involves testing for the presence of THC in the urine which can be present for days or weeks depending on the level of use. Blood tests are also used to detect THC in the bloodstream; however, it is not present in the blood for as long as it is in the urine. Saliva and hair tests are also used to test for THC.

Psychological and Social Effects

Marijuana is viewed by many people as a relatively harmless drug that has positive psychological effects such as relaxation, reduction in anxiety, increased sociability, and relief of pain and discomfort due to its anti-inflammatory properties. This has led to research and policy aimed at the legalization of marijuana. Many states and jurisdictions have legalized marijuana for medical and recreational purposes, although the federal government still recognizes it as an illicit drug.

Drug Interactions and Cross Tolerance

Marijuana's effects and interactions with other drugs can be varied based on the method of consumption, dosage, and potency of the THC and CBD. Combining alcohol and marijuana can enhance impairment and the cognitive effects of both substances. When combined with opioids and benzodiazepines, respiratory depression can occur as well as increase sedation. Combining marijuana with psychedelics can intensify anxiety, paranoia, and the alerted sense of perception. Cross tolerance can occur with marijuana; however, it is not as pronounced as with other substances such as alcohol, opioids, or benzodiazepines. If a tolerance has developed to the effects of marijuana, a reduced response to the effects of other cannabinoids or cannabis-related compounds can occur.

Short- and Long-Terms Effects

Marijuana's short-term effects include euphoria, altered perception, increased appetite, altered motor skills, anxiety, memory and learning problems, dry mouth, and increased heart rate. Long-term effects of marijuana use include decreased cognitive function, poor respiratory health, cardiovascular disease, and mental health issues such as panic attacks, anxiety, and paranoia. Heavy marijuana use also increases the risk of schizophrenia, especially in persons with genetic vulnerability to psychotic disorders.

Withdrawal Effects

Marijuana does not have many of the physical withdrawal effects as other substances. However, there are many behavioral and affective withdrawal symptoms and some physical symptoms that occur when heavy use of marijuana is stopped. These withdrawal effects have been termed cannabis abstinence syndrome or marijuana withdrawal syndrome and include irritability, aggression, anxiety, depression, insomnia, sweating, nausea, decreased appetite, and an intense craving for marijuana. This cluster of symptoms is the most intense in the acute stage of withdrawal (2–10 days) and can linger for as long as 4 months.

HALLUCINOGENS

Pharmacology

Hallucinogens or psychedelic drugs are a group of diverse drugs that produce sensory abnormalities and profound alterations in perception, mood, and cognitive processes when ingested. Scientists have been able to isolate and study the hallucinogenic compounds found in the various plants and mushrooms that produce hallucinogenic effects. Hallucinogens primarily affect the brain's serotonin receptors and dopamine neurotransmitters. Activation of the serotonin receptors lead to the alterations in sensory perception and processing, mood regulation, and cognition. The overlapping of the sensory inputs, referred to as **synesthesia**, often occurs causing one sensation to be translated into another (such as being able to "see" sound, "feel" smells, or "hear" sight). Hallucinogenic drugs excite the CNS which also affects the senses, time, feelings, moods, experiences, and mental processes. Recent studies have suggested that hallucinogens might induce changes in brain plasticity and connectivity, promoting neuroplasticity and synaptic growth. Hallucinogens are metabolized in the liver and excreted through urine, making a urine test the most common drug test for hallucinogens; however, because of the fast metabolism of these drugs they can be difficult to detect in urine tests. Blood tests, hair testing, saliva testing, and specialized medical tests can be used to detect the presence of these substances in a person's system.

Psychological and Social Effects

There are many psychological effects of hallucinogens and psychedelics such as alterations in perception, hallucinations, delusions, changes in sensory experiences, altered sense of time, and profound shifts in consciousness. Some researchers theorize that the default mode network (DMN)—the network of brain regions that are active when a person is not focused on the external environment but on introspection, self-reflection, and internal mental processes—is disrupted when hallucinogens are used. This disruption causes alterations in perception, cognition, and self-awareness. Hallucinogens can create psychological dependence, as people use hallucinogens to change their state of consciousness. They describe the experience as an expansion of the mind with an enhanced sense of clarity and heightened perception of the surrounding environment. Many cultures have used psychedelics in ceremonies and there has been a renewed interest in psychedelics in the treatment of mental health and substance use disorders.

People often believe that psychedelic drugs are not as dangerous as other types of drugs, mainly because there are very little physical, dependence, or withdrawal effects. However, the possibility of a "bad trip" where one experiences intense anxiety or panic that can last for several hours is a concern of this drug class. It appears that the person's overall psychological health, their expectations of the experience, and the setting in which the hallucinogens are used influence the subjective experience and the "trip" taken. Some people who use lysergic acid diethylamide (LSD) also experience "flashbacks" or perceptual distortions when not using the hallucinogens. These can be perceptual, somatic, or emotional experiences and can be very difficult and frightening.

Drug Interactions and Cross Tolerance

The interactions of hallucinogens with other substances can vary widely by substance and by the individual. Because hallucinogens primarily affect serotonin receptors, combining them with other medications that affect serotonin levels, such as antidepressants, can lead to serotonin syndrome, a potentially life-threatening condition. Agitation, confusion, rapid heart rate, and seizures can occur. Combining hallucinogens with alcohol or cannabis can intensify the effects of both substances, causing increased disorientation, impaired judgment, and unpredictable responses. When combined with stimulants, increased heart rate, blood pressure, agitation, anxiety, or panic reactions can occur.

Cross tolerance among the various hallucinogens can occur due to their shared actions on the neurotransmitter systems, primarily serotonin. When a person develops tolerance to one hallucinogen, it may result in reduced sensitivity or tolerance to others that act on similar receptors as is the case with LSD and psilocybin.

Short- and Long-Term Effects

The short-term effects of hallucinogens are altered perception of time, mood dysregulation, delusions, hallucinations, changes in sensory experiences, shifts in consciousness, inability to tell fantasy from reality, panic, memory loss, confusion, muscle relaxation or weakness, problems with movement, enlarged pupils, nausea, vomiting, and drowsiness. The long-term effects of hallucinogens vary by the individual but can include persistent psychotic symptoms, paranoia, hallucinations, disorganized thinking, flashbacks, negative mental health effects, mood swings, and psychological dependence.

Withdrawal Effects

Hallucinogens typically do not induce withdrawal effects because they do not produce significant physical dependence even after regular use. However, flashbacks and other psychological effects may occur such as anxiety, panic, depersonalization, and emotional instability. Disrupted sleep patterns and visual disturbance can also occur that are bothersome and concerning; however they typically remit without medical intervention and diminish over time.

INHALANTS, SOLVENTS, AND AEROSOLS
Pharmacology
Inhalants, solvents, and aerosols are a broad group of substances that can be misused to produce psychoactive effects. Table 3.6 includes a list of commonly misused inhalants, solvents, and aerosols. Most inhalants are common household products, cleaning products, herbicides, pesticides, and forms of glue and paint. Because they are varied and of many different types, it is difficult to broadly assign this class of substance into a type. Some substances have depressant effects, and some have stimulant

Table 3.6 Commonly Abused Inhalants/Solvents

Type	Example	Chemicals in Inhalant/Solvent
Adhesives	Airplane glue	Toluene, ethyl acetate
	Other glue	Hexane, toluene, methyl chloride, acetone, methyl ethyl ketone, and methyl butyl ketone
	Special cements	Trichloroethylene, tetrachlorethylene
Aerosols	Spray paint	Butane, propane (United States), fluorocarbons, toluene, hydrocarbons, "Texas shoe shine" (a spray containing toluene)
	Hair spray	Butane, propane (United States), and CFCs
	Deodorant; air freshener	Butane, propane (United States), and CFCs
	Analgesic spray	CFCs
	Asthma spray	CFCs
	Fabric spray	Butane. Trichloroethane
	PC cleaner	Dimethyl ether, hydro fluorocarbons
Anesthetics	Gaseous	Nitrous oxide
	Liquid	Halothane, enflurane
	Local	Ethyl chloride
Cleaning agents	Dry cleaning	Tetrachloroethylene, trichloroethane
	Spot remover	Xylene, petroleum distillates, and chlorohydrocarbon
	Degreaser	Tetrachloroethylene, trichloroethane, and trichloroethylene
Solvents and gases	Nail polish remover	Acetone, ethyl acetate
	Paint remover	Toluene, methylene chloride, methanol acetone, and ethyl acetate
	Paint thinner	Petroleum distillates, esters, and acetone
	Correction fluid and thinner	Trichloroethylene, trichloroethane
	Fuel gas	Butane, isopropane
	Lighter	Butane, isopropane
	Fire extinguisher	Bromochlorodifluoromethane
Food products	Whipped cream	Nitrous oxide
	Whippets	Nitrous oxide
"Room odorizers"	Locker room, rush, and poppers	Isoamyl, isobutyl, isopropyl or butyl nitrate (now legal), and cyclohexyl

CFCs, chlorofluorocarbons.

Source: From Center for Substance Abuse Treatment. (2015). *Detoxification and substance abuse treatment: Treatment improvement protocol* (TIP) series, No. 45. HHS Publication No. (SMA) 15-4131. U.S. Department of Health and Human Services. https://store.samhsa.gov/sites/default/files/sma15-4131.pdf

or hallucinogen effects. The common factor in this group is the route of administration: inhalation. The inhalant enters the bloodstream via the lungs and quickly reaches the brain where it impacts various neurotransmitters. The effects are dependent on the type of substance. Dilation of the blood vessels and slowing down of brain activity typically occur producing feelings of relaxation and euphoria. Inhalants when misused can have toxic effects on various organs, particularly the brain, lungs, liver, bone marrow, and kidneys.

Psychological and Social Effects

Since inhalants, solvents, and aerosols are common household products, they are mostly misused by adolescents. They are also relatively inexpensive and can be purchased by anyone. The psychological effects are varied based on the substance. Most inhaled substances cause euphoria, a sense of relaxation, and disinhibition. They also can cause confusion, dizziness, disorientation, memory and attention problems, and altered perception of time and space. Mood changes include mood swings, irritability, agitation, and emotional instability. In some cases, the inhalant might cause hallucinations, sensory distortions, or paranoid thoughts.

The social effects of this drug class are consistent across this category of substance misuse. Social isolation, school or work problems, relationship problems, legal issues, health problems, and risk of addiction can all occur with inhalant misuse. Some researchers have made a connection between inhalant use and suicidal behavior, although the cause and effect cannot be clearly stated. It could be that inhalant use leads to depression and suicidal thoughts or, conversely, that the emotional issues lead to inhalant use. There is also the risk of accidental death through the method of inhalation such as using a bag that could cause suffocation. Regardless, it is important to address the emotional and social issues when inhalants are used.

Drug Interactions and Cross Tolerance

Combining inhalants with other substances of misuse can have severe effects depending on the type of inhalant used. In general, when inhalants are used with depressants like alcohol or benzodiazepines, respiratory depression or overdose can occur. When used with stimulants, the interaction can place strain on the heart and suppress breathing. Mixing inhalants with any other substances increases the risk of overdose. There are not enough studies, however, to determine if cross tolerance to inhalants or any other substance occurs.

Short- and Long-Term Effects

The short-term effects of inhalant use are euphoria, increased energy, increased heart rate, decreased appetite, increased focus and attention, insomnia or sleep disturbances, and increased sociability. Long-term effects center on behavioral and mental health effects. Chronic use can lead to serious health effects such as weight loss, malnutrition, heart problems, seizures, brain damage, dementia, and lung disease.

Withdrawal Effects

Little is known about the development of tolerance or withdrawal with inhalant use. A mild withdrawal syndrome has been observed in those who abruptly stop heavy and chronic use of inhalants. Withdrawal effects can include irritability, mood swings, restlessness, insomnia or disturbed sleep, cravings, and physical symptoms such as headaches, nausea, or tremors.

OPIOIDS

Pharmacology

The opioids are a class of drugs used for pain relief; they are also known as "narcotics." There are three kinds of opioids: **natural opioids** which include morphine and codeine; **semisynthetic opioids** which are drugs like oxycodone, heroin, and hydrocodon;, and **synthetic opioids** which include fentanyl and methadone. Opioids can be administered orally, intravenously, intramuscularly, and through the skin or other body membranes. All opioids produce pain relief effects by interacting with the body's naturally occurring opioids receptors that are in the CNS and the gastrointestinal tract. Opioids primarily affect the dopamine, serotonin, norepinephrine, and endorphin neurotransmitters. The body's naturally occurring opioid receptors regulate pain, mood, and other physiological functions. The activation of the receptors inhibits neurotransmitter release which reduces the pain signals along the nervous system, thus dulling and removing pain, but only temporarily. Opioids bind to the receptors in the brain, spinal cord, and other parts of the body mimicking the actions of endorphins and releasing dopamine, activating the reward pathway in the brain, also known as the mesolimbic dopamine system. Opioid tolerance, the need to use more of the substance to feel the same effects, develops quickly, especially to the "rush" or the euphoric effects of the substance created by the release of dopamine. Neuroadaptation occurs to the pain-relieving effects of opioids over time and often hyperalgesia can occur. **Hyperalgesia** occurs when the pain-signaling cells in the nervous system become more sensitive to pain. Individuals need more of the substance to feel the pain-relieving effects of the narcotic; however, increasing the dose exacerbates the pain sensitivity rather than providing pain relief. This is a vicious cycle that leads very quickly to addiction.

Psychological and Social Effects

Opioids provide temporary short-term pain relief by altering the perception of pain in the brain. They also provide a euphoric experience of well-being and relaxation. For someone who experiences pain, physically or psychologically, these are very desirable effects. Individuals who experience this sense of well-being and relief become psychologically dependent on it and seek to stay in that euphoric pain-free place by using more. Unfortunately, using more produces tolerance and hyperalgesia which increases pain and decreases the effectiveness of the substance.

There are generally two categories of people who use opioids: the person in chronic physical pain who overuses prescribed pain medication and the person who misuses illicit drugs like heroin. Overuse of opioids is a serious and chronic problem which has been declared a public health epidemic due to the number of overdose deaths that have occurred. The social effects of opioid use are many including disrupted relationships, social isolation, financial hardships, legal and criminal problems, poor parenting of children, community health issues, workplace problems, stigma, and discrimination.

Drug Interactions and Cross Tolerance

When combined with other substances, opioid use can lead to dangerous drug interactions. There is an increased risk of severe respiratory depression, sedation, coma, or death if opioids are used with other CNS depressants such as benzodiazepines, alcohol, or barbiturates. When used with certain antidepressants, serotonin syndrome may occur which includes symptoms of confusion, rapid heart rate, increased body temperature, and seizures. Some medications such as antibiotics, antihistamines, antipsychotics, or antifungals can intensify the effects of opioids and increase the risk of overdose.

Cross-tolerance between opioids and other various substances that act on the opioid receptors can occur. When a person develops tolerance to one opioid, it may result in reduced sensitivity or tolerance to other opioids. Cross tolerance to endogenous opioids, the body's naturally occurring opioids, can also occur. Some CNS depressants such as benzodiazepines, alcohol, or barbiturates can also exhibit cross tolerance to opioids due to the overall impact on brain function and neurotransmitter systems.

Short- and Long-Term Effects

Short-term effects of opioids are pain relief, drowsiness, nausea, constipation, euphoria, relaxation, confusion, mood changes, itchiness, slowed breathing, or death in the case of overdose. In the case of overdose, medications can be used to reverse the effects of overdose. Naloxone (Narcan) is used to rapidly reverse the respiratory depression caused by opioid overdose by binding to the opioid receptors in the brain and blocking the effects of the opioids that were used. Long-term use of opioids can lead to tolerance, addiction, chronic health issues, hormonal imbalances, increased risk of infections, gastrointestinal issues, and respiratory issues. There are also long-term psychological effects such as mood disorders, depression, anxiety, cognitive changes, and changes in behaviors. Box 3.2 includes the signs and symptoms of opioid intoxication and withdrawal.

Withdrawal Effects

While withdrawal from opioids can be very unpleasant, it is rarely fatal. The severity of symptoms depends on the level and duration of opioid use. Common withdrawal symptoms include flu-like

Box 3.2 Signs and Symptoms of Opioid Intoxication and Withdrawal

Opioid Intoxication	Opioid Withdrawal
Signs • Bradycardia (slow pulse) • Hypotension (low blood pressure) • Hypothermia (low body temperature) • Sedation • Meiosis (pinpoint pupils) • Hypokinesis (slowed movement) • Slurred speech • Head nodding **Symptoms** • Euphoria • Analgesia (pain-killing effects) • Calmness	**Signs** • Tachycardia (fast pulse) • Hypertension (high blood pressure) • Hyperthermia (high body temperature) • Insomnia • Mydriasis (enlarged pupils) • Hyperreflexia (abnormally heightened reflexes) • Diaphoresis (sweating) • Piloerection (gooseflesh) • Increased respiratory rate • Lacrimation (tearing), yawning • Rhinorrhea (runny nose) • Muscle spasms **Symptoms** • Abdominal cramps, nausea, vomiting, and diarrhea • Bone and muscle pain • Anxiety

Source: From Center for Substance Abuse Treatment. (2015). *Detoxification and substance abuse treatment: Treatment improvement protocol* (TIP) series, no. 45. HHS Publication No. (SMA) 15-4131. U.S. Department of Health and Human Services. https://store.samhsa.gov/sites/default/files/sma15-4131.pdf

symptoms, body aches, muscle and joint pain, gastrointestinal problems, nausea, vomiting, diarrhea, abdominal cramping, appetite changes, sweating, chills, goosebumps, increased heart rate and blood pressure, insomnia, nightmares, tingling and itching skin, anxiety, irritability, restlessness, agitation, mood swings, difficulty concentrating, confusion, and intense drug craving (see Box 3.2). The withdrawal can be so uncomfortable that people feel they have no choice but to use the substance again to "get well." This often derails efforts at detoxification and recovery. Medications are very effective in easing the withdrawal and facilitating detoxification as is psychological support and counseling to address cravings and develop a recovery plan. Table 3.5 includes the medications for both opioid and alcohol withdrawal.

SEDATIVES, HYPNOTICS, AND ANXIOLYTICS

Pharmacology

Sedatives, hypnotics, and anxiolytics are three classes of drugs that are CNS depressants. They are synthetic compounds that are prescribed for use under medical supervision. These substances slow down brain activity by affecting the neurotransmitter GABA, causing drowsiness, relaxation, sleepiness, and decreased inhibition; much like alcohol only with greater effectiveness. Commonly used substances in this category that can be misused are benzodiazepines, nonbenzodiazepine hypnotics (Z-drugs), barbiturates, buspirone, and gamma-hydroxybutyrate (GHB).

Benzodiazepines and barbiturates are used to reduce anxiety and panic symptoms, alleviate muscle tension, induce sleep, and manage seizures. There are both short-acting and long-acting benzodiazepines. When taken in larger amounts than prescribed or when injected or snorted to induce rapid absorption, these substances can create a feeling of euphoria through a more pronounced sedative effect. GHB is a sedative-hypnotic that is often termed a "club drug" because it is rapidly absorbed in the body and produces a sense of euphoria, relaxation, and decreased inhibition that lasts for only a few hours.

Psychological and Social Effects

The sedatives, hypnotics, and anxiolytics substances have various psychological effects due to their impact on the neurotransmitter GABA. This inhibitory effect reduces anxiety and worry, allowing the user to feel a sense of tranquility. They also produce a sense of calm and sleepiness that is reassuring for many people who have difficulty sleeping and relaxing. The use of these medications can lead to increased tolerance and dependence on the substance with users becoming even more anxious and worried if they do not use the drugs. This is a never-ending cycle leading to addiction to and dependence on the substance to feel "normal."

In addition to the sedating and relaxation effects, these substances can also lead to impaired concentration, memory problems, and decreased inhibition. The decreased inhibition is a reinforcing social effect that allows many people to engage in social events without worry or anxiety. Increased sociability is often a goal when using GHB. There are other social effects with using these substances such as social behavior change, relationship strain, impact on employment or academic performance, and legal and safety concerns when misuse occurs.

Drug Interactions and Cross Tolerance

Drug interactions with this class of medications and other CNS depressants can be very serious and fatal. When combined with alcohol or other depressant drugs, CNS depression, coma, and even death can occur. When combined with opioids, risks include respiratory depression, sedation, and overdose. These are the most serious drug interactions and must be communicated to the client. Combining sedatives, hypnotics, and anxiolytics with certain older classes of antidepressants or muscle relaxants can increase the sedative effects and, when combined with antipsychotic drugs, can impair cognitive functioning and drowsiness. Over-the-counter antihistamines and even grapefruit juice can amplify the sedating effects of sedatives, hypnotics, and anxiolytics and impair cognitive functioning.

Cross tolerance among the various sedatives, hypnotics, and anxiolytics can occur due to their shared mechanism of action on the CNS involving the activation the neurotransmitter GABA. For example, if an individual develops tolerance to benzodiazepines, they might exhibit reduced responsiveness to barbiturates. There is also the potential of cross tolerance between sedatives, hypnotics, anxiolytics, and other CNS depressant drugs such as alcohol and opioids. The degree of cross tolerance is dependent on many things including the drugs used, the duration of use, and the person's individual biochemistry.

Short- and Long-Term Effects

The short-term effects of sedatives, hypnotics, and anxiolytics include drowsiness, slurred speech, reduced anxiety, poor concentration, confusion, dizziness, decreased reaction time, problems with movement and memory, lowered blood pressure, muscle relaxation, and slowed breathing. The long-term effects of this class of drug can lead to interference with normal sleep patterns, increased risk of falls and injuries, emotional blunting, cognitive impairment, occupational difficulties, social isolation, tolerance, addiction, and misuse.

Withdrawal Effects

The withdrawal effects from sedatives, hypnotics, and anxiolytics can lead to a wide range of symptoms ranging from merely uncomfortable to severe. The withdrawal symptoms include increased anxiety, panic, irritability, confusion, memory problems, restlessness, insomnia, disturbed sleep patterns, tremors, sweats, heart palpitations, increased overall heart rate, nausea, vomiting, diarrhea, numbness, delirium, hallucinations, and seizures. Prolonged use of these classes of drugs lead to the most severe withdrawal symptoms and should only be undertaken under medical supervision, especially if the use of the drugs has been combined with other substance of misuse.

STIMULANTS

Pharmacology

Stimulant drugs come in different forms under two main categories: amphetamines and cocaine. Cocaine, amphetamines, methamphetamine, crack, bath salts, flakka, and other synthetic drugs are the most misused in this category. Stimulant drugs can be ingested, smoked, inhaled, or injected. These drugs are CNS stimulants and are intensely rewarding and highly addictive. When used, stimulants flood the brain with dopamine and simultaneously block dopamine reuptake. In addition to the intense effects on the pleasure centers of the brain, stimulants also increase a sense of alertness and well-being when used. Stimulants also have many physical effects such as increasing blood pressure, heart rate, and temperature, and decreasing appetite.

While both cocaine and amphetamine are CNS stimulants and share similarities in pharmacology, there are some differences. Amphetamines can be used medically in the treatment of some mental health disorders such as attention deficit hyperactivity disorder. When used for a medically prescribed purpose, the effects are longer lasting and can be regulated to a therapeutic dose. They can be misused, however, and become addictive. In addition, methamphetamine is an amphetamine that is highly addictive and does a great deal of damage to the body when used even over a short period of time. Methamphetamine effects can last for days. On the other hand, cocaine has no medical benefits and is a shorter-acting stimulant, with the effects lasing only hours.

Psychological and Social Effects

Due to the pharmacological effects of stimulants, there are many powerful psychological effects connected to stimulant use. The euphoric feeling that is created when stimulants are used for the first time is very intense due to the flooding of dopamine in the brain and the blocking of the reuptake. This creates an intense high that is very hard to recreate after the first use because the brain and body start to compensate for the flood of dopamine that occurs with stimulant use. Often people who misuse stimulants are "chasing the first high" and simultaneously trying to avoid the unpleasantness of withdrawal. Other psychological effects include increased energy, mood changes, anxiety, paranoia, agitation, confusion, memory problems, and irritability.

Because stimulant use leads to increased alertness, increased activity level, and decreased appetite it can be seen as a desirable drug to use in our fast-paced, image-driven culture. The pressure to succeed and excel can drive some people to use stimulants to enhance their performance. These are positive short-term social effects that often lead to longer negative effects such as social isolation, relationship strain, financial problems, and impairment in work or school performance.

Drug Interactions and Cross Tolerance

Combining stimulants can increase the effects of the substances and increase the risk of heart problems, blood pressure issues, anxiety, and paranoia. This can also occur with over-the-counter stimulants such as decongestants or cold medicines. Combining stimulants with selective serotonin reuptake inhibitor (SSRI) antidepressants can increase the risk of serotonin syndrome which is characterized by agitation, confusion, rapid heart rate, and elevated body temperature. Mixing stimulants with alcohol or other depressant substances can increase the effects of both substances, straining the cardiovascular system. As the stimulant use masks its effects, overconsumption of the depressant medication can occur. This is particularly important to recognize with alcohol use due to the serious consequences of overuse leading to alcohol poisoning. Cross tolerance can occur between different drugs within the stimulant class. Individuals who become tolerant to one type of stimulant can have a reduced effect with another stimulant; if this occurs, it will take more of the stimulant to feel the effects.

Short- and Long-Term Effects

Stimulants, both cocaine and amphetamines, have many short-term effects. These include narrowed blood vessels which increases blood pressure, enlarged pupils, increased heart rate and temperature, headaches, increased blood sugar, appetite suppression, anxiety, panic, paranoia, psychosis, and erratic behavior. More severe effects are heart attack, seizure, stroke, or coma. The long-term effects include nasal damage if inhaled, poor nutrition and health, weight loss, heart problems, problems with attention and memory, confusion, insomnia, intense and prolonged itching, and severe dental problems.

Withdrawal Effects

Withdrawal develops within a few hours of the last use of the stimulant. Because of the depletion of the dopamine neurotransmitter, a main effect of withdrawal is depression. Of particular concern is the possibility of suicidal ideation and attempts during this time. This is more pronounced with methamphetamine withdrawal because it is more prolonged and intense than cocaine withdrawal. Other withdrawal effects include hypersomnia or insomnia, fatigue, anxiety, irritability, poor concentration, psychomotor retardation, increased appetite, paranoia, and drug craving.

TOBACCO/NICOTINE

Pharmacology

Nicotine and tobacco come in many forms such as cigarettes, pipes, cigars, chewing tobacco, snuff, vapes, and e-cigarettes. Nicotine is found in tobacco products and acts as a psychostimulant and a mood regulator by its mechanism of action. Nicotine first stimulates and then depresses the CNS. Nicotine increases the heart rate and blood pressure by the release of epinephrine. It also binds to the nicotinic acetylcholine receptors in the brain and stimulates the release of dopamine which is rewarding and pleasurable; creating addictive effects. It then depresses the CNS causing the sensation of relaxation and relief from stress and hunger. The rapid delivery of nicotine throughout the body that occurs with each "puff" ensures a steady stream of the simultaneous stimulant and relaxation effects of the substance. This reinforces the addictive process and promotes use during both low and high arousal situations.

Psychological and Social Effects

Because of its psychostimulant properties and relaxation effect, nicotine is an addictive substance that creates profound psychological effects and cravings. Nicotine is a temporary mood enhancer producing feelings of pleasure, relaxation, and a reduction in anxiety and stress. It can improve concentration and cognitive performance. It also acts as an appetite suppressant which most people perceive as positive. Smoking can be a social activity that is a connecting and bonding point for many people. Social interactions are influenced by the use of tobacco; peer influence to use tobacco is very powerful but over time there has been more social stigma and awareness of the negative health effects of smoking. Secondhand smoke exposure raises concerns for nonsmokers and many policies have been put in place to reduce these risks such as banning indoor use of cigarettes and vaping products.

Drug Interactions and Cross Tolerance

Nicotine interacts with many other drugs and substances which can alter the way that both are metabolized by the body. Caffeine and nicotine are frequently used together (i.e., smoking and drinking coffee). Using them together heightens the stimulant effects and increases heart rate and blood pressure. Nicotine is also used frequently with alcohol. Nicotine has been found to increase the rate at which alcohol is metabolized by the body and can lead to consuming more alcohol to feel the same effects. Nicotine can reduce the effects of antidepressant and antipsychotic medications, oral contraceptives, and certain heart medications.

Cross tolerance with nicotine and other substances is hard to determine based on the mechanism of action that nicotine has in the brain. Nicotine primarily affects the nicotinic acetylcholine receptors in the brain which are very specific to nicotine so the development of tolerance to nicotine might not directly lead to cross tolerance with other substances. However, because of the stimulation effects of nicotine, individuals may develop sensitivity to other stimulants or drugs that affect the dopamine or norepinephrine neurotransmitter system.

Short- and Long-Term Effects

The short-term effects of nicotine include increased heart rate and blood pressure, relaxation, stress relief, and hunger suppression. The long-term effects of nicotine are more serious and include risk of many types of cancers, bronchitis, emphysema, heart disease, leukemia, cataracts, pneumonia, pregnancy risks, poor dental and oral health, reduced immune function, skin damage, reduced bone health, depression, anxiety, and cognitive impairment.

Withdrawal Effects

As a highly addictive drug, the withdrawal symptoms from abruptly stopping tobacco use can be difficult. The withdrawal symptoms can vary in intensity based on the level of dependence, frequency of use, and individual factors. The most common withdrawal symptoms include cravings, irritability, mood changes, difficulty concentrating, increased appetite, sleep problems, fatigue, headaches, and coughing or sore throat. The withdrawal symptoms peak within the first few days and gradually decrease over time.

There are many strategies that can be used to help manage nicotine withdrawal symptoms and increase the chances of successfully quitting tobacco. Using nicotine replacement products such as gums and patches, medications prescribed by medical providers such as bupropion, and participating in support groups can help. Behavioral therapy is also very effective to address stress triggers and develop coping strategies to find ways to replace the positive effects of smoking with healthier ones.

OTHER OR UNKNOWN DRUGS

There are numerous other drugs of misuse that could be included under the category of Other or Unknown in the *DSM*. Steroids, "designer drugs," unregulated drugs, and over-the-counter analgesics and other medications and many more can be misused and lead to intoxicating effects especially when used in high doses and in combination with other drugs. It is important when assessing and screening the client to include questions related to these substances to ensure that a complete picture emerges.

Drug Classes and Summary of Common Substances of Misuse

There are many drugs that can be misused, and it can be difficult to remember them all. An important shortcut to help in understanding substances can come from knowing the drug classes. There are four main classes of drugs found in the common substances of misuse: depressants, stimulants, opioids, and hallucinogens (Table 3.7). **Depressants** slow down the CNS inducing relaxation, sedation, and sometimes euphoria. They can impair coordination, judgment, and memory. The risk of overuse is respiratory depression and overdose. **Stimulants** increase alertness, energy, and attention. They elevate heart rate, blood pressure, and can create a sense of euphoria. Overuse can lead to anxiety, paranoia, and cardiovascular problems. **Opioids** relieve pain and induce feelings of euphoria and relaxation. They can cause drowsiness and respiratory depression. Overuse can lead to overdosing which is fatal. **Hallucinogens** alter perception, mood, and cognitive processes. They can induce hallucinations, intense sensory experiences, and distort reality. The overuse affects vary widely and can be unpredictable.

Table 3.7 Substances of Misuse by Drug Class

Substance	Drug Class
Alcohol	Depressant
Barbiturates	Depressant
Benzodiazepines	Depressant
Buspirone	Depressant
Caffeine	Stimulant
Cocaine	Stimulant
Fentanyl	Depressant/opioid
GHB	Depressant
Hashish	Depressant/hallucinogen
Heroin	Depressant/opioid
Inhalants	Varied depending on substance
Ketamine	Hallucinogen
LSD	Hallucinogen
Marijuana/cannabis	Depressant/hallucinogen
MDMA/ecstasy	Hallucinogen/stimulant
Methamphetamine	Stimulant
Nicotine	Stimulant
Oxycodone	Depressant/opioid
Psilocybin (magic mushrooms)	Hallucinogen

GHB, gamma hydroxybutyrate; LSD, lysergic acid diethylamide; MDMA, methylenedioxy-methylamphetamine.

In addition to knowing the drug class, the signs of intoxication, overdose, and withdrawal are all important when working in the substance use field. It is also helpful to know the names by which the substances are called, both the common name and the street name (Table 3.8).

Table 3.8 Common Substances of Misuse

Substance (Street Names)	Signs of Intoxication	Signs of Overdose	Symptoms of Withdrawal
Alcohol Beer, wine, and hard liquor (Booze, Hooch, Sauce, Brew, Firewater, Juice)	Behavior, impaired judgment, reduced inhibitions, odor of alcohol, confusion, disorientation, delayed reaction time, flushed appearance	Alcohol poisoning can occur which is severe and life-threatening; mental confusion, slow or irregular heartbeat, hypothermia, seizures, unconsciousness, memory blackouts, decrease in temperature, pulse, and blood pressure, coma	Can be life-threatening for those who have been heavy drinkers for a long time; nausea and vomiting, sweating, headaches, insomnia, irritability, increased heart rate, intense dreams, hallucinations, tremors, delirium, grand mal seizures, DTs
Caffeine Beverages and food (Java, Joe, Liquid Energy, Rocket Fuel, Cup of Jolt)	Restlessness, nervousness, excitement, rambling speech or thoughts, increased heart rate, gastrointestinal disturbances, muscle twitching, insomnia	Anxiety, panic, nausea, and vomiting, flushed face, dizziness, rapid heart rate, insomnia, headaches, tremors, shaking, increased urination	Difficulty concentrating, depressed mood, irritability, fatigue, drowsiness, headaches, muscle pain, nausea
Cannabis Marijuana, hashish, hash oil, synthetic cannabinoids (Weed, Pot, Herb, Bud, Ganja, Mary Jane, Reefer, Spice, K2, Black Mamba, Scooby Snax)	Mild sense of euphoria, relaxation, sensory distortion, drowsiness, balance or coordination difficulties, increased heart rate, increased appetite, bloodshot eyes, dry mouth	At high doses THC causes unpleasant symptoms such as anxiety, panic attacks, paranoia, hallucinations, palpitations, disorientation and confusion	Behavioral and affective rather than physical withdrawal symptoms; cannabis abstinence syndrome or marijuana withdrawal syndrome: irritability, trouble sleeping, decreased appetite, anxiety, craving
Hallucinogens LSD, psilocybin, PCP, ketamine, MDMA, DMT, mescaline, salvia divinorum (Acid, Magic Mushrooms, Shrooms, Lucy)	Altered perception of time and reality, delusions, hallucinations, panic, mood changes, sensory abnormalities, impaired coordination, increased heart rate and blood pressure, dilated pupils, nausea, vomiting	Severe and prolonged psychosis, intense and persistent hallucinations, severe anxiety and panic, extreme paranoia, suicidal thoughts and behaviors, seizures	Possible visual disturbances, anxiety, panic, depersonalization, emotional instability, disrupted sleep patterns
Inhalants Volatile alkyl nitrites, nitrous oxide, solvents, fuels, and anesthetics (Whippets, Huffing, Poppers, Glue, Laughing Gas, Bolt, Air Blast)	Varies based on the substance used; common signs include euphoria, dizziness, confusion, blood vessel dilation, excitability, impaired coordination, nausea, vomiting, changes in heart rate, hallucinations, delusions	Varies based on the substance used; generally dizziness, confusion, hallucinations, delusions, slurred speech, nausea, vomiting, irritation of eyes and respiratory tract, difficulty breathing, rapid heartbeat, seizures	Varies based on the substance used but generally like sedative withdrawal; inattentive behaviors, fine tremors, irritability, anxiety, depression, insomnia, tingling sensations, seizures, muscle cramps

(continued)

Table 3.8 Common Substances of Misuse (*continued*)

Substance (Street Names)	Signs of Intoxication	Signs of Overdose	Symptoms of Withdrawal
Opioids Heroin, morphine, oxycodone, codeine, hydrocodone, fentanyl, methadone (Smack, Acy, Roxy, Dope, Percs, Vic)	Can be life-threatening based on type and amount used; generally euphoria, extreme sedation, analgesia (pain reduction), slowed breathing, slowed movements, drowsiness, slurred speech, head nodding, itchiness, slow pulse, pinpoint pupils, low blood pressure, constipation, hypothermia, lack of consciousness, coma, death	Can be life-threatening and requires immediate intervention; blue or grayish skin, unresponsiveness, limp body, fluid in lungs, respiratory depression, loss of consciousness, death	Can vary by substance but generally flulike symptoms such as joint pain, muscle aches, chills, excessive sweating, mood swings, insomnia, frequent yawning, agitation and anxiety, excessive tearing of the eyes, runny nose, increased respiratory and heart rate, increased blood pressure, gastrointestinal distress, heightened reflexes, goosebumps, hyperthermia
Sedatives, hypnotics, and anxiolytics Benzodiazepines, barbiturates, GHB, and Rohypnol (Benzos, Tranks, Downers, Bars, Bennies, Candy)	Drowsiness, slurred speech, impaired coordination, poor concentration, confusion, disorientation, reduced inhibition, memory impairments, slowed breathing, unsteady gait, lowered blood pressure, coma; can lead to death if used with other substances	Can be life-threatening; extreme sedation, slow or shallow breathing, confusion, disorientation, loss of coordination, limp body, low blood pressure, hypothermia, bluish lips or fingertips, unconsciousness, coma, death	Can be life-threatening if physical dependence has occurred; anxiety, panic, insomnia, restlessness, irritability, muscle tension, tremors, increased heart rate, nausea, vomiting, sweating, heightened sensitivity to light, sound, or touch, seizures, possible death
Stimulants Cocaine, amphetamines, methamphetamine (Uppers, Speed, Addy, Ice, Crack, Wake-ups, Go-Fast)	Euphoria, excitement, increased alertness and energy, erratic behavior, panic, paranoia, decreased appetite, elevated heart rate, dilatated pupils, increased body temperature, sweating, tremors or shakiness, agitation or restlessness headaches, erratic behavior, panic, paranoia	Can be life-threatening; severe agitation or anxiety, chest pain, high blood pressure, irregular heartbeat, hyperthermia, hallucinations, delusions, seizures, loss of consciousness, respiratory distress, stroke	Fatigue, exhaustion, disrupted sleep patterns, vivid dreams, anxiety, irritability, poor concentration, slowed thinking, depression, lack of motivation, drug craving, increased appetite, psychomotor retardation
Tobacco and nicotine Cigarettes, cigars, smokeless tobacco, and e-cigarettes (Cigs, Cancer Sticks, Chaw, Snus, Darts, Smokes, Stogies, Heaters)	Increased blood pressure, breathing, and heart rate; elevated mood, decreased hunger, temporary improvement in cognitive function	Excessive nicotine intake can lead to symptoms of nicotine toxicity; nausea, vomiting, dizziness, increased heart rate, headache, excessive sweating, abdominal pain, increased salivation, tremors, confusion, agitation, seizures	Intense cravings, irritability, anxiety, mood swings, difficulty concentrating, increased appetite, insomnia, fatigue, restlessness, headaches

DMT, dimethyltryptamine; DTs, delirium tremens; GHB, gamma-hydroxybutyrate; LSD, lysergic acid diethylamide; MDMA, methylenedioxy-methylamphetamine; PCP, phencyclidine; THC, tetrahydrocannabinol.

ASSESSMENT OF WITHDRAWAL

Assessment core function will be covered fully in Chapter 5, "Assessing the Client"; however, in terms of the scientific principles of substance use in Domain 1 (Box 3.3; Herdman, 2021), it is important to note that assessments can be used for assessing withdrawal symptoms as well as clinical treatment issues under the global criteria "identify appropriate assessment tools" (Cavaiola et al., 2022; Herron & Brennan, 2015; Miller et al., 2019).

Box 3.3 Core Function 4: Assessment

Definition: The procedures by which a counselor/program identifies and evaluates an individual's strengths, weaknesses, problems, and needs for the development of a treatment plan.

Global Criteria:
12. Gather relevant history from client, including but not limited to alcohol and other drug abuse, using appropriate interview techniques.
13. Identify methods and procedures for obtaining corroborative information from significant secondary sources regarding client's alcohol and other drug abuse and psychosocial history.
14. **Identify appropriate assessment tools.**
15. Explain to the client the rationale for use of assessment techniques in order to facilitate understanding.
16. Develop a diagnostic evaluation of the client's substance abuse and **any coexisting conditions** based on the results of all assessments in order to provide an integrated approach to treatment planning based on the client's strengths, weaknesses, and identified problems and needs.

Withdrawal assessments are used to determine potential withdrawal issues clients may experience and to help make recommendations for the appropriate level of care. The ASAM (2023) outlines a multidimensional assessment for providers to use to make treatment recommendations. The first dimension addresses acute intoxication, withdrawal potential, and withdrawal management assessment instruments to avoid any potential hazardous consequences of abrupt discontinuance of substances. There are several substance-specific withdrawal management instruments that can be used when assessing a client; the most frequently used ones are listed in Table 3.9 (DHHS, 2016; Herron & Brennan, 2015).

MEDICATIONS AND MEDICATION-ASSISTED TREATMENT

Medication-assisted treatment (MAT) can play a critical role in treatment of substance use disorders by helping people manage withdrawal symptoms, reduce cravings, and prevent relapse. MAT combined with counseling and behavioral therapies have been shown to be an effective approach to treat substance use disorders. Five medications, approved by the Food and Drug Administration (FDA), have been developed to treat alcohol and opioid use disorders: methadone, buprenorphine, naltrexone, acamprosate, and disulfiram (CSAT, 2015). These medications are listed in Table 3.5 along with their application of use. Currently, there are no approved medications available to treat marijuana, amphetamine, or cocaine use disorders (Doweiko & Evans, 2024; Herron & Brennan, 2015).

POSTACUTE WITHDRAWAL SYNDROME

In addition to acute withdrawal, addiction counselors must be aware of the longer term effects of withdrawal from heavy substance use. The predictable symptoms that follow acute withdrawal are known by many names including protracted withdrawal syndrome, protracted abstinence syndrome, long-term withdrawal, and, mostly commonly, postacute withdrawal syndrome.

Table 3.9 Instruments Commonly Used to Assess Withdrawal Symptoms

Drug of Dependence	Instrument	Notes
Alcohol	CIWA-AR	Not copyrighted and can be accessed online, 10 items, 2 to 5 minutes to complete; scores range from 0 to 67, a score of 10 or greater is clinically significant; requires training to administer
Benzodiazepines	CIWA-B	Adapted from the CIWA assessment instrument for alcohol; higher scores indicate more severe withdrawal symptoms; training is required to administer
Opioids	COWS	A standardized tool used to evaluate opioid withdrawal symptoms, medically based; 11 items scored on a scale from 0 to 4/5; total score is evaluated on a scale from mild to severe withdrawal; special training is required to administer
	SOWS	Assesses withdrawal symptoms like the COWS but with a focus on the client's subjective experience and self-report, 16-item questionnaire with each item scored from 0 to 4; higher scores indicate more severe withdrawal; does not require special training to administer
Cocaine	CSSA	A structured interview that includes 18 questions to assess the physical and psychological symptoms related to cocaine withdrawal; higher scores are associated with poorer treatment outcomes; requires training to administer
Nicotine	FTND	A standardized self-report instrument to assess the intensity of physical addiction to nicotine; contains six items that are scored to yield a total score between 0 and 10; the higher the score, the more intense the physical dependence on nicotine; does not require special training to administer

CIWA-AR, clinical institute withdrawal assessment for alcohol, revised; CIWA-B, clinical institute withdrawal assessment for benzodiazepines, revised; COWS, clinical opiate withdrawal scale; CSSA, cocaine selective severity assessment; FTND, Fagerstrom test for nicotine dependence; SOWS, subjective opiate withdrawal scale.

Postacute withdrawal syndrome (PAWS) is understood as the predictable set of symptoms that occur after a period of abstinence from long-term substance use. PAWS is an important concept to understand when working with clients and for the addiction counseling exam.

Gorski and Miller (1986) were the first to describe PAWS in their work examining the psychosocial stressors that occur in recovery when people are learning to live without the use of substances. Since that time, the understanding of addiction as a medical disease has further enhanced the understanding of PAWS. Long-term chronic use of substances leads to neuroadaptations or changes in the brain because of the continual activation of the reward circuitry system and dopamine depletion. The brain makes changes to restore equilibrium and homeostasis to account for the increased use of substances. Once a person stops using substances the brain must adjust by returning to baseline functioning and healing the nervous system damage done by the substance use. After the period of acute withdrawal, the postacute withdrawal phase starts and can last anywhere from 12 to 18 months or even longer depending on the individual (Alsheikh, 2021; Cavaiola et al., 2022; Gorski & Miller, 1986; Haskell, 2022; Veach & Moro, 2018). The common symptom clusters of PAWS are difficulty thinking clearly, difficulty with memory and recall, dampened emotions or extreme emotional responses, irregular sleep patterns, difficulty with coordination, and sensitivity to stress.

The risk of relapse is high during the PAWS period due to the physical, psychological, and psychosocial stressors that occur after abstinence from long-term substance use. Clients may experience any number of problems in the cluster of symptoms during this time. These may include headaches, cognitive problems, sexual impairment, stomach problems, anxiety, panic, mood swings, depression, chronic pain, intense urges and cravings, insomnia, problems with coordination, and a lack of initiative (Alsheikh, 2021; Haskell, 2022). It is important to note that the number and severity of symptoms experienced are worsened by stress. Addiction counselors must prepare clients for

PAWS and create plans to help them manage stress without returning to substance use. An effective intervention is providing psychoeducation on PAWS to help normalize the experience and give the client hope that the brain and body will heal. Working on coping mechanisms to address PAWS symptoms also helps the client learn to live without substances and decreases the risk of relapse (Cavaiola et al., 2022).

▶ CO-OCCURRING MEDICAL AND MENTAL HEALTH CONDITIONS

The screening core function (Box 3.4; Herdman, 2021) which will be described fully in Chapter 4, "Engaging the Client," contains the global criteria addressing screening for co-occurring medical and mental health conditions. It is important to note that addiction counselors must screen for signs and symptoms of co-occurring medical and mental health conditions to determine the need for additional professional services that are outside of the scope of an addiction counselor's practice. As a group, people with substance use disorders are more likely to need medical care and are more often diagnosed with a mental health disorder than the general population (Cavaiola et al., 2022; Doweiko & Evans, 2024; Meyers & Salt, 2019; Miller et al., 2019; Substance Abuse and Mental Health Administration [SAMHSA], 2020). Substance use impacts many systems of the body and can exacerbate existing health conditions or lead to medical and mental health problems. Substance use can also lead to many infectious diseases because of the inherent risks with using substances and the conditions in which those who become dependent on the substances live. It is important to know the signs and symptoms of the common medical and mental health conditions that co-occur with substance use disorders to provide the necessary referrals for good care.

Box 3.4 Core Function 1: Screening

Definition: The process by which the client is determined appropriate and eligible for admission to a particular program.

Global Criteria:
1. Evaluate psychological, social, and physiological signs and symptoms of alcohol and other drug use and abuse.
2. Determine the client's appropriateness for admission or referral.
3. Determine the client's eligibility for admission or referral.
4. Identify any coexisting conditions (medical, psychiatric, physical, etc.) that indicate the need for additional professional assessment and/or services.
5. Adhere to applicable laws, regulations, and agency policies governing alcohol and other drug abuse services.

The most common medical conditions that occur with substance use disorders include chronic pain, liver diseases, cardiovascular issues, respiratory conditions, gastrointestinal disorders, neurological disorders, pancreatitis, HIV/AIDS, hepatitis, sexually transmitted infections (STIs), pneumonias, and tuberculosis (CSAT, 2015; Doweiko & Evans, 2024). The mental health disorders that most commonly co-occur with substance use disorders include anxiety disorders, depression, bipolar disorders, posttraumatic stress disorder, personality disorders, schizophrenia and psychosis, attention deficit hyperactivity disorders, and feeding and eating disorders (CSAT, 2015; Doweiko & Evans, 2024; SAMHSA, 2020). It is important to note that many licit and illicit substances can cause symptoms that are identical to the symptoms related to mental illness and some mental health disorders are really substance-induced mental health problems. The best practice for the diagnosis of a co-occurring mental health and substance use disorder is to carefully monitor the signs and symptoms of mental health disorders after a period of substance use disorder treatment and abstinence (Table 3.10).

> **Tips From the Field**
>
> Stay in your lane! It is important to know your practice limits in relation to co-occurring disorders. Just as an addiction counselor would never assess and treat medical disorders, you may not be able to assess and treat mental health disorders. Check your scope of practice with your credentialing entity!

Table 3.10 Signs and Symptoms of Co-Occurring Medical, Mental, and Substance Use Disorders

Medical Disorder	Most Common Co-Occurring Substance	Signs and Symptoms
Chronic pain	Opioids	Increased medication use Medication seeking behavior Increased substance use Focus on immediate relief of pain Social and behavioral changes Pain medication tolerance and dependence Functional impairments: inability to perform daily living activities Withdrawal symptoms
Liver disease • Alcohol hepatitis • Fatty liver disease • Cirrhosis	Alcohol Cocaine Methamphetamine	Abdominal pain Jaundice: Yellowing of the skin and eyes Fatigue Swelling in the legs, ankles, or abdomen Easy bruising or bleeding Changes in mental status and functioning Unexplained weight loss Increased sensitivity to medications
Cardiovascular issues • Hypertension • Arrhythmias • Heart attacks	Stimulants Alcohol Nicotine	Elevated heart rate Increased blood pressure Irregular heart rhythms Chest pain Shortness of breath Swelling in the legs, ankles, or abdomen Fainting or dizziness
Respiratory conditions • Asthma • COPD • Lung infections	Nicotine Cannabis, marijuana Inhalants Methamphetamine	Chronic cough Shortness of breath Wheezing or "noisy" breathing Chest pain or tightness Decreased exercise ability Chronic fatigue or weakness
Gastrointestinal disorders • Gastritis • Pancreatitis	Alcohol Nicotine Cocaine Opioids	Abdominal pain Gastrointestinal bleeding Loss of appetite, weight changes Indigestion or heartburn Jaundice or liver pain Nutritional deficiencies
Neurological disorders • Traumatic brain injury • Dementia • Wernicke–Korsakoff's syndrome	Alcohol Stimulants Inhalants Benzodiazepines	Cognitive impairment Mood and behavior changes Motor function problems Seizures Neuropathic pain Sensory changes

(continued)

Table 3.10 Signs and Symptoms of Co-Occurring Medical, Mental, and Substance Use Disorders (*continued*)

Medical Disorder	Most Common Co-Occurring Substance	Signs and Symptoms
Hepatitis • Hepatitis A, B, C, D, E	Alcohol Injectable drugs such as heroin, cocaine, methamphetamine	Fatigue Jaundice Abdominal pain Nausea and vomiting Loss of appetite Dark urine and pale stools Swelling in the abdomen or legs Itchy skin Mental confusion Easy bruising or bleeding
Pneumonias • Fungal pneumonia • Aspiration pneumonia • Community-acquired pneumonia	Nicotine Inhalants Alcohol	Cough Shortness of breath Chest pain Fever and chills Fatigue Confusion or mental changes
Tuberculosis	Alcohol Nicotine Injectable drugs such as heroin, cocaine, methamphetamine	Cough Fever Night sweats Fatigue Weight loss Chest pain Respiratory problems
HIV/AIDS	Injectable drugs such as heroin, cocaine, methamphetamine	Recurrent infections Rapid weight lass Chronic fatigue Fever and night sweats Respiratory problems Skin conditions Cognitive impairment, memory problems
Sexually transmitted infections	Alcohol Stimulants	Genital discharge Rash or skin lesions Genital itching or irritation Pelvic or abdominal pain Painful intercourse
Mental Health Disorder	Most Common Co-Occurring Substance	Signs and Symptoms
Anxiety disorders • Generalized anxiety • Panic disorder • Social anxiety disorder	Alcohol Benzodiazepines Cannabis Nicotine	Persistent worry and fear Restlessness, muscle tension, fatigue Difficulty concentrating Panic attacks Avoidance behaviors Impaired functioning in daily living Heightened sensitivity to environmental stimuli Compulsive behaviors Increased substance use
Depression • Major depressive disorder • Persistent depressive disorder	Alcohol Opioids Cannabis Nicotine	Persistent sadness, hopelessness, and feelings of emptiness Social withdrawal Changes in sleep patterns and appetite Fatigue and lack of energy Difficulty concentrating Irritability and agitation Unexplained aches and pains, digestive issues Suicidal or self-harm thoughts

(*continued*)

Table 3.10 Signs and Symptoms of Co-Occurring Medical, Mental, and
Substance Use Disorders (*continued*)

Mental Health Disorder	Most Common Co-Occurring Substance	Signs and Symptoms
Bipolar disorders	Stimulants Cannabis Alcohol Benzodiazepines	Extreme mood swings Increased impulsivity Agitation or irritability Sleep disturbances Increased energy and restlessness Poor judgment Changes in appetite or weight Difficulty concentrating Psychotic symptoms, dissociating
Posttraumatic stress disorder (PTSD)	Alcohol Cannabis Opioids Nicotine	Flashbacks or intrusive memories Avoiding places and people that may trigger memories Hyperarousal Negative mood and thoughts Sleep problems, insomnia, nightmares, night terrors Self-destructive behaviors Social withdrawal Impaired functioning in daily living Increased substance use to cope
Personality disorders • Antisocial, borderline, and narcissistic personality disorders	Alcohol Stimulants Opioids Cannabis	Mood swings, emotional instability Impulsivity Relationship instability Reckless behavior Self-harm or suicidal ideation/attempts Manipulative behaviors Identity instability or dissociation Isolation or social withdrawal
Schizophrenia	Nicotine Cannabis Alcohol	Increased severity of psychotic symptoms Hallucinations, delusions Impaired cognitive functioning Medication nonadherence Poor insight or judgment Increased risk taking Physical health issues
Attention deficit hyperactivity disorder	Stimulants Cannabis Nicotine Alcohol	Impulsivity Difficulty concentrating Hyperactivity or restlessness Mood swings Risk-taking behaviors Sleep disturbances, insomnia
Feeding and eating disorders • Anorexia nervosa • Bulimia nervosa • Binge eating disorder	Stimulants	Unhealthy eating patterns Preoccupation with body image Compulsive exercise Uses substances as a weight management strategy Social withdrawal Mood disturbances, emotional dysregulation Medical complications, heart issues, stomach problems Denial and secrecy

COPD, chronic obstructive pulmonary disease.

▶ KEY POINTS

- This chapter highlights content on the ADC exam in Domain 1: Scientific Principles of Substance Use and Co-Occurring Disorders and the important global criteria from the Screening and Assessment Core Functions.
- To be effective counselors, addiction counselors need a comprehensive grasp of substance use disorder models, neurobiology, risk factors for substance use disorders, and knowledge of the various substances. Many models, including the moral, disease, biological, psychological, sociocultural, and biopsychosocial models, offer perspectives on addiction. The most currently accepted models are the disease and biopsychosocial models of addiction which are comprehensive and grounded in scientific principles based on the neurobiology of substance use.
- The neurobiology of substance use involves the prefrontal cortex, basal ganglia, and amygdala—the brain structures that impact the reward, habit formation, and emotional responses. Neurotransmission, particularly with use of dopamine and opioids, reinforces addictive behaviors in the brain's reward pathway. The addiction cycle comprises binge/intoxication, withdrawal/negative affect, and preoccupation/anticipation stages, influencing specific brain areas and neurochemical processes. Risk factors such as genetics, environment, and mental health issues increase vulnerability, while protective factors like resilience and positive relationships mitigate substance use risks across diverse contexts. Mastery of these aspects will equip you to pass the exam and effectively address substance use disorders and co-occurring conditions in your clients.
- As outlined by ASAM (2023), addiction is a treatable medical condition influenced by brain complexities, genetics, environment, and life experiences. Substance use, which can potentially lead to compulsive behavior with harmful impacts, evolves in stages along a nonlinear continuum from abstinence to a diagnosed substance use disorder. These stages, detailed in the *DSM*, signify varying degrees of impairment and control over substance use, ranging from mild to severe, where severe cases demonstrate substantial impairment across life domains.
- When diagnosing a client with a substance use disorder and working with them in treatment, you must recognize the drug classes. Understanding the four main drug classes—depressants, stimulants, opioids, and hallucinogens—provides a shortcut in comprehending the diverse effects of common substances of misuse and aids in providing a good assessment and treatment plan. Understanding the specific pharmacological, psychological, and social effects, plus drug interactions, cross-tolerance, short- and long-term impacts, and withdrawal effects of each class of substance, is vital in ensuring proper client care and for passing the exam.
- Assessment, a key component within the scientific principles of substance use in Domain 1, includes evaluating withdrawal symptoms and clinical treatment issues using appropriate assessment tools. Withdrawal assessments aid in predicting potential client issues and recommending suitable care levels. A multidimensional assessment covers acute intoxication, withdrawal potential, and management, employing substance-specific withdrawal instruments to prevent hazardous consequences from abrupt substance discontinuation. Additionally, screening for co-occurring medical and mental health conditions is essential, as substance use disorders often coexist with conditions like chronic pain, liver diseases, anxiety disorders, depression, and schizophrenia, necessitating referrals for comprehensive care outside the counselor's scope.
- Medication-assisted treatment (MAT), when combined with counseling and support, is the most effective treatment in managing withdrawal, reducing cravings, and preventing relapse in substance use disorders. There are several approved and effective drugs for treating alcohol use disorder and opioid use disorder; however, currently there are no approved or effective medications for marijuana, amphetamine, or cocaine use disorders. Behavioral counseling and support are the evidence-based treatments for these substance use disorders.
- Understanding PAWS is crucial when working with clients who are in recovery. PAWS encompasses symptom clusters, such as cognitive difficulties, emotional irregularities, sleep disturbances, and stress sensitivity, all of which can persist 12 to 18 months after substance abstinence. During PAWS, clients face heightened relapse risks due to the physical and psychological stressors, cognitive issues, anxiety, mood swings, and intense cravings. Addiction counselors play a vital role in preparing clients for PAWS, providing psychoeducation to normalize experiences, instill hope in recovery, and develop coping mechanisms to manage stress and mitigate relapse risks.

▶ **REFERENCES**

Alsheikh, M. Y. (2021). Post-acute withdrawal syndrome: The major cause of relapse among psychoactive substances addicted users. *Archives of Pharmacy Practices*, 12(4), 91–97. https://doi.org/10.51847/iOICfUjpnm

American Psychiatric Association. (2022). *Diagnostic and statistical manual of mental disorders* (5th ed., text rev.). https://doi.org/10.1176/appi.books.9780890425787

American Society of Addiction Medicine. (2019, September 15). *Definition of addiction.* https://www.asam.org/quality-care/definition-of-addiction

American Society of Addiction Medicine. (2023). *The ASAM criteria* (4th ed.). Hazelden.

Brown-Rice, K., & Moro, R. R. (2018). Biological theory: Genetics and brain chemistry. In R. Lassiter, & J. R. Culbreth (Eds.), *Theory and practice of addiction counseling* (pp. 47–75). Sage.

Cavaiola, A., Giordana, A. L., & Golubovic, N. (2022). *Addiction counseling: A practical approach.* Springer Publishing Company.

Center for Substance Abuse Treatment. (2015). *Detoxification and substance abuse treatment:* Treatment improvement protocol (TIP) series, No. 45. HHS Publication No. (SMA) 15-4131. U.S. Department of Health and Human Services. https://store.samhsa.gov/sites/default/files/sma15-4131.pdf

Doweiko, H. E., & Evans, A. (2024). *Concepts of chemical dependency* (11th ed.). Cengage Learning.

Erickson, C. K. (2018). *The science of addiction: From neurobiology to treatment* (2nd ed.). W.W. Norton & Co.

Fluyau, D., & Charlton, T. E. (2022). *Drug addiction.* National Library of Medicine. https://www.ncbi.nlm.nih.gov/books/NBK549783/

Gorski, T. T., & Miller, M. (1986). *Staying sober: A guide for relapse prevention.* Herald House/Independence Press.

Haskell, B. (2022). Identification and evidence-based treatment of post-acute withdrawal syndrome. *The Journal for Nurse Practitioners*, 18(3), 272–275. https://doi.org/10.1016/j.nurpra.2021.12.021

Herdman, J. W. (2021). *Global criteria: The 12 core functions of the substance abuse counselor* (8th ed.).

Herron, A. J., & Brennan, T. K. (2015). *The ASAM essentials of addiction medicine.* Wolters Kluwer.

Lassiter, P. S., & Spivey, M. S. (2018). Historical perspectives and the moral model. In R. Lassiter, & J. R. Culbreth (Eds.), *Theory and practice of addiction counseling* (pp. 27–46). Sage.

Meyers, P. L., & Salt, N. R. (2019). *Becoming an addictions counselor: A comprehensive text* (4th ed.). Jones & Bartlett Learning.

Miller, W. R., Forcehimes, A. A., & Zweben, A. (2019). *Treating addiction: A guide for professionals* (4th ed.). The Guilford Press.

Substance Abuse and Mental Health Services Administration. (2020). *Substance use disorder treatment for people with co-occurring disorders:* Treatment improvement protocol (TIP) series, No. 42. SAMHSA Publication No. PEP20-02-01-004. U.S. Department of Health and Human Services. https://store.samhsa.gov/sites/default/files/pep20-02-01-004.pdf

U.S. Department of Health and Human Services, Office of the Surgeon General. (2016, November). *Facing addiction in America: The Surgeon General's Report on alcohol, drugs, and health.* https://www.ncbi.nlm.nih.gov/books/NBK424849/figure/ch2.f3

Veach, L. J., & Moro, R. R. (2018). *The spectrum of addiction: Evidence-based assessment, prevention, and treatment across the lifespan.* Sage.

Volkow, N. D., & Blanco, C. (2023). Substance use disorders: A comprehensive update of classification, epidemiology, neurobiology, clinical aspects, treatment, and prevention. *World Psychiatry*, 22(2), 203–229. https://doi.org/10.1002/wps.21073

Waller, R. C. (2023). *The ASAM criteria: Treatment criteria for addictive, substance-related and co-occurring conditions* (4th ed.). Hazelden Betty Ford Foundation.

CASE STUDY 3.1

A 54-year-old White male presents to an emergency clinic complaining of a headache, vomiting, insomnia, racing heart, and odd perceptual experiences that include seeing and hearing things that are not real. The physician notes that the man is sweating heavily, has a strong odor of alcohol, and his hands are shaking. A counselor is called in to complete a substance use evaluation after the doctor's examination. During the evaluation, the client shares that he drinks alcohol daily, mostly hard liquor, and that he has recently been fired from his job for violating the substance use policy. He came to work under the influence of alcohol several times and has had numerous accidents at work. He estimates that he drinks roughly a fifth of whiskey every other day. His last drink was yesterday (about 20 hours ago) and he started feeling sick when he woke up this morning. He shares that he stopped because he feels he may have a problem with alcohol and wants to prove to his wife that he can stop drinking. He also reports he has been smoking marijuana daily and has used a benzodiazepine for anxiety as prescribed by his doctor, however, his prescription was not refilled at the last visit. The doctor refused to refill it after learning that the client was drinking daily. The client is requesting medication to help him sleep. The counselor is very concerned because the client states he has been very depressed and has had suicidal thoughts. He also reports seeing things that no one else does and this scares him.

1. Based on the information presented, what substance of use should concern the counselor the most?

2. What withdrawal assessment instruments should be used with this client?

3. What recommendations should the counselor make to the doctor based on the information they have gathered from the client?

(See answers on the next page.)

CASE STUDY 3.1 ANSWERS

1. The use of alcohol and benzodiazepines together are the most concerning for this client. Both substances are CNS depressants and their use together can be life-threatening. Their effects are amplified and can lead to severe consequences such as increased sedation, loss of consciousness, respiratory depression, risk of overdose, impaired judgment or coordination, memory impairment, and heart problems. Stopping heavy alcohol and benzodiazepines suddenly can trigger life-threatening alcohol withdrawal symptoms such as hallucinations, hypothermia, sepsis, seizures, delirium tremens, or cardiac arrest. Based on the symptoms presented by this client there are concerns that withdrawal would be severe and life-threatening.

2. The CIWA-AR would be an appropriate assessment instrument to use with this client. The CIWA-AR helps determine the severity of alcohol withdrawal and whether medical intervention is necessary to manage the symptoms safely. Using the ASAM criteria will also help in determining the appropriate level of care for the client.

3. Based on the results of the evaluation, consulting with the doctor would include recommending using the ASAM level of care dimensions to determine the best options for safe detoxification. This client is at risk for serious life-threatening withdrawal that needs medical intervention. The counselor should also address the need for counseling and psychological support following the period of detoxification based on the level of depression and suicidal ideation.

CASE STUDY 3.2

Katie is a 35-year-old Caucasian woman who is a wife, mother of two young children, and a rising professional. Katie calls to set up an appointment with an addiction counselor because her husband, Lewis, is threatening to leave her. He believes she has relapsed and is using pain medication again without a prescription. The counselor schedules a counseling appointment with Katie and Lewis together. During the session, Katie shares her substance use history and previous treatment. Katie went to residential treatment 1 year ago. The reason for her admission was using too much oxycodone and pain medication that was not prescribed to her. Katie initially began taking oxycodone because of a back injury she experienced after a car accident 5 years ago. At the time, she took the medication as prescribed but enjoyed how wonderful it made her feel about her whole life. Over the next few years, there were times she had reasons to visit her doctor and she was usually able to walk out of the doctor's office with a prescription for oxycodone.

As Katie's life became more complicated with her marriage, children, her career, and the day-to-day pressures of life, Katie looked for ways to make herself feel better. She began to seek out oxycodone or any prescription pain medication from friends, family, and coworkers. If someone she knew had injured themselves in some way, she was quick to inquire whether the doctor had given them any pain medication. She lost many friends because they were annoyed with her.

When Katie found out how to get oxycodone through the internet, she began buying large quantities because her pain was increasing, and she did not feel well if she ran out. This was very expensive. Lewis became aware of the situation because of the financial stress on the family. He talked with her about this, and she claimed she was only getting vitamins and other natural remedies for pain. He did not think she was telling the truth and suspected she was buying oxycodone. After being confronted by her husband and parents, Katie agreed to go to treatment.

Katie spent 4 weeks in the treatment center and completed the program. Upon discharge it was recommended that she continue in an aftercare program in the community. Katie reports she did not do follow-up counseling or attend the aftercare program. She felt that she had gotten the oxycodone use under control and that it was all "behind her now." Lewis did not attend the family program offered at the treatment center and did not attend any follow-up care or support group meetings. They both agreed they could put this unfortunate incident behind them and move on with their lives.

In the session, Katie and Lewis share that over the past several months, Katie's pain medication-seeking behaviors returned. Katie was able to get oxycodone from her doctor after the birth of her last child due to medical complications. To add to this, Lewis had an accident at work resulting in a torn Achilles tendon and was prescribed hydrocodone, which Katie took from him. Lewis was very upset but agreed it was better than buying the medication from the internet. He is off work but must use crutches to get around. Katie does not help much around the house or with the children because she is too stressed with work. Lewis has become the at-home parent taking care of the children while Katie goes off to work. Lewis and Katie are also in the middle of a major home improvement project which Lewis is doing himself. The stress is high.

The other day while Lewis was home tending to the family, a courier delivered a package for Katie. Lewis had to sign for it. It felt and sounded like a bottle of pills to Lewis. He opened it and found oxycodone. Lewis was beside himself. He later found evidence of several other deliveries from the same courier during the past few months. Lewis is very concerned she is falling back into her opioid use disorder. Her parents are also worried about her because they have heard a lot of news reports about people overdosing on "fake pain medication" that contains fentanyl. Katie is aware of this risk but does not believe that anything bad will happen. She insists she needs the medication because her pain is worse than it has ever been and she gets very sick if she is does not take it. She refuses to go back to treatment because they will not be able to manage her pain and she believes she will lose her job if she misses work.

1. What are the psychological and social effects of Katie's opioid use?

2. Based on the information presented, should the counselor assume Katie has developed tolerance to the pain medication? Why or why not?

3. Based on the information presented, is it likely that Katie might go through withdrawal if she stops taking the pain medication? Why or why not?

4. If Katie were your client, what are reasonable next steps for you to take?

(See answers on the next page.)

CASE STUDY 3.2 ANSWERS

1. Katie experienced temporary short-term pain relief when she first started using oxycodone for her back injury. She then started to experience euphoric feelings of well-being and relaxation from the medication on which she became psychologically dependent. Despite the initial feelings of well-being and relaxation, Katie is experiencing many social effects of her use including difficulties in her marriage, loss of friendships, financial hardships, and family problems.

2. Yes, it is likely that Katie is experiencing tolerance to the medication. As she has continued to use more of the medication over the years, she started to buy more and more of the medication indicating it was taking more of the substance to feel the same effects. She is likely experiencing hyperalgesia which increases the pain sensitivity and decreases the effectiveness of the substance. This is assumed from the reports that the pain is the worst that it has ever been despite taking larger amounts of the medication.

3. Yes, it is likely that Katie is and will experience withdrawal if she stops taking the pain medication. Her report that she gets "very sick" if she doesn't take the pain medication indicates that she is experiencing withdrawal symptoms when she does not take the medication.

4. It would be helpful to administer an assessment to determine and clarify the withdrawal effects that Katie is experiencing. The Clinical Opiate Withdrawal Scale (COWS) or the Subjective Opiate Withdrawal Scale (SOWS) would be good instruments to use. Based on the results, researching treatment programs that include medications and psychological support and counseling would be the next step for treatment planning.

KNOWLEDGE CHECK: CHAPTER 3

1. An instructor asks a student to give an example of a central nervous system (CNS) depressant. Which response requires correction?
   A) Alprazolam (Xanax)
   B) Pentobarbital (Nembutal)
   C) Amphetamine (Benzedrine)
   D) Alcohol

2. Abstinence is to harm reduction as:
   A) Controlled drinking is to willpower
   B) Methadone is to disulfiram (Antabuse)
   C) Alcoholics Anonymous is to needle exchange
   D) IV drug use is to smoking marijuana

3. The goal of complete abstinence as the only treatment choice is most consistent with the _____ model of addiction.
   A) Disease
   B) Moral
   C) Sociocultural
   D) Psychological

4. An instructor asks a student to name a drug that is considered to have potentially life-threatening withdrawal symptoms in an otherwise healthy adult. Which response is correct?
   A) Benzodiazepines
   B) Alcohol
   C) Opioids
   D) Alcohol and benzodiazepines taken together

5. Sensitivity to light, sound, and touch, muscle tension, nausea or vomiting, psychomotor agitation, and seizures are all signs or symptoms of:
   A) Cannabis withdrawal
   B) Cocaine withdrawal
   C) Sedative, hypnotic, or anxiolytic withdrawal
   D) Opioid withdrawal

6. Which of the following substance does not belong with the others?
   A) Alcohol
   B) Methamphetamine
   C) Alprazolam
   D) Lorazepam

7. Which of the following neurotransmitter is primarily affected by opioid use, leading to pain relief and euphoria?
   A) Glutamate
   B) Gamma-aminobutyric acid (GABA)
   C) Norepinephrine
   D) Endorphins

(See answers on the next page.)

1. C) Amphetamine (Benzedrine)

CNS depressants are drugs that slow down brain activity by affecting the neurotransmitter gamma-aminobutyric acid (GABA). There are three major types of CNS depressants: sedatives, hypnotics, and tranquilizers. CNS depressants cause drowsiness, relaxation, and decreased inhibition. Alprazolam, pentobarbital, and alcohol are all in the sedative-hypnotic class of drugs that can be abused leading to addiction. Benzedrine is a CNS stimulant drug first introduced as a drug in the 1930s to treat narcolepsy and is now known as amphetamine.

2. C) Alcoholics Anonymous is to needle exchange

The relationship between abstinence and harm reduction is understood in the context of approaches to addressing substance use disorders. Alcoholics Anonymous is an abstinence-based approach to substance use disorder treatment. Needle exchange is a harm reduction-based approach that aims to reduce disease among substance users. Controlled drinking could be considered a treatment approach, however, willpower is a cognitive state and not a treatment approach. Methadone and disulfiram are both medications for substance use treatment and not two different approaches. IV drug use and smoking marijuana are centered on substance use and not a treatment approach.

3. B) Moral

The moral model conceptualizes the use of substances as a moral failing with complete abstinence as the treatment of choice to address moral shortcomings. The disease model of addiction views addiction as a chronic and relapsing brain disorder characterized by compulsive substance seeking. Complete abstinence aligns with this model as well because substances can trigger uncontrollable cravings and behaviors; however, there are also other treatment methods that are acceptable such as harm reduction and medications.

4. C) Opioids

Reading the question carefully, we can see that this is about life-threatening *withdrawal* symptoms and not intoxication effects. Both alcohol and benzodiazepines affect the central nervous system, and if the person has used to the point of dependence, sudden withdrawal from alcohol and benzodiazepines can become life-threatening due to seizures, delirium tremens, cardiovascular instability, and respiratory issues. Opioids can be life-threatening if overdose occurs when a person is using the substance; however, withdrawal from opioids is not life-threatening, but it can be rather unpleasant.

5. C) Sedative, hypnotic, or anxiolytic withdrawal

These symptoms are most closely aligned with withdrawal from sedatives, hypnotics, or anxiolytics. While there are many withdrawal symptoms that overlap among substances of misuse, look for the key defining characteristics of each choice. In this instance, muscle tension versus muscles aches differentiates the symptoms from opioid withdrawal. Because there is no mention of behavioral or affective withdrawal symptoms, cannabis withdrawal can safely be eliminated as a choice. Because withdrawal from stimulants is often associated with depressed activity of the mind and body, cocaine can also be safely eliminated as a choice due to the psychomotor agitation that is included in the symptom list.

6. B) Methamphetamine

This question requires knowledge of the class of drugs that substances belong to. Alcohol, alprazolam, and lorazepam are all central nervous system depressants. Methamphetamine is a stimulant. Knowing the drug class is important and equally important is knowing the generic names of the drugs in the class. Alprazolam and lorazepam are benzodiazepines. A key indicator to look for in the benzodiazepine class of drugs is the "-ams" or "-pams" in the name, such as alprazolam, lorazepam, diazepam, clonazepam, and oxazepam among others.

7. D) Endorphins

This question requires a basic understanding of the main neurotransmitters impacted by opioid use. Dopamine, serotonin, endorphins, and norepinephrine are the neurotransmitters primarily affected by opioid use. Opioids bind to endorphin receptors in the brain, mimicking the effects of naturally occurring endorphins and releasing dopamine, which leads to the euphoric effects of opioid use. This binding results in pain relief and a sense of euphoria. GABA and glutamate are neurotransmitters involved in alcohol use and impact learning memory and neural excitability rather than euphoria.

8. Which of the following is a primary factor influencing the rate at which alcohol is absorbed into the bloodstream?
   A) Drinking two drinks over 3 hours
   B) Alternating alcoholic drinks with water
   C) Drinking slowly
   D) Drinking on an empty stomach

9. Which neurotransmitter is significantly affected by alcohol consumption, leading to the sedation effects of intoxication?
   A) Serotonin
   B) Dopamine
   C) Gamma-aminobutyric acid (GABA)
   D) Endorphins

Doug is a 40-year-old Caucasian father of two teenage boys whose partner forced him to talk to a counselor about his marijuana use. He is not happy to be in the counselor's office. "What's the big deal?" he asks. "It's just pot." Doug's partner had given him an ultimatum: either he quits smoking marijuana or she moves out. She delivered this ultimatum when their 15-year-old son was suspended from school for smoking marijuana.

When they were younger, Doug and his partner smoked pot together. As their children grew older, however, his partner stopped smoking. Doug tried to quit a few times, but always went back to smoking to manage his stress. For a long time, Doug's partner tolerated his continued use, and Doug agreed that he would be discreet to avoid others knowing he was smoking pot. Both Doug and his partner felt that the children should not know about Doug smoking marijuana. Doug tried to be careful, but a few times his son walked in on him while smoking. Doug would often miss family events due to being high and he would make up excuses for why he was absent. Doug's partner indicates that Doug has hidden money in the past and that the family has been late on bills due to Doug buying marijuana instead of using the money for household needs. Doug has been buying more and more marijuana and is always searching for the "bud" with the best potency so he can feel the effects like he did when he first started smoking. Doug nearly lost his last job due to a positive drug screen for THC; however, he ultimately quit his job because of the continued drug screens that he could not pass. Doug took a different job that does not require drug screens, but it pays much less than he made before. His partner is not happy about that decision, and it has led to financial problems.

"Why can't you settle for my promising to try harder to hide it from the kids?," he argues to his partner. "It's not as if it's really a problem. I still work and do all the things you want me to. You even told me I am easier to get along with when I smoke. Remember when I quit a few years ago, how grumpy and depressed I was?" Given this, the counselor gets the sense that Doug sees his problem as his wife's refusal to be reasonable. However, Doug does share that he wonders what people at his job will think if word gets out that he smokes marijuana and how miserable he will be if he stops smoking.

---

10. Based on the information presented in the vignette, what is the best diagnosis for Doug?
    A) Cannabis Use: Mild
    B) Cannabis Use: Moderate
    C) Cannabis Use: Severe
    D) None of the above, he does not exhibit symptoms that indicate a substance use disorder

11. Doug has started to buy and use edible products that contain delta-9-tetrahydrocannabinol (THC) in addition to smoking multiple times a day. What is the most likely explanation to account for this behavior?
    A) Doug likes to experiment with new things
    B) Doug is tolerant to the effects of THC
    C) Doug is fearful he will again get caught smoking by his son and using edibles is easier to hide
    D) Edibles are cheaper to buy

(See answers on the next page.)

8. D) Drinking on an empty stomach

This question asks what influences the rate of absorption of alcohol into the bloodstream, not what impacts the blood alcohol concentration (BAC) after it is in the bloodstream. Drinking alcohol on an empty stomach will increase the rate of absorption because consuming alcohol with food slows down the absorption process, reducing the impact on the body. Drinking two drinks over 3 hours, alternating alcoholic drinks with water, and drinking slower will decrease the BAC because less alcohol enters the body and thus the bloodstream.

9. C) Gamma-aminobutyric acid (GABA)

Alcohol enhances the inhibitory effects of GABA, leading to sedation and relaxation, which are characteristic features of alcohol intoxication. Alcohol also releases dopamine, endorphins, and serotonin, the feel-good neurotransmitters. However, these neurotransmitters are connected to the reward center of the brain leading to feelings of pleasure and well-being with little impact on the sedation aspect of intoxication.

10. C) Cannabis Use: Severe

Doug exhibits many symptoms of a severe cannabis use disorder: relationship problems, family problems, attempts to stop without success, financial problems, giving up important events to use the substance, loss of job, tolerance, and withdrawal symptoms when he stops using marijuana. At least six *Diagnostic and Statistical Manual of Mental Disorders* (DSM) criteria can be identified in this case which is the minimum needed for a severe substance use disorder diagnosis.

11. B) Doug is tolerant to the effects of THC

Doug is experiencing tolerance and needs to increase the amount of THC in his system to feel the intoxicating effects. Ingesting edibles would be possible to do in many settings. In addition to smoking, which is the most effective route of administration, being able to ingest edibles throughout the day will keep more THC in his system on an on-going basis.

12. The counselor suspects Doug experienced some withdrawal symptoms when he stopped smoking based on his comments that his partner did not like that he was grumpy and depressed the last time he stopped smoking. What other things might the counselor expect Doug to say about that time?
    A) "I had tremors and a seizure the last time I tried to quit."
    B) "I was very sensitive to light and felt like I had the flu."
    C) "I couldn't stay warm, and my muscles hurt really bad."
    D) "I was very angry, irritated with everyone, and couldn't sleep without thinking of smoking."

13. Which of the following factors contribute most significantly to Doug's reluctance to acknowledge the severity of his marijuana use?
    A) His son's suspension from school due to his substance use
    B) His partner's ultimatum about quitting marijuana or she will leave
    C) Financial difficulties arising from purchasing marijuana
    D) Doug's perception that marijuana helps him manage stress, improves his mental state of mind, and his fear of withdrawal

14. Doug states he is worried about how miserable he will feel if he quits smoking. When talking more about this, he shares that before he started smoking, he was very anxious and had difficulty interacting with others. He feels like this will come back even more if he stops smoking because he will be anxious and depressed. He worries he will lose his job because he will not be able to get along with other people. These statements indicate to the counselor that
    A) Doug may have a co-occurring mental health issue
    B) Doug is making excuses about why he should continue to smoke
    C) Doug might have a co-occurring medical condition
    D) None of the above

15. Doug has agreed to start counseling to work on his marijuana use. During the intake session, the counselor completes an evaluation and discusses other areas of Doug's life and substance use. Which substance would increase the cognitive impairment Doug may be experiencing because of his marijuana use?
    A) Alcohol
    B) Cocaine
    C) Opioids
    D) Tobacco

16. What is a potential risk associated with the concurrent use of alcohol and benzodiazepines?
    A) Increased alertness
    B) Reduced sedation
    C) Enhanced respiratory function
    D) Heighted central nervous system depression

17. How do alcohol and caffeine differ in their effects on the central nervous system?
    A) Both act as stimulants, enhancing alertness and energy levels
    B) Alcohol acts as a stimulant and caffeine acts as a depressant
    C) Both act as depressants, causing sedation and relaxation
    D) Alcohol acts as a depressant and caffeine acts as a stimulant

18. Alcohol and caffeine are often consumed together. However, there are troubling drug interactions that can occur with this combination. Which statement is the most correct regarding the drug interactions between alcohol and caffeine?
    A) Both alcohol and caffeine are stimulants, and the interactions can lead to increased alertness and heart rate
    B) Caffeine can mask the depressant effect of alcohol leading people to feel less impaired than they really are, increasing the risk of alcohol overconsumption
    C) Alcohol and caffeine can be consumed together safely
    D) Caffeine can counteract the depressant effect of alcohol and decrease the level of impairment caused by the alcohol

(See answers on the next page.)

12. D) "I was very angry, irritated with everyone, and couldn't sleep without thinking of smoking."

The withdrawal symptoms for delta-9-tetrahydrocannabinol (THC) are mostly behavioral, psychological, and emotional rather than physical making choice D the best choice. Tremors, seizures, light sensitivity, flu-like symptoms, muscle aches, and feeling cold are physical symptoms which are more common with withdrawal from opioids, alcohol, sedatives, and hypnotics.

13. D) Doug's perception that marijuana helps him manage stress, improves his mental state of mind, and his fear of withdrawal

Doug's reluctance to acknowledge the severity of his marijuana use primarily stems from his belief that marijuana helps him manage stress and it enhances his mood to be better able to interact with life. Doug repeatedly refers to how marijuana makes him more agreeable and more able to cope with stress; he downplays the other problems such as family issues and money problems. He has an unrealistic idea that he can continue to use and not experience any more consequences. He also indicates he does not want to feel the withdrawal effects.

14. A) Doug may have a co-occurring mental health issue

Doug's statements that he was very anxious prior to smoking marijuana could indicate that he was experiencing a mental health disorder that smoking marijuana is alleviating. It is minimizing to classify Doug's concerns as excuses. There is no indication that Doug has a medical concern.

15. A) Alcohol

Using alcohol and marijuana together increases the cognitive impairments of both substances.

16. D) Heighted central nervous system depression

The simultaneous use of alcohol and benzodiazepines can lead to an additive effect on the central nervous system. Both alcohol and benzodiazepines are central nervous system depressants, and the interaction can lead to severe sedation, respiratory depression, coma, or even death.

17. D) Alcohol acts as a depressant and caffeine acts as a stimulant

Alcohol is a depressant causing sedation and slowing down of neural activity and caffeine acts as a stimulant increasing alertness and neural activity.

18. B) Caffeine can mask the depressant effect of alcohol leading people to feel less impaired than they really are, increasing the risk of alcohol overconsumption

When combined with alcohol (a depressant), caffeine (a stimulant) can mask or partially counteract the depressant effect of the alcohol. This leads to people being more awake and feel less impaired than they really are. This can increase the risk of overconsuming alcohol or engaging in more risky behaviors while drinking, leading to serious injury.

19. Among the following choices, which is most likely to be considered a significant risk factor contributing to substance use initiation in adolescents?
A) High academic achievement
B) Strong family support and communication
C) Peer pressure and social influence
D) Participation in structured extracurricular activities

20. What is the primary factor that contributes to the potential for overdose when individuals misuse prescription opioids?
A) Increased tolerance
B) Enhanced pain relief
C) Risk of respiratory depression
D) Strict adherence to prescribed dosages

Joy is a 20-year-old Native American woman admitted to an inpatient substance use treatment program after a suicide attempt while she was drinking. She started drinking alcohol at age 12 and has tried a wide variety of benzodiazepine and opioid pills. She prefers alcohol as her sole substance of choice after having a scary incident where she became unresponsive and was taken to the hospital after she drank and used opioids. She has increased her alcohol use over time from drinking a few beers to drinking a fifth of alcohol each day to feel the effects. She was the victim of date rape at age 15 when she and her friends were drinking. She did not tell her family for fear that they would think less of her for not preventing or fighting off the attack. She shared that she does not feel very close to her family. Both of her parents have been in treatment for substance use and were absent during most of her growing up. Joy also has a history of depression and sometimes regulates her emotions by intentionally burning her arms with cigarettes. When she has tried to stop drinking in the past, she experienced significant cravings and could not sustain abstinence for any length of time. In treatment, she has worked to gain control over her repeated self-destructive behavior. When she has the urge to drink, use drugs, or burn herself, she was guided in treatment to try to "bring down" the feelings through grounding, rethinking the situation, and reassuring herself that she could get through it. She is beginning to see that her substance use had been a way to numb pain.

21. What underlying factor from Joy's history and experiences may significantly contribute to her current pattern of substance use?
A) Family problems
B) Early exposure to substance use
C) History of depression and past traumatic experiences
D) Cultural background and heritage

22. Identify the stage of substance use that best aligns with Joy's current situation based on the provided information?
A) Regular use
B) Substance use disorder
C) Experimentation
D) Initiation

23. What short-term effects might be happening to Joy based on her alcohol use that could have contributed to the trauma she experienced?
A) Enhanced memory and cognitive function
B) Increased coordination and motor skills
C) Sedation and impaired judgment
D) Elevated heart rate and alertness

(See answers on the next page.)

19. C) Peer pressure and social influence

There are both protective and risk factors among the choices. The question asks for risk factors making peer pressure and social influence as the only correct choice, as high academic achievement, strong family support and communication, and participation in structured extracurricular activities are protective factors.

20. A) Increased tolerance

Misuse of prescription opioids, such as taking higher doses than prescribed, can lead to increased tolerance, raising the risk of overdose as individuals may take larger amounts to achieve the desired effects.

21. C) History of depression and past traumatic experiences

Co-occurring mental health disorders are significant contributors for substance use to cope with the symptoms. Family problems and early exposure are risk factors for substance use but may not be factors in their current substance use. Cultural background and heritage can be protective factors.

22. B) Substance use disorder

Joy has been drinking for 8 years with increasing amounts to feel the effects. She has experienced tolerance and withdrawal and negative consequences as a result of her use.

23. C) Sedation and impaired judgment

The short-term effects of alcohol are common and include decreased coordination, memory problems, decreased alertness, and impaired judgement. This can lead to being in risky situations.

24. Based on drug interactions, what might have happened to Joy when she drank alcohol and used opioids?
    A) The depressant effects of both substances were intensified leading to increased sedation and respiratory depression causing her to become unresponsive
    B) The stimulant effects of the opioids combined with the depressant effects of the alcohol lead to a change in neurotransmitter activity
    C) Joy likely used heroin instead of prescription opioids
    D) Joy might have had a co-occurring medical condition that leads to respiratory problems that was intensified by the alcohol use

25. "Drinking too much alcohol and getting drunk is a choice. If someone breaks the law while under the influence, they should go to jail, not treatment!" This statement is consistent with which model of substance use?
    A) Disease
    B) Social
    C) Moral
    D) Biopsychosocial

26. Which of the following medication is commonly used to reverse opioid overdose by restoring normal breathing patterns?
    A) Naloxone (Narcan)
    B) Diazepam
    C) Methadone
    D) Buprenorphine

27. What is the primary purpose of medication-assisted treatment (MAT) for opioid use disorder?
    A) To intensify the effects of opioids
    B) To provide a substitute opioid for long-term use
    C) To facilitate a rapid detoxification process
    D) To reduce cravings and withdrawal symptoms while supporting recovery

28. Tina frequently drinks coffee and smokes cigarettes. She experiences a heightened stimulating effect when she does and can tell when she needs to slow down on the coffee. What physiological effects are likely occurring when she combines nicotine and caffeine, leading her to know that she needs to slow down?
    A) Decreased heart rate and blood pressure
    B) Increased relaxation and stress relief
    C) Heightened stimulant effects, increased heart rate and blood pressure
    D) Reduced effects of caffeine on alertness and focus

29. How does cross tolerance between cocaine and amphetamines affect an individual's response to both substances?
    A) Increased sensitivity to the effects of both drugs
    B) Reduced tolerance to amphetamines but an increased tolerance to cocaine
    C) Decreased sensitivity to the effects of both drugs
    D) None of the above; cross tolerance cannot happen within the same class of drugs

30. John is experiencing mood swings, sleep problems, difficulty concentrating, and an intense craving for alcohol. He has been abstinent from alcohol for 10 months and he thought things would get better after the withdrawal he went through. What is John experiencing?
    A) He has relapsed and has not told anyone about it
    B) He is experiencing postacute withdrawal; the lingering of withdrawal symptoms that persist beyond the initial acute phase of withdrawal
    C) He has had a sudden relapse into substance use after his first period of abstinence
    D) He has likely damaged his brain beyond repair due to his heavy alcohol use over several years

(See answers on the next page.)

24. A) The depressant effects of both substances were intensified leading to increased sedation and respiratory depression causing her to become unresponsive

Combining alcohol and opioids can result in potentially dangerous interactions intensifying the central nervous system depressants' effects. When used together the effects are additive, leading to increased drowsiness, sedation, slowed breathing, and a higher risk of overdose, coma, or even death.

25. C) Moral

The moral model conceptualizes substance use as a moral failing with punishment as the preferred method of correcting the problem behavior; the statement in the question certainly falls under this model. The sociocultural model emphasizes the social environment as a contributor to substance use, the disease model conceptualizes addiction as a chronic medical disease that is biologically based, and the biopsychosocial model of addiction combines the disease model with the psychological and social/cultural models of substance use disorders to arrive at a comprehensive conceptualization of addiction.

26. A) Naloxone (Narcan)

Naloxone is an opioid receptor antagonist used as an emergency intervention to rapidly reverse the effects of opioid overdose, particularly respiratory depression.

27. D) To reduce cravings and withdrawal symptoms while supporting recovery

MAT combines medications with counseling and behavioral therapies to address opioid use disorder. It helps reduce cravings, withdrawal symptoms, and the risk of relapse.

28. C) Heightened stimulant effects, increased heart rate and blood pressure

Nicotine and caffeine, when used together, enhance the stimulant effects of each substance. This interaction leads to heightened stimulant effects, including increased heart rate and blood pressure due to the synergistic action of both nicotine and caffeine.

29. B) Reduced tolerance to amphetamines but an increased tolerance to cocaine

Cross tolerance pertains to the phenomenon where tolerance to one substance can influence or affect the body's response or tolerance level to another substance within the same class of drugs; this makes choice D incorrect. Often, cross tolerance refers to the increasing tolerance to one substance and decreasing tolerance to the other.

30. B) He is experiencing postacute withdrawal; the lingering of withdrawal symptoms that persist beyond the initial acute phase of withdrawal

Postacute withdrawal refers to a prolonged phase following the initial withdrawal period where individuals might experience persistent but milder withdrawal symptoms including mood swings, sleep disturbances, cognitive difficulties, fatigue, low energy, decreased physical coordination, cravings, and stress sensitivity.

31. Which brain structure is primarily associated with the reward and motivation system leading to the habitual use of substances?
A) Amygdala
B) Hippocampus
C) Basal ganglia
D) Prefrontal cortex

32. During which stage of the addiction cycle do we see tolerance start to develop?
A) Binge/intoxication
B) Withdrawal/negative affect stage
C) Preoccupation/anticipation stage
D) All of the above

33. During which stage of the addiction cycle does the prefrontal cortex play a significant role?
A) Binge/intoxication
B) Withdrawal/negative affect stage
C) Preoccupation/anticipation stage
D) All of the above

34. How might the activation of the amygdala contribute to the development of a substance use disorder?
A) It initiates the pleasurable effects of substances during the binge/intoxication stage
B) It triggers the prefrontal cortex to control impulsive substance-seeking behavior
C) It induces negative emotions during the withdrawal/negative affect stage
D) It maintains habit circuitry in the basal ganglia to reinforce substance cravings

35. How does the involvement of the prefrontal cortex contribute to the addiction cycle?
A) The prefrontal cortex has no role in the addiction cycle
B) The activation of theprefrontal cortex promotes relaxation and decreases substance seeking
C) Overactivation of the prefrontal cortex's "go" system drives substance-seeking behaviors
D) The prefrontal cortex regulates withdrawal symptoms and diminishes negative emotions

(See answers on the next page.)

31. C) Basal ganglia
The basal ganglia, located deep in the brain and part of the limbic system, houses a high concentration of dopamine projections and is responsible for the rewarding or pleasure effects of substances, contributing to the formation of habitual substance use patterns.

32. B) Withdrawal/negative affect stage
Over time decreases in the dopamine system as occurs in the withdrawal/negative affect stage, lead to using more of the substance to regain pleasurable effects. This is defined as tolerance.

33. C) Preoccupation/anticipation stage
The prefrontal cortex, known as the executive center responsible for decision-making, plays a substantial role during the preoccupation/anticipation stage of the addiction cycle. During this stage, individuals experience cravings and engage in substance-seeking behaviors driven by the overactivation of the prefrontal cortex's "go" system and underactivation of the "stop" system. This phase involves decision-making and the manifestation of craving behavior, characteristic of the prefrontal cortex involvement.

34. C) It induces negative emotions during the withdrawal/negative affect stage
The amygdala, a crucial brain structure in processing emotions and threats, gets activated during the withdrawal/negative affect stage. The activation leads to the experience of negative emotions due to reduced activity in the reward circuitry, causing diminished dopamine release and the activation of the brain's stress system. The combination of decreased dopamine and increase stress chemicals reinforces the neurochemical basis driving compulsive substance use.

35. C) Overactivation of the prefrontal cortex's "go" system drives substance-seeking behaviors
The overactivation of the prefrontal cortex's "go" system during the preoccupation/anticipation stage drives substance-seeking behaviors in individuals with substance use disorders. This overactivation contributes to impulsive and compulsive substance-seeking behaviors characteristic of this stage of the addiction cycle.

Engaging the Client

Thomas Maxson

▶ INTRODUCTION

The next five chapters focus on counseling a client from initial contact until discharge through discussion and application of the 12 core functions of a substance use counselor (Kulewicz, 2000). This chapter covers the process of engaging the client in services through application of the core functions of screening, intake, and orientation. Chapter 5, "Assessing the Client," covers Domain 2: Evidence-Based Screening and Assessment. Chapter 6, "Planning Treatment With the Client," and Chapter 7, "Counseling With the Client," cover Domain 3: Evidence Based Treatment, Counseling, and Referral. This section concludes with addressing Domain 4: Professional, Ethical and Legal Responsibilities.

The 12 core functions of an alcohol and drug counselor provide a framework for the treatment process in substance use disorder treatment. These functions serve as a guide for counselors to effectively assess, plan, and implement treatment for individuals struggling with substance use disorders. The 12 core functions provide a structured and comprehensive framework for counselors to guide the treatment process, tailor interventions to individual needs, and support clients in their journey toward recovery from substance use disorders. In the next five chapters, each of these core functions are detailed with the underlying global criteria and tasks of the counselor explained.

When conceptualizing alcohol and drug counseling, it is helpful to consider the "flow of treatment" through the 12 core functions. Figure 4.1 outlines the flow of treatment from initial contact to discharge.

▶ WHAT IS ENGAGEMENT?

Engagement is the process of connecting with a client for the purpose of screening, admitting, and orienting a client so counseling services can begin.

Unfolding Case Study

Insight Counseling, where you are employed, offers individual and family outpatient counseling for adults and adolescents. It does not offer detoxification and withdrawal management services nor emergency psychiatric hospitalization services. Jim calls a counselor at insight counseling first thing Monday morning and states "I need help. I had a terrible weekend; I can't keep going like this." As an alcohol and drug counselor, it is essential that you have the skills to handle a call such as this, but where do you start?

Engaging a potential client and continuing to engage ongoing clients are essential functions of the alcohol and drug counselor. The first three core functions are about building engagement with the client. Upon first contact, whether this be by phone, text, e-mail, or in person, the process of screening begins.

Unfolding Case Study

We have Jim on the phone. What do we do now?

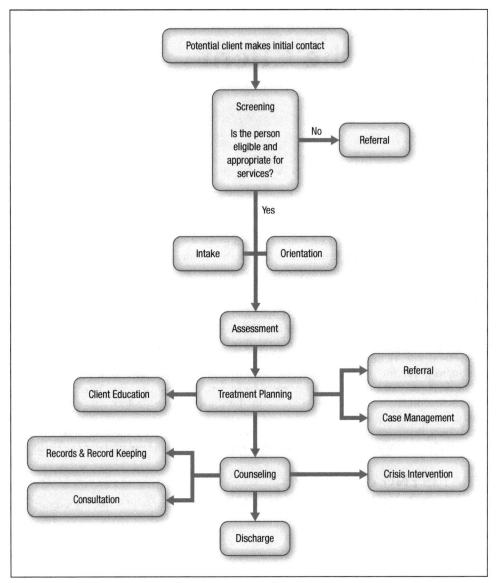

Figure 4.1 12 core functions.

▶ SCREENING

In the core function of **screening**, the global criteria are broken down into four tasks.

GLOBAL CRITERION 1: EVALUATE SIGNS AND SYMPTOMS

The first task of screening is addressed by Global Criterion 1: *Evaluate a client's psychological, social, and physiological signs and symptoms of alcohol and other drug use* (Box 4.1; Herdman, 2021).

Unfolding Case Study

Since Jim is on the phone, we must listen carefully to the words he is using as well as the tone, volume, clarity, and language choice. Jim sounds like he is expressing serious concern about his situation. He is speaking rapidly, he has a slight slur to his speech, and he uses the words "I can't keep going like this."

Box 4.1 Core Function 1: Screening

Definition: The process by which the client is determined appropriate and eligible for admission to a particular program.

Global Criteria:
1. Evaluate psychological, social, and physiological signs and symptoms of alcohol and other drug use and abuse.
2. Determine the client's **appropriateness** for admission or referral.
3. Determine the client's **eligibility** for admission or referral.
4. Identify coexisting conditions (medical, psychiatric, physical, etc.) that indicate the need for additional professional assessment and/or services.
5. Adhere to applicable laws, regulations, and agency policies governing alcohol and other drug abuse services.

As an alcohol and drug counselor, you would be working now to **engage** Jim to better understand his needs and to see if you can offer the services he needs. It is essential the counselor maintains a warm, positive regard and curiosity about the client's situation. Just as we are screening Jim for our services, Jim is also screening us to determine if he believes we can be of help to him.

Establishing a rapport during screening aids in the client's willingness to follow through with accessing services or with a referral if one is made. The client is not being diagnosed during screening; however, the person engaging in the screening process needs to have sufficient knowledge about substance use in order to ask effective questions. In the next interaction, you will see the counselor inquire about Jim's presenting concern and support him for reaching out for help. We are specifically listening for psychological, social, and physiological signs and symptoms of alcohol and other drug use. Psychological symptoms are changes in emotion and thinking patterns due to or a consequence of alcohol and other drug use. Social symptoms are changes in a person's relationships as a consequence of alcohol and other drug use. Physiological symptoms are physical symptoms that are the result of alcohol or other drug use (Table 4.1).

Table 4.1 Psychological, Social, and Physiological Symptoms of Alcohol and Other Drug Use

Psychological Symptoms	Social Symptoms	Physiological Symptoms
Fear due to consequences of substance use	Negative impact on employment (job loss, reduced hours, employed below education and skill levels)	Withdrawal symptoms (shakes, tremors, hallucinations, and seizure)
Limited nonsubstance-related coping strategies	Negative impact on relationships (increased conflict, divorce, and loss of friends)	Sleep and appetite disruption
Thoughts and actions increasingly focus on obtaining, using, and recovering from substance use	Difficulty engaging in social situations without using substances	Physical injury (tooth loss, organ damage, and injection site infection)
Lying about substance use	Planning activities where substance use is available and avoiding activities it is not	Increased tolerance
Blaming others for the reasons to use	Increased association with others who use substances	Failed attempts to quit using substances
Creating excuses to explain consequences	Isolation from others	Craving to use a substance
Denying impact of substance use	Engaging in hazardous activities related to substance use	Using more than intended

Unfolding Case Study

Counselor: Jim, I am glad you called Insight Counseling this morning. How can I help you?

Jim: I really need help. I can't have another weekend like the one I just had. I am scared I am going to lose my job today. My boss e-mailed me this morning and told me to meet him in his office at 10 o'clock (**psychological and social symptoms**).

(continued)

(continued)

Counselor:	It sounds like you are very worried about your job and that you had a very difficult weekend. Can you tell me more about what happened this weekend?
Jim:	Our company had a weekend retreat with all the management staff. On Saturday night, several of us went downtown to a bar. One thing led to another and I ended up having too many drinks. The police were called and one of my coworkers had to promise to take me back to the hotel and watch me for the night. I missed the morning session on Sunday because I was still drunk. I made it to the luncheon later in the day, but everyone could tell I was hungover. My boss was really mad because I was supposed to present the new sales plan that afternoon. He told me just to go home (*social symptom*).
Counselor:	You mentioned you can't keep going like this?
Jim:	Well, I don't like to admit it, but it seems more often than not when I drink, I end up drinking too much and end up in situations I don't want to be in. My wife has complained about my drinking, but she is going to be really mad if I lose my job over it (*social symptom*). I think I may have a drinking problem.
Counselor:	I am glad you called us, Jim. We offer outpatient counseling services in this office. It sounds like you are interested in scheduling an appointment?
Jim:	I need to do something.

The counselor engages Jim in conversation through active listening, inquires about Jim's initial concerns, and listens for possible psychological, social, and physiological symptoms. Jim provides a great deal of valuable information throughout the exchange that helps the counselor better understand Jim's needs. Jim reveals several symptoms consistent with an alcohol use disorder. He indicates that he is experiencing work problems and marital concerns and that there has been law enforcement contact, as well as psychological and physiological symptoms. As you can see through the initial screening process, the counselor is evaluating/assessing Jim's current situation and symptoms. The skills required for screening are similar to those required by the core function of assessment but are not as in depth. The counselor needs to gather enough information to determine if the client is a good fit for the facility's services but does not complete a full assessment, as this is beyond the scope of the screening core function.

GLOBAL CRITERION 2: APPROPRIATENESS FOR ADMISSION OR REFERRAL

Now that we have a general understanding of Jim's concern and why he is calling, the second task of screening is addressed by Global Criterion 2: *Determine the client's **appropriateness** for admission or referral*. This determination is based on a counselor's ability to meet the current needs of the client. The key question to determine appropriateness is "Can I offer the level of care this client needs right now?" To determine appropriateness for admission, the counselor will ask more specific questions about Jim's current symptoms. If the counselor cannot meet Jim's needs, they will make a referral to another facility that can.

Unfolding Case Study

Counselor:	Jim, I need to ask you some specific questions to determine if I can be of service to you. Is that OK?
Jim:	Sure.
Counselor:	Jim, when was the last time you drank?
Jim:	Last night, I had a couple of beers after I got home. I was feeling really bad and just needed something to take the edge off. I haven't drunk anything this morning though, I don't want my boss to think I really do have a drinking problem.
Counselor:	Have you ever experienced any withdrawal symptoms such as shakes, tremors, seizures, or hallucinations?
Jim:	No, never anything like that. I don't drink that much.
Counselor:	You mentioned you "can't keep going like this?"
Jim:	Yeah, something has to change. I can't keep having this sort of problem.

(continued)

(continued)

Counselor:	Some people will say they can't keep going like this when they are really ready for life to change and some people say it when they are having thoughts of killing themselves. Have you had thoughts about suicide?
Jim:	*Gosh no, life isn't that bad. I would never do something like that.*

As mentioned previously, Insight Counseling offers outpatient counseling but does not offer detoxification and withdrawal management services or emergency psychiatric hospitalization services. Through the conversation, the counselor screens if Jim needs detoxification or withdrawal management services. Jim does not report a history of withdrawal. The counselor also briefly screens Jim for possible suicidal ideation. Jim denies any thoughts of suicide. Given these responses, Jim is considered initially appropriate for individual outpatient counseling. If Jim's answers indicated the need for detoxification and withdrawal management or emergency psychiatric services, the counselor would have facilitated a referral to another agency that can offer the services Jim needed.

GLOBAL CRITERION 3: ELIGIBILITY FOR ADMISSION OR REFERRAL

The third task of screening is addressed by Global Criterion 3: *Determine the client's **eligibility** for admission or referral*. The determination of a client's eligibility for admission or referral is based on the client's unique characteristics. The key question to determine eligibility is "Is this the right agency to meet the client's needs?" The information we are seeking is related to demographics. The counselor will ask questions to assess if Jim meets the client demographic (Box 4.2) served by the agency.

Unfolding Case Study

Counselor:	Jim, is it okay if I ask you a few more questions?
Jim:	Yes, but I really want to get something scheduled before I see my boss this morning.
Counselor:	At Insight Counseling, we offer both telehealth and in-person sessions. Do you have a preference for a type of session?
Jim:	I don't know about all this technology stuff. I want to go there. I looked up your address and I live close by.
Counselor:	Do you have insurance that you will be using to help pay for services?
Jim:	Yes, I have coverage through my wife's job. Will that work?
Counselor:	Yes. Let's get an appointment scheduled for you. How about tomorrow at 10?
Jim:	Yes, that will work. If I still have a job, I am sure my boss will give me the time off for the appointment.

Box 4.2 Demographic Considerations

Age
Sex
Gender
Race
Ethnicity
Legal status
Marital status
Income
Education status
Veteran status
Overall health stability
Insurance coverage/payor source
Housing status
Geographic area
Telehealth versus in-person sessions
Scheduling availability

As mentioned previously, Insight Counseling offers counseling to adults and adolescents. Jim is an adult and has insurance coverage to assist in paying for services. We know he lives in the area based on his responses; therefore, there are no geographic concerns related to state licensure. Because Jim meets the eligibility requirements for Insight Counseling, an appointment can be scheduled for him.

GLOBAL CRITERION 4: IDENTIFYING COEXISTING CONDITIONS

The fourth task of screening is addressed by Global Criterion 4: *Identify coexisting conditions (medical, psychiatric, physical, etc.) that indicate the need for additional professional assessment and/or services.* The identification of coexisting conditions is an important aspect of screening; however, as noted previously, we are not completing a comprehensive evaluation during screening. We are seeking to identify concerns that may need immediate referral or result in the person not being appropriate for services at a particular agency.

Unfolding Case Study

Jim does not identify any coexisting conditions. The counselor initially screens Jim for possible suicidal ideation, which he denies. Though not as essential for an outpatient treatment program, residential substance use treatment programs frequently require a physical examination by a medical provider to ensure the client is healthy enough to actively participate in treatment and that any medical needs can be managed while the client is at the facility. When Jim completes his assessment, the counselor will further assess possible coexisting conditions.

GLOBAL CRITERION 5: LAWS, REGULATIONS, AND AGENCY POLICIES

The fifth task of screening is addressed by Global Criterion 5: *Adhere to applicable laws, regulations, and agency policies governing alcohol and other drug abuse services.* Global Criterion 5 does not directly involve the client; rather, the criteria is focused on the protection of the client. The successful completion of Global Criterion 5 requires the alcohol and drug counselor to understand the applicable rules, regulations, and agency policies of where the alcohol and drug counselor provides services. Examples of this include the Health Insurance Portability and Accountability Act (HIPAA), 42 code of federal regulation (CFR) pt 2, state laws governing substance abuse counselors, and local agency policies and procedures. Further information regarding this will be covered in Chapter 8, "Legal, Ethical, and Professional Issues." One of the most important considerations for the counselor to remember about the core function of screening is that although the person being screened is not yet officially a client, the counselor is required to treat the inquiry as confidential and cannot disclose the person's identity or identifying information just as if they were a client.

Tips From the Field

Agencies with more specific appropriateness and eligibility requirements (such as withdrawal management, residential treatment, and halfway house programs) usually have written screening forms or request prior evaluations to assist in collecting the necessary information for a screening team to decide if a client is a good fit for the program.

▶ INTAKE

Unfolding Case Study

Jim arrives at Insight Counseling for his scheduled appointment.

The next step in engaging Jim in the counseling process is to complete the tasks of the core function of **Intake** (Box 4.3; Herdman, 2021). Intake involves the completion of the administrative and initial assessment procedures for admission to a program. The procedures completed during the intake process are

Box 4.3 Core Function 2: Intake

Definition: The administrative and initial assessment procedures for admission to a program.

Global Criteria:
6. Complete required documents for admission to the program.
7. Complete required documents for program eligibility and appropriateness.
8. Obtain appropriately signed consents when soliciting from or providing information to outside sources to protect confidentiality and rights.

typically the same for all clients. Often agencies will have an "intake packet" that is completed prior to the initiation of clinical services. The global criteria for the intake function specify the types of documents to be completed.

GLOBAL CRITERION 6: COMPLETE REQUIRED DOCUMENTS FOR ADMISSION

The completion of Global Criterion 6 involves the completion of required documents for admission to the program. These documents vary from agency to agency but typically will involve the gathering of basic demographic information as well as obtaining the client's signature to demonstrate understanding and consent of program practices and policies. Examples of this include:

- consent to receive treatment,
- authorization to bill a client's insurance company and receive payment,
- authorization to send reminder texts or e-mails for upcoming appointments,
- consent for telehealth services should this be a utilized modality,
- acknowledgment of a client's rights and responsibilities,
- acknowledgment of fees for services the client will receive, and
- notice of privacy practices to address the requirements of HIPAA.

Clients are asked to acknowledge they either received or were offered written information regarding the privacy protection policy.

GLOBAL CRITERION 7: COMPLETE REQUIRED DOCUMENTS FOR ELIGIBILITY AND APPROPRIATENESS

Global Criterion 7 focuses on the completion of required documents for program eligibility and appropriateness. Global Criteria 2 and 3 focus on screening for eligibility and appropriateness whereas in Global Criterion 7, the agency documents this information. The documentation of eligibility and appropriateness may be completed by the client by completing a well-written demographic form specifying their name, address, sex, age, insurance information, and other information required by the agency to establish necessary eligibility and appropriateness requirements. To reduce the risk of insurance fraud, agencies make a copy of a client's insurance card and driver's license to be stored with the client chart. This documentation verifies the client's self-reported information gathered during the screening process. Agencies that offer sliding fee services will also request a client to bring documentation of their income either through recent paystubs or the prior year tax filing. Copies of this information are kept in the client chart to document the eligibility to receive a fee reduction based on the sliding fee scale.

GLOBAL CRITERION 8: OBTAIN SIGNED CONSENTS

Global Criterion 8 specifies the importance of obtaining appropriately signed consents when soliciting from or providing information to outside sources to protect confidentiality and rights. The key to successfully completing this task is acquiring the freely given consent of the client. The client's chart must contain a signed consent document which specifies to whom the client consents sharing of their protected health information and from whom the agency may request information about the client. HIPAA and 42 CFR pt 2 are very clear about the importance of confidentiality of client information.

More information regarding the requirements of a valid consent form is found in Chapter 6, "Planning With the Client."

The core function of intake establishes a foundation from which the rest of the counseling process grows. The documentation that is created during the intake process verifies that the client is aware of the services they are receiving, consents to receive these services, is aware of the fees they will pay for these services, and understands who will have access to their information. In other words, these documents result in a contract for services and establish the rules around which the services are performed.

Tips From the Field

Well-written and organized initial documents create the basis for which agencies can demonstrate compliance with local, state, and federal laws as well as helping to meet the guidelines of credentialing agencies. Clear initial documentation along with effective orientation also assist in engaging a client in a trusting and open relationship with the agency and the counselor.

▶ ORIENTATION

Often completed simultaneously with the core function of intake, the core function of **orientation** (Box 4.4; Herdman, 2021) involves describing to the client:

- general nature and goals of the program,
- rules governing client conduct and infractions that can lead to disciplinary action or discharge,
- hours when services are available (in a nonresidential program),
- treatment costs to be borne by the client (if any), and
- client rights.

Box 4.4 Core Function 3: Orientation

Definition: Describe to the client the following: general nature and goals of the program; rules governing client conduct and infractions that can lead to disciplinary action or discharge from the program; in a nonresidential program, the hours during which services are available; treatment costs to be borne by the client, if any; and client rights.

Global Criteria:
9. Provide an overview to the client by describing program goals and objectives for client care.
10. Provide an overview to the client by describing program rules and client obligations and rights.
11. Provide an overview to the client of program operations.

It is essential that counselors recognize that the completion of the documents and the explanation of the services are two different, yet essential, activities. Without signed documentation, there is no verification that the client was informed of the contract for services and without explanation, we cannot expect that a client will be an active and informed participant in services.

The tasks of orientation complete the initial engagement with the client. The goal of orienting a client to the program is to help the client be as fully informed as possible as to what will be expected during participation in services. A client who knows what to expect during services and knows what will be expected of them during services has a greater likelihood of success and reduced likelihood of program discontinuation.

GLOBAL CRITERION 9: PROGRAM GOALS AND OBJECTIVES

The initial task of orientation is specified in Global Criterion 9: *Provide an overview to the client by describing program goals and objectives for client care.* Program goals are not the same as a client's individual treatment plan goals. Program goals are broad goals that are the same for all participants, whereas individual goals are tailored to the unique needs and presenting concerns of each client. To help understand Global Criterion 9, we return to Jim.

Unfolding Case Study

Counselor:	Jim, here at Insight Counseling we have several broad program goals that we help each of our clients attain. May I share these with you?
Jim:	Yes.
Counselor:	Our program goals are to help you increase your awareness of the impacts of your substance use and to assist you in exploring your options regarding substance use. Through the assessment process, we will offer you recommendations for treatment and then we can work together to create your individual treatment plan. Additionally, we have the goal of providing quality information and education about substance use to you and to your family members if you so choose. We also want to help you identify triggers for substance use, develop alternate healthy coping strategies, and build a positive support system to help you meet your goals. Are these goals of interest to you?
Jim:	Yes, I think this is what I need. I don't know what is happening, but I know I can't keep going like this. I know my wife would like to come with me, but I don't know if I am ready for that yet.
Counselor:	I will make a note of that regarding your wife. When you are ready, you are welcome to have her accompany you to a session.

Through this first part of orientation, we have invited Jim to participate in our services by describing the nature of Insight's program goals and objectives. Jim freely consents to participate and, given his comment about inviting his wife to join him in the future, we can see he is beginning to see himself staying in services for a period of time.

GLOBAL CRITERION 10: RULES, CLIENT OBLIGATIONS, AND RIGHTS

The second task of orientation is explained in Global Criterion 10: *Provide an overview to the client by describing program rules, and client obligations and rights.* Completing this task will vary greatly depending on the type of program a client is entering. A residential substance use program will have an extensive rules list, or possibly a client handbook, covering items such as curfew, cell phone usage, visiting hours, dress code expectations, and so forth; whereas a small outpatient program is more likely to have implied rules that are common for all public places such as hygiene, respect for the space of others in common areas, and bringing animals to the office; these rules are clarified as the need arises.

Providing orientation to client obligations is similar to helping a person understand their part of a contract. Client obligations are often referred to as "client responsibilities." The alcohol and drug counselor agrees to offer counseling services and, in exchange the client agrees to the client responsibilities. Examples of client responsibilities include: treat those providing care with dignity and respect, attend scheduled appointments, call in advance if there is a need to cancel an appointment, pay the agreed fee in a timely manner, and actively participate throughout the treatment process.

In addition to obligations, all clients have rights when receiving services. Examples of client rights include:

- being treated with dignity and respect;
- having treatment records kept confidential and being informed of the limits to this confidentiality;
- having the ability to file a complaint if a concern arises;
- sharing in the development of a treatment plan;
- receiving a clear explanation of conditions, symptoms, and treatment options;
- the ability to decline participation or withdraw from services at any time and receive referral information if requested; and
- inquiring about and being informed of the counselor's work history, training, education background, and qualifications.

Alcohol and drug counselors will orient the client to these rights and responsibilities and will have the client sign a document acknowledging these rights and responsibilities/obligations. Signing and retention of this document is also part of the intake process.

Tips From the Field

Many insurance companies provide example client rights and responsibilities forms on their websites for counselors to use.

It is essential to orient the client to their rights and responsibilities. This orientation assists the client in understanding what is expected of them through the treatment process, thereby increasing active participation. Orientation to client rights helps the client be an informed consumer of counseling services and empowers the client to make decisions in their care. Client rights and responsibilities as well as other rules and regulations followed by the program should be explained to the client in a way the client can understand.

GLOBAL CRITERION 11: PROGRAM OPERATIONS

The final task in the core function of orientation is Global Criterion 11: *Provide an overview to the client of program operations*. Program operations include the hours the counselor's office or agency is open; how crisis calls are handled during hours of operation and after hours of operation; orientation to the use of e-mail, text messages and other forms of electronic interaction; and the use of telehealth services. Orientation to program operations also include more general topics that are often covered by support staff or by the counselor when the client first arrives to the building including the location of the restroom, where to wait for an appointment, and where to park when arriving for an appointment.

Clients vary in their expectations for access to their counselor, thus orientation at the beginning of services is essential. Some clients have the expectation that if they call, their call will be returned within a short period of time. If the counselor's policy is to return a call within 24 hours, the client needs to be aware of this. If the counselor uses e-mail or other electronic forms of communication, the client must be oriented to what level of response they can expect as well as what types of information are acceptable to communicate via electronic means. The ethics of electronic communication are discussed in Chapter 6, "Planning Treatment With the Client" and Chapter 8, "Legal, Ethical, and Professional Issues."

The process of orientation can take many formats. Orientation is often completed through a combination of informing the client orally and having written information for the client to read. Counselors balance oral versus written orientation based on the client's individual needs and ability to understand the orientation. Some clients will need minimal oral orientation and prefer to read the information either at the time of their appointment or through signing documentation online prior to the appointment; whereas other clients will need more extensive explanation. In the end, it is the counselor's responsibility to adequately orient the client and not assume the client "should" know. A brief excerpt of the orientation between Jim and his counselor is as follows.

Unfolding Case Study

Counselor: I appreciate you completing the registration and intake packet and reviewing the rights and responsibilities of receiving counseling services at Insight Counseling. I want to review a few of the points covered in the packet. Counseling involves an agreement between me, as the counselor, and you, as the client. I am a licensed alcohol and drug counselor. I agree to complete a thorough assessment and advise you of my recommendations and treatment options. You can then decide if you want to continue services. Everything you tell me is confidential in that I will not reveal to anyone that you attend counseling and I will not reveal anything we talk about to anyone else unless you sign a disclosure indicating whom I can speak to and what I can speak to them about. There are exceptions to this confidentiality, however. If you tell me that you are going to harm yourself or are going to harm someone else, I am required by law to take steps to ensure your or the other person's safety. If you tell me about abuse that has occurred to a child, I am a mandatory reporter and must inform law enforcement to ensure the safety of the child. Finally, if I receive an order signed by a judge to release your records, I am required by law to disclose the information that is ordered. Do you have any questions about this?

Jim: What if my wife calls and wants to know if I am coming and what I am talking about in counseling?

(continued)

(continued)

Counselor:	I cannot disclose any information to her unless you sign a disclosure form indicating what you are permitting me to speak to her about.
Jim:	Good; I am not sure I am ready for her to know everything.
Counselor:	For you to be successful in counseling, it is essential that you attend all of your scheduled appointments and that you agree to work on the treatment plan that we create. If you are not able to attend an appointment, I ask that you call a minimum of 24 hours ahead of time to cancel the appointment. We will bill your insurance; however, any cost not covered by your insurance company will be your responsibility. Do you have any questions about this?
Jim:	No, I understand.
Counselor:	If you need to get hold of me between sessions, please call and leave a message. I will do my best to return your call within 24 hours.
Jim:	Can I just e-mail you instead or send you a text message?
Counselor:	As we get to know each other better, we can discuss how e-mail may be beneficial for the therapy process. I have found it is better initially to keep all communication within the face-to-face session to reduce misunderstandings as well as allowing me to give you my full attention when we are communicating. In the event of a crisis where you do not feel you can wait for me to call you back, I encourage you to call the local crisis support line or the local emergency department for assistance as I cannot guarantee I can get back to you quickly enough in a crisis.
Jim:	I understand.
Counselor:	Do you have any other questions?
Jim:	It all works for me.
Counselor:	Excellent; if you do ever have any questions, please let me know. Let's begin the assessment.

At this point in the conversation the counselor has completed all the tasks of screening, intake, and orientation, has worked to engage Jim, and has begun the transition to the next core function, assessment.

▶ KEY POINTS

■ Screening is completed upon initial contact with the client. If the client is eligible and appropriate, an offer is made to engage services. If the client is found not to be eligible or appropriate, the client is referred to other services.

■ Intake involves the completion of the written documents required for entry into services. The client's signature is gathered as evidence that the client has been provided information about the program.

■ Orientation is when the counselor explains to the client the program operations, the rights of being a client, and the obligations/responsibilities of being a client, as well as any other pertinent information regarding the program.

■ From the point of view of the client, these three core functions and the tasks associated with each may appear simply administrative in nature; however, for the counselor the interactions that occur between the counselor and client form the beginning of the counseling relationship both from a legal and interpersonal standpoint. The quality of engagement, completeness of the intake paperwork, and thoroughness of orientation lay the foundation for the treatment process. Counselors may be tempted to overlook the importance of the first three core functions, which would be unfortunate and not advised. Many problems that arise during the course of treatment can be traced back to failure to adequately complete the early tasks of treatment.

▶ REFERENCES

Herdman, J. W. (2021). *Global criteria: The 12 core functions of the substance abuse counselor* (8th ed.).

Kulewicz, S. F. (2000). *The twelve core functions of a counselor* (4th ed.). Stanley Kulewicz.

CASE STUDY 4.1

Jan places a call to the Freedom House, a halfway house for men in recovery. She shares with the admission staff who answers her call that she has been drinking every day for the past 90 days—ever since her husband left her for her best friend. She indicates she wants to quit drinking and heard that people could live at the halfway house and get help with sobriety.

The admission staff shares with Jan that the Freedom House is for men only and they do not have any services for women. The staff inquires if Jan is interested in a referral for other services. Jan indicates she is open to this as she knows she needs to do something different. The staff inquires if Jan has experienced any withdrawal symptoms such as shakes, tremors, night sweats, hallucinations, or seizures. Jan reports that she has been drinking every day for the past 90 days—typically three to four bottles of wine each night on top of the glass or two she has during her lunch break. She shares she did try earlier this week to not drink but felt very ill and "not right" until she drank two glasses of wine. The staff, recognizing Jan's high probability of needing detoxification and withdrawal services, provides Jan with the name and number of the local agency that offers detoxification and withdrawal management services. Jan takes down the information and agrees to call right after she hangs up.

1. The admission staff completed the tasks of which core function in the case scenario?
   A) Intake
   B) Orientation
   C) Crisis management
   D) Screening

2. Though the admission staff who answered the phone did not know Jan directly, the staff had previously heard part of her story from a friend who discussed how one of her coworker's husbands walked out on her a few months ago. Which of the following is correct?
   A) The admission staff is free to tell her friend about the call because Jan did not become a client
   B) The admission staff can tell her friend about what happened to Jan as long as she does not tell her Jan called asking about admission to a substance treatment program
   C) The admission staff cannot say anything about the call as Jan has the legal right to confidentiality even if she only requested information about services
   D) The admission staff should have told Jan that her coworkers are talking about her

3. The admission staff referred Jan to alternate services because:
   A) Jan was not appropriate for services at a men's halfway house
   B) Jan was not eligible for services at a men's halfway house
   C) Jan did not have the correct insurance to be admitted to a men's halfway house
   D) Jan was still blaming her husband for why she started drinking

4. The admission staff asked about withdrawal symptoms because:
   A) The staff was curious about Jan's story so she could tell her friend
   B) The staff was evaluating Jan's psychological, social, and physiological signs and symptoms as a part of the screening process and to aid in making an appropriate referral
   C) The staff was determining if Jan was appropriate for the halfway house services
   D) The staff is required by law to ask about how much a person is drinking when they call about services

(*See answers on the next page.*)

CASE STUDY 4.1 ANSWERS

1. D) Screening

Through a series of questions, the admission staff determines if Jan is appropriate and eligible for services. Intake involves the administrative and initial procedures for admission to a program whereas orientation involves discussing the client's rights and responsibilities. Jan requested assistance, but was not in crisis.

2. C) The admission staff cannot say anything about the call as Jan has the legal right to confidentiality even if she only requested information about services

Confidentiality is legally guaranteed beginning at initial screening. The admission staff is not allowed to discuss the call or any information learned from the call. It is not ethical to tell Jan that her coworkers are talking about her as this is not the role of the admission staff.

3. B) Jan was not eligible for services at a men's halfway house

Eligibility criteria focus on demographic characteristics. Jan is woman and the halfway house only accepts men; therefore, she is not eligible for services. Though Jan is not appropriate for the halfway house level of care due to needing detoxification and withdrawal services, this is not the primary reason she was referred to other services—even if she did not need detoxification and withdrawal services, Jan would still not be eligible for services at a men's halfway house. Further, no insurance information was collected as she is not eligible for services and her reasons for drinking have no bearing on her eligibility for services.

4. B) The staff was evaluating Jan's psychological, social, and physiological signs and symptoms as a part of the screening process and to aid in making an appropriate referral

Evaluating signs and symptoms is a part of the screening core function and aids in making an appropriate referral. The staff is legally obligated to maintain confidentiality. Jan is not eligible for services, thus there is no reason to further assess if she is appropriate, and the staff is not required by law to ask how much a person is drinking.

KNOWLEDGE CHECK: CHAPTER 4

1. Screening is:
   A) The process by which the client is determined appropriate and eligible for admission to a particular program
   B) The administrative and initial assessment procedures for admission to a program
   C) Describing to the client the general nature and goals of the program, rules governing client conduct, and infractions that can lead to disciplinary action or discharge from the program
   D) Developing a treatment plan with the client to direct service provision

2. Orientation is:
   A) The process by which the client is determined appropriate and eligible for admission to a particular program
   B) The administrative and initial assessment procedures for admission to a program
   C) Describing to the client the general nature and goals of the program, rules governing client conduct, and infractions that can lead to disciplinary action or discharge from the program
   D) Developing a treatment plan with the client to direct service provision

3. Intake is:
   A) The process by which the client is determined appropriate and eligible for admission to a particular program
   B) The administrative and initial assessment procedures for admission to a program
   C) Describing to the client the general nature and goals of the program, rules governing client conduct, and infractions that can lead to disciplinary action or discharge from the program
   D) Developing a treatment plan with the client to direct service provision

4. Which of the following is an example of program operations?
   A) Hours of operation
   B) Rules regarding reporting suspected abuse or neglect
   C) The program only accepts veterans as clients
   D) A client can decide to change counselors if they feel uncomfortable with their current counselor

5. Which is an example of an eligibility requirement?
   A) Over the age of 18
   B) Have not used any substances in 5 days
   C) Medically stable
   D) Willing to sign a disclosure to a support person

6. Which is an example of an appropriateness requirement?
   A) Over the age of 18
   B) Homelessness
   C) Involvement in the legal system
   D) Current symptoms can be managed at the level of care offered by the program

7. Obtaining appropriately signed consents is a task of which core function?
   A) Intake
   B) Screening
   C) Orientation
   D) Counseling

8. Evaluating psychological, social, and physiological signs and symptoms of alcohol and other drug use and abuse is a task of which core function?
   A) Case management
   B) Intake
   C) Screening
   D) Orientation

(See answers on the next page.)

1. A) The process by which the client is determined appropriate and eligible for admission to a particular program

The definition of screening is the process by which the client is determined appropriate and eligible for admission to a particular program. The administrative and initial assessment procedures for admission to a program comprise the definition of the core function of intake. Describing to the client the general nature and goals of the program, rules governing client conduct, and infractions that can lead to disciplinary action or discharge from the program is the definition of the core function of orientation. Developing a treatment plan with the client to direct service provision refers to the core function of treatment planning.

2. C) Describing to the client the general nature and goals of the program, rules governing client conduct, and infractions that can lead to disciplinary action or discharge from the program

Describing the general nature and rules of a program to a client is the definition of the core function of orientation. The process by which the client is determined appropriate and eligible for admission to a particular program is the definition of screening. The administrative and initial assessment procedures for admission to a program comprise the definition of intake. Developing a treatment plan with the client to direct service provision refers to the core function of treatment planning.

3. B) The administrative and initial assessment procedures for admission to a program

The definition of intake is the administration and initial assessment procedures for admission to a program. The process by which the client is determined appropriate and eligible for admission to a particular program is the definition of screening. Describing to the client the general nature and goals of the program, rules governing client conduct, and infractions that can lead to disciplinary action or discharge from the program is the definition of the core function of orientation. Developing a treatment plan with the client to direct service provision refers to the core function of treatment planning.

4. A) Hours of operation

Hours of operation is an example of program operations. Rules regarding reporting suspected abuse or neglect is an example of a program rule. The program only accepts veterans as clients is an example of an eligibility requirement. A client can decide to change counselors if they feel uncomfortable with the current counselor is an example of a client right.

5. A) Over the age of 18

Being over the age of 18 is an example of an eligibility requirement. Having not used any substances in 5 days is an example of an appropriateness requirement. Being medically stable is an example of an appropriateness requirement. Willing to sign a disclosure to a support person is an example of a program rule.

6. D) Current symptoms can be managed at the level of care offered by the program

An example of an appropriateness requirement is whether or not a client's current symptoms can be managed at the program's level of care. Over the age of 18 is an example of an eligibility requirement. Homelessness is an example of an eligibility requirement. Involvement in the legal system is an example of an eligibility requirement.

7. A) Intake

Obtaining appropriately signed consents is a task of the core function of intake. An example of a screening task is evaluating the client's appropriateness for admission. An example of an orientation task is providing an overview of program operations to the client. Counseling would not occur until after screening, intake, and orientation.

8. C) Screening

Evaluating psychological, social, and physiological signs and symptoms of alcohol and other drug use and abuse is the definition of screening. Obtaining appropriately signed consents is a task of the core function of intake. An example of an orientation task is providing an overview of program operations to the client. Case management would not occur until after screening, intake, and orientation.

9. Once a person is deemed eligible and appropriate for services the next step is to:
   A) Begin arrangements for intake and admission to the program
   B) Refer the potential client to other services
   C) Immediately contact the client's significant other to gather additional information
   D) Continue assessing the potential client to determine a diagnosis

10. Which of the following is correct regarding the core function of orientation?
    A) It is the client's responsibility to read and orient themselves to the rules of the program
    B) It is the counselor's responsibility to adequately orient the client to the rules of the program
    C) It is the client's responsibility to ask other clients in the program about the rules
    D) The counselor bears no responsibility for the client understanding the rules of the program if the rules are clearly posted on the wall for all clients to read

11. Providing a tour of the facility occurs during the process of what core function?
    A) Intake
    B) Orientation
    C) Assessment
    D) Screening

12. Asking the client to sign the rights and responsibilities form occurs during the process of what core function?
    A) Intake
    B) Orientation
    C) Assessment
    D) Screening

13. During the orientation phase, the counselor ensures that the client understands:
    A) The need for immediate detoxification
    B) The importance of medication-assisted treatment (MAT)
    C) Their rights and responsibilities while in treatment
    D) The consequences of relapse

14. A client reports that they were arrested for possession of methamphetamine. The counselor should note this as:
    A) A social symptom of alcohol and other drug use
    B) A psychological symptom of alcohol and other drug use
    C) A physiological symptom of alcohol and other drug use
    D) Not relevant to the client's presenting concerns

An alcohol and drug counselor works at an adult female-specific residential substance use treatment center. Their job is to review evaluations of clients requesting admission to treatment and complete the admission process when admitted. The counselor receives an application from a 19-year-old female who is requesting admission because she was arrested for possession of methamphetamine. The evaluation indicates she has been using methamphetamine multiple times per week for the past year and has been unsuccessful in stopping her use in outpatient counseling. The evaluation recommends residential substance use treatment. She has a prior admission to a psychiatric hospital due to suicidal ideation and was diagnosed with major depressive disorder, moderate. The evaluation reports the symptoms of her depression are stabilized and no suicidal thinking is reported. The potential client has not used any substances for the past 3 days as she is staying with her mother until she can be admitted to treatment.

15. Based on the information presented, the potential client is eligible for admission to the program due to:
    A) Being sober for a minimum of 3 days
    B) Being an adult female
    C) Not having current suicidal ideation
    D) Not being able to maintain sobriety in outpatient counseling

(See answers on the next page.)

9. A) Begin arrangements for intake and admission to the program

Once a person is deemed eligible for services, arrangements can begin for intake and admission. Referring the potential client to other services is incorrect, no referral needs to occur if the potential client was deemed eligible and appropriate. Immediately contacting the client's significant other to gather additional information is incorrect and could not be done without the potential client's consent. Continuing to assess the potential client to determine a diagnosis is incorrect. A diagnosis will not be made until during the assessment process.

10. B) It is the counselor's responsibility to adequately orient the client to the rules of the program

It is the counselor's responsibility to orient the client to the rules of the program. The client has the responsibility to follow these rules and ask if they do not understand the program rules. Posting the rules is not sufficient to meet the requirements of the core function of orientation.

11. B) Orientation

Providing a tour is an example of an orientation task. Neither intake, assessment, and screening include a tour.

12. A) Intake

Collecting signatures is a criteria of the intake core function. The orientation core function consists of informing the client, whereas collecting signatures is an intake core function criteria. Signatures are not collected during the completion of the core functions of assessment or screening.

13. C) Their rights and responsibilities while in treatment

Orientation focuses on helping the client understand the program whereas the need for intoxication, importance of MAT, and the consequences of relapse are counseling interventions.

14. A) A social symptom of alcohol and other drug use

Legal charges fall in the social symptom category as they relate to a person's interactions or relationship with others or the community. Psychological symptoms refer to thoughts and emotion regulation and physiological symptoms refer to how a substance affects a person's body. The legal charge is relevant to the client's presenting concern as often a legal charge is indicative of an increase in severity of a person's use.

15. B) Being an adult female

The client is eligible for admission to a treatment center which only treats adult females. Being sober for a minimum of 3 days, not having current suicidal ideation, and not being able to maintain sobriety in outpatient counseling are all appropriateness criteria.

Assessing the Client

Thomas Maxson

In Chapter 4, "Engaging the Client," the tasks of engaging a client were introduced. Initial engagement is completed through the core functions of screening, intake, and orientation. This chapter focuses on the skills and tasks of assessing a client. The process of assessment is addressed under Domain 2: Evidence-Based Screening and Assessment.

▶ ASSESSMENT

Assessment refers to the procedures by which a counselor identifies and evaluates an individual's strengths, weaknesses, problems, and needs for the development of a treatment plan.

Unfolding Case Study

At the end of Chapter 4, "Engaging the Client," we had completed the tasks of engagement with Jim. Jim initially made contact due to concerns about the impact his alcohol use was having on his life. We initially **screened** Jim to see if he was eligible and appropriate for outpatient services at Insight Counseling. We then invited Jim to the office and completed the initial **intake** paperwork that demonstrated his eligibility and appropriateness for our services. Finally, we engaged in the tasks of **orientation** to help Jim understand what he can expect from services. Now that the engagement process is complete, the next step is to complete an assessment of Jim. An assessment provides the counselor with the information necessary to complete a treatment plan with Jim. The tasks of assessment are described by the core function of assessment (Box 5.1; Herdman, 2021).

Box 5.1 Core Function 4: Assessment

Definition: The procedures by which a counselor/program identifies and evaluates an individual's strengths, weaknesses, problems, and needs for the development of a treatment plan.

Global Criteria:
12. Gather relevant history from the client including but not limited to alcohol and other drug abuse using appropriate interview techniques.
13. Identify methods and procedures for obtaining corroborative information from significant secondary sources regarding the client's alcohol and other drug abuse and psychosocial history.
14. Identify appropriate assessment tools.
15. Explain to the client the rationale for the use of assessment techniques in order to facilitate understanding.
16. Develop a diagnostic evaluation of the client's substance abuse and any coexisting conditions based on the results of all assessments in order to provide an integrated approach to treatment planning based on the client's strengths, weaknesses, and identified problems and needs.

The assessment process in substance use counseling involves gathering relevant, comprehensive information about the client's substance use history, physical and mental health, family dynamics, social support, and other relevant factors. The purpose of assessment is to gain a holistic understanding of the client's needs, strengths, and treatment goals. Various approaches are used to complete an assessment. These include:

1. **Biopsychosocial assessment:** Considers biological, psychological, and social factors that contribute to substance use. Gathers information about the client's physical and mental health, family history, social environment, and cultural background.

2. **Motivational interviewing (MI):** A client-centered approach that explores the motivation and readiness for change through empathetic listening, open-ended questions, and collaboratively set treatment goals.
3. **Cognitive behavioral assessment:** Focuses on identifying the client's thoughts, beliefs, and behavioral patterns and examines the client's triggers, cravings, coping skills, and the consequences related to substance abuse.
4. **Dual diagnosis assessment/co-occurring assessment:** Used when there is a co-occurring mental health disorder alongside substance use. The counselor assesses the presence and severity of both conditions to develop an integrated treatment plan.
5. **Addiction Severity Index (ASI):** Provides a structured interview format to gather information across several domains such as medical, employment, legal, family, and substance use history. The ASI is widely used to assess the severity of substance use and to identify areas of impairment or need.
6. **Standardized screening tools:** Substance Abuse Subtle Screening Inventory (SASSI), the drug abuse screening test (DAST-10), or the Alcohol Use Disorders Identification Test (AUDIT) may be utilized to assess substance use severity, patterns, and related problems.
7. **Observation and clinical interviews:** Client behaviors, affect, and interactions that counselors use to assess the client's level of substance use, cognitive functioning, and emotional well-being.
8. **Collateral information:** Obtained from other sources such as family members, friends, or healthcare providers who have knowledge of the client's substance use history and its impact on their life.

By using a combination of these assessment techniques and theories, substance use counselors can gather a comprehensive understanding of the client's unique circumstances, formulate an accurate diagnosis, and develop an individualized treatment plan to address their specific needs.

Tips From the Field

A quality assessment helps the counselor and the client understand why the individual is seeking services today and answers the question "What now?"

The skills necessary to complete an assessment are summarized by the International Certification & Reciprocity Consortium's (IC&RC) job analysis under Domain 2: Evidence-Based Screening and Assessment (Box 5.2; IC&RC, 2022).

Box 5.2 DOMAIN 2: Evidence-Based Screening and Assessment

A. Utilize established interviewing techniques (e.g., MI, probing, questioning)
B. Utilize established screening and assessment methods and instruments (e.g., ASI, adverse childhood experiences [ACEs], and Substance Abuse Subtle Screening Inventory [SASSI]).
C. Identify methods and interpret results from drug and alcohol testing
D. Utilize established diagnostic criteria for evaluating substance use (i.e., *Diagnostic and Statistical Manual of Mental Disorders* [DSM])
E. Assemble a comprehensive client biopsychosocial history (e.g., health, family, employment, collateral sources)
F. Determine the course of action to meet the individual's immediate and ongoing needs
G. Determine level of care based on placement criteria

The first task of assessment is gathering relevant history from the client including but not limited to alcohol and other drug use using appropriate interview techniques (Global Criteria 12). To effectively complete an assessment, the counselor must understand what needs to be gathered from the client. A comprehensive assessment is one that includes a complete biopsychosocial history (Domain 2: E). A biopsychosocial history encompasses a review of all areas of the client's life. The word biopsychosocial is a combination of three parts. "Bio" refers to assessing relevant biological facets of the client. This includes current medications, current and relevant past medical concerns, the experience of chronic pain, and any physical disabilities or need for specific physical accommodations to be successful in treatment. For some clients, their biological or physical functioning significantly impacts their day-to-day life and may have a significant correlation to their substance use. For other clients, their physical functioning is not a concern and does not correlate to their substance use. "Psycho" refers to assessing relevant psychological facets of the client. This includes current and past mental health and substance use symptoms; current and past treatment experiences; the attitudes and beliefs the client has toward themselves, others, and the world; as well as the client's current awareness of or insight into the concerns that are facing them. Finally, "social" refers to assessing the client's experiences and views of their present and past relationships. This includes current and past peers, current and past romantic partners, and current and past relationships with their family. Social history also refers to school history, work history, and military history. Completing a biopsychosocial assessment connects to the information that was gathered to complete Global Criteria 1, *Evaluate psychological, social, and physiological signs and symptoms of alcohol and other drug use and abuse* as a part of the core function of screening.

As discussed in Chapter 8, "Legal, Ethical, and Professional Issues," prior to beginning the assessment the client is oriented to the limits of confidentiality. As you are completing the substance use assessment, the client may ask about these limits again prior to reporting certain information. It is essential for the counselor to be factual and forthcoming in reviewing the limits of confidentiality as well as to have a willingness to discuss with the client a hypothetical scenario so the client can be informed of their options. For example, a client inquires if the counselor would have to report to the police if "someone" were to say they got drunk and drove home last week. The counselor should reply that confidentiality laws would protect "that person." The client is also oriented to the rationale for the use of assessment techniques (Global Criteria 15). Explaining to the client the rationale for the use of assessment techniques assists the client in understanding what is happening during the assessment process and often reduces a client's defensiveness.

In completing the assessment, the counselor will use established interviewing techniques, such as MI (Domain 2: A; MI is explored in Chapter 7, "Counseling With the Client"). The key skill for completing an assessment is the intentional use of open-ended versus close-ended questions. Open-ended questions refer to questions that evoke a broad answer from the client. We are asking them to "tell us a story" about themselves such as their alcohol use history or how they maintained sobriety for over a year during their last period of abstinence. Close-ended questions seek to elicit a single word or short-answer response. Close-ended questions are used when the counselor is seeking an initial response such as "Are you taking any medications?" Have you completed a substance evaluation in the past?" "Do you have any military history?" to determine if further probing of the topic area is needed.

A quality assessment does not rely on the self-report of the client alone. As part of the interview the counselor identifies methods and procedures for obtaining corroborative information from significant secondary sources regarding the client's alcohol and other drug use and psychosocial history (Global Criteria 13). The counselor will orient the client as to the purpose of the collateral information and complete a release of information prior to contacting any sources of collateral contact. The counselor also utilizes appropriate assessment tools and instruments (Global Criteria 14, Domain 2: B). If a counselor utilizes drug and alcohol testing either administered by the counselor or received from an outside entity, the counselor will establish competence in interpreting the results or will seek consultation in interpreting the results (Domain 2: C).

Once the interview is complete and the corroborative information is integrated, the counselor will utilize established diagnostic criteria to develop a diagnostic evaluation of the client's substance use and any coexisting conditions based on the results of all assessments in order to provide an integrated approach to treatment planning based on the client's strengths, weaknesses, and identified problems and needs (Global Criteria 16, Domain 2: D). Based on the entirety of the information, the counselor will then determine the course of action to meet the individual's immediate and ongoing needs and determine the level of care based on placement criteria (Domain 2: F and G).

Counselors are sensitive to the age, culture, primary language, cognitive level, and possible trauma history of the individual being assessed. To complete a valid assessment, the counselor needs to make modifications to the standard assessment process to account for individual client needs.

Counseling agencies and most insurance companies have assessment templates that can be utilized for the completion of an assessment. This chapter offers one example of a biopsychosocial assessment template. Each section of the assessment is discussed and then a completed assessment is presented with the information gathered from Jim.

Tips From the Field

The template you choose to use may vary from the one presented here. The key is for all of the areas to be covered in a way that is understandable and usable to assist the counselor and client in understanding the client's current strengths, weaknesses, problems, and needs so that a treatment plan can be developed.

The template is a roadmap that helps guide the interview. It is arranged in such a way as to allow time for the client to build trust and become comfortable with answering questions about themselves without feeling threatened. This then leads to questions that require increased vulnerability on the client's part. Responding to questions about substance use history, family history, and behavioral health history requires greater divulgence of information that some clients may find uncomfortable. It is the responsibility of the counselor to recognize and validate a client's discomfort and work to build engagement and rapport with the client.

The counselor should expect that that client will be somewhat defensive during an assessment interview and may attempt to minimize facts they feel will be viewed as unfavorable or possibly cause greater intervention recommendations than they are willing to accept. This is especially the case when clients are requested to complete an assessment by the criminal justice system or some other formal system (e.g., child and family services, employer concern, custody dispute; Box 5.3).

▶ DEMOGRAPHICS

The assessment begins with inquiring about demographic information. Much of this information is gathered from the initial intake paperwork the client fills out prior to the beginning of the assessment. The demographic information begins to inform the counselor of possible important areas to explore. For example, the school history of a 15-year-old client is likely to be more relevant to understanding the client than the school history of a 45-year-old client.

▶ PRESENTING PROBLEM/PRIMARY COMPLAINT

The presenting problem/primary complaint section offers the counselor an opportunity to understand the "Why now?" question. It also allows the client to begin to share their concerns about their substance use and their own conceptualization of their current situation in life. The counselor can gain valuable information regarding the client by asking the open-ended question, "What brings you to see me today?" During this section of the assessment, the counselor can build rapport and trust by validating the client for attending the evaluation as well as begin to identify the client's motivation for change and their areas of ambivalence. The counselor must be cautious to not spend too much time in this section, otherwise sufficient time will not be available to complete the rest of the assessment.

▶ MEDICAL HISTORY

Depending on their unique characteristics, a client's medical history can be a brief or extensive section of their assessment. The 15-year-old mentioned earlier may be very healthy and have no significant medical history; however, this same 15-year-old may have had knee surgery at age 13 after a baseball injury. The teen was prescribed an opiate pain reliever and felt relief from both the physical pain and the sadness he feels due to the death of his younger sister. He then began seeking additional refills from his doctor and eventually began stealing opiates from family and friends. The counselor needs to specifically ask about any history of hospitalizations, surgery, and chronic medical conditions.

Questions in the medical history section also cover the history of brain injury. It is estimated that at least one out of five people presenting for treatment of a substance use disorder is also living with the effects of brain injury (Lemsky, 2021). People with traumatic brain injury seeking services for

Box 5.3 Substance Use Assessment

Name: Date of Evaluation:
Referred by: DOB: Age:

A. **DEMOGRAPHICS**
   a. Name, age, and race/ethnicity

B. **PRESENTING PROBLEM/PRIMARY COMPLAINT**
   a. Summary of what led client to schedule this assessment
   b. "Why now?"

C. **MEDICAL HISTORY**
   a. Current medications
   b. Current relevant medical concerns
   c. Major past surgeries or other medical concerns including history of head/brain injury
   d. Ongoing medical needs that may impact substance use treatment
   e. Family history of medical concerns
   f. Significant allergies
   g. Prenatal, birth, or developmental concerns or complications

D. **WORK/SCHOOL/MILITARY HISTORY**
   a. Relevant school history based on age of client
   b. Relevant work history based on age of client
   c. Military history including history of deployment and traumatic experiences

E. **ALCOHOL/OTHER DRUG HISTORY**
   a. Frequency and amount of each substance including nicotine
   b. Alcohol or drug of choice
   c. History of substance-induced/use disorder
   d. Use patterns
   e. Consequences of use (physiological, legal, interpersonal, familial, vocational, etc.)
   f. Periods of abstinence/when and why
   g. Tolerance level
   h. Withdrawal history and potential
   i. Influence of living situation on use
   j. Other addictive behaviors (e.g., gambling)
   k. IV drug use

F. **LEGAL HISTORY**
   a. Criminal history and other information (self-report or from legal system)

G. **FAMILY/SOCIAL/PEER HISTORY**
   a. Family of origin history including past and current relationship with siblings and parents
   b. History of childhood trauma and abuse and self-assessment of current impact
   c. Social/peer history
   d. History of significant relationships/marriages
   e. Children
   f. Current social supports and quality of these supports
   g. Hobbies/fun
   h. Spirituality/religion

H. **BEHAVIORAL HEALTH HISTORY**
   a. Prior substance use assessments and findings
   b. Prior substance use disorder treatment and outcome
   c. Prior mental health diagnosis
   d. Prior mental health treatment and outcome
   e. Family history of mental health or substance concerns
   f. Risk of danger to self or others
   g. Screening for mental health symptoms

I. **COLLATERAL INFORMATION**
   a. Report any information about the client's use history, pattern, and/or consequences learned from other sources

(continued)

Box 5.3 Substance Use Assessment (*continued*)

J.   OTHER DIAGNOSTIC/SCREENING TOOLS—SCORES AND RESULTS
   a.   Report the results and scores from any other substance abuse assessment tool

K.   AMERICAN SOCIETY OF ADDICTION MEDICINE (ASAM) MULTIDIMENSIONAL ASSESSMENT
   Dimension 1: Acute intoxication and/or withdrawal potential
       i.   Intensity:
       ii. Justification:
   Dimension 2: Biomedical conditions and complications
       i.   Intensity:
       ii. Justification:
   Dimension 3: Emotional, behavioral, or cognitive conditions and complications
       i.   Intensity:
       ii. Justification:
   Dimension 4: Readiness to change
       i.   Intensity:
       ii. Justification:
   Dimension 5: Relapse, continued use, or continued problem potential
       i.   Intensity:
       ii. Justification:
   Dimension 6: Recovery/living environment
       i.   Intensity:
       ii. Justification:

L.   CLINICAL IMPRESSION
   a.   Summary of evaluation
       i.   Behavior during evaluation (agitation level, mood, and level of cooperation)
       ii. Motivation to change
       iii. Level of denial or defensiveness
       iv. Personal agenda
       v.   Discrepancies of information provided
   b.   Strengths of the individual/family identified
   c.   Needs of the individual/family identified
   d.   Substance use or substance use disorder diagnostic impression (including justification)
       i.   Identify the substance use and substance use disorder diagnostic impression

M.   DIAGNOSIS (*DSM-5-TR*)

N.   RECOMMENDATIONS
   a.   Primary/ideal level of care recommendation
       i.   Identify the level of care and service(s) that would best meet the needs of the client
   b.   Available level of care/barriers to ideal recommendation
       i.   If the level of care and service(s) are not available or there is some other reason the client cannot re-
            ceive that service, identify those reasons. Include the next best substance use level of care and service
            that the client can be referred to
   c.   Client response to recommendation
       i.   Document the client's response to the level of care and service recommendation
   d.   Identification of who needs to be involved in the client's treatment
   e.   Treatment plan goals including transitioning to lower levels of care and discharge planning
   f.   A means to evaluate the client's progress throughout their treatment and outcome measures at discharge
   g.   Recommended referrals for community resources

substance use may experience subtle but significant changes in memory, attention, problem solving, sensation, social behavior, and self-regulation, which make it difficult to remember appointments, understand expectations, follow through with tasks, and participate in group settings (Lemsky, 2021).

In addition to inquiring about a client's prescribed medications, it is essential to follow up and ask about the client's consistency or compliance with taking medications as directed. If a client is not consistent in taking prescribed medications, their treatment outcomes will be negatively impacted. Noncompliance may suggest a client's mistrust in their provider or ambivalence about needing outside assistance in treating their condition.

Other information documented in this section includes prenatal, birth and developmental concerns, allergies, and family history of medical concerns.

▶ SCHOOL/WORK/MILITARY HISTORY

The school/work/military history section begins to provide a developmental and historical perspective of a client's life. Most clients are willing to discuss their school and work experiences more readily than other parts of their history. The counselor can begin to ascertain if the client experienced difficulty in school which may suggest the presence of a learning disability or other academic concern. This is relevant information when the counselor considers treatment recommendations and accommodations the client may need to be successful in treatment. Conversely, if a client experienced success in school and sees reading and academics as strengths, they may respond better to a treatment plan which includes reading books on recovery. Difficulties in completing high school may also begin to suggest early consequences related to a client's substance use.

Frequent job changes or job losses may be a sign of substance use concerns that are significant enough to impact employment. A skilled counselor can begin to assess the signs and symptoms of a substance use disorder through targeted open-ended questions regarding job losses. Questions such as "How long was your longest full-time job?" and "What was your usual pattern of employment over the past 2 years?" are useful beginning questions in exploring an individual's employment history. However, it is important to recognize that stable employment does not rule out the possibility that a person has a substance use disorder.

Military history is included in this section as it fits within the developmental structure of this function of a person's life. Assessing a person's history of military experiences and their adjustment after the military can also begin to signal areas for further inquiry later in the assessment. It is essential to directly ask about experiences of deployment-related and nondeployment-related trauma and substance use.

▶ ALCOHOL/OTHER DRUG HISTORY

The alcohol/other drug history directly assesses a client's history of substance use. A full history of each drug used, the pattern of use, and impact of use is gathered. For some clients with poly drug use that occurred during the same period of time, a chronological history fits the best, whereas for other clients, assessing each drug individually is a better fit. Counselors need to include nicotine and caffeine as a part of their assessment, as well as nonsubstance addictive behaviors.

When assessing a person's alcohol and other drug use, it is helpful to the counselor to have a standard approach to gathering this information. Asking the client about their age of first use and their experience of first use can offer the counselor valuable insight into the original motivations for substance use. Initiation of substance use typically begins for one of three primary reasons: impulsivity, positive reinforcement, or relief of negative feelings (Substance Abuse and Mental Health Services Administration [SAMHSA], 2016). Impulsivity is characterized by acting without foresight or regard for the consequences. For example, an adolescent may impulsively take a first drink, smoke a cigarette, begin experimenting with marijuana, or succumb to peer pressure to try a party drug. Impulsivity continues into adulthood; for example, imagine a 28-year-old woman agreeing to try cocaine for the first time when out with friends after a breakup. She does not leave her home that evening intending to use cocaine but decides to experiment because an opportunity presents itself. After the initial experimentation with a substance, individuals make a choice as to which substances to continue to use. The 28-year-old female may choose to never use cocaine again; however, if she received positive reinforcement for the use or experienced relief of a negative feeling, she may choose to continue.

Positive reinforcement refers to a pleasurable experience of substance use and/or the person using the substance receiving approval from others. If either is experienced, the person is more likely to use the substance again. The substance may also bring relief from negative feelings such as stress, anxiety, social isolation, or depression. The temporary relief from the negative feelings the substance brings increases the likelihood that the person will use again. The 28-year-old female using cocaine after a breakup may have greatly enjoyed the extra energy and feeling of euphoria that enhanced her experience of going out with friends. Further, if she connects the use of cocaine to relief of the sadness from the breakup and begins looking forward to using again to relieve the negative feeling, this increases her chances of engaging in ongoing use, possibly leading to a cocaine use disorder.

Understanding an individual's reason for initiating and then choosing to continue to use a substance also aids in developing an individualized treatment plan which focuses on the core purpose for the use of the substance. If this same 28-year-old woman enters a treatment program at age 31 with a cocaine use disorder, understanding the initiation of her use provides the counselor with clues as to her treatment needs as well as relapse risk. Development of an individualized treatment plan is further explored in Chapter 6, "Planning Treatment With the Client."

After learning the person's age of first use and the reasons for initiation and continued use, the counselor continues to gather historical information about the person's use. The counselor assesses the frequency and amount of each substance used as well as use patterns. The counselor seeks to identify the impact and consequences of use on a person's life, including their relationships, thinking, and behavior patterns. The counselor gathers information about tolerance, craving, and withdrawal as well as periods of abstinence. When assessing periods of abstinence, the counselor inquires about when, and why, the abstinence period began and ended. The counselor also inquires about route of administration and changes in the route of administration, including specifically asking about IV use as appropriate for each substance. Other addictive behaviors are also assessed in the alcohol and other drug history including gambling, pornography, sexual compulsivity, and internet/gaming use. With each substance and nonsubstance addictive behavior, the counselor documents the last use. At the conclusion of the alcohol and other drug history, the counselor and the client identify and document which substance is the individual's preferred substance (Box 5.4).

Box 5.4 Commonly Assessed Substances of Use and Nonsubstance Addictive Behaviors

- Alcohol
- Cannabis (marijuana, wax): Complete this regardless of the legal status of marijuana in the individual's state of residence.
- Synthetic and cannabis-related substances (K2, cannabinoids)
- Cocaine/crack
- Amphetamines/methamphetamines
- Heroin
- Methadone
- Other opiates (including Kratom)
- Sedatives/tranquilizers/hypnotics/dissociatives
- Benzodiazepines
- Hallucinogens
- Inhalants
- Other medications: For example diphenhydramine (Benadryl), acetaminophen (Tylenol), dextromethorphan, and so forth
- Caffeine
- Nicotine
- Gambling
- Internet/gaming
- Pornography
- Sexual compulsivity

▶ LEGAL HISTORY

The legal history section provides an understanding of the person's involvement in the criminal justice system. It is important to indicate if the counselor gathered the information in this section from the individual's self-report or if the counselor was provided or gathered collateral information from the justice system. By assessing an individual's criminal justice system involvement, the counselor learns the impact of an individual's substance use. This history provides helpful information in building a more robust and accurate history of the individual's substance use; however, remember that legal problems due to substance use are not a defining criteria of a substance use disorder according to *DSM-5-TR*. Nonsubstance-related legal history is also important to formulate a holistic understanding of the individual and their treatment needs. This history should include all episodes of incarceration as well as their last episode of incarceration.

▶ FAMILY/SOCIAL/PEER HISTORY

The family/social/peer history section offers an essential snapshot into the developmental, environmental, and relational factors that shaped the individual being assessed. An individual's family of origin and early environmental and peer influences provide the foundation for the individual's development, which then establishes relational patterns that are often carried into adult relationships.

In this section, the counselor assesses a person's family of origin, including past and current relationship status with parents and siblings. The counselor also assesses significant environmental influences including the neighborhood where the individual lived and the impact of peer relationships. A history of childhood trauma and abuse, either as the victim or the perpetrator, and the current impact of these experiences is also assessed in this section. A counselor should be cautious in assessing childhood abuse as the individual may experience a traumatic response upon reporting such events. Further, a counselor also must be aware of, and follow through on, child abuse reporting requirements as dictated by state law.

In addition to family of origin, significant adult relationships, including marriages or long-term relationships, are also assessed in this section. Identifying patterns in these relationships aids the counselor in identifying the possible impact of substance use on relationships. The relationship the individual has with their children is assessed, including barriers to the relationship and impact of substance use on these relationships.

The next area assessed in this section is social support. The counselor needs to determine if the individual has informal supports that promote sobriety and recovery or if a majority of the person's informal supports use substances in a problematic manner. Along with social support, identifying a person's hobbies and spiritual/religious preferences assists in understanding the needs of the individual as well as strengths and supports that can be drawn upon during the treatment planning and counseling process.

▶ BEHAVIORAL HEALTH HISTORY

The behavioral health history section focuses on past and current behavioral health interventions. This includes past psychiatric hospitalizations, partial hospitalization stays, and outpatient mental health counseling. The behavioral health history section is also where the counselor documents if the client has participated in past or present substance use treatment including outpatient, intensive outpatient, or residential substance use treatment. Asking the client about past assessment and past diagnoses aids the counselor in identifying additional potential sources of collateral information as well as providing a better understanding of an individual's insight regarding their behavioral health needs. The counselor also inquires about any mental health or substance use concerns that the individual's direct family members may have or are currently experiencing.

The substance use counselor is expected to screen for mental health symptoms and recommend a referral for further assessment if mental health symptoms are identified. The counselor also screens for suicidal or homicidal ideation. It is important to be aware of the scope of practice for your particular license or credential when it comes to mental health treatment, screening and referral. If the counselor identifies concerns in either of these areas, appropriate action must be taken. Further discussion of this is covered in Chapter 8, "Legal, Ethical, and Professional Issues."

Common questions for screening for mental health symptoms include:

- Have you had periods of time not directly related to your substance use in which you experienced:
  - Sadness or depression?
  - Significant anxiety or worry that was difficult to control?
  - Hearing or seeing things that others do not see or hear (i.e., hallucinations)?
  - Difficulty focusing, concentrating, or sustaining attention?
  - Difficulty managing violent thoughts or engaging in violent behavior?

  If yes:
    - ○ Have you had thoughts of hurting others in the past week?
    - ○ Are you having thoughts of hurting someone right now?
    - ○ **If yes: The counselor must assess who the client is thinking of hurting and what means of harm they are considering. Seek consultation and make a safety plan for the individual and consider if there is a duty to warn the potential victim.**

● Suicidal thoughts or engaged in a suicide attempt?

If yes:

○ In the past few weeks, have you wished you were dead?

○ In the past few weeks, have you felt that you or your family would be better off if you were dead?

○ In the past week, have you been having thoughts about killing yourself?

○ Have you ever tried to kill yourself?

If yes, how? When?

○ *If the client answers* yes *to any of the above questions about suicide, ask the following acuity question:*

○ Are you having thoughts of killing yourself right now?

○ If yes, please describe.

○ **Seek consultation and make a safety plan for the individual and consider if there is a need for psychiatric hospitalization or further assessment for emergency protective custody.**

▶ COLLATERAL INFORMATION

Gathering collateral information with the appropriate consents in place, is essential to the completion of a quality assessment. Without collateral information, the recommendations are based entirely on the self-report of the individual completing the assessment. Given that many individuals are referred for a substance use assessment at the request of others, sometimes based on threat of jail, divorce, or other consequence, the possibility of the individual minimizing or presenting false information is significantly increased.

Possible sources of collateral information include parents, siblings, a spouse or long-term partner, long-term friends, employer, teacher, school records, probation/parole officer, attorney, prior treatment records or treatment providers. Anyone who has relevant knowledge about the individual may be a source of collateral information. When selecting a source of collateral information, it is important for the counselor to consider the possible motives of the person providing the information. A woman who is referred by an employer for an evaluation before returning to work may offer her husband as a source of collateral information. This husband may have a strong motive to minimize his wife's substance use so that she does not lose her job and can quickly return to work. On the other hand, past treatment records or probation officers will provide unbiased information.

In addition to reviewing records and speaking to those with client information, a counselor may be provided with results from drug and alcohol body fluid screening completed externally, such as from the criminal justice system or a private company contracted by the client's employer. Some counselors also choose to complete drug and alcohol screening as a part of the evaluation and treatment process. Common screening methods include breathalyzers, urine screening, or mouth swabs.

Drug and alcohol body fluid screening results assist in offering objective information as to the client's substance use. Employer-provided screening results often impact a person's eligibility to continue with their current employment and may result in an employee's termination. It is important for counselors to avoid engaging in debates about the validity of the test results but rather to use the results as one part of the assessment process.

If a counselor chooses to administer alcohol and drug screening onsite, the counselor must become knowledgeable in the various methods of testing, the appropriate storage and disposal of testing supplies, as well as the risks and benefits of administering body fluid screening onsite. The acquisition, storage, administration, and disposal of body fluid screening tests, as well as the body fluids themselves, require specific policies and procedures. Questions include whether the counselor will conduct observed or unobserved urine testing; how will the counselor manage privacy concerns; what if the client does not consent to observed testing; how does the counselor dispose of breathalyzer tubes, urine cups, or mouth swab devices after use; and what does the counselor do if the result is nonnegative (positive for a substance)? The criminal justice system and private testing companies have specific procedures for verifying any nonnegative results, thereby increasing the reliability and validity of the results; counselors, however, typically do not have these resources. For some clients, a nonnegative result can spur a productive conversation around recovery; for other clients, a nonnegative result may create increased defensiveness and justifications about why the test is not accurate. In summary, counselors must be prepared, knowledgeable, and intentional when using drug and alcohol body fluid screenings.

Tips From the Field

All requests for collateral information can only be initiated after the client has been oriented to the scope and purpose of what will be disclosed to the collateral contact and has completed a valid release of information. The counselor also informs the source of collateral information why they are being contacted, that their information will be included in the assessment document, and will likely be read by the client.

▶ DIAGNOSTIC/SCREENING TOOLS: SCORE AND RESULTS

Counselors utilize established screening and assessment methods and instruments to aid in the completion of an assessment. There are a wide variety of assessment instruments available for use. Counselors are responsible for being knowledgeable about the reliability and validity of the instruments they choose as well as being competent in the use and interpretation of the instrument. Table 5.1 describes many of the frequently used diagnostic and screening tools alcohol and drug counselors use. You should be familiar with them for your clinical practice and to pass the exam.

Table 5.1 Diagnosis/Screening Instruments

Adolescent Diagnostic/ Screening Instruments	Description
ASI	A guided interview assessment tool used to assess an adult's condition in areas that are typically affected by substance abuse, including medical status, employment, family/social functioning, behavioral health, and legal status (McLellan et al., 1992).
AUDIT	Developed by WHO, the 10-question AUDIT has been found to provide an accurate measure of risky alcohol use across gender, age, and cultures. The AUDIT is available in multiple languages (available from WHO).
ASSIST	Developed by WHO and an international team of substance use researchers, ASSIST screens for all levels of problem or risky substance use in adults. ASSIST consists of eight questions covering tobacco, alcohol, cannabis, cocaine, amphetamine-type stimulants (including ecstasy), inhalants, sedatives, hallucinogens, opioids and "other drugs" (available from WHO).
TAPS	The TAPS tool has two components. The first component (TAPS-1) is a four-item screen for tobacco, alcohol, illicit drugs, and nonmedical use of prescription drugs. If an individual screens positive on TAPS-1 (i.e., reports other than "never"), the tool will automatically begin the second component (TAPS-2), which consists of brief substance-specific assessment questions (TAPS-2) to arrive at a risk level for that substance, ranging in severity from "problem use" to the more severe SUD (McNeely et al., 2016; National Institute on Drug Abuse, n.d.). Clinicians are encouraged to provide positive feedback to clients who screen negative and support their choice to abstain from substances.
DAST-10	A 10-item self-report instrument that asks about use of drugs, not including alcoholic beverages, during the past 12 months. "Drug use" refers to the use of prescribed or over-the-counter drugs in excess of wha is directed and any nonmedical and/or illegal use of drugs (available from the Centre for Addiction and Mental Health, Toronto, Canada).
CUDIT-R	An 8-item measure used to screen for cannabis use disorder (CUD; Adamson et al., 2010).
SASSI-4	SASSI-4 identifies high or low probability of substance use disorders and includes a prescription drug scale that identifies individuals likely to be abusing prescription medications. It also provides a measure of profile validity and clinical insight into level of defensiveness and willingness to acknowledge experienced consequences of substance use disorder (available from the SASSI Institute).
SOGS	SOGS is a lifetime measure of problem gambling that has been found to be reliable and valid. This screening tool places individuals in one of three categories: nonproblem, problem gambler, and probable pathological gambling (available from www.ncpgambling.org/files/NPGAW/SOGS_Eng.pdf).
ACE questionnaire	The ACEs questionnaire asks a series of 10 questions about common traumatic experiences that occur in early life (Felitti et al., 1998).

(continued)

Table 5.1 Diagnosis/Screening Instruments *(continued)*

Adolescent Diagnostic/ Screening Instruments	Description
CRAFFT	CRAFFT screens youth under 21 for alcohol and other drug use and is recommended by the American Academy of Pediatrics. CRAFFT Version 2.1 has three questions which screen for alcohol and other drug use; the 2.1+N version has four questions including a screening question for tobacco use and vaping. There are self-administered and clinician interview versions of the CRAFFT. It is available in English and Spanish (Center for Adolescent Behavioral Health Research, 2021).
S2BI	S2BI is a seven-item tool used to assess the frequency of alcohol and substance use (e.g., tobacco, marijuana, prescription drugs, illegal drugs, inhalants, herbs, synthetic drugs) among adolescents from 12 to 17 years of age (Levy et al., 2014).
NIAAA screening for youth	NIAAA screening for youth uses a two-item scale to assess alcohol use among youth and adolescents between 9 and 18 years of age. The first question determines the frequency of friends' drinking, and the second question assesses personal drinking frequency (National Institute on Alcohol Abuse and Alcoholism, 2011).
CASI	A guided interview assessment tool used to assess an adolescent's condition in areas that are typically affected by substance use including education, use of free time, leisure activities, peer relationships, family relationships, and psychiatric status (Meyers et al., 1995).
SASSI-A3	SASSI-A3 identifies high or low probability of substance use disorders in clients 13 to 18 years of age. SASSI-A3 also provides clinical insight into family and social risk factors, level of defensive responding, consequences of substance misuse teens endorsed, and a prescription drug use scale that identifies teens likely to be abusing prescription medication (available from the SASSI Institute).
SOGS-RA	This instrument is composed of 12 items and has been found to be valid and reliable for detecting gambling problems among adolescent populations (Winters et al., 1993).

ACE, Adverse Childhood Experiences; ASI, Addiction Severity Index; ASSIST, Alcohol, Smoking, and Substance Abuse Involvement Screen Test; AUDIT, Alcohol Use Disorder Identification Test; CASI, Comprehensive Adolescent Severity Inventory; CRAFFT, Car, Relax, Alone, Forget, Family or Friends, Trouble; CUD, Cannabis Use Disorders; CUDIT-R, Cannabis Use Disorder Identification Test-Revised; DAST, Drug Abuse Screening Test; NIAAA, National Institute on Alcohol Abuse and Alcoholism; S2BI, Screening to Brief Intervention; SASSI, Substance Abuse Subtle Screening Inventory; SASSI-A, Substance Abuse Subtle Screening Inventory for Adolescent; SOGS, South Oaks Gambling Screen; SOGS-RA, South Oaks Gambling Screen-Revised for Adolescents; SUD, Substance Use Disorder; TAPS, Tobacco, Alcohol, Prescription medication and other Substance use; WHO, World Health Organization.

THE AMERICAN SOCIETY OF ADDICTION MEDICINE MULTIDIMENSIONAL ASSESSMENT

After all of the assessment information is gathered, the decision of the appropriate level of care for the client is guided by the completion of a multidimensional assessment based on the ASAM criteria (Mee-Lee et al., 2013). The six dimensions of the multidimensional assessment provide the counselor a way of organizing, categorizing, and prioritizing information to make decisions about treatment recommendations and the appropriate service and level of care across the treatment continuum.

The information that follows provides an overview of the six ASAM dimensions (Table 5.2), how to assign risk, and the services and levels of care most commonly available. For more information on the application of the ASAM criteria counselors are encouraged to reference the fourth edition of *The ASAM Criteria: Treatment Criteria for Addictive, Substance-Related, and Co-Occurring Conditions.*

The fourth edition of The ASAM Criteria was released in late 2023 (Waller et al., 2023). There are significant changes between the third edition and the fourth edition. As an introduction to the changes, Box 5.5 summarizes the changes to the six ASAM dimensions.

Risk Rating

Minimal Impairment or Very Low Risk

A rating of 0 indicates no or very low concern or need in this dimension. The individual is not experiencing any symptoms and this dimension may be a positive contributing factor for the individual.

Mild Impairment or Low Risk

A rating of 1 indicates mild or low concern or need in this dimension. The individual is experiencing only mild symptoms which can be resolved in a short period of time and with minimal intervention.

Table 5.2 The ASAM Dimensions

Dimension	Dimension Name	Description
Dimension 1	Acute intoxication and/or withdrawal	Understanding the client's past and current symptoms of intoxication and/or withdrawal
Dimension 2	Biomedical conditions and complications	Understanding the client's health history and current physical health needs
Dimension 3	Emotional, behavioral, or cognitive conditions and complications	Understanding the client's mental health history and current mental health or cognitive needs
Dimension 4	Readiness to change	Understanding the client's readiness to engage in change behavior
Dimension 5	Relapse, continued use, or continued problem potential	Understanding the client's relapse or risk of continued use
Dimension 6	Recovery/living environment	Understanding the client's recovery and living environment

ASAM, American Society of Addiction Medicine.

Box 5.5 The ASAM Criteria Subdimensions

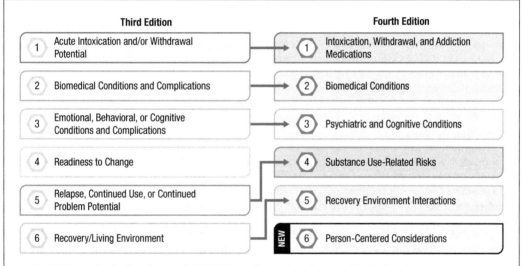

The Fourth Edition reorders the dimensions from the Third Edition. Readiness to change is now considered within each dimension, and the Third Edition Dimensions 5 and 6 were shifted to Dimensions 4 and 5, respectively, in the Fourth Edition. The new Dimension 6: Person-Centered Considerations considers barriers to care (including social determinants of health), client preferences, and need for motivational enhancement.

Dimension 1 – Intoxication, Withdrawal, and Addiction Medications

- Intoxication and associated risks
- Withdrawal and associated risks
- Addiction medications needs

Dimension 2 – Biomedical Conditions

- Physical health concerns
- Pregnancy-related concerns
- Sleep problems

Dimension 3 – Psychiatric and Cognitive Conditions

- Active psychiatric concerns
- Persistent Disability
- Cognitive Functioning
- Trauma exposure and related needs
- Psychiatric and cognitive history

Dimension 4 – Substance Use Related Risks

- Likelihood of risky substance use
- Likelihood of risky SUD-related behaviors

Dimension 5 – Recovery Environment Interactions

- Ability to function in current environment
- Safety in current environment
- Support in current environment
- Cultural perceptions of substance use

Dimension 6 – Person-Centered Considerations

- Client preferences
- Barriers to care
- Need for motivational enhancement

ASAM, American Society of Addiction Medicine.

Moderate Impairment or Moderate Risk

A rating of 2 indicates moderate concern or risk in this dimension. The individual is experiencing moderate symptoms which will require assistance; however, the individual likely has skills and supports to aid in ameliorating this risk.

Severe Impairment or Severe Risk

A rating of 3 indicates severe concern or risk in this dimension. The individual is experiencing significant impairment in coping in this dimension and will require significant support to manage the current symptoms.

Profound Impairment or Imminent Risk

A rating of 4 indicates imminent concern for the safety and wellbeing of the individual. The individual is experiencing profound impairment in coping and functioning in this dimension and requires immediate intervention to manage the current symptoms. A rating of 4 suggests the individual is experiencing life threatening symptomology (Acute Intoxication and/or Withdrawal Potential or Biomedical Conditions and Complications) or their safety is currently at risk (Emotional, Behavioral or Cognitive Conditions and Complications, Relapse, Continued Use, or Continued Problem Potential, or Recovery/Living Environment).

Each dimension is assigned a risk rating from 0 to 4 based on the strengths and needs of the individual at the time of the assessment. The risk rating assists in identifying and prioritizing treatment needs. It is important to recognize that the risk ratings are not static and unchanging; thus it is essential to revisit the multidimensional assessment and corresponding risk rating throughout an individual's treatment.

Risk is rated on a scale of 0 to 4 with 0 considered very low risk and 4 indicating imminent risk and the person needs immediate intervention in this area due to experiencing significant symptoms that are interfering with day-to-day functioning and safety.

The counselor assigns a risk rating to each dimension and the justification for this risk rating. After this is completed, the counselor reviews the multidimensional assessment to determine the most appropriate level of care and service for the individual. A score of 4 requires immediate intervention and the counselor must make arrangements for services and referrals to address this dimension.

In selecting the appropriate service, the counselor utilizes information from the other dimensions to determine if the client has areas of strength to draw on as well as areas of need that may intensify risk or danger. For example, an individual may report that their significant other threatened to harm them if they seek counseling. The individual is afraid to go home as their significant other has followed through on threats in the past, resulting in injuries that required hospitalization. However, the individual also reports they are ready to make a change and contacted their sister to come pick them up after assessment. Alternatively, if the individual reported they had nowhere else to go and their significant other is in the parking lot outside the office waiting for the client, the counselor will need to provide immediate assistance to aid the individual in finding a safe exit from the building and a connection with resources to arrange where to stay for the night.

Level of Care

After careful consideration of the risk rating of each dimension and the individual's unique strengths and needs, the counselor determines the appropriate level of care and service for client referral (Figure 5.1). If the ideal service is not available due to financial, geographical, or other reasons, the counselor notes this and recommends the next best service. Each level of care has a corresponding dimensional profile. For more information, see the most recent edition of the *The ASAM Criteria: Treatment Criteria for Addictive, Substance-Related, and Co-Occurring Conditions.*

The counselor initially considers the appropriate level of care the individual needs. The key to thinking about level of care is "where" the service is delivered and "how much" intervention or support is required to reduce the individual's risk and impact of the individual's symptoms. The counselor aims to recommend the least restrictive level of care that meets the individual's needs (Box 5.6).

▶ CLINICAL IMPRESSION

The clinical impression is the section of the assessment where the counselor summarizes their impression of the individual's behavior during the evaluation, including motivation to change, willingness to

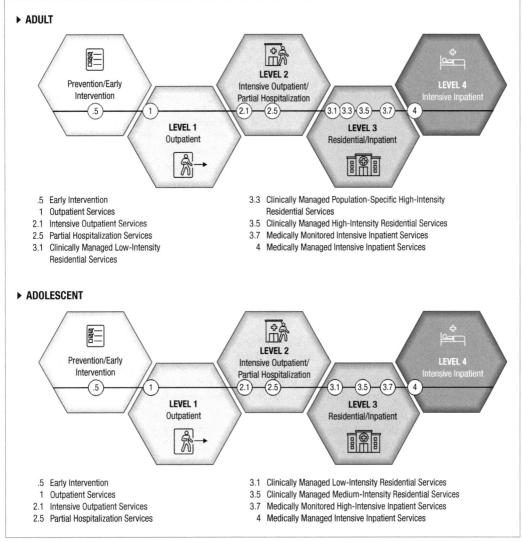

Figure 5.1 ASAM continuum of care.

Source: Guyer, J., Traube, A., & Deshchenko, O. (2021, November 9). *Speaking the same language: A toolkit for strengthening patient-centered addiction care in the United States*. American Society of Addiction Medicine. https://www.asam.org/asam-criteria/toolkit

acknowledge and accept the need for change of substance use behavior, and any discrepancies in the information provided. Based on the information gathered from the individual, the counselor summarizes the individual's strengths and needs as well as specifies a diagnosis or diagnoses and the justification for the diagnosis. The counselor may also include other relevant information that the counselor believes should be highlighted for the treatment provider or referring party.

DIAGNOSIS

The counselor carefully reviews the individual's self-reported information, the collateral contact, and the results of the diagnostic and screening tools and arrives at a diagnosis based on the *Diagnostic and Statistical Manual of Mental Disorders,* Fifth edition, Text Revision (*DSM-5-TR*; American Psychiatric Association [APA], 2022; often referred to simply as *DSM*) criteria. The *DSM* diagnosis criteria and process are also outlined in Chapter 3, "Physiology and Psychopharmacology." If the counselor is appropriately licensed, the counselor will diagnose both mental health and substance use disorders. If the counselor is not licensed to diagnose mental health disorders, they will diagnosis the substance use disorders and make referral for further assessment of a possible mental health disorder, if appropriate, based on the screening that was completed in the substance use assessment.

Box 5.6 Levels of Care

Level .5: Early intervention is delivered in the community with low intensity. The purpose of this level of care is for prevention of future substance use and offering education and strategies to aid the individual in engaging in healthy and low-risk behavior.

Level 1: Outpatient services are delivered in the community through regularly scheduled sessions with the counselor. The client does not remain at the treatment facility overnight. The frequency of these sessions typically ranges from 1 to 9 hours per week for adults and 1 to 6 hours per week for adolescents involving individual and/or group sessions. Outpatient services may be an initial level of care recommendation or may be used as a step-down level of care from a more intense level of care. Opioid treatment programs are also considered a Level 1 service. The length of stay in a Level 1 level of care is individualized based on need.

Level 2: Intensive outpatient (Level 2.1) and partial hospitalization services (Level 2.5) offer more hours of treatment and typically more group intervention than standard outpatient services (Level 1). Level 2 services are offered in the community and the client does not typically remain at the treatment facility overnight. If the program does offer overnight housing, the client does not require 24-hour supervision or access to services. The frequency of sessions typically ranges from 9 to 19 hours of service per week for adults and 6 to 19 hours per week for adolescents for intensive outpatient, and more than 20 hours per week for partial hospitalization services. The length of stay in a Level 2 level of care is individualized based on need.

Level 3: Residential and inpatient services (Levels 3.1, 3.3, 3.5, and 3.7) offer 24-hour staffing with increasing intensity of services, structure, and support. The focus of Level 3 is to develop and practice recovery skills in a structured treatment setting. Individuals requiring Level 3 services are unable to consistently demonstrate adaptive skills in the community without consistent structure and support. The length of stay in a Level 3 level of care is individualized based onneed.

Level 4: Medically managed intensive inpatient services offers 24-hour care in an acute care hospital setting. The care is managed by a physician and the full resources of an acute care or psychiatric hospital are available. Individuals requiring Level 4 services are experiencing a medical emergency or require ongoing medical monitoring and intervention to manage their symptoms. The length of stay in a Level 4 level of care is individualized based on need but is frequently only a few days until stabilization can be achieved and the individual transferred to a lower level of care.

Source: From Mee-Lee, D., Shulman, G. D., Fishman, M. J., Gastfriend, D. R., Miller, M. M., & Provence, S. M. (Eds.). (2013). *The ASAM criteria: Treatment criteria for addictive, substance-related, and co-occurring conditions* (3rd ed.). The Change Companies, Copyright 2013 by the American Society of Addiction Medicine.

A counselor makes the best diagnosis based on the information available at the time of the evaluation. If new information becomes available, the diagnosis may be amended.

The *DSM* specifies the symptoms required for each diagnosis. Counselors reference the *DSM* in arriving at the appropriate diagnosis and appropriate specifiers. Each substance is diagnosed independently based on the symptoms assessed during the interview with the individual.

The *DSM-5-TR* (APA, 2022) Substance-Related and Addictive Disorders chapter describes 10 separate classes of drugs. These substances include alcohol, caffeine, cannabis, hallucinogens, inhalants, opioids, sedatives, hypnotics and anxiolytics, stimulants (amphetamine-type substances, cocaine, and other stimulants), tobacco and other (or unknown) substances. According to the *DSM-5-TR*,

> All drugs that are taken in excess have in common direct activation of the brain reward systems, which are involved in the reinforcement of behaviors and establishment of memories. Instead of achieving reward system activation through adaptive behaviors, these substances produce such an intense activation of the reward system that normal activities may be neglected. Instead of achieving reward activation through adaptive behaviors, drugs of abuse directly activate reward pathways (APA, 2022, p. 543).

This definition makes clear the role that the brain plays in developing and maintaining substance use disorder. Keeping this description in mind will aid the counselor in diagnosing and making a prudent recommendation. The *DSM-5-TR* further states,

> The phrase drug addiction is not applied as a diagnostic term in this classification. The more neutral term substance use disorder is used to describe the wide range of the disorder from a mild form to a severe state of chronically relapsing compulsive pattern of drug taking. The

phrase drug addiction is omitted from the official DSM because of its uncertain definition and its potentially negative connotation (APA, 2022, p. 543).

The Substance-Related and Addictive Disorders chapter of the *DSM-5-TR* also includes Gambling Disorder. The *DSM-5-TR* explains that "gambling behaviors activate the reward systems similar to those activated by drugs of abuse and produce some behaviors symptoms that appear comparable to those produced by substance use disorders" (APA, 2022, p. 517). The *DSM-5-TR* does not include internet gaming disorder (IGD) as a diagnosable condition. IGD is included in the section recommending further research. Caffeine use disorder is also included in the section recommending further research. These disorders are not included in the substance-related and addictive disorders chapter as additional research was deemed to be needed to validate the diagnoses.

Substance related disorders are divided into two groups: substance induced disorders and substance use disorders. Substance induced disorders result from recent ingestion of a substance. Substance use disorders are related to the 10 separate classes of drugs (caffeine is not included).

Substance induced disorders includes diagnoses related to intoxication, withdrawal, and other substance induced mental disorders that directly arise from the use of the substance including substance induced psychotic disorder or substance induced anxiety disorder (tobacco is not included).

The substance use disorders directly result from a change in brain function that continues even after the discontinuation of the substance and the detoxification period. The impact of the brain changes results in cravings for the substance when exposed to stimuli associated with the use of the drug (people, places, objects, and emotions) resulting in repeated periods of returning to active use. The diagnostic criteria are divided into four primary groups (Table 5.3).

Substance use disorders are specified based on the number of symptoms that are present ranging from two to 11 symptoms. The presence of only one symptom does not support a diagnosis of a substance use disorder. It is important for the counselor to remember that legal problems by themselves are not one of the 11 criteria; this was changed with *DSM-5*. Further, an individual may experience tolerance and withdrawal (Criteria 10 and 11) based on the use of prescription medications during medical treatment. This is considered an effect of the prescribed medication and does not support the diagnosis of a substance use disorder.

Tips From the Field

A person can be considered "reliant" on a medication taken as prescribed. Counselors must educate their clients on the difference between withdrawal symptoms due to a prescribed medication taken as directed and the symptoms of a substance use disorder. Frequently, individuals in recovery will misconstrue or fear withdrawal from an antidepressant or other prescribed medication which is being taken as directed as a sign they are "addicted," or they will get suggestions from others that they are "addicted" and need to quit this substance as well.

If the individual experiences other symptoms of a substance use disorder (e.g., taking larger amounts than prescribed, neglecting activities to continue to use), a diagnosis of a substance use disorder is appropriate. Mild use disorder refers to the presence of two to three symptoms, moderate use disorder refers to the presence of four to five symptoms, and severe use disorder refers to the presence of six or more symptoms.

Substance use disorders are also specified based on length of time since the last use as well as if this period of abstinence was based on being in a controlled environment. The counselor recognizes that once the function of the brain adapts to the use of a substance, resulting in meeting criteria for a diagnosis of a substance use disorder, this adaptation is lifelong. Therefore, once a person is diagnosed with a substance use disorder or met the criteria of a substance use disorder in the past, even without formal diagnosis at that time, this diagnosis does not "disappear" from their medical records. The disorder may enter remission, during which the disorder is not active. However, upon resumption of the substance use, the disorder becomes active again, the brain continues to adapt, and the reward system begins to seek (crave) activation by the substance.

A specifier of "in early remission" is utilized if "after full criteria for the disorder were previously met, none of the criteria has been met for at least 3 months but for <12 months (with the exception of craving)" (APA, 2022, p. 554). Craving is not considered when assigning this specifier as a person could experience craving for a substance throughout much of the rest of their lives.

Table 5.3 *DSM-5-TR* Diagnostic Criteria for Diagnosing and Classifying Substance Use Disorders

Criteria Type	Descriptions
Impaired control over substance use (Criteria 1 to 4)	1. The substance is taken in larger amounts and for a longer amount of time than intended. 2. The individual has a persistent desire to cut down or regulate use. The individual may have unsuccessfully attempted to stop in the past. 3. The individual spends a great deal of time obtaining, using, or recovering from the effects of substance use. 4. The individual experiences craving or an immediate desire to use the substance.
Social impairment (Criteria 5 to 7)	5. Ongoing use impairs the individual's ability to fulfill major obligations at work, school, or home. 6. The individual continues substance use despite it causing significant social or interpersonal problems. 7. The individual reduces or discontinues recreational, social, or occupational activities because of substance use.
Risky use (Criteria 8 and 9)	8. The individual continues substance use despite placing themselves in physically risky situations. 9. The individual continues to use the substance despite knowledge that it may cause or exacerbate physical or psychological problems.
Pharmacological (Criteria 10 and 11)	10. **Tolerance:** Individual requires increasingly higher doses of the substance to achieve the desired effect, or the usual dose has a reduced effect; individuals may build tolerance to specific substances at different rates. 11. **Withdrawal:** An individual experiences the characteristic signs and symptoms of withdrawal when they discontinue using the substance or an individual will seek a related substance to relieve or avoid withdrawal symptoms; no documented withdrawal symptoms from hallucinogens, PCP, or inhalants. Note: Individuals can have an SUD with prescription medications, thus tolerance and withdrawal (criteria 10 and 11) in the context of appropriate medical treatment do not count as criteria for an SUD.

Notes: SUDs are classified as mild, moderate, or severe based on how many of the 11 criteria are fulfilled: mild, any 2 or 3 criteria; moderate, any 4 or 5 criteria; severe, any 6 or more criteria.
DSM-5-TR, Diagnostic and Statistical Manual of Mental Disorders, Fifth Edition, Text Revision; PCP, phencyclidine; SUD, substance use disorder.
Source: Adapted and updated from McNeely, J., & Adam, A. (2020, October). *Substance use screening and risk assessment in adults.* Johns Hopkins University. https://www.ncbi.nlm.nih.gov/books/NBK565474

A specifier of "in sustained remission" is utilized if "after full criteria for the disorder were previously met, none of the criteria has been met at any time during a 12-month period or longer (with the exception of craving)" (APA, 2022, p. 554). Craving is not considered when assigning this specifier.

A specifier of "in a controlled environment" is utilized if an individual has been confined to an environment where substance use is restricted. The counselor should not assume just because an individual has been in a controlled environment that they did not have access to various substances and the counselor must not assume that if an individual has been in a controlled environment that they did not engage in substance use.

Diagnosis of a substance use disorder is based on the International Classification of Diseases, Tenth Revision, Clinical Modification (ICD-10-CM) coding system. The diagnosis code that applies to the class of substance should be used, but the counselor documents the name of the specific substance in the assessment (i.e., moderate amphetamine use disorder rather than moderate stimulant use disorder). If criteria are met for more than one substance use disorder, all disorders should be diagnosed separately.

All diagnoses begin with an F, followed by two digits that specify the type of substance. A period separates the first two and the last two digits. The final three digits indicate the severity specifier or any substance induced disorders. Therefore, a substance use disorder and a substance induced disorder cannot be diagnosed simultaneously per ICD-10-CM guidelines.

The counselor is cautious and thorough when assigning a diagnosis. If a person requests an assessment due to a charge of driving under the influence (DUI), the counselor will not assign a diagnosis of alcohol intoxication unless the person is actively intoxicated at the time of the assessment. If this is the case, it is not ethical to continue with the assessment. Substance induced disorders are typically diagnosed by licensed medical staff who are interacting with the individual after a recent ingestion of a substance. Substance use counselors working on detoxification and withdrawal management facilities are likely to encounter individuals meeting the criteria for a substance induced disorder with far greater frequency than a counselor providing outpatient services. All counselors must be aware of the signs and symptoms of a substance induced disorder (Table 5.3).

RECOMMENDATIONS

The recommendation section is where all the information from the assessment culminates into the plan for the client. The recommendation section must be clear and concise so there is no question as to what the recommended course of treatment is. The recommendation section is meant to reflect the least restrictive level of care to meet the needs of the client based on their history and diagnosis. Other treatment providers, the court system, and the client themselves look to the recommendation section for the plan of action to reduce the impairment the symptoms of the diagnosis create.

The counselor puts forth a primary/ideal recommendation to address the client's needs. Unfortunately, due to availability of treatment because of geography, financial accessibility, waiting lists, medical needs, or other factors, the ideal level of care may not be possible. The counselor then identifies the level of care that is available to the client and recommends modifications that can be made to the secondary level of care to make it more ideal; an example: If an intensive outpatient program (Level 2.1) is the ideal recommendation but is not available, an outpatient (Level 1.0) is then recommended. The counselor may recommend the client be seen two times per week or attend three self-help meetings per week along with one-time per week outpatient counseling. The counselor also documents the client's response to the recommendation. The client's response often informs the counselor as to the motivation and willingness of the client to follow through with the recommendation.

The counselor also identifies who needs to be involved in the client's treatment. This may include the client's significant other, a supportive parent, pastor, sponsor, close friend, medical provider, probation officer, or other members of the client's support system.

Initial goals for the client are identified in the recommendation section. These initial goals form the basis for the development of the client's treatment plan. As these goals are met, the client will transition to lower levels of care. The counselor identifies a means to evaluate the client's progress through treatment and criteria for discharge. Discharge planning begins during the assessment process. Finally, the counselor identifies any referrals that need to be made to community agencies such as case management, medication management, housing, employment services, or other supportive services.

Once the assessment is complete, the counselor begins the process of the next core function, treatment planning with the client, which is the focus of the next chapter, Chapter 6 "Planning Treatment with the Client."

Tips From the Field

Your assessment may be the only means a referral source has to form an impression as to your ability and professionalism as a counselor. It is essential that each assessment you complete is accurate, written in a professional manner, and proofread. Further, the decisions made from the assessment results may significantly impact the client's future. Failure to complete an accurate assessment may result in loss of reputation, a complaint against your professional license, or a civil lawsuit.

Unfolding Case Study

When we began this chapter, Jim presented to our office for an assessment. The following is the assessment completed with Jim. As you review the assessment, reflect on what has been discussed throughout this chapter regarding the elements of the assessment process. The counselor used **observation and a clinical interview** utilizing **motivational interviewing**, to complete a **biopsychosocial assessment**. The counselor also explored Jim's **thinking patterns** and **co-occurring** symptoms. The counselor utilized **standardized screening tools** to aid in assessing Jim. Finally, the counselor gathered **collateral information** to verify Jim's self-report and additional information about Jim and his substance use. All this information was integrated into a clinical impression to develop a diagnosis and treatment recommendations for Jim (Box 5.7).

Box 5.7 Sample Substance Use Assessment

Counselor Letterhead
Substance Use Assessment

Name: Jim   **Date of Evaluation:** 08/15/2023
Referred by: Self-referred   **DOB:** 08/31/1985   **Age:** 38

A.   DEMOGRAPHICS
Jim is a 38-year-old White married male.

B.   PRESENTING PROBLEM/PRIMARY COMPLAINT
Jim is self-referred for a substance use assessment. He indicated he attended a work retreat this past weekend. He became very intoxicated on Saturday night and had to be helped back to his room. He reported the police were called due to his behavior, but he was not arrested. He missed the retreat's Sunday morning session and was very hungover all day Sunday. Jim had a meeting with his boss yesterday morning and was informed that if there were any more concerns regarding his behavior, his employment would be terminated.

Jim desires to begin counseling to help him "get my alcohol use under control." He reports that he cannot have any more problems when he drinks and wants to "figure out how to drink without having problems."

C.   MEDICAL HISTORY
Jim is not taking any medication. He previously was prescribed sertraline (Zoloft) 50 mg due to social anxiety. He took this for several months but never liked the idea of being on medication, so he quit. His wife told him he seemed happier when he was taking the medication but is not totally sure. Jim denies any current medical concerns. He had knee surgery several years ago. He denies any concerns after the surgery. Jim denies any significant family history of medical concerns. He does not report any significant allergies. Jim met all developmental milestones and reports no prenatal or birth complications.

D.   WORK/SCHOOL/MILITARY HISTORY
Jim reports he graduated high school in 2003. He was active in various clubs and generally enjoyed school and did well academically. He completed a bachelor's degree with a major in business management. He has been employed full time since graduating college in 2007. Jim is currently employed with a company called X-am Consulting as a consultant and trainer. He has worked for X-am for the past 5 years. He is usually away from home 1 week a month either consulting or training. Jim enjoys his job and prefers to remain employed with X-am. Jim reports he has no military history.

E.   ALCOHOL/OTHER DRUG HISTORY
Alcohol: Jim reported he began drinking when he was 14. He and his friends would drink off and on throughout high school. During his freshman year of college, he began drinking most weekends to intoxication. He felt it was the only way he had enough courage to talk to women. This pattern continued throughout college. He admitted that he had to drink more to get the same effect by the time he was a senior in college. He received a minor in possession (MIP) charge in his sophomore year. He feels this was "just something that happens to everyone in college." After college, he and his wife Samantha stayed together and she became pregnant. He quit drinking while she was pregnant, noting he was "trying to be a good husband." After their the baby was born, Samantha had to spend a lot of time with their son as he was ill a great deal. Jim started drinking more as he felt lonely and left out. He was unsure if he was really ready to be in a committed relationship and have a child but felt he could not get out of it by then.

(continued)

(*continued*)

Jim does not feel his alcohol use really became a problem until 8 years ago. He was drinking every weekend, "because Samantha was always out with her friends somewhere." He then got a DUI on the way back from a work dinner. Jim stated, "Everyone else was drinking just as much as me; I don't know why I was the one that got pulled over. I was almost home even." The DUI scared him, and he quit drinking for 2 years. He started again after Samantha's mother died. He once again felt very alone as he reports she became depressed and withdrawn. He hid his drinking from Samantha for about 2 years, only drinking after she went to bed. At some point, she caught him drinking. He promised to cut back but admits he did not in actuality.

Once he started his current job, he began traveling more often. When he was away from home, he would drink in the hotel bar each night, or stop and get a bottle to drink in the room before bed. This past year he feels his drinking has impacted his work performance. He knows that he is on his last warning with his boss and does not want to lose his job.

Jim states that in this past year, he will have two or three mixed drinks most nights of the week at home, but when he is traveling for work, he will drink eight to 10 drinks per night. He admits he needs to drink more to feel the same effect. He has attempted to quit drinking this past year on a few occasions after Samantha yelled at him but does not make it more than about 5 days. When he does drink, he has a hard time stopping after three drinks, usually drinking far more than intended. Jim denies that he has ever experienced withdrawal symptoms when he quits drinking but indicated strong physical urges and psychological cravings. Jim feels his relationship with Samantha has issues and reluctantly acknowledged his drinking has made the situation worse. Jim reports he drank 25 days out of the past 30. His last drink was Sunday night.

Opioids: Jim reported he was prescribed oxycodone/paracetamol (Percocet) after his knee surgery. He initially took it as prescribed but then reported he began looking forward to taking the medication at night. He went back to his doctor for two more refills, but eventually his doctor said no. Jim admits he has asked around the office for people that have had surgery to see if they will give him/sell him their extra pills. He stated that he can see how this could be a problem, but he likes how the opioid helps him relax after a difficult day at work. He estimates his last use was over 2 years ago, though admits he still thinks about the feeling he had when he was taking them and wishes he could have this feeling every once in a while.

Jim denies any history of tobacco use.

Jim denies any other illicit or licit drug use or abuse.

Caffeine: Jim reports during the past 6 months he typically consumes one or two 16-oz energy drinks per day.

Gambling: Jim reports he first began playing poker on his phone in 2020 when he was at home more during the COVID-19 pandemic. He played most days during 2020 but cut back when he had to start traveling again in late 2021. Since then, he has been playing poker and slot machine apps several times per week. He estimates he spends $100 or so per week on these apps. His wife does not know that he is spending money on these apps as he uses a separate credit card to pay for them. She has complained that he seems more "distracted" by his phone. He does not see it as a big deal but does feel he is starting to spend too much, especially since his daughter wants to attend a private school and they are going to have to start paying tuition. Jim does not report his gambling has caused financial problems for the family.

Pornography: Jim indicated he was first exposed to pornography about the time he started drinking. He and his friends would have his friend's brother get them movies. He has viewed pornography off and on over the years. In 2020, when he was home, he began viewing pornography more often. He would watch pornography when he stayed up and drank after his wife went to bed. He reports his use has increased in the past 3 years as he and Samantha have been arguing more. He estimates he views pornography three or four times per week over the past 6 months. He indicated he feels guilty, but that he has created profiles on various dating sites and chatted with other women. He reported he only does this after he has had a few drinks. His wife has found pornographic pictures on his phone in the past and was upset by them. She accused him of cheating on her when she saw he downloaded a dating app. He reports that he thinks he was able to convince her he was just helping a friend learn how to use it. He has met a couple of women at the hotel bar when he is out of town, but never went any further than talking. Jim stated, "I don't want to completely lose my marriage."

F. LEGAL HISTORY (per self-report)
10/22/2004—Minor in Possession; 2 days in jail.
05/23/15—Driving Under the Influence 1st; 12 months unsupervised probation successfully completed.
08/31/21—Disturbing the Peace; $75 ticket.

(*continued*)

(*continued*)

G.   FAMILY/SOCIAL/PEER HISTORY

Jim was born to Elwood and Fionna. He is their only child. Jim reports growing up was generally positive. His parents remain married and are currently retired living in southern California. He gets along well with his parents and sees them usually once a year. He denies any childhood trauma or abuse. He reflects that he spent a lot of time on his own as there were not very many other children in the neighborhood. Jim reports he had friends in school and a close friend group in high school.

Jim met his wife, Samantha, during his second year of college. They dated off and on for 2 years until during his senior year they decided to move in together as roommates with two other friends. They continued to live together as a couple after the other two friends moved out. Samantha became pregnant just after they both graduated from college. They got married shortly after finding out she was pregnant. Jim indicated this was a stressful time as he was not sure he really wanted to be with Samantha but since she was pregnant, felt he needed to stay with her. Jim and Samantha have three children, a son age 16 and two daughters ages 12 and 10.

Jim described his relationship with his wife as "confusing." He never was certain that he really wanted to be with her in the beginning, but now they have been together for so long and have three children, he does not want to leave. He feels she likely feels the same way about him. Life just continues to happen around them, and they continue to live much like the roommates they started out as. Jim denies ever cheating on Samantha, but she has accused him many times. He knows that she has talked to a few men from her job over the years but does not feel anything more than flirting has happened. They have not talked about divorce but admits they really "don't talk much about anything."

Jim does not feel he has any close friends. He talks to people at work and will visit his high school friends every few months. He does not report any hobbies. For fun, he mainly stays at home, plays internet games, or looks up various topics online. Jim does not attend any organized religious services. He would not describe himself as an atheist but is not sure what he really believes.

H.   BEHAVIORAL HEALTH HISTORY

Jim completed a substance use assessment after the DUI charge in 2015. He remembers he had a blood alcohol level (BAC) of .12. He was coming back from a work dinner and was arrested just outside of his house. He feels bad because his son saw him get arrested when he was getting a ride home from a friend's house. His wife did not talk to him for a week and threatened that something "had better change." Jim completed three counseling sessions. He got the first bill and realized all of the cost was going to his deductible and stopped attending. He does not remember if the counselor told him if he had a diagnosis. He just remembers the counselor kept telling him to go to Alcoholics Anonymous (AA) meetings and that he "had" to stop drinking. Jim stated that he did not like it because the counselor kept saying that he was an "alcoholic." Jim does not feel he fits this definition because he goes to work every day, does not have to drink in the morning, and is sure he could stop if he really wanted to. Jim attended one AA meeting back then. He did not go back, noting, "the people at those meetings really had problems; they aren't like me."

Jim has never been diagnosed with a mental health condition. He took sertraline, an antidepressant medication, for a few months, but this was because his wife was upset that he was withdrawn when attending work functions with her and would never speak to anyone. She thought he was anxious and depressed. Jim commented, "I would have been fine if she would have let me drink before going, but she wouldn't let me. She told me she thought I would embarrass her."

Jim does not identify any family history of mental health or substance use concerns.

Jim denies any history of suicidal thoughts or attempts. He denies that he has ever wanted to hurt anyone else and indicated no one has ever complained about his anger. He denies any significant episodes of depression or ever having a panic attack. He denies ever having any symptoms of psychosis.

I.   COLLATERAL INFORMATION

Jim consented to have his wife, Samantha, being called as a collateral contact. Samantha reported she has been concerned about Jim's drinking ever since she knew him. In college, he would occasionally drink too much, but they laughed it off because it was college. After their son was born, he was sober for a few weeks. Their son was often sick in the first year, so Samantha had to spend a lot of time with him. She feels Jim felt left out. He began isolating and drinking more about that time. They argued about his drinking, and he cut back for a while, but then if there were stress, he would start to drink at home after she went to bed. She did not say anything because they would just argue more. He lost one job about 6 months before the DUI 7 years ago. Jim did not admit it, but Samantha feels he was fired because of his alcohol use. After the DUI, she believes Jim was sober for about 4 years. They became closer during this time, but then he started

(*continued*)

(continued)

traveling more with his current job. His drinking picked up again. Samantha indicated she has asked Jim to stop drinking, to go to AA meetings, to spend more time with the kids, or just do something different. She feels he does care about the family, but she does not know how much longer she wants to stay with him. She has considered leaving him but does not want to for the kids' sake. Samantha indicated the past year has been the worst. He has been talked to several times by his boss about being late to work. She has asked him to quit drinking, but he only stops for about 10 days and then starts again. When he starts drinking, he will drink too much and he has started hiding his alcohol use so she does not yell at him. Samantha has stopped asking him to go to her work functions because of an incident this year at a country club. He started drinking and embarrassed her in front of all of her coworkers. Samantha reported she is open to attending marriage counseling with Jim as she would like their home to be better for the kids. Samantha stated that she does drink rarely and is willing to abstain from alcohol use if it helps Jim.

J.   OTHER DIAGNOSTIC/SCREENING TOOLS—SCORE AND RESULTS
Jim completed the SASSI-4. It indicated a high probability of Jim having a substance use disorder. His results suggest he completed the questions in a valid manner.

Jim completed the South Oaks Gambling Screen (SOGS). He scored a 3 indicating Jim may be a potential pathological gambler (problem gambler).

K.   ASAM MULTIDIMENSIONAL ASSESSMENT
    Dimension 1: Acute intoxication and/or withdrawal potential
        i.   Intensity: 1
        ii.   Justification: Jim has been drinking on a consistent basis. Jim does not have a history of withdrawal symptoms. Jim should self-monitor for symptoms
    Dimension 2: Biomedical conditions and complications
        i.   Intensity: 0
        ii.   Justification: There are no medical concerns or complications indicated
    Dimension 3: Emotional, behavioral, or cognitive conditions and complications
        i.   Intensity: 1
        ii.   Justification: Jim self-reports some anxiety related to social situations. It is not expected this will impact his ability to participate in treatment but may impact his willingness to participate in activities to build informal support
    Dimension 4: Readiness to change
        i.   Intensity: 2
        ii.   Justification: Jim reports he wants to "get his alcohol use under control and figure out how to drink without having problems." Though Jim is seeking counseling voluntarily, he appears to be in the contemplation stage of change
    Dimension 5: Relapse, continued use, or continued problem potential
        i.   Intensity: 3
        ii.   Justification: Jim is at high risk for continued use and continuing to have problems related to his drinking. Recently, Jim has not been successful staying sober for more than 5 to 10 days
    Dimension 6: Recovery/living environment
        i.   Intensity: 2
        ii.   Justification: Jim's wife is supportive of his recovery. She does not engage in problematic alcohol use. However, Jim frequently drinks at home when his wife is sleeping

L.   CLINICAL IMPRESSION
Jim presented for a substance use evaluation voluntarily, but at the encouragement of his wife and implication of consequences from his boss if he did not. Jim appeared forthcoming and cooperative throughout the evaluation. He voiced a willingness to make changes in his behavior, but his comment of wanting to "figure out" how to drink without having problems is telling of his stage of change and will need to be a target of his treatment plan. Jim was not defensive about his alcohol use but does not recognize the extent alcohol use is impacting his life. Jim would prefer to learn enough to be able to continue to drink and not have complaints from his wife or employer. There are discrepancies noted between the information reported and the information his wife, Samantha, reported especially in regard to his period of sobriety after the DUI 7 years ago, the length of sobriety in his recent attempts to cut back, as well as the amount he is drinking. Strengths for Jim include his desire to remain with his family, his willingness to attend counseling, a recognition his alcohol use is causing concern, and a successful period of sobriety in the past. Jim needs to build increased awareness of the impact of his alcohol use, further assess his gambling and pornography

(continued)

(*continued*)

use and how these behaviors impact his thinking and relationships, build alternate coping strategies and supports, and consider conjoint counseling with his wife.

Jim meets criteria for alcohol use disorder, moderate based on symptoms of tolerance, drinking larger amounts and for a longer amount of time than intended, a persistent desire to quit without success in these attempts, continued use despite it causing significant interpersonal problems, and discontinued social activities due to alcohol use. Jim does not meet criteria for a gambling disorder; however, his gambling behavior should be a part of his treatment plan. Jim's difficulty in social situations should continue to be screened for possible referral for further assessment.

M. DIAGNOSIS (*DSM-5-TR*)
F10.20 Alcohol Use Disorder-Moderate

N. RECOMMENDATIONS
Based on the information gathered in this assessment, the primary recommendation for Jim is to participate in individual outpatient counseling, ASAM Level 1. This level of care is available to Jim in his community. Jim is in agreement with this recommendation and willing to participate. Jim's wife should be included in his treatment and family sessions with Jim, his wife, and children should be considered.

Treatment plan goals will include increasing awareness of the impact of alcohol use, increasing awareness of the impact of his gambling and pornography use, developing alternate coping strategies, and building informal supports. Jim needs to identify his goal regarding alcohol use; deciding if he wants to be sober and build a recovery program or if he wants to maintain his initial goal of attempting to learn how to drink without having problems. Progress will be evaluated based on reduced number of days of drinking per month, increased adaptive coping skill use, and increased positive social support interaction. A referral for a medication assessment to assist with managing cravings will be considered if Jim continues to express difficulty managing alcohol-related cravings. If Jim is unable to maintain sobriety despite his ongoing efforts to do so, a referral will be made to a higher level of care. Discharge will be considered when Jim has developed a stable recovery program.

Counselor Signature and Credentials

Based on the results of Jim's evaluation, a diagnosis of alcohol use disorder, moderate was found to be appropriate with a recommendation of outpatient treatment, ASAM 1.0. In addition to addressing his alcohol use, the recommendation is to also explore further Jim's gambling behavior and pornography use. Jim also self-reported concerns about anxiety. If he continues to report concerns about symptoms of anxiety after he has experienced a period of sobriety, a referral for a mental health assessment is warranted if the diagnosis and treatment of an anxiety disorder is not in the counselor's scope of practice.

Reflecting back to earlier in the chapter, we consider the overall purpose of an assessment: "A quality assessment helps the counselor and the client understand the *why* the individual is seeking services *today* and answers the question *what now*." For Jim, the *why he* sought services was due to concern about the impact of his alcohol use. Jim is seeking services *today* because of fear of losing his job and the recommendation section answers the question as to *what now*.

▶ KEY POINTS

- Assessment involves the history gathering from a client as well as utilizing collateral information, assessment tools, and drug and alcohol testing as appropriate to develop a comprehensive biopsychosocial history. The assessment data are integrated to develop a diagnostic evaluation to determine the appropriate level of care to meet the client's treatment needs.
- From the point of view of the client, the assessment can seem uncomfortable and at times intrusive.
- The counselor must engage in effective orientation to explain to the client the purpose of the assessment process, use appropriate interview techniques, and be sensitive to unique differences between clients.

■ The assessment provides the basis for all treatment that the client receives. The more complete the assessment, the more valid a treatment recommendation will be. Incomplete or poorly completed assessments will cause the client to receive inadequate or inappropriate treatment, costing the client money and time, and, at worst, may cause the client to be hospitalized, or experience further legal, social, or physical problems, or even death.

▶ STUDY RESOURCES

The Substance Abuse and Mental Health Services Administration (SAMHSA) offers many free publications available for download that are key documents in the field for treatment of substance use disorders. The following study resources can be found on SAMHSA's webpage (https://store.samhsa.gov):

TIP 31 Screening and Assessing Adolescents for Substance Use Disorders
TIP 47 Substance Abuse: Clinical Issues in Intensive Outpatient Treatment

▶ REFERENCES

Adamson, S. J., Kay-Lambkin, F. J., Baker, A. L., Lewin, T. J., Thornton, L., Kelly, B. J., & Sellman, J. D. (2010). An improved brief measure of cannabis misuse: The cannabis use disorders identification test-revised (CUDIT-R). *Drug and Alcohol Dependence, 110*(1–2), 137–143. https://doi.org/10.1016/j.drugalcdep.2010.02.017

American Psychiatric Association. (2022). *Diagnostic and statistical manual of mental disorders* (5th ed., text rev.). https://doi.org/10.1176/appi.books.9780890425787

Center for Adolescent Behavioral Health Research. (2021). *The CRAFFT 2.1 Manual*. CABHRe.

Felitti, V. J., Anda, R. F., Nordenberg, D., Williamson, D. F., Spitz, A. M., Edwards, V., & Marks, J. S. (1998). Relationship of childhood abuse and household dysfunction to many of the leading causes of death in adults: The adverse childhood experiences (ACE) study. *American Journal of Preventive Medicine, 14*, 245–258.

Herdman, J. W. (2021). *Global criteria: The 12 core functions of the substance abuse counselor* (8th ed.).

International Certification and Reciprocity Consortium. (2022). *Candidate guide for the IC&RC alcohol and drug counselor examination*. https://internationalcredentialing.org/wp-content/uploads/2024/01/ADC-Candidate-Guide-09.2022_Final-Edit_10.31.22.pdf

Lemsky, C. (2021). *Traumatic brain injury and substance use disorders: Making the connections*. Substance Abuse and Mental Health Services Administration.

Levy, S., Weiss, R., Sherritt, L., Ziemnik, R., Spalding, A., Van Hook, S., & Shrier, L. A. (2014). An electronic screen for triaging adolescent substance use by risk levels. *JAMA Pediatrics, 168*(9), 822–828. http://www.ncbi.nlm.nih.gov/pmc/articles/PMC4270364

McLellan, A. T., Kushner, H., Metzger, D., Peters, R., Smith, H., Grissom, G., & Argeriou, M. (1992). The fifth edition of the addiction severity index. *Journal of Substance Abuse Treatment, 9*(3), 199–213.

McNeely, J., Wu, L., Subramaniam, G., Sharma, G., Cathers, L. A., Svikis, D., Sleiter, L., Russell, L., Nordeck, C., Sharma, A., & O'Grady, K. E. (2016). Performance of the tobacco, alcohol, prescription medication, and other substance use (TAPS) tool for substance use screening in primary care patients. *Annals of Internal Medicine, 165*, 690–699. https://doi.org/10.7326/M16-0317

Mee-Lee, D., Shulman, G. D., Fishman, M. J., Gastfriend, D. R., Miller, M. M., & Provence, S. M. (Eds.). (2013). *The ASAM criteria: Treatment criteria for addictive, substance-related, and co-occurring conditions* (3rd ed.). The Change Companies, Copyright 2013 by the American Society of Addiction Medicine.

Meyers, K., McLellan, A. T., Jaeger, J. L., & Pettinati, H. M. (1995, May–June). The development of the comprehensive addiction severity index for adolescents (CASI-A). An interview for assessing multiple problems of adolescents. *Journal of Substance Abuse Treatment, 12*(3), 181–193. https://doi.org/10.1016/0740-5472(95)00009-t

National Institute on Alcohol Abuse and Alcoholism. (2011). *Alcohol screening and brief intervention for youth*. NIH Publication.

Substance Abuse and Mental Health Services Administration, Office of the Surgeon General. (2016, November). *Facing addiction in America: The Surgeon General's Report on alcohol, drugs, and health* (Chapter 2). U.S. Department of Health and Human Services. https://www.ncbi.nlm.nih .gov/books/NBK424849

Waller, R. C., Boyle, M. P., & Daviss, S. R. (Eds.). (2023). *The ASAM Criteria: Treatment criteria for addictive, substance-related, and co-occurring conditions* (Vol. 1: Adults, 4th ed.). Hazelden Publishing.

Winters, K. C., Stinchfield, R. D., & Fulkerson, J. (1993). Toward the development of an adolescent problem severity scale. *Journal of Gambling Studies, 9*, 63–84.

CASE STUDY 5.1

Markus is a 27-year-old Hispanic male. He presents for an assessment after testing nonnegative for marijuana and amphetamines on a random drug test as required by his employer. Markus has been taken off his forklift driving duties by his supervisor until he completes a substance use assessment and follows the recommendations of the assessment. Markus shares during the assessment that he has been smoking marijuana off and on for the past several months. He was introduced to marijuana by a friend he met at work shortly after the start of the year. He reported he only smokes it when he plays darts at the friend's house. He believes he can easily stop using marijuana by not going over to this friend's house. He feels more confident about this as he reports this friend was fired the same day Markus took the drug test so he will not see his friend at work any longer. Markus reported he has been taking dextroamphetamine-amphetamine (Adderall) on occasion over the past 2 months when he has a hard time getting out of bed in the morning. Last year, he moved out of his mother's house and started sharing an apartment with his girlfriend. He reports his girlfriend has a prescription for dextroamphetamine-amphetamine and he "borrows" some from her. They recently had a child together resulting in Markus not getting as much sleep as he used to. He does not report a pattern of use of amphetamines and stated that he only started because he missed 2 days in a row at work from being tired. He believes he will have no problem stopping using substances as this job is important to him.

1. Given the information presented in the case study, the most likely level of care recommendation is:
   A) .5 Early intervention
   B) 1.0 Outpatient counseling
   C) 2.1 Intensive outpatient services
   D) 2.5 Partial hospitalization services

2. To help verify the information Markus reported regarding his drug use history, the best collateral contact is Markus's:
   A) Boss
   B) Friend from work
   C) Girlfriend
   D) Mother

3. An appropriate assessment instrument to use during the assessment process is:
   A) Alcohol Use Disorder Identification Test (AUDIT)
   B) South Oaks Gambling Screen (SOGS)
   C) Cannabis Use Disorder Identification Test-Revised (CUDIT-R)
   D) Screening to Brief Intervention (S2BI)

4. Because Markus was referred by his supervisor, a release of information for the counselor to speak to his supervisor is
   A) Not needed because the supervisor made the referral
   B) Needed because Markus has a right of confidentiality regarding his records
   C) Not needed because Markus violated the employment contract
   D) Needed for the counselor to use the drug testing results provided by the supervisor

(See answers on the next page.)

CASE STUDY 5.1 ANSWERS

1. A) .5 Early intervention

Based on the information presented, it is unlikely Markus has a substance use disorder, thus a prevention level of care is appropriate. The other levels of care would involve information and treatment methods that would be of greater intensity than Markus requires.

2. C) Girlfriend

Markus's girlfriend has the most recent observations of Markus's behavior and can speak to his "borrowing" of her dextroamphetamine-amphetamine. Though there is some concern she may minimize her report to try to keep Markus out of trouble, she still remains the best option. He has not lived with his mother for a year, his boss only observes him at work, and his friend was using with him and is of lower likelihood of being honest.

3. C) Cannabis Use Disorder Identification Test-Revised (CUDIT-R)

Markus presented due to cannabis use. Therefore, the CUDIT-R is the most appropriate screening instrument. The AUDIT focuses on alcohol use, which is not a referral concern; the SOGS is an assessment for gambling; and the S2BI is for adolescents.

4. B) Needed because Markus has a right of confidentiality regarding his records

A release of information is needed as Markus has the right to confidentiality. He can choose to not release the evaluation or any other information to his employer. The employer does not need a release of information to provide information to the counselor.

KNOWLEDGE CHECK: CHAPTER 5

1. In substance use counseling, assessment involves:
   A) Developing a relapse prevention plan
   B) Identifying the client's strengths and needs
   C) Conducting individual counseling sessions
   D) Providing immediate support during emergencies

2. The primary purpose of the assessment process is to:
   A) Develop treatment goals for the client
   B) Determine the severity of substance use
   C) Screen for co-occurring mental health disorders
   D) Gather comprehensive information about the client

3. An example of a psychological factor in a biopsychosocial assessment is:
   A) Social anxiety
   B) Spirituality
   C) History of concussion
   D) Military history

4. An example of a current social factor in a biopsychosocial assessment is:
   A) Peer group
   B) Being fired from a job 3 years ago
   C) Cancer diagnosis
   D) Suicidal thoughts

Naya, a 17-year-old female, presents intoxicated on oxycontin. Her parents found her passed out in the bathroom with a bottle of oxycontin near her. They were able to wake her enough to get her to come to counseling but she still does not look well, is having a hard time staying awake, and seems to have very shallow breathing. The counselor has concern about her medical stability. She has type 1 diabetes and her parents do not know if she has been taking her insulin consistently. Her parents state she has been talking about wanting to die for the past 2 years and has been hospitalized on two occasions for overdosing on pills. She has been in outpatient counseling for 2 months and seemed to have some motivation to change. However, she seems to only be able to be substance free for about 2 weeks at a time. Her parents are both marijuana users and smoke openly at home, but do not think this has anything to do with their daughter's substance concerns.

---

5. Which American Society of Addiction Medicine (ASAM) dimension is most pressing to address first for Naya?
   A) Dimension 1: Acute intoxication and/or withdrawal potential
   B) Dimension 3: Emotional, behavioral, or cognitive conditions and complications
   C) Dimension 4: Readiness for change
   D) Dimension 6: Recovering/living environment

6. Naya's parents' use of marijuana fits best on which ASAM dimension?
   A) Dimension 3: Emotional, behavioral, or cognitive conditions and complications
   B) Dimension 4: Readiness to change
   C) Dimension 5: Relapse, continued use, or continued problem potential
   D) Dimension 6: Recovery/living environment

7. Based on the information presented in Naya's case, what should the counselor do next?
   A) Advise the parents to take their daughter home and let her get a good night's sleep
   B) Advise the parents to take their daughter to the emergency department for assessment
   C) Monitor the daughter's condition while talking to the parents about their marijuana use
   D) Engage in counseling with the daughter around the importance of sobriety

(See answers on the next page.)

1. B) Identifying the client's strengths and needs

Identifying the client's strengths and needs is part of assessment. Developing a relapse prevention plan, conducting individual counseling sessions, and providing support during emergencies are not part of the assessment process.

2. D) Gather comprehensive information about the client

The purpose of the assessment is to gather comprehensive information about the client to understand the needs of the client. Developing treatment goals, determining the severity of substance use, and screening for co-occurring mental health disorders are not part of the assessment process.

3. A) Social anxiety

Social anxiety is a psychological factor. Spirituality and military history are considered social factors; a history of concussion is a biological factor.

4. A) Peer group

A client's peer group is an essential social factor when completing an assessment. Being fired from a job 3 years ago may be considered a social factor but is likely not relevant to the present assessment of social factors. A cancer diagnosis is a biological factor and suicidal thoughts are a psychological factor.

5. A) Dimension 1: Acute intoxication and/or withdrawal potential

For Naya's care and safety, it is most pressing to address acute intoxication and/or withdrawal potential. The client is experiencing current effects of intoxication and is at risk of increasingly problematic symptoms if medical care is not rendered soon. Dimensions 3, 4, and 6 can be addressed after Dimension 1.

6. D) Dimension 6: Recovery/living environment

The client is currently living in an environment where drug use is commonplace and accepted. Though they are using different drugs, recovery is likely going to be more difficult given the parents' drug use in the home. Naya sharing that she has wanted to die would be addressed in Dimension 3, her observed motivation for change would be noted in Dimension 4, and her history of staying substance free for 2 weeks at a time would be addressed in Dimension 5.

7. B) Advise the parents to take their daughter to the emergency department for assessment

Given the concerns about medical stability, the parents should be advised to take their daughter immediately to the emergency department at the closest hospital for assessment. It is critical for the client's health and safety that she receive treatment immediately. Monitoring her condition, attempting to counsel with her, and telling the parents to take her home for a good night's sleep are not sufficient care for her current state.

8. A co-occurring assessment is completed when:
   A) Both the client and their significant other are interviewed for the assessment
   B) There is suspicion of a mental health disorder occurring with the substance use disorder
   C) A counselor believes the client has more than one substance use disorder diagnosis
   D) By two different providers

9. The completion of a multidimensional assessment
   A) Provides the counselor a way of organizing, categorizing, and prioritizing information
   B) Occurs when multiple people are interviewed to gather information to complete an assessment
   C) Provides information to the treating counselor about multiple areas of a client's life
   D) Is used to make a diagnosis of the client

10. One limitation of the Alcohol Use Disorder Identification Test (AUDIT) is it
    A) Is only available in English
    B) Relies on self-reported data from the client
    C) Is difficult to score
    D) Is expensive to administer

11. During an assessment, it is important for the counselor to:
    A) Give advice to the client about how to better their life
    B) Set clear treatment goals with the client
    C) Observe the client's behavior for clues to their current functioning and well-being
    D) Make it clear that the client has a problem with substance use

12. During an assessment, the counselor is engaged in which of the following?
    A) Observing the client's behavior and affect
    B) Creating goals with the client
    C) Taking notes to report to the client's probation officer
    D) Ignoring nonverbal cues as the client is likely just nervous

13. The client's recommended level of care is primary determined by
    A) Placement criteria
    B) Recommendation by the referring party
    C) The preference of the client
    D) The recommendation of the client's significant other

14. *DSM* stands for:
    A) *Determination and Standardization Manual of Mental Disorders*
    B) *Diagnostic and Standards Manual of Disorders*
    C) *Diagnostic and Statistical Manual of Mental Disorders*
    D) *Direction and Standards Manual for Counselors*

15. Determining the best course of action to meet the client's immediate and ongoing needs corresponds to which section of the assessment document?
    A) Diagnostic formulation
    B) Recommendations
    C) Collateral contact
    D) Client placement criteria

16. Which of the following will aid the counselor in completing a valid assessment?
    A) Ask each client the same questions, in the same order, in the same way
    B) Consider each client's cultural background when completing the assessment
    C) Presume each client is being dishonest during the assessment
    D) Disregard any preference the client has in considering recommendations for level of care

(*See answers on the next page.*)

8. B) There is suspicion of a mental health disorder occurring with the substance use disorder

This type of assessment includes gathering symptoms of mental health disorders with the goal of a more complete diagnostic picture and to develop a treatment plan that addresses both the mental health and substance use disorder. While a client's significant other may need to be involved in their treatment, two or more providers may treat a client, and a client may have more than one substance use disorder, these factors are not what is known as a co-occurring disorder.

9. A) Provides the counselor a way of organizing, categorizing, and prioritizing information

A multidimensional assessment is completed based on the American Society of Addiction Medicine (ASAM) criteria. A multidimensional assessment is not used to make a diagnosis and may or may not be completed after interviews with multiple other people are interviewed. Though it does provide information about a client's life, this is not the primary goal.

10. B) Relies on self-reported data from the client

A limitation of the AUDIT is that it relies on self-reports from the client. This is why it is important for the counselor to obtain corroboration information from significant secondary sources. The AUDIT is available in multiple languages, is free of charge, and a counselor can become competent in the use of the AUDIT with little training.

11. C) Observe the client's behavior for clues to their current functioning and well-being

The counselor is active in observing a client's behavior during the course of the assessment. The counselor is not giving advice during the assessment and is not setting treatment goals, as treatment planning happens after the assessment is completed. Whether the client has a problem with substance use or not, the purpose of the assessment is to gather information, not try to convince the client that they have a problem with substance use.

12. A) Observing the client's behavior and affect

The counselor actively observes a client's behavior and affect throughout the assessment to better understand the client. The counselor creates goals with the client after the assessment is complete. Though the counselor and probation officer may communicate as a part of gathering collateral information, the purpose of the assessment is not to take notes to report to the probation officer. The counselor is in tune with nonverbal cues as this may provide valuable information about the client's current functioning and ability to interact with others.

13. A) Placement criteria

Client placement criteria determines the most appropriate level of care for a client. The recommendation of the referring party, preference of the client, and recommendation of a significant other may affect a counselor's final decision when considering the unique needs of the client; however, the placement criteria is the primary starting point.

14. C) *Diagnostic and Statistical Manual of Mental Disorders*

The *DSM* is currently in its Fifth Edition, with a text revision released in 2022.

15. B) Recommendations

The recommendations section spells out the course of action to meet the immediate and ongoing needs of the client. The diagnostic formulation identifies the symptoms of a substance use disorder the client may meet. The collateral contact section summarizes additional information which was gathered during the completion of the assessment. The client placement criteria section aids in deciding on the appropriate level of care for the client.

16. B) Consider a person's cultural background when completing the assessment

The counselor considers the unique needs of each client. Asking the same questions in the same order in the same way may not be the best for the client. Presuming the client is being dishonest during the assessment will negatively affect the rapport between the client and the counselor. Disregarding any client preference will have a negative effect on client engagement and participation in the recommended treatment.

17. An instructor teaching a class on assessing clients asks a student what considerations a counselor should have if a client has a significant reading impairment. What response by the student requires correction from the instructor?
    A) The counselor should encourage the client to take their time completing the screening instruments
    B) The counselor should not utilize a screening instrument as the results would not be valid if it is not completed in the same way as other clients
    C) The counselor should offer to read the screening instrument questions to the client
    D) The counselor should choose a screening instrument that has a lower reading comprehension level

18. The best screening instrument is the one that
    A) Is most readily available
    B) Is most cost-effective
    C) Is most reliable and valid
    D) Is used the most often

19. An instructor presents a case study to the class in which a client has been charged with first offense driving under the influence of alcohol two nights previously. The instructor asks a student for the client's likely diagnosis. Which response from the student requires correction from the instructor?
    A) Alcohol use disorder, moderate
    B) Alcohol intoxication
    C) Alcohol use disorder, mild
    D) Alcohol use disorder, moderate, and in partial remission

20. A client was referred for an assessment due to four citations for possession of marijuana over the course of the past 6 months. As well, the client was fired from two jobs in the past year due to marijuana use. The client does not report any other symptoms of a marijuana use disorder. Based on the diagnostic criteria, the client's most likely diagnosis is:
    A) Cannabis use disorder, mild
    B) No diagnosis
    C) Cannabis use disorder, moderate
    D) Cannabis use disorder, severe

(See answers on the next page.)

17. B) The counselor should not utilize a screening instrument as the results would not be valid if it is not completed in the same way as other clients

The counselor must make adaptations for each client's unique needs. Not using a screening instrument due to a reading impairment may be convenient for the counselor but is not in the best interest of the client. Encouraging the client to take their time, offering to read the questions to the client, or choosing a valid instrument with a lower reading comprehension level are all acceptable options for an accommodation for a client with a reading impairment.

18. C) Is most reliable and valid

The counselor selects the best screening instrument for each client which is more reliable and valid based on their unique circumstances. Being most readily available, most cost effective or used the most often are conveniences for the counselor, not the most beneficial for the client.

19. B) Alcohol intoxication

The counselor should not have completed an assessment on a client who is actively intoxicated. Further, a diagnosis of alcohol intoxication is not given based on past intoxication at the time of the offense. The other diagnoses are all possible.

20. B) No diagnosis

The client is only reporting information to meet one criteria for a substance use disorder. Repeated legal charges do not count as a criteria alone.

Planning Treatment With the Client

Thomas Maxson

Unfolding Case Study

We return to your client, Jim. Now that his assessment is complete, the next step for the counselor is to summarize the assessment information with Jim and collaboratively develop a treatment plan. The core function of treatment planning is described in Box 6.1 (Herdman, 2021).

Box 6.1 Core Function 5: Treatment Planning

Definition: Process by which the counselor and the client identify and rank problems needing resolution; establish agreed upon immediate and long-term goals; and decide upon a treatment process and the resources to be utilized.

Global Criteria

17. **Explain** assessment **results** to client in an understandable manner.
18. **Identify** and **rank** problems based on individual client needs in the written treatment plan.
19. Formulate **agreed** upon **immediate** and **long-term goals** using **behavioral** terms in the written treatment plan.
20. Identify the treatment **methods** and **resources** to be utilized as appropriate for the individual client.

Treatment planning is aligned with Domain 3: Evidence-Based Treatment, Counseling and Referral, and is further defined within the Core Competencies of a substance use counselor. This chapter will cover the following tasks and skills from Domain 3 (IC&RC, 2022):

E. Recognize when to utilize and how to facilitate referrals for clients (e.g., case management, follow-up)

F. Identify and respond to concerns related to specific populations (e.g., LGBTQ+, pregnancy, youth, justice-involved, housing insecure)

G. Collaborate with multidisciplinary team, other professionals, and client supports (e.g., family) to determine and provide care

J. Utilize best practices in developing and updating a treatment plan
   1. Goals and objectives
   2. Strategies and interventions (e.g., relapse prevention, coping skills)

K. Identify available resources to meet client needs

Throughout this chapter, the process and steps of treatment planning will be covered along with the application of the core functions of Referral and Case Management to assist with a client's treatment.

Before treatment planning can begin, the counselor must explain the results of the assessment in a way that is understandable to the client. The counselor explains the diagnostic impression, findings of the assessment, and recommendations to the client and to any designated significant others from the client's life. This is an ideal time for a counselor to encourage the client to bring a supportive individual with them to counseling to begin to develop the client's informal support network. Not all clients will be willing or interested in having others present; nevertheless, the offer begins to plant seeds to include others in the future.

For the client who is entering counseling voluntarily or with a desire to make changes in their life, the review of the assessment results will likely be confirmation of what they already knew or strongly suspected. In this case, the counselor is helping the client more clearly understand their current situation as well as the path forward. Whereas if a client is mandated to attend counseling and does not believe there is a concern, explaining the results of the assessment may be met with strong defensiveness or resistance to accepting the results and, in some cases, a refusal to accept the assessment results as a valid reflection of the current situation. Counselors recognize that defensiveness is a part of the counseling process and indicates where to begin counseling and that it is not a sign of when to end counseling. This is all part of the treatment planning process.

Once the client indicates an understanding of the findings of the assessment and recommendations, the client must decide what to do next. A client may decide not to continue to seek treatment, may agree to some but not all the counselor's recommendations, or may agree to and be willing to begin treatment as recommended. It is not uncommon for clients to "negotiate" with the counselor regarding recommendations. Counselors must be able to clearly explain, based on the data from the assessment, the rationale for their recommendations. Utilizing the American Society of Addiction Medicine (ASAM) client placement criteria will assist the counselor in explaining the reasons for the recommendations that were made. It is ultimately the client's choice to engage in treatment and it is the counselor's responsibility to actively engage the client in the treatment process and work to understand the client's ambivalence in committing to treatment.

▶ RESISTANT OR AMBIVALENT?

If a client does not readily accept and commit to the counselor's recommendation, some counselors may call this "resistant behavior" or that the person is "in denial." Counselors must work to avoid this kind of labeling and making this sort of assumption about clients. Holding negative views of clients as "resistant" or "in denial" creates an unnecessary barrier between the client and counselor that is difficult to overcome and may inadvertently sabotage the relationship.

Clients are frequently "ambivalent" about committing to a counselor's recommendation. Ambivalence is standing between two equally appealing (or unappealing) paths and being uncertain of which path to take. If a counselor can understand the client's uncertainty from this point of view, the client and counselor can engage in productive discussion about the challenge of making a decision and committing to a path. Ambivalence is an expected part of any change process and should not be viewed in a negative manner but rather as an opportunity to better understand the client and develop connection and engagement. All behavior has a purpose. Until the purpose of the behavior is understood or met in an alternate way, the behavior will continue.

Counselors who understand and know how to embrace ambivalence will have greater engagement and success with their clients. However, counselors also need to balance their awareness of the impact of substance use with the client's preferences and work to educate their clients on the pros and cons of the options that are available.

Unfolding Case Study

Scenario No. 1: During a session, Jim tells you about Frieda, his friend of several years. Jim says yesterday Frieda called him as she left her counselor's office after hearing the results of the substance use assessment she completed last week. Frieda was very upset. She told Jim that the counselor wants her to go to residential substance use treatment. Frieda continued, "She didn't give me a choice; she just told me that is what I have to do. I tried to tell her I have only used twice this past week and am really trying to improve, but she just wouldn't listen. I know treatment may help me, but I will lose my job, my apartment, and don't have anyone to watch my kids. It is like she didn't care; she just kept saying I was being resistant to her treatment recommendation, that I am in denial about my problem, and that I have to go treatment and if I don't, she isn't going to be my counselor anymore. I don't know what to do."

Based on Jim's description, is Frieda being resistant or in denial or is she ambivalent about going to treatment due to all the costs she feels will come as a result?

Frieda is in a challenging situation. She is beginning to make changes on her own (cutting back on her use) and has the desire to engage in counseling; however, the thought of losing her job, her apartment, and not having anyone to watch her kids are all very real considerations in her life. Further, the threat of losing access to her counselor if she doesn't comply adds more fear and uncertainty.

What will Frieda do? There is a good likelihood Frieda will drop out of counseling altogether and be fearful of returning to counseling in the future as the experience may cause her to believe all counselors will expect the same thing of her.

If we consider this example with a counselor who understands behavior change and ambivalence, the situation likely would have turned out differently.

(continued)

(*continued*)

Scenario No. 2: Jim says Frieda called him as she left her counselor's office after hearing the results of the substance use assessment she completed last week. Frieda sounded hopeful. She told Jim her counselor wanted her to go to residential substance use treatment. She continued, "I told my counselor I have only used twice this past week and am trying really hard to improve. I told her I know treatment may help me, but I will lose my job and my apartment and don't have anyone to watch my kids. She heard me and encouraged me for the changes I was making. She seemed to understand the challenges treatment would cause and we worked out a plan for me to see her twice a week, to go to three self-help meetings a week, and to call my sober friend and tell her I want to stop getting high and ask if I can call her if I have thoughts of using. I feel like she really got how hard this is and how hard I am willing to work. I agreed that if I was unable to stay sober after we try this plan for a while, I would be willing to go to residential treatment. She even told me that she would make a referral to help me find resources so I don't lose my apartment and that I will have time to find someone to watch my kids. I think I can do this."

What will Frieda do? She has already started the plan. She called her friend, asked for help, committed to a counseling plan, and is willing to accept she may need residential treatment if the current plan doesn't offer enough support. She has hope for her future. Frieda is much more likely to follow through with counseling, wherever the treatment path may take her.

▶ TREATMENT PLAN DEVELOPMENT

After the assessment results are explained to the client and the client indicates an understanding of the results, treatment plan development begins.

Treatment planning begins with the client and the counselor collaborating to prioritize the problems or challenges that need to be addressed and identifying the strengths a client possesses to aid in their recovery (Domain 3: J). This is often called "creating the problem list." The treatment plan and goals should be person-centered and include strength-based approaches or ones that draw upon an individual's strengths, resources, potential, and ability to recover, to keep the client engaged in care. Individualized treatment plans should consider age, gender identity, race, ethnicity, language, health literacy, religion/spirituality, sexual orientation, culture, trauma history, and co-occurring physical and mental health problems (U.S. Department of Health and Human Services [DHHS], 2016).

Reviewing the risk rating of the ASAM domains offers a valuable place to begin treatment planning. For example, if a client is experiencing significant withdrawal symptoms from heroin, this issue is going to be the number one treatment target. However, if they are experiencing withdrawal symptoms and they have a profound infection at the injection site, a referral for a medical consult regarding the infection will be the number one priority while concurrently planning on how to address withdrawal symptoms.

Tips From the Field

While withdrawal management is highly effective in preventing immediate and serious medical consequences associated with discontinuing substance use, it is not by itself an effective treatment for any substance use disorder. Unfortunately, many individuals who receive withdrawal management do not become engaged in treatment, resulting in increased risk of resumption of use as well as increased risk of overdose. Individuals with opioid use disorders may be left particularly vulnerable to overdose and even death (DHHS, 2016).

If a person has stability in ASAM Domains 1 and 2, attention is turned to the next agreed upon priority between the client and the counselor. This may be relationship concerns, behavioral or emotional symptoms, managing triggers, a difficult work environment, acute trauma symptoms, or a living environment that does not support sobriety. In addition to this, the identification of strengths aids the client and counselor in understanding what inter- and intrapersonal resources a client possesses to draw on to meet their goals. Some clients may have extensive support from family who can offer a safe place to stay or are willing to check in with the person daily. Clients may have previous successes with sobriety and can reflect on these successes as a way of establishing their goals for this episode of recovery. Counselors should take the time to explore the strengths of clients not only to identify resources that can be tapped into, but also to remind clients of hope and the value of their experience.

Unfolding Case Study

Let's return to Frieda. She identifies her number one concern/problem as her living situation. She lives with her sister who drinks alcohol every day after she gets off work. Though Frieda does not like drinking and does not feel she has a problem with alcohol, she knows that when she does drink, she typically ends up using methamphetamine. She is uncertain if she can continue to live with her sister and be methamphetamine free. She is uncertain about what to do. She does not feel she can afford to live on her own and she sees her sister as one of her best friends as they have only really been able to count on each other. Frieda does not feel moving out is an option. How would you prioritize the treatment needs and plan with Frieda? What would come first? What are the strengths and successes you could build on?

▶ CREATING A RECOVERY PATHWAY

Overall, recovery tends to follow a consistent path. Though the following is not an all-encompassing list, it provides a general framework for the progression of substance use treatment.

- Explain the assessment results to the client in an understandable manner.
- Educate the client about substance use disorders and their biopsychosocial impact.
- Educate the client about treatment options.
- Attend to medical, detoxification, and withdrawal management needs.
- Understand the client's goal which may include harm reduction or complete abstinence.
- Educate the client often about the treatment and recovery process based on their goal.
- Assist the client in identifying the strengths they possess and past successes they have experienced to build hope for the challenges of making change.
- Identify needs beyond what the counselor is able to offer which require case management or referral to other providers to build stabilization in the client's life (housing, employment, financial assistance, medical coverage, and legal support).
- Help the client build awareness of the effects of the substance use disorder in their life through tracking the impact of current use as well as exploring the client's history of use.
- Continue monitoring for symptoms related to possible co-occurring disorders and refer for additional assessment as appropriate.
- Educate the client and rehearse strategies for coping with triggers and cravings.
- Encourage the client to build an informal support network with whom they develop trust and who share their commitment to their goal and to their struggles and successes.
- As appropriate, educate the client's loved ones about the substance use disorder, triggers, and how to be supportive.
- Educate and practice new problem-solving strategies rather than relying on substance use or other compulsive behaviors.
- Refine the new strategies and assist the client in incorporating the strategies in day-to-day life.
- As appropriate, build acceptance of chronic illness and a commitment to daily recovery tasks.
- Help the client grieve the impact of their past behavior and build hope for the future.
- Identify signs and symptoms that may indicate the disorder is becoming active again.
- Develop strategies to ameliorate the symptoms and increase support for recovery.
- Help the client address prior trauma and family-of-origin concerns.
- Help the client integrate into their identity what it means have a substance use disorder and what is means to be in recovery.

To help guide the overarching path of treatment and recovery, counselors benefit from an understanding of treatment and recovery models including principles for effective treatment of substance use disorders, harm reduction programs such as moderation management, and Gorski's Developmental Model of Recovery (Gorski & Miller, 1986; Table 6.1).

Tips From the Field

In general, it is recommended that individuals with serious substance use disorders stay engaged in the treatment process for at least 1 year. This may involve participation in three or four different programs or services at reduced levels of intensity, all of which are ideally designed to help the client prepare for continued self-management after treatment ends (DHHS, 2016).

Table 6.1 Principles of Effective Treatment

Adults	Adolescents
1. Addiction is a complex but treatable disease that affects brain function and behavior 2. No single treatment is appropriate for everyone 3. Treatment needs to be readily available 4. Effective treatment attends to the multiple needs of the individual, not just their substance use 5. Remaining in treatment for an adequate period of time is critical 6. Behavioral therapies, including individual, family, or group counseling, are the most commonly used forms of substance use treatment 7. Medications are an important element of treatment for many clients, especially when combined with counseling and other behavioral therapies 8. An individual's treatment and services plan must be assessed continually and modified as necessary to ensure that it meets their needs 9. Many individuals may have **co-occurring** disorders 10. Medically assisted detoxification is only the first stage of addiction treatment and by itself does little to change **long-term** substance use 11. Treatment does not need to be voluntary to be effective 12. Substance use during treatment must be monitored continuously, as lapses during treatment do occur 13. Treatment programs should test clients for the presence of HIV/AIDS, hepatitis B and C, tuberculosis, and other infectious diseases; provide **risk-reduction** counseling; and link clients to other treatment if necessary	1. Adolescent substance use needs to be identified and addressed as soon as possible 2. Adolescents can benefit from interventions early in their substance use 3. Routine annual medical visits are an opportunity to ask adolescents about substance use 4. Legal interventions and sanctions or family pressure may play an important role in getting adolescents to enter, stay in, and complete treatment 5. Substance use disorder treatment should be tailored to the unique needs of the adolescent 6. Treatment should address the needs of the whole person, rather than just focusing on their substance use 7. Behavioral therapies are effective in addressing adolescent drug use 8. Families and the community are important aspects of treatment 9. Effectively treating substance use disorders in adolescents requires also identifying and treating any other mental health conditions they may have 10. Sensitive issues such as violence and child abuse or risk of suicide should be identified and addressed 11. It is important to monitor substance use during treatment 12. Staying in treatment for an adequate period of time and continuity of care afterward are important 13. Testing adolescents for sexually transmitted infections such as HIV and hepatitis B and C, is an important part of substance use treatment

HARM REDUCTION

Counselors recognize that not all clients enter counseling seeking abstinence. Meeting a client "where they are" is an essential skill for counselors. Whereas some clients utilizing harm reduction principles may have the goal of sobriety, others may have the goal of continuing to use the substance but to minimize damaging consequences. The goal of harm reduction is to reduce the negative impact substance use is having on a person's life. This may take the form of safer-use locations or methods, reduction in the amount of use, or establishing guidelines or rules around use (e.g., designating a driver prior to a night of drinking, only using heroin if there is a friend who has naloxone to treat an overdose, always using a clean needle). Harm reduction may also involve changing the substance used to one that causes less disruption to the person's goals.

Some individuals use harm reduction methods as a way to begin exploring sobriety and recovery prior to committing to full abstinence. These individuals typically have moderate to severe substance use disorders and eventually identify that harm reduction is not sufficient to meet the goals they have for their life. Others, often with mild or moderate substance use disorders, utilize harm reduction strategies to reduce the impact of their substance use while continuing to use at reduced amounts or frequencies. Moderation Management™ is a self-help support group that utilizes harm reduction principles and may be used as an alternative to 12-step models (see Moderation.org for more information).

DEVELOPMENTAL MODEL OF RECOVERY

Gorski and Miller (1986) developed the abstinence-focused developmental model of recovery based on the interviews and chart reviews with clients they treated. Gorski discovered there are common warnings signs those with substance use disorders experience prior to returning to use. He identified recovery as a process with "six developmental periods" or stages described in Table 6.2. The developmental model of recovery aids a counselor in understanding where a client is in the recovery process and aids the client in understanding what lies ahead to ideally develop a lifelong recovery program. Helping the client understand recovery is a process and not an event. It helps the client develop hope for their future as well as having a better understanding and expectation of what is to come.

Table 6.2 Six Developmental Stages and Goals

Developmental Stages	Goal
Pretreatment	Recognition of addiction, learning by consequences that you cannot safely use addictive chemicals
Stabilization	Regaining control of thought processes, emotional processes, memory, judgment, and behavior
Early recovery	Accepting the disease of addiction and learning to function without drugs and alcohol
Middle recovery	Developing a normal, balanced lifestyle
Late recovery	Development of healthy self-esteem, spiritual growth, healthy intimacy, and meaningful living
Maintenance	Staying sober and living productively

Source: Adapted from Gorski, T., & Miller, M. (1986). *Staying sober: A guide for relapse prevention.* Herald House/Independence Press.

Gorski and Miller (1986) also suggested recovery is not a straight line and that persons may recover over a period of time, often advancing to one stage of recovery and then falling back either into active use or to the behavior from an earlier period of life. They referred to this as "partial recovery." Individuals will advance until they encounter a "stuck point" in their recovery. A stuck point can occur when an individual does not have sufficient skill to advance further, encounter a significant stressor in their life, or become complacent in their own growth and development.

The developmental model of recovery (Table 6.3) offers detail regarding the tasks associated with each developmental stage and provides language that can be used for goal and objective development. A counselor can help guide a client through the stages by integrating the skills of each stage into the treatment plan, leading the client to the next developmental task, teaching skills to support the client, and monitoring for stress, anxiety, and overwhelming feelings the client may present that foretell an approaching stuck point. The counselor encourages the client forward and recognizes when the client needs a rest to consolidate the gains they have made.

There are two primary crises that clients experience when working through the developmental model. The first is a crisis of use or a "motivational crisis." This is typically an event which disrupts the client's pattern of use, creates discomfort in their life, and causes the client to seriously consider making changes to their substance use. Examples of motivational crises include the death of a close friend to an overdose, the birth of a child, a significant other threatening or actually leaving due to the client's substance use, an injury or accident, or an arrest. Some clients will also talk about a "spiritual awakening" where they have a moment of realization that they do not want to use substances anymore. This crisis of use or motivational crisis can result in a period of sobriety (either voluntary or involuntary) or may result in a desire to not use. Counselors recognize that as a result of outside forces (e.g., threat of jail, hospitalization, incarceration) a client may be sober and not want to be, and as well how a client may be actively using and want to be sober but not know how to stop. Only through collaboration with the client will the counselor discover the client's goal.

The second crisis is a "crisis of identity." The values and behaviors demonstrated during active use come in direct conflict with the new sobriety-centered values and behaviors. This may be a single moment or a series of events that force a client to ask "Who am I now?" This often takes the form of having to make decisions about friends that the client used to drink or use with, letting go of old clothing or music, redirecting old thoughts, or embracing new activities that would not have fit in the old lifestyle. Clients begin to actively manage and self-direct their recovery program by recognizing when to ask for help, choosing nonaddictive coping mechanisms, resisting the urge for substitute addictions, and being willing to listen to feedback from others about their behaviors.

Unfortunately, clients may not embrace the crisis of identity and instead settle for "good enough recovery." Though settling is not a conscious choice, it often occurs because of the resolution or reduction of the consequences from the crisis of use, reduced treatment interactions, and increases in the

Table 6.3 Developmental Model of Recovery

Pretreatment		Stabilization	Early Recovery		Middle Recovery	Late Recovery	Maintenance
Giving up the need to control use	Crisis of use	Recuperation from the damage of substance use	Internal change related to substance use	Crisis of identity	External repair of lifestyle damage	Growing beyond childhood limitations	Continued growth and development
1. Development of motivating problems 2. Attempts at normal problem solving 3. Attempts at controlled use 4. Accepting the need for abstinence 5. Recognizing chemical dependency or behavioral loss of control		1. Attempts at abstinence without help 2. Acceptance of the need for help 3. Recovery from withdrawal 4. Interrupting addictive preoccupation 5. Learning nonchemical stress management 6. Developing hope and motivation 7. Stabilizing housing, finances, supports, and day-to-day functioning	1. Short term social stabilization 2. Recognition of addictive disease 3. Acceptance and integration of the substance use disorder 4. Learning nonchemical coping skills 5. Developing a **sobriety-centered** value system 6. Trying to keep old friends 7. Still externally regulated 8. "Good enough recovery"		1. Resolving the crisis of identity 2. Repair of substance **use-caused** social damage 3. Starting a **self-regulated** recovery program 4. Developing new friends and genuinely discarding prior friends 5. Establishing lifestyle balance (work, social, family, and intimate) 6. **Self-management** of change	1. Resolution of family of origin issues 2. Develop intimacy skills 3. Establish a basic integrated sense of self 4. Reorganize lifestyle around new role/identity 5. Developing stable **long-term** intimate relationships 6. **Self-regulated** identity	1. Maintain a recovery program 2. Effective **day-today** coping 3. Continued growth and development 4. Effective coping with life transitions and complicating factors 5. Recognizes need for further therapy as necessary

expectations of day-to-day life. Others in the client's life begin "expecting" the person to be sober and do not understand the ongoing nature of a recovery program. The client begins skipping self-help meetings, reducing counseling appointments, and often will slide back to addictive-based coping and imbalanced living to navigate the stresses of life, all the while justifying the behavior because "I am sober."

Counselors prepare clients for this part of their recovery journey through consistent treatment plan review. The counselor helps the client reflect on what they have done, consolidate gains, encourage progress, and introduce the rewards and potential perils of the path ahead. Through this review process, the counselor works to keep the client engaged, encouraged, and challenged, all within a window that is tolerable for the client. If the counselor does not engage and encourage the client, the client may lose interest and motivation for change and discontinue the change process. Chapter 7, "Counseling With the Client," also discusses pathways of recovery to consider when working with clients. Fitting the pathway to the client is critical for recovery to be long lasting.

STAGE-BASED TREATMENT PLANNING

To develop an effective treatment plan, the counselor must consider the current awareness and acceptance the client has regarding the substance use disorder. If a client readily acknowledges they have a substance use disorder, or at least that the substance is causing difficulty for them in meeting their life goals, treatment planning proceeds differently than with a client who does not acknowledge or accept that their substance use is causing difficulty or that they have a substance use disorder.

Counselors utilize their knowledge of the stages of change and the use of motivational interviewing (MI) to engage clients where they are in the change process. MI is covered more in depth in Chapter 7, "Counseling With the Client."

Stage-based treatment planning helps the counselor align goals and objectives based on the level of awareness and acceptance a client has regarding the impact of their substance use. It is important to note a client may be in the action stage of treatment regarding one concern but still in the precontemplative stage regarding another. For example, a client may readily admit they have an alcohol use disorder and be more than 6 months sober while at the same time does not recognize their gambling behaviors are causing similar family problems as the alcohol was causing. A client in this situation may comment "No one seems to care I quit drinking. That's what they said they wanted. Now they just complain about my gambling. I can't seem to please them." This statement suggests the client does not understand or have awareness of the impact of their gambling behavior and may be beginning to question why they should remain sober, as people are still complaining. The counselor will work with this client to develop different goals and objectives regarding alcohol use versus gambling behavior based on the different stages of change the client is in regarding each behavior.

The stages of change as described by Prochaska and DiClemente (1994) and outlined in Chapter 7, "Counseling With the Client," includes 5 distinct categories: (1) precontemplation, (2) contemplation, (3) preparation, (4) action, and (5) maintenance. As a part of the treatment planning process, the counselor utilizes the stages of change (DiClemente, 2018) to identify appropriate goals and objectives (Box 6.2). The client tasks can be utilized as objectives in a client's treatment plan. The counselor's tasks allow them to be effective when counseling a client in each stage. If a client is not engaging in counseling, is not completing homework tasks, or seems disinterested or defensive in session, the counselor should evaluate if they are interacting with the client based on the appropriate stage. If the counselor is engaging in counseling strategies that do not match the client's stage of change, counseling will be less effective, and the client is more likely to disengage from counseling. For additional information, TIP 35 offers comprehensive coverage regarding stages of change and the application to counseling (Substance Abuse and Mental Health Services Administration [SAMHSA], 2019). Additional information regarding the stages of change can be found in DiClemente (2018) and Prochaska and DiClemente (1994).

As the client and the counselor develop treatment goals and objectives, as indicated above, the counselor identifies the client's stage of change and guides objectives respectively. Table 6.4 outlines corresponding client change processes that can be utilized to assist the client in meeting the goal of the stage. These processes guide the creation of treatment assignments the client can engage in outside of session and which can be reviewed in session to specifically target the client's stage-based need.

The first two change processes, Consciousness Raising and Emotional Arousal, help a client reflect and gain perspective of the impact their substance use is having on their life. Clients often have become accustomed to the impact of their substance use and over time fail to recognize that the impact of the substance use is the cause of the problems they are experiencing. The counselor assigns homework

Box 6.2 Stages of Change

Precontemplation: Not seriously considering change

- *Goal*: Raise doubts and concerns about the target behavior.
- *Objectives (client tasks)*: Increase awareness of the need for change and concern about the current pattern of behavior.
- *Counselor tasks*: Establish rapport, ask permission and build trust; understand reward for current behavior, review negative effects of continued substance use.

Contemplation: Thinking about change

- *Goal*: Reflection on the current situation that leads to a decision to change.
- *Objectives (client tasks)*: Analyze the pros and cons of the current behavior pattern and of the costs and benefits of change, complete decisional balance.
- *Counselor tasks*: Understand, normalize, and validate ambivalence, facilitate decision-making.

Preparation: Getting ready to make change

- *Goal*: Create an action plan to be implemented in the near term.
- *Objectives (client tasks)*: Increase commitment to change and create a change plan. Identify When, How and Who can help with the plan.
- *Counselor tasks*: Build belief and hope for change.

Action: Making the change

- *Goal*: Engage in behavior to change the current pattern of behavior. New patterns of behavior are established for a significant period of time (6 months).
- *Objectives (client tasks)*: Implement strategies of change: revising plan as needed; sustaining commitment in face of difficulties. Taking action, sharing with others, discarding the old behavior and thinking.
- *Counselor tasks*: Provide support and reflection for actions leading toward the goal.

Maintenance: Sustaining behavior change until integrated into lifestyle

- *Goal*: Long-term sustained change of the old pattern and establishment of a new pattern of behavior.
- *Objectives (client tasks)*: Sustaining change over time and across a wide range of different situations. Avoiding slips and relapses back to the old pattern of behavior.
- *Counselor tasks*: Affirm resolve and encourage self-efficacy.

Relapse and recycling: Returning to previous behavior and reentering the cycle of change

- *Goal*: Client has renewed determination and confidence to resume change efforts.
- *Objectives (client tasks)*: Reestablish recovery behavior patterns; identify warning signs and behaviors that contributed to the lapse.
- *Counselor tasks*: Help reframe lapses into learning experiences and help client to avoid discouragement and demoralization.

---

assignments such as tracking cravings, use and impact of current substance use, as well as completing a history of their substance use, to assist the client in raising their awareness of the impact of the substance use. The counselor also works to identify the client's use of minimization, rationalization, and justification of the impact and assists the client in seeing more clearly the actual impact of the past and present substance use. As the client reduces the use of these defense mechanisms, the client begins to experience increased emotional arousal and distress when consequences of their current substance use occur as well as when reviewing past substance use. The counselor recognizes the distress the client begins to feel and assists the client in both coping with the grief and pain from this increased awareness as well as utilizes this grief and pain as a motivator for the client to make further change.

As the client becomes more aware of the impact of their current substance use, the counselor guides the client to consider the pros and cons of their substance use behaviors and the impact on their relationships using Environmental Reevaluation strategies. This aligns with assisting the client in engaging in Self-Reevaluation and considering the impact of the substance use behaviors on how they are living out their values in their lives.

If the client has participated in the first four processes, they begin to recognize that their substance use behaviors are impacting their relationships and community as well as impacting their ability to

Table 6.4 Catalysts for Change

Type	Specific Client Change Processes	Stage of Change
Experiential	Consciousness raising: Gains new awareness and understanding of substance use behavior	Precontemplation/contemplation
	Emotional arousal: Is motivated to contemplate change after an important emotional reaction to current substance use behavior or the need to change	Precontemplation/contemplation
	Environmental reevaluation: Evaluates pros and cons of current substance use behavior and its effects on others and the community	Precontemplation/contemplation
	Self-reevaluation: Explores the current substance use behavior and the possibility of change in relation to own values	Contemplation
	Social liberation: Recognizes and increases available positive social supports	Contemplation/preparation
Behavioral	Counterconditioning: Begins to recognize the links between internal and external cues to use substances and experiments with substituting more healthful behaviors and activities in response to those cues	Preparation/action
	Helping relationships: Seeks and cultivates relationships that offer support, acceptance, and reinforcement for positive behavioral change	Preparation/action/maintenance
	Self-liberation: Begins to believe in ability to make choices/to change. Develops enhanced self-efficacy and commits to changing substance use behaviors	Preparation/action/maintenance
	Stimulus control: Avoids stimuli and cues that could trigger substance use	Action
	Reinforcement management: Begins to self-reward positive behavioral changes and eliminates reinforcements for substance use	Action/maintenance

Source: Substance Abuse and Mental Health Services Administration. (2019). *Enhancing motivation for change in substance use disorder treatment: Treatment improvement protocol (TIP) Series No. 35.* SAMHSA Publication No. PEP19-02-01-003. Substance Abuse and Mental Health Services Administration.

live out their values in life—in both the present and the past. At this point, the client must decide if they want to consider making changes in their behavior or if they want to stay their current course. Along with discussing this decision, counselors encourage the process of Social Liberation, wherein clients recognize and increase positive social support. A client may not be ready to commit to making a change, but they may be willing to begin associating with those that do not engaging in problematic substance use and reduce the time spent with people and in places that promote problematic substance use behaviors.

When a client decides to make a change to their substance use behaviors, they leave the precontemplation and contemplation stages of changes and move to the preparation and action stages of change. The preparation and action stages of change utilize behavioral processes to assist the client's change. The counselor guides the client in the use of Counterconditioning and the establishment of Helping Relationships. These processes involve the client learning and utilizing effective coping responses to triggers or cues to substance use. Additionally, the client begins to establish relationships and support for their behavior changes. At this point the client is actively involved in the change process. They have moved from the stabilization developmental stage to the stage of early recovery. The client will typically freely acknowledge that their substance use causes problems in their lives and they must make changes in the substance use behavior to reduce or eliminate these problems. The client recognizes what cues a desire to engage in the substance use behavior and is practicing new skills and strategies in response to these cues. Further, they have reduced associating with the people and in the places that promote the substance use behavior and are exploring new supportive people and locations.

As the client becomes more confident in their ability to use the new skills, the process of Self-Liberation emerges. The counselor reinforces and encourages the client's behavior, changes in thinking, and in independently making different choices than before while also believing they have the ability to make different choices. At this point, the client begins to verbalize that they are choosing to change their substance use behavior to improve their lives and to meet their values rather than feeling they "have" to make the change due to the risk of an external consequence. The process of self-liberation corresponds to the developmental stage of middle recovery.

Tips From the Field

Integrating the language of "choice" such as "I choose to," "I get to," "I want to" assists a client in becoming active in their recovery. Using the language of "have to" such as "I can't," "they want me to," "they are making me" keeps a client in a passive role or may prompt them to resist change to maintain a sense of agency and control. Counselors can begin integrating the language of "choice" within the first interaction with the client by encouraging them for "choosing" to attend the assessment or "making a choice" to explore treatment rather than continuing to experience the consequences of ongoing substance use.

The client then begins to engage in the processes of Stimulus Control and Reinforcement Management by actively avoiding stimuli and cues that may trigger substance use, self-rewarding positive behavioral change, and eliminating reinforcements for substance use. At this point, the counselor is affirming the client's resolve and encourages self-efficacy.

It is essential the counselor understands how the developmental model of recovery, stages of change, stage-based treatment planning, and stage-based change processes weave together. Each contributes to the counselor's ability to assist the client to form treatment goals and objectives. The client is the expert on themselves, and the counselor is the expert guide to help on their change journey. As a guide, the counselor must be aware of the client's current desire to change and current skills and abilities as well as how to best assist the client in progressing through the Stages of Change and the development of new skills and abilities.

ZONE OF PROXIMAL DEVELOPMENT

The zone of proximal development (ZPD), developed by Vygotsky (1978), represents the space between what a learner (client) is capable of doing without support and what the learner (client) cannot do even with support. It is in this range where the learner (client) can perform with support from a counselor or a peer with more knowledge or experience.

Counselors utilize the theory of ZPD to develop achievable goals and utilize well-written objectives to build a client's skills to help them reach the goal. The counselor teaches and encourages the client's use of new skills. Clients are also encouraged to engage in peer support groups to learn and practice new skills. Interaction with peers that have more skill and/or longer periods of sobriety assists the client in building hope they can achieve ongoing sobriety as well using observational learning of how the peers are being successful. Individuals with more skill or knowledge than the learner (client) are considered a more knowledgeable person or more knowledgeable other.

When developing goals and objectives with a client, it is crucial to determine if the goal is achievable or attainable by the client. As previously mentioned, if a goal is met too easily, it can decrease the client's motivation to continue; however, if the goal is too difficult to meet, the client's self-confidence will reduce along with their belief they can reach any counseling goal resulting in increased risk of dropping out of the change process.

It is essential that the counselor is aware of and considers the outside influences in the client's life. The client's informal interactions will either reinforce new skill development or hinder the new goal-directed skill development. In the ideal situation, a client begins interacting with peers who are supportive and engaged in recovery, offer encouragement and suggestions to manage cravings, and invite the client to sober social activities to build new nonsubstance-involved recreation and fun. In the worst case, the informal interactions work against the intentional new goal-directed skill development and the client begins to practice skills that work against their progress toward the stated goal. This can occur in situations wherein clients learn how to better conceal their substance use, utilize adulterants to pass drug testing, or use substances that create intoxication without being detected by a drug test.

Counselors also utilize the skill of scaffolding to build skill and support to assist the client in reaching their goals. Scaffolding begins with the counselor offering consistent support and direct teaching of skills. This occurs through frequent therapeutic interactions, often multiple times per week with a mix of individual and group counseling. As the client practices the skill and becomes more consistent and proficient in the use of the new skills, the counselor becomes a guide offering pointers and assisting with problem solving. Finally, as the client begins to use the skill independently, the counselor encourages the client to continue to practice the skill and begins to introduce the next skill or moves to the next objective to reach the goal.

Skill development in treatment planning is an intentional and progressive process which requires the counselor to have knowledge not only of substances and their effects, but also the process of recovery and learning theory. Counselors must also maintain a keen awareness of the interactive effects between the client, the counselor, the client's peer interactions, the environment the client lives in, the client's history, experiences, and strengths, and the clients own cultural views and beliefs.

GOAL AND OBJECTIVE DEVELOPMENT

Once the client and the counselor have prioritized the problem list, goals can be developed. Goal development in treatment planning typically has two main targets. The first is a reduction of impairment caused by the symptoms of the diagnosis. The second is an improvement of the client's functioning and satisfaction with life. The ideal outcome of treatment is the achievement of both goals.

In substance use counseling, the overall goal is not to cure the disorder, but to use new skills and strategies to move the disorder into remission and help the client develop a long-term lifestyle of recovery that supports maintaining remission of the substance use disorder. Further, the counselor will assist the client to recognize signs the disorder is becoming active and learn strategies to manage the symptoms effectively. This overall goal is similar to the management of any chronic health condition.

There are entire books and software programs dedicated to treatment planning (e.g., Klott and Jongsma, 2015). These offer helpful ideas for possible goals and objectives depending on the client's concern. As we review the definition of treatment planning, one of the key elements is the collaborative process between the client and counselor. The suggested goals in treatment planning books and software are a starting point for the collaboration and should not be utilized without client input.

Goals should be measurable and time limited. Both the client and counselor should know what "success" or "meeting the goal" is. Ideally, goals should include the client's words. For example, "I want to stop using alcohol within the next 30 days" or "I want to learn how to say no when someone asks me to work a double shift. I know I am successful if I go a full month without any doubles" or "I want to identify what I enjoy doing for fun and have a list of three things I have tried and enjoy within the next 60 days." These goals can be measured—Has the person stopped using alcohol? Have they stopped working double shifts? Can they identify what they enjoy doing for fun?—and are time limited: "within 30 days," "no doubles for a month," and "three fun things within 60 days."

Utilizing the SMART goal model assists a counselor in writing effective goals and objectives (Table 6.5). As mentioned, the goal is one sentence—a broad statement about the long-term expectation of what should happen. The goal is achieved through the objectives and interventions or services that are offered.

Table 6.5 Tips for Writing SMART Goals

Specific	Define what you expect Determine who will do it Detail accountability Use action verbs, expressing physical or mental action, as much as possible Provide enough detail; this depends on the goal but should be enough to be clear
Measurable	Identify how you will know the goal was accomplished—usually this means quantity but can also be quality (for instance, "I will communicate with my sponsor 5 out of 7 days each week")
Achievable/attainable	Does the person have the time, skill, and support to accomplish the goal? Consider if there may be factors beyond the client's control
Relevant	The goal is related to the client's needs The goal will make a meaningful difference if accomplished and is meaningful to the client Why am I setting this goal now?
Time bound	Specify when the goal should be completed. Is this realistic? Include time-lined benchmarks for long-range goals and all objectives

SMART, specific, measurable, achievable, relevant, and time bound.
Source: Adapted from Substance Abuse and Mental Health Services Administration. (2023, May 6). *Developing goals and measurable objectives.* https://www.samhsa.gov/grants/how-to-apply/writing-completing-application/goals-measurable-objectives

The characteristics of effective goals include (SAMHSA, 2023):

- Address outcomes, not how outcomes will be achieved.
- Describe the behavior or condition that is expected to change.

- Describe who will be affected by the change.
- Lead clearly to one or more measurable results.
- Are concise.

Objectives are steps toward the goal. Objectives are "how" a person will get to the goal. When writing objectives, think about labeling the steps it takes before one can reach the next "landing" and rest. If you want to climb to the top of a tall building or climb a mountain, it is important to establish rest points to pause and reflect on where you have been, how you got there, and allow yourself to gather the strength and resources to continue the climb. If a person must take too many steps to get to a place to rest and reflect, they may get tired and give up; conversely, if there is only one step to get to the next landing, the person may be lulled into a sense of "good enough" and stop trying to climb. The counselor helps the client develop realistic goals based on their current skill level, so the client must stretch to get to the goal without feeling hopeless and overextended.

In addition to goals and objectives, treatment plans typically contain interventions (Box 6.3). The definition of an intervention as a part of a treatment plan may vary depending on the agency a counselor works for or the electronic health record that is being used. Most frequently, interventions are either considered additional steps to meet an objective or the services that will be utilized to support the client in reaching their goal. This chapter considers the latter definition wherein interventions are the services that will be utilized to support the client reaching the goal. Examples of services include individual, family or group counseling, case management services, medication management, and self-help meetings.

Box 6.3 **Treatment Plan Summary and Example**

The following are the steps involved in creating a treatment plan with the client.

1. *Identify the needs of the client and create a problem list: Throughout the initial assessment, identify the client's needs with the client. These needs will be related to the diagnosis as well.*
    From these identified needs, the counselor may summarize the list, asking the client if there are any more, and then prioritize with the client which needs are most important to work on first.

Example:
Client needs:

- Stable housing
- Abstinence from substances
- Reduced depressive symptoms.
- Medication assessment
- Increased activities during the day
- Improved social support

2. *Goals: The goal is the expected outcome or condition stated in relatively broad terms and based on the identified need. The goal needs to have a timeline by which the goal will be completed or reviewed.*
    Helpful questions to ask in the interview to identify the goals may be:
    - "If this (need) were to be different or better for you in 3 months, what would that be like or what would that look like?"
    - "How will I know, or what will I see, if this is different?"
    Questions such as these will elicit what the client envisions for their life and guide the creation of specific, measurable, achievable, relevant, and time bound (SMART) goals. Client quotes may be used in the goal statement. The counselor can then summarize the goal in clinical terms if need be.

Example:
Client statement: "I would like to not have to use drugs to feel okay about life."
  Goal: Client will feel "okay about life" without using drugs as evidenced by abstaining from drugs for 4 weeks and attending narcotics anonymous to meet new friends.

3. *Objectives (steps): The objectives are a step-by-step procedure involving behavioral or thinking change and practice activities to reach the goal. There should be at least two objectives per goal but usually <4 to keep it manageable. Each step or objective should lead the client closer to the goal.*
    Helpful questions to lead to identifying objectives may be:
    - "How can you reach your goal?"
    - "What things need to happen to get you to where you want to be?"

(continued)

Box 6.3 Treatment Plan Summary and Example *(continued)*

This will start the client thinking and problem solving on their own behalf (a skill we want to teach all clients). The counselor can be creative and actively assist in this process by suggesting ideas. Once again, ensure that the objectives are behavioral, measurable, attainable, and timeline oriented.

Example:

- (Client name) will journal four core feelings daily.
- (Client name) will monitor cravings for substance use daily.
- (Client name) will learn, use, and journal coping skills to manage cravings.
- (Client name) will develop a positive support group.
- (Client name) will attend two events sober.

4. *Interventions (method): Interventions refer to the service that is being provided. You must have a counseling intervention on your treatment plan if you are going to be a provider of the plan.*
   The interventions are the services you are providing to the client. They are the "things you are doing" as the counselor to help the client.

Example:

- Individual counseling
- Family counseling
- Cognitive Behavioral Therapy
- Mindfulness Based Relapse Prevention
- Self-help/support groups
- Referral to a medical doctor
- Referral to a housing provider

In short, treatment planning is as follows:

- Start with a good assessment
- Identify need areas or a problem list
- Identify strengths, supports, and resources
- Prioritize needs/problems
- Create goals (desired outcomes)
- Create objectives (steps to the goal)
- Develop interventions
- Review and update as needed

Example:

Brief assessment: Jill is a 25-year-old female. She is currently living in a friend's basement but needs to move. She indicated a significant history of anxiety and panic attacks which resulted in the loss of her previous job. She has had positive results with anti-anxiety medication in the past and would desire to start medication again. She is unaware of coping strategies for anxiety and does not feel that her friends are supportive or understand her anxiety. Several months ago, she discovered that if she drinks around three shots of vodka before she goes somewhere, she has less anxiety. However, she has now been carrying vodka with her to keep her anxiety at bay during the day. She is concerned about how much money she is spending on vodka.

Needs:

- Learn new coping skills for anxiety
- Reduce alcohol use
- Develop positive support system
- Explore medication options

Goal 1: Jill will "not drink so much" as evidenced by elimination of alcohol use within 90 days

Objective a. Jill will track the times that she does drink.
Objective b. Jill will leave her alcohol at home rather than taking it with her.
Objective c. Jill will speak with others before she takes a drink.
Objective d. Jill will not buy another bottle of alcohol after the current one is gone.
Objective e. Jill will journal triggering events, thoughts, and feelings when she thinks about drinking.

Intervention 1. Individual therapy
Intervention 2. Attend self-help meetings

(continued)

Box 6.3 Treatment Plan Summary and Example *(continued)*

Goal 2: Jill will "not be scared anymore" of panic attacks as evidenced by increasing healthy coping strategies within 90 days.

Objective a. Identify warning signs and triggers for anxiety and panic.
Objective b. Develop distraction and escape strategies when anxiety begins to build.
Objective c. Learn thought stopping and relaxation strategies to prevent increase in anxiety.
Objective d. Develop list of supportive individuals to call when feeling anxious.

Intervention 1. Attend individual cognitive behavioral therapy weekly.

▶ REFERRAL AND CASE MANAGEMENT

Counselors recognize that they are not able to provide all the services a client needs. Clients may need medication management, assistance with securing housing, access to medical care, or financial or legal assistance. Some clients need transportation assistance to get to appointments, an advocate to help them through a challenging situation, parenting assistance, or a variety of other services and supports. A counselor includes these other services within the treatment plan as these services support the client reaching their goal. Counselors utilize the skills of referral and case management to facilitate and collaborate with these other services.

When a counselor and client identify a need or problem the counselor cannot meet, "the counselor must have the ability to recognize when to utilize and how to facilitate referrals for clients (e.g., case management, follow-up)" (Domain 3: E; Box 6.4; Herdman, 2021) and "identify available resources to meet client needs" (Domain 3: K). With this, the counselor "identifies and responds to concerns related to specific populations (e.g., LGBTQ+, pregnant, youth, justice-involved, and housing insecure)" (Domain 3: F; Box 6.4). The process of identifying and responding to a need the client cannot meet is also described in the core function of referral.

Box 6.4 Core Function 10: Referral

Definition: Identifying the needs of a client that cannot be met by the counselor or agency and assisting the client to utilize the support systems and community resources available.

Global Criteria:
35. Identifying **need(s)** and/or **problem(s)** that the agency and/or counselor **cannot meet**.
36. **Explain** the **rationale** for the referral to the client.
37. **Match** client **needs** and/or problems **to** appropriate **resources**.
38. Adhere to applicable laws, regulations, and agency policies governing procedures related to the protection of the client's **confidentiality**.
39. Assist the client in **utilizing** the support **systems** and community **resources** available.

The core function of referral requires two tasks of the counselor. The first is to identify the needs of the client that cannot be met by the counselor and the second is to assist the client to utilize the resource or support. It is important to note that simply identifying the unmet need is insufficient. Without actually connecting the client to the service, the need will remain unmet.

Once a need has been identified, the counselor explains the rationale for a referral to the client as well as the options that are available to assist with this need. In order to match the client's needs to appropriate resources, the counselor must be aware of the options available in the community to assist their client, whether this be a referral to a specific agency (e.g., an agency that offers a parenting class) or to a service that will help the client connect to resources (e.g., an agency that provides case management services). If the client agrees to the referral, the counselor must adhere to applicable laws, regulations, and policies regarding confidentiality. More information on confidentiality can be found in Chapter 8, "Legal, Ethical, and Professional Issues."

For some situations, a referral may mean the counselor is referring the client to a different service provider and discontinuing services, whereas in other situations, the counselor is referring a client to an additional service while also continuing to offer counseling services to the client. If the counselor discontinues services after the facilitation of the referral is complete, the counselor will not have further contact with the client unless the client is referred back to them for additional counseling. For example, a counselor completes a substance use assessment on a client with a recommendation of residential substance use treatment. The assessing counselor does not offer this level of care and thus refers the client to a provider offering residential treatment services. The counselor then discontinues interactions with the client once the referral is complete. However, the client may be referred back to the assessing counselor for continued care counseling once the residential substance treatment program is completed.

▶ CASE MANAGEMENT

If the counselor refers a client to additional services and continues to offer counseling services to the client, the counselor is expected to: "Collaborate with the multidisciplinary team, other professionals, and client supports (e.g., family) to determine and provide care" (Domain 3: G). This is described in the core function of case management (Box 6.5; Herdman, 2021).

Box 6.5 Core Function 7: Case Management

Definition: Activities which bring services, agencies, resources, or people together within a planned framework of action toward the achievement of established goals. It may involve liaison activities and collateral contacts.

Global Criteria:
28. **Coordinate services** for client care.
29. **Explain** the **rationale** of case management activities to the client.

When a counselor engages in case management activities, the counselor is coordinating services for the client to assist them in reaching their goals. As a part of this coordination, the counselor collaborates with the providers involved in the client's care to ensure all services and supports involved are working toward the same goal.

Clients with multiple and complex needs are more likely to have multiple services and supports involved with their care. These services, along with the counselor and the client, form what is referred to as a **multidisciplinary team**. A multidisciplinary team is formed when varying supports are engaged in the client's care. Some team members are very active in the client's care; others may have very specific and time limited roles. In some situations, formal team meetings are held when the client and the other members of the multidisciplinary team gather to discuss the client's successes and ongoing needs to reach their goals as well as coordinating resources and interventions so that there is not duplication of or divergent services being offered. In other situations, the services are monitored through informal communication such as phone calls or e-mails by a case manager.

Counselors are cognizant of their role in case management services. Counselor collaboration with the multidisciplinary team may mean the counselor is also the case manager and responsible for the monitoring and coordination of services, whereas in other circumstances the counselor is a team member and another provider is in the role of the case manager. It is essential that the team members collaborate with each other to ensure all services are helping the client advance toward a common and agreed upon goal. Further, it is essential the client is the lead voice on the multidisciplinary team, as the purpose of the team is to assist the client in reaching their desired goal.

Tips From the Field

To assist clients, counselors must be knowledgeable regarding resources that are available in the community. This requires ongoing networking and engagement with other service providers.

Unfolding Case Study

Let's return to Frieda once again to develop a treatment plan. Frieda is uncertain of what to do regarding her living situation. She identified her living situation as her number one concern and reported she does not feel leaving her living situation is an option. Frieda and the counselor work together to develop a goal and objectives regarding her living situation. The counselor respects that Frieda is not willing to leave her home or her sister. Frieda does express

(continued)

(continued)

a goal that she wants her home to be "drug and alcohol free." She feels this is going to be an ongoing goal that can be reviewed at each session. After some discussion, she concludes that if this goal cannot be met within 60 days, she will need to reconsider her living situation. This goal reflects "what" Frieda wants.

Frieda and the counselor then discuss the steps or objectives to reach the goal. The objectives describe the "how" of Frieda going to get to her goal. The counselor is aware that Frieda has had a hard time telling her sister "no" in the past, leaving the house if her sister is drinking, and often avoids confrontation with her sister. The counselor reflects on Frieda's zone of proximal development. Frieda can tell her sister she wants to be drug-free and that it is hard for her to be drug-free if there is alcohol in the house. She has not been able to tell her sister that she does not want her to bring alcohol in the house as she is afraid her sister will get angry and remind her of how many times she did things she did not want to do to protect Frieda in the past. Upon further discussion, Frieda shared that asking her sister for support makes her feel guilty, ashamed, and overwhelmed. Frieda also indicated that she tends to talk to her sister only when her sister is intoxicated. She wonders if the conversation would be different if she approached her sister when her sister is sober.

Frieda and the counselor developed the following goal and objectives.

Goal: Frieda will be in "a home that is drug and alcohol free" within 60 days. (This connects to Frieda's overall goal of her not using alcohol or drugs anymore.)

Objectives: Frieda will:

Share with her sister her goal of sobriety within the next 14 days

Speak to her sister when she is sober about not bringing alcohol into the house within the next 14 days

Identify the feelings of guilt and shame and the triggers to these feelings

Develop and practice alternate coping strategies for guilt and shame

Speak to friends and identify a safe place she and her kids can go for the night if her sister is actively drinking at home

Identify activities she, her children, and her sister can do for fun to reduce stress and decrease the risk of alcohol use in the home

Begin to look for alternate housing options in 30 days if her sister is not receptive to not having alcohol in the home

Interventions:

Outpatient counseling two times per week

Three self-help meetings per week

Case management services

Frieda agrees to this goal and set of objectives. This goal targets the developmental period of stabilization. Frieda is working on creating a foundation on which to begin to build a recovery program. She hopes this can be with her sister, but if her sister is not willing, Frieda acknowledges she may have to develop a stable foundation elsewhere. She commits to completing the first two objectives within the next 14 days; the other objectives she agrees to work on and complete prior to 60 days. Frieda expresses that making a decision to move out now seems impossible (outside of her ZPD), but she feels if she takes each of these steps over the next 60 days, she feels making the decision will be more possible and she will not feel as guilty (scaffolding with support). It is agreed that she will attend outpatient counseling twice weekly. In addition, she agrees to a referral to case management services to assist her in exploring housing options, daycare options, and financial assistance programs that may be available for her. She feels the extra support from working with a case manager will be helpful for her sobriety as well. Frieda also agrees to attend three self-help meetings per week to build informal supports (gaining support and observing skills from peers).

The counselor is aware of an agency that offers case management services which will assist Frieda in exploring housing options, access to available daycare, and connect Frieda with financial assistance programs. The case manager will be in charge of these additional referrals. Frieda agrees to this referral and the counselor has Frieda sign a release of information so the counselor may speak to the case management agency. The counselor will collaborate with the assigned case manager throughout her time as Freida´s counselor.

▶ TREATMENT PLAN REVIEWS

The counselor collaborates with the client in reviewing and modifying the treatment plan based on an assessment of progress at regular intervals. Regular intervals are typically presumed to be every 90 days in an outpatient setting or sooner as need be to reflect the completion of objectives. Goals for clients in detoxification or hospitalization services are reviewed daily. Goals in residential programs are typically reviewed weekly, whereas goals in intensive outpatient programs are usually reviewed every 14 days. However, goals can and should be reviewed and updated in a frequency that reflects the client's progress.

When reviewing a treatment plan, the counselor and the client review the progress on each objective as well as the overall goal. If the objectives and goals are met, the achievement is encouraged and celebrated and the goal is retired and a new goal is developed. If the goal is not met, the counselor and the client reflect on the challenges in achieving the objectives and meeting the goal. The counselor explores with the client what went well and what progress was made, as well as the barriers that were encountered. The counselor reflects on their knowledge of the stages of change as well as ZPD. Questions a counselor considers include:

- Were the objectives achievable based on the client's skill level and what the client learned while in counseling?
- Did the client have sufficient support and guidance to advance toward the goal?
- Were there other events that interrupted the achievement of the goal that were within or not within the control of the client?
- Were the goal and objectives appropriate based on the client's stage of change?
- Does the client want to continue to pursue this goal? If so, what additional supports do they need to be successful?

As a part of the treatment plan review, new goals and objectives are developed as appropriate based on stage of change and the client's current skill and support level. The entire process is repeated until the client has met their goals, is ready to transition out of formal services, and is able to continue to utilize informal supports and services.

Unfolding Case Study

After 60 days, Frieda and the counselor reviewed her treatment plan. Frieda reported she did talk to her sister and her sister was receptive to not drinking in the home. Frieda did attend self-help meetings and has developed several new acquaintances as well as met an older woman in her church group who agreed to serve as her mentor. This woman is teaching Frieda about how to better manage her money as well as assisting in parenting ideas and parenting support when Frieda becomes frustrated. She has also accompanied Frieda to a school meeting to help Frieda understand what was said. Frieda felt this was very helpful as she did not do well in school and talking to a teacher is very intimidating for her. Frieda has been participating in case management services and has identified several options for housing for her and her children if this becomes necessary. She has also been able to access food assistance and learned how to use the city bus to help her get around more easily.

Frieda reports her sister continued drinking in the house twice a week the first month but only twice in the past 30 days. Frieda drank with her sister and then got high four times the first month and drank one night in the past 30 days but did not get high. She was able to go to her room and did not engage with her sister the second night her sister drank. When asked how she was successful in making this change, Frieda reported she was able to use new skills for coping with cravings and felt less guilty the next day when she talked to her sister about how much the drinking hurt her as she did not respect Frieda's request. Frieda is choosing to continue to live with her sister and keep working on their relationship and agreement regarding no alcohol in the house. Frieda has also asked her sister to come to a counseling session with her, but her sister has not committed yet.

New goals were created focusing on stabilization in her recovery. Frieda wants to work with her case manager to find a new job with better hours and better pay as well as work on the feelings of shame her children have because of her drug and alcohol use. She is recognizing that she is spending too much money on toys for her kids, buying them whatever they ask as she feels she needs to make up for being absent when she was getting high. Frieda is also noticing increased memories of her past experiences interfering with her ability to trust others and make friends.

The case example of Frieda illustrates that while the initial goal wasn't specifically related to her sobriety, being able to stay in her home was a significant need that ultimately addressed her substance use. The counselor and Frieda developed objectives related to the factors that contributed to Frieda's substance use. Frieda already was committed to becoming sober, she just was not sure how to do it. Think all the way back to Frieda's initial assessment review: If the counselor had insisted on Frieda's going to residential treatment, she likely would have dropped out of treatment. Instead, Frieda and the counselor were able to develop a support plan that met her needs, created a goal that was important to Frieda, and as a result Frieda was able to develop a support and recovery program within her home community. During the treatment plan review process, the counselor and Frieda reviewed her goal and objectives. The counselor focused on Frieda's successes of talking to her sister, developing informal supports, and reducing her substance use. The counselor did not focus on the five times Frieda did use a substance aside from the problem solving that had already occurred in the counseling sessions. Frieda is actively taking steps and making modifications to her plan (action stage of change), therefore the counselor continues to support Frieda in her plan.

Unfolding Case Study

We now turn our attention back to Jim. Jim has arrived for the second session and the counselor and Jim are ready to review the results of the assessment and develop his treatment plan.

Jim returned to the office to review the results of his assessment. He was encouraged to invite his wife to attend this session. Jim declined, fearing his wife may respond negatively to the information presented. He is not ready to reveal to her all the information he shared during the assessment.

The counselor shared the assessment results with Jim. Jim was surprised the counselor was concerned about his gambling and pornography use. He does not see these as a problem as no one has "really" complained about them to him. He agreed that he is uncomfortable in social settings and uses alcohol to feel more "comfortable" interacting with others. He is willing to monitor this feeling. He does agree that he needs to do something about his alcohol use so that he does not lose his job. He also indicates that between the assessment and this session, his boss gave him a written warning and created a performance-improvement plan Jim must follow. One of the expectations was for Jim to continue in counseling. Jim was asked if he wanted to continue with counseling based on the assessment recommendation. He indicates that he does want to continue.

The counselor and Jim begin identifying and ranking problems as well as formulating agreed-upon goals. Jim identifies keeping his job and marriage as his top two concerns and the threat of the loss of either of them as his number one problem. From this, he states his goal is:

"I don't want my drinking to cause me problems."

The counselor asks Jim what this means to him and how he will know if he is successful in this goal, as well as his timeframe to meet this goal. These questions are important so Jim and the counselor can identify the desired outcome for the goal. Jim states, "I don't want my drinking to cause me problems. I will know I am successful if for the next 3 months, my wife and boss don't complain about my drinking."

The counselor recognizes that Jim's stated goal is not to be alcohol free (abstinent) but rather to not have his wife or boss complain. In his mind, their complaining is the problem. He desires to find a way to drink and not have anyone complain about his drinking.

The counselor makes a mental note of this and continues to work with Jim by asking him to identify the steps (objectives) he sees he will need to take to meet this goal. Jim replies that he is unsure and hopes the counselor can help him with this. The counselor, recognizing that Jim is in the early part of the contemplation stage of change and is going in between the developmental stages of pretreatment and stabilization, suggests to Jim objectives (steps) that align with these stages. The tasks for Jim in these stages are to increase both the awareness of the need for change and the concern about the current pattern of behavior. The tasks for the counselor are to establish rapport, ask permission and build trust, understand reward for current behavior, and review negative effects of continued substance use.

The counselor refers to the catalysts of change and identifies consciousness-raising activities that create increased emotional arousal which fit within the contemplation stage of change and the developmental stage. The counselor will utilize environmental reevaluation which will help Jim assess the pros and cons of his substance use. The counselor recognizes that Jim is not ready to commit to abstaining from alcohol and that Jim is unsure if his alcohol use is the actual problem. Further, the counselor recognizes that in order to keep Jim in his ZPD, the counselor needs to guide Jim to engage in tasks related to discovery. Jim is not ready to take action and does not yet have the ability to intervene consistently when he encounters cues/triggers to drink. The counselor will teach Jim additional skills and help him build social supports as a part of engaging in scaffolding as Jim begins to experiment with making thinking and behavior changes.

As the counselor and Jim discuss treatment objectives, they agree upon the following initial treatment plan. Due to Jim's ambivalence, one treatment goal with four objectives was chosen to avoid overwhelming Jim in the early stages of his treatment.

Goal: "I don't want my drinking to cause me problems. I will know I am successful if for the next 3 months, my wife and boss don't complain about my drinking."

Objective 1: Jim will track each time he has the desire to or does use alcohol.

Objective 2: Jim will complete a written history of his alcohol use to better understand the impact of and what has sustained his alcohol use.

Objective 3: Jim will evaluate the pros and cons of continued alcohol use and the effect on his marriage, employment, and other relationships.

Objective 4: Jim will communicate with his wife regarding her feelings about his alcohol use.

Intervention 1: Individual counseling three to four times per month.

Intervention 2: Couples counseling as needed.

The counselor discusses each of the objectives with Jim. Jim agrees with this plan and agrees to attend counseling on a weekly basis. He is willing to complete his alcohol use history, track his desire for alcohol, and the outcome of the desire weekly. He agrees to include his gambling behavior in this history, but reiterates he does not think it is a problem.

Now that Jim's treatment plan is complete, the next step for the counselor is to engage in the counseling process, intentionally utilizing counseling theories and techniques.

▶ KEY POINTS

- The core function of treatment planning takes place after the assessment.
- During treatment planning, the counselor must recognize when to utilize and how to facilitate referrals for clients; collaborate with a multidisciplinary team to determine and provide care; develop a treatment plan that sets goals, objectives, strategies, and interventions; and identify available resources to meet client needs.
- Ambivalence is an expected part of any change process. Counselors who understand and know how to embrace ambivalence will have greater engagement and success with their clients.
- Treatment planning begins with the client and the counselor collaborating to prioritize the problems or challenges that need to be addressed and identifying the strengths a client possesses to aid in their recovery.
- There are multiple pathways to recovery including harm reduction and abstinence-based programs.
- Counselors utilize their knowledge of the stages of change and the use of motivational interviewing to engage clients where they are in the change process.
- It is essential that the counselor is aware of and considers the outside influences in the client's life. The client's informal interactions will either reinforce new skill development or hinder the new goal-directed skill development. Counselors utilize the skill of scaffolding to build skill and support to assist the client in reaching their goals.
- Once the client and the counselor have prioritized the problem list, goals can be developed. Goal development in treatment planning typically has two main targets. The first is a reduction of impairment caused by the symptoms of the diagnosis. The second is an improvement of the client's functioning and satisfaction with life. The ideal outcome of treatment is the achievement of both goals.
- Counselors utilize the skills of referral and case management to facilitate and collaborate with these other services.

▶ REFERENCES

DiClemente, C. C. (2018). *Addiction and change: How addictions develop and addicted people recover* (2nd ed.). Guilford Publications.

Gorski, T., & Miller, M. (1986). *Staying sober: A guide for relapse prevention.* Herald House/Independence Press.

Herdman, J. W. (2021). *Global criteria: The 12 core functions of the substance abuse counselor* (8th ed.).

International Certification and Reciprocity Consortium. (2022). *Candidate guide for the IC&RC alcohol and drug counselor examination.* https://internationalcredentialing.org/wp-content/uploads/2024/01/ADC-Candidate-Guide-09.2022_Final-Edit_10.31.22.pdf

Klott, J., & Jongsma, A. E. (2015). *The co-occurring disorders treatment planner, with DSM-5 updates.* Wiley.

Prochaska, J. O., & DiClemente, C. C. (1994). *The transtheoretical approach: Crossing traditional boundaries of therapy.* R. E. Krieger.

Substance Abuse and Mental Health Services Administration. (2019). *Enhancing motivation for change in substance use disorder treatment: Treatment improvement protocol (TIP) Series No. 35. SAMHSA Publication No. PEP19-02-01-003.* Substance Abuse and Mental Health Services Administration.

Substance Abuse and Mental Health Services Administration. (2023, May 6). *Developing goals and measurable objectives.* https://www.samhsa.gov/grants/how-to-apply/writing-completing-application/goals-measurable-objectives

U.S. Department of Health and Human Services, & Office of the Surgeon General. (2016, November). *Facing addiction in America: The Surgeon General's Report on alcohol, drugs, and health.* https://www.ncbi.nlm.nih.gov/books/NBK424857

Vygotsky, L. S. (1978). *Mind in society: The development of higher psychological processes.* Harvard University Press.

⬤ CASE STUDY 6.1

Patrice completed a substance use assessment last week. Her diagnosis is opioid use disorder-mild, cannabis use disorder-mild, and alcohol use disorder-moderate. The recommendation of the evaluation is to attend individual outpatient counseling once per week and group counseling once per week. Patrice arrives today to begin counseling. When Patrice arrives, the counselor presents Patrice with her treatment plan and tells her the primary goal is for her to be abstinent from all substances. To do this she is going to stop going to see her mom and sister as they both drink, attend the local Catholic church weekly because she mentioned she used to attend there, track times she thinks about drinking, and bring her husband with her to the next session so he can hear about the things she needs to change in her life.

Patrice objects to this plan, stating that she is uncertain if she even wants to stop drinking or stop smoking marijuana and she absolutely knows that she does not want to go back to the Catholic church. She also does not want to bring her husband to session as he has a history of being physically abusive to her. She indicates that she only came to counseling because her husband told her she has a substance use problem, and he would not stop bothering her until she did. She confides that she would really like to leave her husband but knows he would try to hurt her if he found out she wanted to leave him.

1. What is Patrice's current stage of change in regard to her substance use?
   A) Contemplation
   B) Preparation
   C) Precontemplation
   D) Action

2. What is an appropriate referral the counselor could make if Patrice consents to the referral?
   A) A spiritual advisor to help her with her concerns about the Catholic church
   B) A marriage counselor to help Patrice and her husband improve their communication
   C) A hotline for women experiencing intimate partner violence
   D) A local Alcoholics Anonymous (AA) meeting to help her find a sponsor

3. What did the counselor do wrong in the treatment planning process?
   A) The counselor did not review the assessment results with Patrice
   B) The counselor did not include Patrice in developing the treatment plan
   C) The counselor did not consider Patrice's current stage of change
   D) All of the above

(*See answers on the next page.*)

CASE STUDY 6.1 ANSWERS

1. C) Precontemplation
Patrice indicated that she is not sure she wants to stop using substances. Given this statement she is in the precontemplative stage or is not currently considering change.

2. C) A hotline for women experiencing intimate partner violence
Patrice stated that she is considering leaving her marriage and is worried about her safety if she attempts to do so. Patrice was clear she is not interested in pursuing returning to the Catholic church, she is not seeking marriage counseling, and is not asking for help with sobriety right now.

3. D) All of the above
The first task is for the counselor to review the assessment results with Patrice. The counselor then should have included Patrice in the treatment planning process. Finally, the counselor must consider Patrice's stage of change when considering recommendations and in the creation of the treatment plan. Unfortunately, the counselor did not do any of these.

KNOWLEDGE CHECK: CHAPTER 6

1. In which stage of change does an individual have no intention to quit substance use and may be unaware of the negative consequences?
   A) Precontemplation
   B) Contemplation
   C) Preparation
   D) Action

2. During which stage of change does an individual begin to recognize the need to change, but may still be ambivalent about taking action?
   A) Contemplation
   B) Preparation
   C) Maintenance
   D) Relapse

3. What is the primary focus of the preparation stage in the stages of change model for substance use counseling?
   A) Developing coping strategies
   B) Taking concrete steps toward change
   C) Maintaining change over the long term
   D) Building awareness of the issue

4. Which stage of change involves actively modifying behaviors, thoughts, and environment to overcome substance use?
   A) Action
   B) Contemplation
   C) Maintenance
   D) Precontemplation

5. What is the key focus of the maintenance stage in substance use counseling?
   A) Building awareness of the issue
   B) Taking concrete steps toward change
   C) Preventing relapse and consolidating gains
   D) Assessing readiness for change

6. What is the term for the return to substance use after a period of abstinence or successful behavior change?
   A) Recovery
   B) Lapse
   C) Relapse
   D) Regression

7. During which stage of change are individuals actively exploring and weighing the pros and cons of substance use behavior change?
   A) Precontemplation
   B) Contemplation
   C) Preparation
   D) Action

8. How does the zone of proximal development (ZPD) relate to treatment planning?
   A) Encourages a one-size-fits-all treatment planning approach
   B) Highlights the importance of uniform curriculum for all clients
   C) Supports tailoring treatment to meet individual clients' needs
   D) Is irrelevant to the concept of treatment planning

(See answers on the next page.)

1. A) Precontemplation

Precontemplation is the stage where individuals are not considering changing their behavior and may lack awareness of the need for change. Contemplation is the stage characterized by an awareness of the problem and the consideration of change, but no commitment to action has occurred. In the preparation stage, individuals start taking specific actions to address their substance use, such as setting a quit date or seeking support. The action stage is where individuals are engaged in efforts to modify their behavior and environment to overcome substance use.

2. A) Contemplation

Contemplation is the stage characterized by an awareness of the problem and the consideration of change, but no commitment to action has occurred. Precontemplation is the stage where individuals are not considering changing their behavior and may lack awareness of the need for change. In the preparation stage, individuals start taking specific actions to address their substance use, such as setting a quit date or seeking support. The action stage is where individuals are engaged in efforts to modify their behavior and environment to overcome substance use.

3. B) Taking concrete steps toward change

In the preparation stage, individuals start taking specific actions to address their substance use, such as setting a quit date or seeking support. Precontemplation is the stage where individuals are not considering changing their behavior and may lack awareness of the need for change. Contemplation is the stage characterized by an awareness of the problem and the consideration of change, but no commitment to action has occurred. The action stage is where individuals are engaged in efforts to modify their behavior and environment to overcome substance use.

4. A) Action

The action stage is where individuals are engaged in efforts to modify their behavior and environment to overcome substance use. Maintenance involves efforts to prevent relapse and consolidate the gains made during the action stage. Precontemplation is the stage where individuals are not considering changing their behavior and may lack awareness of the need for change. Contemplation is the stage characterized by an awareness of the problem and the consideration of change, but no commitment to action has occurred.

5. C) Preventing relapse and consolidating gains

Maintenance involves efforts to prevent relapse and consolidate the gains made during the action stage. The focus of the action plan is taking concrete steps toward change. The counselor seeks to build awareness of the issue during the precontemplation stage. The counselor assesses readiness for change during the contemplation stage.

6. C) Relapse

Relapse refers to the return to substance use after a period of abstinence or successful behavior change.

7. B) Contemplation

Contemplation involves the consideration of the pros and cons of behavior change. In the precontemplation stage, the client is not considering changing their behavior and may lack awareness of the need for change. In the preparation stage, individuals start taking specific actions to address their substance use, such as setting a quit date or seeking support. The action stage is where individuals are engaged in efforts to modify their behavior and environment to overcome substance use.

8. C) Supports tailoring treatment to meet individual clients' needs

The ZPD emphasizes the need for personalized and targeted treatment to meet each client's specific developmental level.

9. In Vygotsky's theory, what is the significance of social interaction within the zone of proximal development (ZPD)?
   A) Social interaction has no impact on learning within the ZPD
   B) Social interaction is necessary for learning within the ZPD, as it provides support and guidance
   C) Social interaction hinders the learning process
   D) Social interaction is only relevant outside the ZPD

10. What distinguishes the zone of proximal development (ZPD) from the concept of the client's comfort zone?
    A) ZPD includes tasks that are too easy for the client
    B) The comfort zone is the same as the ZPD
    C) ZPD involves tasks that are challenging but achievable with support
    D) Comfort zone tasks are always beyond the client's capabilities

11. What is the significance of addressing lifestyle imbalances as a part of treatment planning?
    A) It is unnecessary for sustained recovery
    B) It contributes to stabilization and reduces relapse risk
    C) It only impacts the advanced stages of recovery
    D) It is only relevant for individuals with co-occurring disorders

12. How does the concept of specificity contribute to the effectiveness of specific, measurable, achievable, relevant, and time-bound (SMART) goals in substance use counseling?
    A) Makes goals more abstract and open-ended
    B) Helps avoid accountability
    C) Provides clarity and focus on what needs to be achieved
    D) Increases the likelihood of relapse

13. What is the primary purpose of the "R" in SMART goals in substance use counseling?
    A) To ensure the goal is realistic and achievable for the client
    B) To ensure the goal is relevant to the client's desires and values
    C) To ensure the goal is regularly reviewed
    D) To ensure the goal can be reliably measured.

14. How does the "A" in SMART goals contribute to goal achievement in substance use counseling?
    A) Making goals arbitrary and capricious
    B) Emphasizing adaptability
    C) Ensuring accountability and action-oriented objectives
    D) Promoting ambiguity in goal setting

15. How does the concept of measurability enhance the effectiveness of SMART goals in substance use counseling?
    A) Makes goals more abstract and subjective
    B) Allows for clear tracking and evaluation of progress
    C) Decreases the need for accountability
    D) Reduces the relevance of goals

16. What is the primary responsibility of a substance use counselor in the referral process?
    A) Create a comprehensive treatment plan
    B) Transfer responsibility to other professionals
    C) Link clients with appropriate resources and services
    D) Avoid direct involvement with clients

17. How does the case management function contribute to the continuity of care in substance use counseling?
    A) Reducing the cost of counseling to clients
    B) Limiting collaboration with other professionals
    C) Coordinating and overseeing the various aspects of a client's treatment
    D) Avoiding involvement in clients' lives outside of counseling sessions

(See answers on the next page.)

9. B) Social interaction is necessary for learning within the ZPD, as it provides support and guidance
Vygotsky emphasized the role of social interaction, where a more knowledgeable person guides the learner through tasks within the ZPD.

10. C) ZPD involves tasks that are challenging but achievable with support
The ZPD includes tasks that are just beyond the client's current abilities but can be accomplished with assistance, distinguishing it from the comfort zone.

11. B) It contributes to stabilization and reduces relapse risk
Addressing lifestyle imbalances is important for stabilizing abstinence and reduces relapse risk throughout the recovery process.

12. C) Provides clarity and focus on what needs to be achieved
Specificity in SMART goals ensures that objectives are clearly defined, reducing ambiguity and enhancing focus on the desired outcomes.

13. B) To ensure the goal is relevant to the client's desires and values
The "R" in SMART goals emphasizes the importance of ensuring that goals are relevant and aligned with the individual's overall treatment plan and recovery objectives.

14. C) Ensuring accountability and action-oriented objectives
The "A" in SMART goals emphasizes that objectives should be achievable and action-oriented, contributing to accountability and progress.

15. B) Allows for clear tracking and evaluation of progress
Measurability ensures that goals are quantifiable, allowing for clear tracking, evaluation, and adjustment of objectives based on progress.

16. C) Link clients with appropriate resources and services
The referral function aims to connect clients with services that address their specific needs and contribute to their overall well-being.

17. C) Coordinating and overseeing the various aspects of a client's treatment
Case management ensures that different elements of a client's treatment plan are coordinated, promoting continuity of care and comprehensive support.

18. What role does cultural competence play in the referral and case management core functions of substance use counseling?
    A) Is not important in referral or case management
    B) Limits collaboration with diverse professionals
    C) Enhances the ability to address the unique needs of diverse clients
    D) Reduces the options available to meet client's needs

19. How does confidentiality play a role in the referral and case management core functions in substance use counseling?
    A) Because it is for referral, sensitive information can be disclosed without consent of the client
    B) By fostering fear of what can be shared with other professionals
    C) By fostering trust and ensuring the protection of client information
    D) Reduces communication with external service providers

20. How does the contemplation stage differ from the precontemplation stage in stage-based treatment planning?
    A) Clients in contemplation are actively seeking change
    B) Clients in contemplation are unaware of the need for change
    C) Clients in contemplation are considering the possibility of change
    D) Clients in contemplation are fully committed to change

21. How does stage-based treatment planning address the unique needs of clients in different stages of change?
    A) By customizing interventions to meet the specific needs of clients in each stage
    B) By overlooking individual differences
    C) By offering a standardized treatment approach
    D) By avoiding consideration of client readiness for change so everyone is treated equally

22. How does stage-based treatment planning address the potential challenges of resistance and ambivalence in clients?
    A) By ignoring resistance and ambivalence to maintain a positive therapeutic alliance
    B) By emphasizing the counselor's authority over the client's concerns
    C) By avoiding discussions about client readiness for change
    D) By acknowledging and addressing resistance and ambivalence as normal stages in the change process

---

Francesca is a 16-year-old female. She is under supervision of juvenile probation for possession of a controlled substance. She was referred to counseling after a substance use evaluation recommended individual and family counseling. Francesca was caught on school grounds with a marijuana vape and a bottle containing 22 amphetamine/dextroamphetamine (Adderall) pills. The pills were prescribed to Francesca's brother. Francesca's mom, Katrina, reports Francesca has been more "moody and irritable" lately and has been sneaking out of the house at night. Katrina feels Francesca's behavior changed after her father moved out of the house 3 months ago. Francesca admits she was selling her brother's pills at school. After some discussion, she reported she was selling the pills to help pay for food for her and her brother as she heard her mom talking on the phone about how she cannot pay the bills this month. Francesca also overheard the landlord telling her mom that if she did not pay the rent soon, he will evict them and they will have to move out next month.

Katrina is not sure what to do. She does not make enough money to pay the bills unless she gets a second job, but if she gets a second job, she will not be home in the morning to get the kids to school and will have to rely on Francesca to get her brother ready and walk him to school. Francesca will then be late to school herself if she does this. She also knows she needs to be home to support and supervise Francesca.

---

23. Who are considered members of Francesca's multidisciplinary team?
    A) The counselor and Francesca
    B) The counselor, the probation officer, and Francesca's mom
    C) Francesca's mom, Francesca, and the probation officer
    D) The counselor, the probation officer, Francesca's mom, and Francesca

(*See answers on the next page.*)

18. C) Enhances the ability to address the unique needs of diverse clients
Cultural competence is crucial in understanding and addressing the unique needs of diverse clients in both referral and case management.

19. C) By fostering trust and ensuring the protection of client information
Maintaining confidentiality fosters trust and ensures the protection of client information, supporting effective collaboration in both referral and case management.

20. C) Clients in contemplation are considering the possibility of change
In the contemplation stage, clients are aware of the need for change and are actively considering the possibility of making changes in their behavior.

21. A) By customizing interventions to meet the specific needs of clients in each stage
Stage-based treatment planning customizes interventions to address the specific needs and readiness for change of clients in different stages.

22. D) By acknowledging and addressing resistance and ambivalence as normal stages in the change process
Stage-based treatment planning recognizes resistance and ambivalence as natural stages, allowing counselors to address these challenges as part of the change process.

23. D) The counselor, the probation officer, Francesca's mom, and Francesca
All individuals working with Francesca are members of the team. As the client, Francesca is a key member of the team. A school representative will be included as a team member if the family consents to this.

24. Based on the family's needs, what should be the first point of focus for the treatment plan?
    A) Making contact with Francesca's dad so he can attend family counseling
    B) Telling the school Francesca has been selling pills so they can watch her more closely and intervene with the students who were buying the pills
    C) Connecting the family with resources for housing and financial support
    D) Getting Katrina drug test kits so she can make sure Francesca is not using marijuana or other drugs

25. Which of the following is correct regarding referral and case management for Francesca?
    A) The counselor must have Katrina complete and sign a release of information before providing information to the family about housing assistance
    B) The counselor must have Katrina complete and sign a release of information before talking to the school about Francesca
    C) The counselor must call the police because Francesca admitted she was selling pills at school
    D) None of the above

(See answers on the next page.)

24. C) Connecting the family with resources for housing and financial support

While all aspects mentioned are important to address, the treatment plan must prioritize the immediate needs of the family. A stable foundation is essential to addressing other concerns with Francesca's behavior. Connecting the family with resources and financial support should be the counselor's first priority.

25. B) The counselor must have Katrina complete and sign a release of information before talking to the school about Francesca

Francesca and her mom must consent to the communication before the counselor talks to the school. The counselor does not need a signed release of information to provide information regarding housing assistance or other community resources. Confidentiality laws prevent the counselor from informing the police about Francesca's behavior of selling pills at school.

Counseling With the Client

Christine Tina Chasek

▶ INTRODUCTION

An addiction counselor must attend to many different things in the service of helping others, but no task is more important than counseling. In the addiction counseling performance domains, Domain 3 contains the critical tasks of counseling and evidence-based treatment. This chapter covers the global criteria in the counseling core function which includes individual, group, family, and significant other counseling along with evidence-based treatment. We cover major counseling theories and techniques along with the impact of trauma on the client and counselor. Pathways of recovery, co-occurring disorders (CODs), and considerations for special populations are also addressed. Crisis intervention and client education as core functions are highlighted with the global criteria for each core function.

Tips From the Field

The 12 core functions are critical to know and understand to pass the alcohol and drug counselor (ADC) exam. Equally important are the global criteria, or tasks, under each core function. It is helpful to think of the global criteria as the steps needed when working with clients in that core function area.

▶ COUNSELING WITH THE CLIENT

The 2022 International Certification and Reciprocity Consortium (IC&RC) ADC job analysis identified four performance domains for an ADC with several tasks included in each domain (see Chapter 1, "Introduction to Addiction Counseling and the Alcohol and Drug Counselor" for the four domains and the related knowledge, skills, and tasks; IC&RC, 2022). Domain 3 covers the task of evidence-based treatment, counseling, and referral and includes the highest percentage of questions on the ADC exam. The knowledge and skills needed for this domain are included in the counseling, crisis intervention, and client education core function (Herdman, 2021). The areas covered in this chapter are important to focus on when studying for the exam.

▶ COUNSELING CORE FUNCTION AND GLOBAL CRITERIA

The **counseling core function** is defined as the utilization of special skills to assist individuals, families, or groups in achieving objectives through exploration of a problem and its ramifications; examination of attitudes and feelings; consideration of alternative solutions; and decision-making (Herdman, 2021). The global criteria in the counseling core function contain the theories and techniques used in the counseling process as well as tools for interacting with clients in a therapeutic setting.

Counseling is a relationship between the counselor and the client (or client system) that helps the client identify and use resources to resolve the issues that brought them into counseling. Counseling with individuals is an intensive one-on-one personal process based in the counselor's ability to listen and help the client clarify and resolve the presenting issues. Counseling with groups and loved ones requires special knowledge about group interactions and family dynamics (Box 7.1; Herdman, 2021).

The Twelve Steps are reprinted with permission of Alcoholics Anonymous World Services, Inc. ("A.A.W.S."). Permission to reprint the Twelve Steps does not mean that A.A.W.S. has reviewed or approved the contents of this publication, or that A.A. necessarily agrees with the views expressed herein. A.A. is a program of recovery from alcoholism only - use of the Twelve Steps in connection with programs and activities which are patterned after A.A., but which address other problems, or in any other non-A.A. context, does not imply otherwise.

Box 7.1 Core Function 6: Counseling: Individual, Group and Significant Others

Definition: The utilization of special skills to assist individuals, families, or groups in achieving objectives through exploration of a problem and its ramifications; examination of attitudes and feelings; consideration of alternative solutions; and decision-making.

Global Criteria:
21. Select the counseling **theories** that apply.
22. Apply **techniques** to assist the client, group, and/or family in exploring problems and ramifications.
23. Apply **techniques** to assist the client, group, and/or family in examining the client's **behavior, attitudes, and/or feelings** if appropriate in the treatment setting.
24. **Individualize** counseling in accordance with cultural, gender, and lifestyle **differences**.
25. **Interact** with the client in an appropriate **therapeutic** manner.
26. Elicit **solutions** and decisions from the **client**.
27. **Implement** the treatment plan.

▶ COUNSELING THEORIES AND EVIDENCE-BASED TREATMENTS

An addiction counselor must be aware of many counseling theories that encompass and inform their work. This section covers the major counseling theories in the addiction counseling field that are commonly used by counselors to provide evidence-based treatment. Each theory is summarized and reviewed, including identifying the major theorist, an overview of the theory, key concepts of the theory, therapeutic goals, and treatment techniques.

Before embarking on a review of the theories, it is important to know that all client work begins and ends with the therapeutic relationship. Each theory covered in this section has at its core the assumption that a good working therapeutic alliance is a necessary condition for a successful outcome. The **therapeutic relationship** can be defined as the way the counselor and the client connect, engage, and work together toward treatment goals and tasks. A good therapeutic relationship consists of three essential qualities: (1) an emotional bond of trust, caring, and respect; (2) agreement on the goals of therapy; and (3) collaboration on the work or tasks of treatment (Bordin, 1979). Engaging with the client and developing a good therapeutic relationship is the connecting factor across all the counseling theories—and for good reason. A good therapeutic relationship is one of the strongest predictors of successful treatment regardless of the presenting issue or the therapy approach used (Ardito & Rabellino, 2011; Horvath, 2001; Miller & Moyers, 2015; Norcross & Lambert, 2019; Stubbe, 2018).

▶ PSYCHODYNAMIC APPROACHES

Psychodynamic approaches to counseling include psychoanalytic theory, Adlerian therapy, and **transactional analysis (TA)** (Table 7.1).

PSYCHOANALYTIC THEORY

The earliest and most recognized theorist in the field of psychology is Sigmund Freud. Freud's views and psychoanalytic theory make up the foundation of psychodynamic approaches that include theories developed by Carl Jung and Erik Erickson (Corey, 2023). Psychoanalytic theory continues to influence counseling practice today.

Psychoanalytic theory is a model of deterministic personality development that is driven by biological and instinctual drives as well as unconscious motivations. Freud theorized that humans are driven by life and death instincts that serve the purpose of survival, personal growth, and development. This results in three primary personality structures that are set in early childhood: The **id, ego,** and **superego.**

- ■ **Id:** The unconscious drives and impulses that are biologically determined. Operates out of the pleasure principle. The goal is instant gratification, regardless of the consequences.

Table 7.1 Summary of Psychodynamic Approaches

Psychodynamic Approaches	Key Figures	Major Focus	Key Concepts	Techniques
Psychoanalytic therapy	• Sigmund Freud • Carl Jung • Erik Erikson	• Personality theory • Philosophy of human nature • Self-psychology • Social and cultural factors	• Biological and instinctual drives • Unconscious motivation • Id, ego, superego • Defense mechanisms • Transference/countertransference • Object relations	• Analytic insight • Free association • Interpretation • Dream analysis • Analysis of transference
Adlerian therapy	• Alfred Adler • Rudolf Dreikurs	• Social relatedness • Consciousness drives behavior • Individual psychology • Strive for meaning and success • Systems approach	• Choice • Responsibility • Inferiority feelings • Reeducate individuals and reshape society • Values, beliefs, goals	• Birth order determination • Life tasks analysis • "The Question" • Reorientation reeducation
TA	• Eric Bern • Robert Goulding • Mary Goulding	• Personality theory • "Games" played to avoid intimacy • Rewriting early scripts through awareness • Antideterministic	• Parent, adult, child personality traits • Ego states • "Games" • Scripting • Injunctions • Counter injunctions • Autonomous choice	• Script analysis • Structural analysis • Sculpting • Redecisioning

TA, transactional analysis.

- **Ego:** Operates out of the reality principle and is a partially conscious system that organizes and mediates between the id and the superego.
- **Superego:** The conscience moral guide that internalizes the rules of society and caregivers and strives for perfection. Functions to inhibit the impulses of the id and to convince the ego to pursue moralistic goals rather than realistic ones.

To negotiate the conflict between the id and superego, the ego develops **defense mechanisms** (Table 7.2). The goal of therapy is to identify and understand the defense mechanisms to bring about change.

Freud theorized that there are levels of consciousness and the that key to understanding problems of personality and behavior lies in accessing the **unconscious** parts of the mind. The unconscious stores all experiences, memories, and repressed material built up over time to develop unhealthy behaviors and neurotic symptoms such as anxiety and depression.

A key task of therapy is to make the unconscious motives conscious and to strengthen the ego. This is done through numerous psychoanalytic techniques such as free association, interpretation of dreams, and analysis of **transference** and **countertransference** in the therapeutic relationship.

- **Transference:** A client views the counselor through the lens of past experiences, important caregivers, and significant others, and then "transfers" the feelings, attitudes, thoughts, and fantasies they have toward them onto the counselor.
- **Countertransference:** The counselor's response to the client based on their past.

In psychoanalysis, both transference and countertransference are substance for interpretation, insight, and "*working through*" problems. By uncovering the past and working through the transference, a person reconstructs their basic personality to moves toward health and well-being.

Because Freud's theory is heavily based in basic biological drives, he developed a stage model of psychosexual and psychosocial personality development from birth through adulthood. The psychosexual stages are chronological starting in infancy and carried through to adulthood.

Table 7.2 Defense Mechanisms

Defense Mechanism	Definition	Example
Repression	Forcing painful, threatening, or unacceptable thoughts and feelings from awareness into the unconscious mind	Client may show repressed feelings by behaving inappropriately, such as laughing when it is clearly not appropriate
Denial	Denying the existence of a threatening aspect of reality, operates at preconscious or conscious levels	A smoker denies that a chain-smoking habit will have any negative health consequences
Projection	Attributing to others one's own unacceptable desires and impulses	A partner having an affair accuses their significant other of being unfaithful
Reaction formation	Exchanging an unacceptable urge or feeling for a more acceptable one, often exaggerated	A person who drinks in secret but in public and to the family demands abstinence from alcohol
Displacement	Directing energy toward another object or person when the original object or person is not accessible	Coming home from a bad day at work angry with the boss but yelling at the kids or "kicking the dog"
Regression	Going back to an earlier phase of development when there were fewer demands	Children who are under stress in school go back to earlier behaviors such thumb sucking
Rationalization	Finding a satisfactory way for doing something unacceptable	Stealing clothes from a large luxury store because the store can afford the loss and the clothes are way overpriced anyway
Sublimation	Diverting sexual or aggressive energy into other things	Playing tackle football and hitting people as hard as possible to express anger toward a controlling parent
Introjection	Taking in and accepting the values and standards of others; can be positive or negative	Accepting parental values (positive) or identifying with an abuser and accepting the abuse (negative)
Intellectualization	Understanding a very difficult situation cognitively but not allowing any feelings about it	A person who is sexually abused explains, while not expressing any emotion, that the abuser was an alcoholic and couldn't help what they did
Compensation	Masking perceived weakness or developing positive traits to make up for limitations; can be positive or negative	Hiding feelings of inferiority, that is, people with low self-esteem talking about themselves all the time

- **Stage 1: Oral stage:** Birth to 18 months. Based on trust and the ability (or inability) to trust others and oneself through the feeding and care of the infant.
- **Stage 2: Anal stage:** Ages 1 to 3. The child begins to form autonomy and independence through controlling bodily functions. Parental discipline patterns and attitudes play a significant part of personality development during this stage.
- **Stage 3: Phallic stage:** Ages 3 to 6. The child's basic conflict centers on the unconscious incestuous desires the child has for the parent which is suppressed. The striving for the love and approval of the opposite sex parent is described as the *Electra complex* for cisgender females and the *Oedipus complex* for the cisgender males.

Another psychoanalytic theorist, Erik Erikson, expanded the psychoanalytic personality theory by developing psychosocial stages of development that extend from childhood into adulthood. Psychosocial stages refer to the psychological and social tasks that individuals must master to develop and grow (Table 7.3). According to Erickson's developmental theory, growth occurs by successfully resolving the psychosocial **crisis** that happens at each psychosocial stage. The developmental crisis is defined as a turning point in life that requires establishing equilibrium between two crucial tasks. Successful resolution allows an individual to move toward growth while failing to resolve the conflict, which is seen as regression in development.

Table 7.3 Erikson Psychosocial Stages

Psychosocial Stage	Basic Conflict	Description
Infancy 0 to 1 year	Trust versus mistrust	Trusting that basic needs such as nourishment and affection will be met
Early childhood 1 to 3 years	Autonomy versus shame/doubt	Developing a sense of independence in tasks
Play age 3 to 6 years	Initiative versus guilt	Taking initiative on activities; guilt can develop when initiative is unsuccessful or boundaries are overstepped
School age 7 to 11 years	Industry versus inferiority	Developing self-confidence in abilities or a sense of inferiority
Adolescence 12 to 18 years	Identity versus confusion	Experimenting with and developing identity and roles
Early adulthood 12 to 29 years	Intimacy versus isolation	Establishing intimacy and healthy relationships with others
Middle age 30 to 64 years	Generativity versus stagnation	Contributing to society and family legacy
Old age 65+	Integrity versus despair	Assessing and making sense of life and meaningful contributions

Carl Jung was a contemporary and colleague of Freud, however, Jung ultimately developed his own theory of personality that was very different from the Freudian view. Jung described his theory and approach as **analytical psychology**, an elaborate explanation of human nature that combines ideas from history, mythology, anthropology, and religion. Jung abandoned the psychosexual stages of development and focused instead on an individual's midlife as an important time of development where the primary goal is achieving **individuation**, the harmonious integration between the conscious and unconscious aspects of personality. He also referred frequently to the **collective unconscious** as the deepest but least accessible parts of personality that included inherited parts of all human experiences labeled as **archetypes**. These common human experiences are the **persona** (a mask, or public face that we all wear to protect ourselves), the **anima** and **animus** (the biological and psychological aspects of gender), and the **shadow** (the dark side of feelings, thoughts, and actions). These archetypes are accessed through dream work, which is central to Jungian therapy.

ADLERIAN THERAPY

Alfred Adler developed a theory and system of therapy that broke with Freud's notion of biological and instinctual determinism. Adler believed that people were motivated by social relatedness rather than sexual urges and that behavior was purposeful and goal directed. At an early age, each person creates an approach to living built on choice, responsibility, and meaning that remains consistent throughout their life. His view of human nature was positive and his theory growth oriented. Key components of Adlerian therapy are lifestyle assessments addressing the three universal **life tasks**: (1) building friendships (social tasks), (2) establishing intimacy (love tasks), and (3) contributing to society (work tasks). Other key concepts in Adlerian theory are social connection, goal orientation, and private logic. Isolation, self-absorption, and other maladaptive responses to life are experienced by those who are only concerned with the self (Corey, 2023).

TRANSACTIONAL ANALYSIS

TA is both a theory of personality and an organized system of interactional therapy built on the philosophy that decisions are made on past premises even though those premises may no longer be valid. Eric Berne, the key figure in TA, stressed that people always have the potential for choice, change, and to move towards autonomy by becoming aware of past "scripts and transactions." Three ego states are continuously functioning in all interactions: The **parent, adult**, and **child**.

■ **Parent:** The collection of unquestioned messages received when growing up along with the values, rules, and judgments about self, others, and the world.

- **Adult:** The rational, reality- and present-oriented state that is objective and operates on data.
- **Child:** A collection of the thoughts, feelings, and behaviors that were experienced as a child.

When a person's ego states interact with the ego states of another person, this is a "transaction," which can be complementary or problematic. A series of interactions ending with a "negative payoff" is called a **game**. Counselors help clients become more autonomous by becoming aware of the games they play to make new decisions about their behavior and rewrite their life script (Corey, 2023).

▶ HUMANISTIC- AND RELATIONSHIP-ORIENTED APPROACHES

The humanistic- and relationship-oriented approaches (Table 7.4) emerged as the field was moving away from psychoanalysis and biological drives toward a humanistic psychology that emphasized human growth and potential. Maslow (1943) proposed a motivation theory of human development that organized human needs into a hierarchical structure with the most basic needs at the bottom and the more complex at the top. He postulated that humans could reach their full potential and become

Table 7.4 Humanistic and Relationship-Oriented Approaches of Counseling

Humanistic and Relationship-Oriented Approaches	Key Figures	Major Focus	Key Concepts	Techniques
Person-centered therapy	• Carl Rogers • Natalie Rogers	• Humanistic philosophy • Trust clients to move forward in a positive manner • Congruence of ideal self to Real self	• Congruence • Unconditional positive regard • Accurate empathic understanding • Actualizing tendency • Trust in the therapeutic process • Nondirective	• Reflection of feelings • Immediacy • Full therapist engagement with client • Relationship and rapport building
Existential therapy	• Victor Frankl • Rollo May • Irvin Yalom	• Philosophical approach • Way of thinking and an attitude about therapy • Morality, meaning, freedom, and responsibility • Reflection on life and meaning	• Choice, we are what we choose to be • Self-awareness • Existential tradition • Freedom and responsibility • Courage to be • Aloneness • Search for meaning • Awareness of death and nonbeing	• Increase self-awareness • Challenge clients to take responsibility • Move toward authenticity • Use of techniques from other theories
Gestalt therapy	• Fritz Perls • Linda Perls • Erving and Miriam Polster	• Integration of thinking, feeling, behaving • Wholeness • Antideterministic • Confrontation	• Here and now experiencing • Personal responsibility • Unfinished business • "Re-own" parts of self	• Empty chair technique • Internal dialogue • Future projection • Exaggeration exercise
Motivational enhancement therapy; motivational interviewing	• Bill Miller • Steven Rollnick	• Client centered humanistic approach • Semidirective • Collaboration with client • A way of being • Evoke motivation from the client	• Motivational interviewing spirit • Self-responsibility • Stages of change • Reduce ambivalence • Change talk • Sustain talk	• Express empathy • Roll with resistance • Develop discrepancy • Support self-efficacy • Change plan

"self-actualized" when lower basic needs were met in a sequential fashion up the hierarchy (Maslow, 1943; Figure 7.1). The approaches under the humanistic- and relationship-oriented self-growth models are described here in the counseling and evidence-based treatment domain.

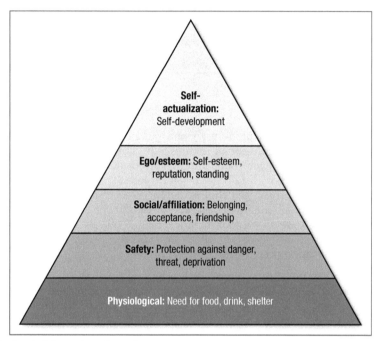

Figure 7.1 Maslow's hierarchy of needs.

Sources: Data from Maslow, A. H. (1943). A theory of human motivation. *Psychological Review, 50*(4), 370–396. https://doi.org/10.1037/h0054346; Maslow, A. H. (1962). *Toward a psychology of being.* Van Nostrand Company; Maslow, A. (1970). *Motivation and personality* (2nd ed.). Harper and Row; Maslow, A. H. (1971). *The farther reaches of human nature.* Viking; Maslow, A. H. (1987). *Motivation and personality* (3rd ed.). Pearson Education.

PERSON-CENTERED THERAPY

Carl Rogers had a profound impact on the counseling field when he introduced his person-centered humanistic approach to counseling (Corey, 2023). Person-centered therapy is nondirective and has at its base a belief that people are good and capable of natural healing if the right conditions are met in the counseling experience. Faith is placed in the client's ability to become self-aware throughout the process and move toward living a full and meaningful life by becoming the ideal self. This **actualizing tendency** is a core tenet of the theory and places the responsibility on the client for healing and growth, rejecting the idea that the counselor is the expert in the process. The counselor is responsible for the therapeutic relationship and the client is responsible for actualizing their potential.

Based heavily in the therapeutic relationship, Rogers maintained that three therapist attributes are necessary and sufficient to help a client change and grow.

- **Congruence/genuineness:** Be genuine and themselves in the therapeutic relationship which may include some self-disclosure and sharing.
- **Unconditional positive regard:** Show respect and acceptance of the client without judgement.
- **Accurate empathic understanding:** Be able to grasp and feel the world of the client from the client's point of view.

If these conditions are met the client will feel safe, understood, and able to grow to their full potential achieving a positive counseling outcome. Over the years, there has been much research that supports the importance of the therapeutic relationship and client-centered counseling, making the client-centered approach a key piece of many counseling therapies.

Tips From the Field

Creating mnemonics is a good strategy to use to remember counseling theory concepts. Mnemonics are shortcuts to recall details of complex topics. For example, to remember the core conditions of client-centered therapy developed by Carl Rogers, remember the word **CUE**:

- **C**ongruence/genuineness
- **U**nconditional positive regard
- **E**mpathy

EXISTENTIAL THERAPY

Existential therapy is less of a structured theory and more of a counseling approach focusing on themes such as mortality, meaning, freedom, responsibility, anxiety, and aloneness as they relate to the client's presenting concerns. Victor Frankl and Rollo May are the leading theorists connected to this therapeutic approach. The goal is to help clients explore their life, maximizing self-awareness and growth to become more aware of their choices and the freedom to fulfill their personal potential. Basic dimensions of the human condition include the capacity for self-awareness freedom, and responsibility; creating one's identity; establishing meaningful relationships with others; the search for meaning, purpose, values, and goals; anxiety as a condition of living; and an awareness of death and nonbeing. Two important concepts are:

- **Freedom:** Clients are responsible for their lives and actions and that failures are a call to action.
- **Existential anxiety:** The unavoidable result of being confronted with the givens of life, including death, freedom, choice, isolation, and meaninglessness. Man strives to make meaning in life and counseling is the perfect place to do the work.

GESTALT

Gestalt is a system of therapy that is processes-based, suggesting that individuals must be understood in the context of the environment and the things around them. Fritz Perls established this therapy and has had the biggest influence on its development across time. The view of the person is **antideterministic**; that is, people strive for wholeness and health and have the capability to make the choices and changes necessary to achieve that goal when it is brought into their awareness. The focus of therapy is on the **here and now**, living in the present and taking responsibility for the thoughts, feelings, and actions that occur. Counselors create a safe space in the therapy room that helps the client gain awareness of the moment-to-moment things they are experiencing and saying. The client does the work of making their own meaning and interpretations of the issues that arise while the therapist acts as a catalyst to speed up the process.

The client is expected to work on the **unfinished business** that is uncovered from the past that interferes with their current functioning. Other key concepts in Gestalt therapy include personal responsibility, avoiding experiencing, and the awareness of the now. Gestalt therapy is very experiential and includes techniques such as the exaggerating exercise and the empty chair technique (Corey, 2023).

MOTIVATIONAL INTERVIEWING

Motivational interviewing (MI) is built on the client-centered counseling principles of accurate empathy, unconditional positive regard, and genuineness. Miller and Rollnick (2023) developed MI to challenge the confrontational model of addiction counseling treatment that had evolved over time in the profession. MI relies on the **transtheoretical model of change** developed by Prochaska et al. (1994) that describes change as occurring in a person through a series of stages.

1. **Precontemplation:** The person is not considering a change and may in fact not even be aware that a need to change exists.
2. **Contemplation:** The person is aware a problem exists but is ambivalent about change. They have reasons both for and against change and often stay stuck between those two states.

3. **Preparation:** The person has determined that the advantages of change outweigh the consequences of staying the same, tipping the ambivalence scale toward change. Preparation includes making plans for change and starting the steps needed.
4. **Action:** The person chooses change strategies and pursue the change plan. Clients in the stage are active and engaged in the treatment process.
5. **Maintenance:** The person makes efforts to sustain the changes and to prevent slipping into previous behavior patterns. This is the long-term lifestyle change needed to maintain new behaviors.

The stages of change are not a linear process, but rather circular. Clients may go in and out of the motivation to change in a spiral-like pattern. The movement through change must be monitored and addressed as a client goes through treatment with the spiral moving upward through each step of the process. MI is built on this idea and is a nonconfrontational directive model of counseling that is designed to elicit the client's own internal motivation to change.

MI is most commonly noted by three overarching areas: spirit, principles, and change strategies. These areas are visualized as a triangle, with the spirit of MI forming the base and the strategies forming the tip (Figure 7.2).

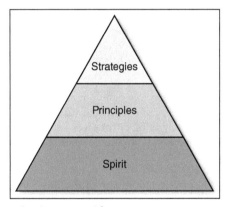

Figure 7.2 Motivational interviewing pyramid.

A key concept of MI is a positive, collaborative counseling relationship that addresses the client's **ambivalence to change** by evoking their reasons for change and strengthening their motivation and commitment. Ambivalence in not seen as resistance or denial but as a normal part of the change process and an important motivational barrier to address.

Ambivalence is resolved by exploring the client's values and own intrinsic motivations while developing a partnership that forms the **spirit of MI**. Miller and Rollnick (2023) describe the spirit of MI as a *way of being with people* that encompassed the following elements:

- **Partnership:** A collaborative process where the counselor is seen as the expert in helping people change and the client is honored as the expert in their own lives.
- **Evocation:** The belief that people have within themselves the resources and skills needed for change. The goal of the MI process is to draw this out of the client.
- **Acceptance:** The counselor takes a nonjudgmental stance and seeks to understand the client's experience through *expressing accurate empathy, using affirmations, supporting autonomy,* and *seeing the client as having absolute worth.*
- **Compassion:** The counselor promotes the client's welfare and well-being in a selfless manner.

Four principles of MI form the basis of the MI approach (Table 7.5). These are (1) expressing empathy (EE), (2) developing discrepancy (DD), (3) rolling with resistance (RR), and (4) supporting self-efficacy (SS). These four principles guide the practice of MI and should always be in the forefront of the counseling experience.

Motivational Interviewing Strategies

In addition to spirit and the principles of MI, the addiction counselor uses strategies that help move the client through the stages of change. While there are several strategies that can be found in more

Table 7.5 Principles of Motivational Interviewing

MI Principle	Key Concepts
EE: Expressing empathy	• Demonstrate empathy and reflective listening • Acceptance facilitates change • Ambivalence is a normal part of the process
DD: Developing discrepancy	• Guide conversation to highlight the differences between the client's goals and values and their current behavior • The client rather than the counselor should argue for change
RR: Rolling with resistance	• Resistance is not opposed directly • The counselor must avoid arguing for the status quo or unwanted change • The client is the primary resource for finding answers and solutions • When resistance is present, it is a signal *to the counselor* to respond differently
SS: Supporting self-efficacy	• The belief in change is an important motivator • Support the client's belief that changes are possible • The client, not the counselor, is responsible for choosing and carrying out change • The counselor's own belief in the client's ability to change becomes a self-fulfilling prophecy

comprehensive texts such as Miller and Rollnick (2023) and Substance Abuse and Mental Health Services Administration (SAMHSA, 2019), the foundational and most common strategies are as follows:

- **OARS:** The intentional use of four basic counseling microskills: **o**pen ended questions, **a**ffirmations, **r**eflective listening, and **s**ummarizations **(OARS)**. These core counseling skills ensure a higher level of success in engaging clients, less incidences of rupture in the client–counselor relationship, and adherence to the principles of MI.
  - **Open ended questions:** Invite the client to tell their story, be a part of the process, and be in control of the information shared.
  - **Affirmations:** Strengths-based way to help the counseling conversation move forward. The counselor's affirming boosts the client's confidence to act and promotes their self-efficacy; a key principle of MI.
  - **Reflective listening:** The key to expressing empathy (EE)—the fundamental MI approach to counseling. Encourages a nonjudgmental relationship that communicates respect and acceptance of the client, establishes trust and exploration of values, thoughts, and feelings; and allows the counselor to be supportive using specific client statements. Reflective listening should be used when resistance is present in the counseling conversation, this facilitates "rolling with resistance."
  - **Summarizations:** A form of reflective listening that distills down the essence of several client statements and reflects them back. Help the client see a fuller picture of the issue and connects things together to help them move toward change.
- **Tipping the ambivalence scale:** Ambivalence is a normal experience in the change process. In MI, recognizing "change talk" and "sustain talk" is a strategy used to explore the client's ambivalence.
  - **Change talk:** Statements such as "I want to find an Alcoholics Anonymous (AA) meeting" and "I would probably learn a lot if I went to AA meetings."
  - **Sustain talk:** Statements such as "I do just fine handling things when I'm drinking." or "I really enjoy drinking and can't imagine myself ever giving it up." These statements do not necessarily mean the client is not willing to change, but that they are ambivalent and stuck.

The counselor's job is to engage and encourage more change talk than sustain talk. This can be accomplished by ensuring there is an empathic therapeutic relationship, recognizing the type of talk the client is engaged in, using reflective listening to encourage more change talk, and minimizing sustain talk. Counselors should not argue with the client's sustain talk or try to persuade the client to take a "side"—these actions only strengthen the client's motivation toward staying the same rather than changing.

Open-ended "DARN" questions target the **d**esire for change, the **a**bility to change, the **r**easons to change, and the **n**eed to change—thus labeled the DARN questions. Another strategy for evoking change talk is using the **importance ruler** (Figure 7.3) and the **confidence ruler** (Figure 7.4). These rulers are very practical and helpful strategies that allow the client to explore the ambivalence and move closer toward change. A few other strategies used frequently in MI are the **decisional balance exercise, querying extremes, looking back, looking forward, exploring goals and values,**

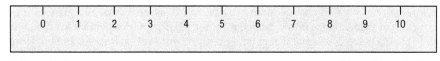

Not Important   **Extremely Important**

- Initial question: "On a scale of 0 to 10, how important is it for you to change *[name the target behavior, like how much the client drinks]* if you decided to?"
- Follow-up question 1: "How are you at a *[fill in the number on the scale]* instead of a *[choose a lower number on the scale]*?" When you use a lower number, you are inviting the client to reflect on how he or she is already considering change. If you use a higher number, it will likely evoke sustain talk (Miller & Rollnick, 2013). Notice the difference in the following examples:

Lower number
  - **Counselor:** You mention that you are at a 6 on the importance of quitting drinking. How are you at a 6 instead of a 3?
  - **Client:** I'm realizing that drinking causes more problems in my life now than when I was younger.

Higher number
  - **Counselor:** You mention that you are at a 6 on the importance of quitting drinking. How are you at a 6 instead of a 9?
  - **Client:** Well, I am just not ready to quit right this second.

  In the higher number example, the counselor evokes sustain talk, but it is still useful information and can be the beginning of a deep conversation about the client's readiness to change.
- Follow-up question 2: "What would help move from a *[fill in the number on the scale]* to a *[choose a slightly higher number on the scale]*?" This question invites the client to reflect on reasons to increase readiness to change.

Figure 7.3 The importance ruler.

Source: From Substance Abuse and Mental Health Services Administration. (2021). *Treatment for stimulant use disorders: Treatment improvement protocol (TIP) series No. 33. SAMHSA Publication No. PEP21-02-01-004.* Substance Abuse and Mental Health Services Administration.

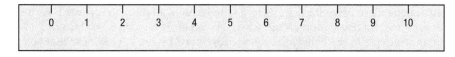

Not Confident   **Extremely Confident**

- Initial question: "On a scale of 0 to 10, how confident are you that you could change *[name the target behavior, like stop drinking]* if you decided to?"
- Follow-up questions:
  - "How are you at a *[fill in the number on the scale]* instead of a *[choose a lower number on the scale]*?" Using a lower number helps clients reflect on how far they've come on the confidence scale. Using a higher number with this question may discourage clients, which can elicit sustain talk. If that should happen, use strategies discussed previously for responding to sustain talk.
  - "What would help you get from a *[fill in the number on the scale]* to a *[choose a slightly higher number on the scale]*?" This open question invites clients to reflect on strategies to build confidence. Don't jump to a much higher number, which can overwhelm clients and lower confidence.

  Whatever the client's response to these scaling questions, use it as an opportunity to begin a conversation about his or her confidence or perceived ability to move forward in the change process.

Figure 7.4 The confidence ruler.

Source: From Substance Abuse and Mental Health Services Administration. (2021). *Treatment for stimulant use disorders: Treatment improvement protocol (TIP) series No. 33. SAMHSA Publication No. PEP21-02-01-004.* Substance Abuse and Mental Health Services Administration.

developing discrepancy, the Columbo approach, and writing a **change plan** found in SAMHSA (2019) and Miller and Rollnick (2023).

MOTIVATIONAL ENHANCEMENT THERAPY

Developed out of the MI approach, **motivational enhancement therapy (MET)** is designed to produce internally motivated change quickly by using MI, assessments, and goal setting to help the client move out of ambivalence into a change mindset. MET provides personalized, neutral, MI-style feedback to clients using assessments that enhance the client's self-awareness of behaviors to change. Counselors elicit the client's understanding of assessment feedback and use reflections to emphasize the change the clients is considering. Goal setting occurs based on the client's new self-awareness and motivation toward change (SAMHSA, 2019).

▶ COGNITIVE BEHAVIORAL APPROACHES

In contrast to the antideterministic psychodynamic theories and the semidirective approach of the humanistic theories, the cognitive behavioral approaches are largely deterministic, active, and directive (Corey, 2023; Table 7.6). These approaches have the most empirical support and are widely used in the addiction counseling field.

BEHAVIORISM

In the behavioral theory of psychology, human behavior is seen as the product of learning and change is a process of classical and operant conditioning based on a stimulus and response model. In **classical conditioning**, an unconditioned stimulus leads to an unconditioned response; for example, a dog will salivate when presented with food, an automatic response based on biology. When an unconditioned stimulus (ringing a bell) is paired with food given to the dog, over time the conditioned stimulus (the ringing bell) will trigger a response (salivating). If the conditioned stimulus (ringing the bell) is no longer paired with the unconditioned response, (salivating), the conditioned response (salivating to the bell) will no longer occur, and the behavior will be extinguished. This example is from the famous experiment by Ian Pavlov who trained dogs to salivate to a bell ringing and then extinguished this response to demonstrate the principles of classical conditioning (Corey, 2023). **Operant conditioning** on the other hand is learning that occurs mainly from the consequences that follow behaviors. If the consequences that follow a behavior are reinforcing, chances are, the behavior will be repeated. This can be a **positive reinforcement** (e.g., a student earns money for good grades on a report card) or **negative reinforcement** (e.g., a student who has good grades on a report card does not have to do chores for a month). Behaviors are also shaped in operant conditioning by **punishment**, adding a negative consequence to behavior (e.g., a child who receives a failing grade in a class loses driving privileges for a month). **Extinction** occurs when a behavior is no longer reinforced. These concepts are important concepts in the behavioral theory developed by Dr. B. F. Skinner that is the basis for behavioral approaches to counseling (Corey, 2023).

Behavior theory is concerned with observable behavior rather than the client's inner world and stresses action over thought and feelings. Behavioral counselors are concerned with rigorous assessment, observable behaviors, determinants of behavior, learning experiences that promote change, actionable treatment strategies, and evaluating the outcome of the interventions. The approach stresses present behavior and has little concern with the past, the origins of disorders, or insight. Counselors help clients identify and eliminate maladaptive behavior patterns by helping them learn more constructive patterns through behavior modification. This is done by conducting a very thorough behavioral assessment and developing very clear treatment goals that are action oriented. Homework is given to clients to practice between sessions and reviewed in subsequent sessions adjusting the plan as needed. Clients are expected to be very active in the process and to experiment with new behaviors. There is less emphasis on the therapeutic relationship between the counselor and client in the behavioral approach, however, a collaborative relationship is an important part of treatment. Unlike client-centered therapy where the client-counselor relationship is seen as *necessary **and** sufficient for change*, the behavioral therapy approach sees the relationship as *necessary but **not** sufficient* for behavior change.

Table 7.6 Cognitive Behavioral Approaches to Counseling

Cognitive Behavioral Approaches	Key Figures	Major Focus	Key Concepts	Techniques
Behaviorism	• B. F. Skinner • Albert Bandura • Marsha Linehan	• Behavior change • Behavior as product of learning • Mindfulness	• Classical conditioning • Operant conditioning • Awareness and perception • Self-compassion	• Social skills training • Role playing • Modeling • Systemic desensitization • Exposure therapy • Relaxation training • Mindfulness • EMDR • ACT
Cognitive therapy	• Aaron T. Beck • Judith Beck	• Empirical evidence • Present centered, problem oriented • Perception and meaning influence feeling and behaving • Thoughts are accessible to introspection	• Negative cognitive triad • Psychological distress is an exaggeration of adaptive functioning • Cognitive distortions • Beliefs play a role in psychological distress • Change in beliefs leads to change in behaviors and emotions	• Therapeutic relationship • Empathy with technical competence • Socratic dialogue • Educating the client • Bibliotherapy • Homework assignments • Thought records
CBT	• Albert Ellis (REBT) • Christine Padesky (SF-CBT) • Donald Meichenbaum (CBM)	• Collaborative therapeutic relationship/ therapist is active • Psychological distress is maintained by cognitive processes • Changing cognitions changes behavior and affect • Educational format • Present-centered, time-limited	REBT focus is to challenge irrational beliefs. ABC framework SF-CBT identifies and incorporates clients' strengths into therapy process CBM posits that clients must become aware of how they think, feel, and behave and their impact on others; change behavior first	• Homework • Operant conditioning • Modeling • Behavioral reversal • ABC-DE model • Identify and integrate strengths • Self-instructional training • Develop and practice coping skills • Stress inoculation training
Reality therapy/ choice theory	• William Glasser • Robert Wubbolding	• Humans are driven by encoded needs • Rejects the medical model • Behavior is an attempt to get needs met • Acceptance and responsibility	• Survival • Love and belonging • Power • Freedom • Fun	• Build therapy relationship • WDEP system

ABC, activating event, beliefs about the event, and consequences/emotional reaction; ABC-DE, activating event, beliefs, consequences, dispute, and effective philosophy; ACT, acceptance and commitment therapy; CBM, cognitive behavior modification; CBT, cognitive behavior therapy; EMDR, eye movement desensitization and reprocessing; REBT, rational emotive behavior therapy; SF-CBT, strength focused cognitive behavioral therapy; WDEP, wants, doing, self-evaluation, plans, and planning.

There are several treatment techniques used in behavior therapy to effect change. The major behavioral therapy techniques are summarized in the following to highlight the more common counseling techniques used in addiction counseling.

Behavior Modification

Behavior modification is a very clear and distinct pattern of reinforcement to shape behavior. Systematic use of reinforcement can be seen in drug courts and other treatment models such as contingency management, to help substance use disorder clients change. Examples of behavior modification include:

- **Contingency management:** An effective evidence-based treatment that uses the systematic use of reinforcement in response shaping where positive reinforcement is consistently used to shape a client's behavior, such as a getting a reward when a drug screen is negative.
- **Token economics:** Clients earn tokens when they display the desired behaviors and over time the tokens can be exchanged for a reinforcing reward.
- **Behavioral contracting:** Two parties agree upon what behavior to change and what tangible rewards will be available when the contract is fulfilled. Behavioral contracting can be facilitated in therapy through the treatment planning process and throughout therapy as an intervention for targeted behaviors.
- **Modeling:** Learning of skills through imitating another person. In modeling, the counselor has the client observe the behavior that is desired by watching others demonstrate it. The client then mimics that behavior until it becomes an automatic learned behavior. Modeling can be used in combination with other behavioral techniques to strengthen the probability of success.

Progressive Muscle Relaxation

Progressive muscle relaxation is a behavioral technique that helps clients learn how to cope with the stressors they experience in everyday life. Clients are taught to tense and relax muscle groups in a relaxed environment. Through tensing and relaxing the muscles and focusing on deep and regular breathing, clients can achieve a state of relaxation in both body and mind. Clients are instructed to practice the technique outside of therapy as homework so that the relaxation becomes a habitual pattern of behavior that can be paired with stressful stimuli.

Systematic Desensitization

Systematic desensitization is a technique that pairs relaxation of the mind and body (often achieved using the progressive muscle relaxation exercise) with a hierarchy of anxiety-producing stimuli. In the relaxed state, clients are exposed to anxiety-provoking stimuli in a systematic hierarchy. When clients become anxious, they are taught to return to relaxation until the anxiety subsides. This process continues up the anxiety hierarchy until desensitization to the stimuli occurs. This process works to desensitize the client to the anxiety producing stimuli based on the assumption that a person cannot be relaxed and anxious at the same time.

Exposure Therapies

In **exposure therapies**, clients are exposed to the very things that contributed to the anxiety or the fears in a systematic way either through imaging the fear or through actual live exposure (**in vivo exposure therapy**).

Flooding is an exposure therapy that exposes the client to anxiety provoking stimuli for longer and more prolonged periods of time. During these exposures, clients are taught to use relaxation exercises to bring down their anxiety as they move through the therapy.

Eye movement desensitization and reprocessing (EMDR) is a newer exposure therapy that pairs rapid eye movements or other bilateral stimulation with cognitive processing of traumatic events and memories to allow for new and less anxiety provoking associations to be paired with the memory. The exposure to the trauma is thought to be less triggering for clients because it does not require the client to describe or experience the trauma in detail. The end goal of EMDR is to formulate new processing, new learning, and new insights to the trauma to lessen the emotional response.

In all the exposure therapies, clients should be well informed of the therapy, give consent, and be allowed to terminate the exposure if they choose.

Aversion Therapy

Aversion therapy is commonly used in addiction counseling treatment. This approach combines an adverse stimulus (usually punishment) to an undesired behavior. Its goal is to lessen and eventually extinguish the undesired behavior. An example of aversion therapy is giving the medication disulfiram (Antabuse) to clients who drink alcohol heavily. The disulfiram is "punishment" for drinking because it makes the person very ill when they drink. Aversion therapy is effective in the short term for stopping behaviors during which time the goal is to help clients develop more effective and healthy behaviors to replace the undesired behavior. This is a very important step in aversion therapy to maintain the gains made.

Biofeedback Treatment

Biofeedback treatment aims to combat stress and anxiety through relaxation training and learning to control physiological processes such as heart rate, blood pressure, and skin temperature. During biofeedback sessions, physiological responses are monitored and the client learns to recognize the physical signs and symptoms of stress and anxiety. By learning how to control the physical and psychological effects of stress using biofeedback, clients are better able to learn how to relax their mind and body to cope with anxiety and control emotionality. Biofeedback is a type of training that is effectively used with many other treatment techniques to help clients with many issues including stress, anxiety, mood disorders, and substance use disorders.

Social Skills Training

Social skills training involves educating the client on appropriate social interactions, modeling the behavior, rehearsing the desired behavior in social settings, and receiving feedback on the skills displayed. A key component of the training is action, having the client engage in the skills learned and being reinforced for using the skills effectively. Anger management training, an issue that frequently comes up when working with substance use disorder clients, is an example of social skills training.

Mindfulness and Acceptance

These are considered the "third wave" of behavior therapy that incorporates things that have not traditionally been included in the therapy such as spirituality, values, being in the moment, emotional expression, and acceptance. **Mindfulness** is the intentional awareness of the present moment, while **acceptance** is having attention in the present that is nonjudgmental. In mindfulness- and acceptance-based approaches, clients are taught to become aware of the present with acceptance and without judgment. There are several mindfulness- and acceptance-based treatment approaches that combine elements of cognitive and behavioral therapy.

COGNITIVE THERAPY

Cognitive therapy is built on the cognitive model, postulating that thoughts, feelings, and behaviors are all connected, with change occurring when clients change their thinking. Aaron and Judith Beck are most associated with originating this system of therapy that has clients challenging their cognitive thought distortions and developing more flexible ways of thinking (Beck, 2010). Automatic problematic thoughts, or **cognitive thought distortions**, are the biased perspectives we hold about ourselves or the world that come in many forms but fall into a few identifiable categories. Some common examples of cognitive thought distortions include **catastrophizing**, always assuming the worst-case scenario; **personalization**, taking responsibility for events or situations that are beyond your control; **all-or-nothing thinking**, viewing events in black and white with no gray areas; and **overgeneralizing**, drawing broad conclusions based on limited evidence. Therapist help clients identify these thought distortions in the cognitive restructuring process to identify their automatic problematic thoughts (cognitions), dispute the automatic thoughts, and develop a rational rebuttal that is practiced frequently to change the problematic thinking patterns. Cognitive therapy is very structured, directive, active, and time limited. When combined with behavioral therapies, it is known as cognitive behavioral therapy (CBT).

COGNITIVE BEHAVIORAL THERAPY

The most widely used approach in psychotherapy, and the most heavily researched, is the cognitive behavioral approach (Corey, 2023; Padesky & Mooney, 2012). Combining the behavioral and the cognitive approach creates **cognitive behavioral therapy (CBT)**. CBT is grounded in the theory that thoughts, beliefs, behaviors, emotions, and physical reactions are all linked and that a change in one area will lead to changes in other areas. CBT therapists use behavioral techniques such as operant conditioning, modeling, behavioral rehearsal to the client's thinking and cognitions to help change behavior and address the presenting concerns. All of the CBT approaches share the following premises: (a) a collaborative relationship between the client and therapist is necessary, (b) psychological distress is maintained by cognitive processes, (c) changing cognitions produces the desired changes in affect and behavior, (d) therapy is present focused and time limited, (e) the therapist is active and directive, and (f) treatment is educational and focused on specific targeted problems.

Rational Emotive Behavior Therapy

Albert Ellis developed **rational emotive behavior therapy (REBT)** as an active and directive form of therapy that uses cognitive, behavioral, and emotive techniques to facilitate client change (Corey, 2023). Counseling is a process of reeducation; helping clients challenge the **irrational beliefs** that developed in childhood because of early messages about the world, self, and others. Clients are directed to examine the validity of their irrational beliefs and reject them as illogical and unhelpful by developing more **rational beliefs** that are true, sensible, and constructive. According to REBT, emotional difficulties do not originate from events or incidents; it is the irrational beliefs, the "shoulds," "musts," and "oughts" about the events that cause the self-defeating emotions and behaviors. Clients are taught to eliminate these irrational beliefs by attacking them using the **ABC (DE) model** where $\underline{A}$ is the activating event, $\underline{B}$ is the beliefs about the event, and $\underline{C}$ is the consequences, both emotional and behavioral, of holding on to the irrational beliefs. It is the irrational beliefs in $\underline{B}$ that are targeted in counseling. Counselors have the client dispute ($\underline{D}$) the irrational beliefs and work toward embracing more rational beliefs which leads to a new effective philosophy ($\underline{E}$) that has healthier behavioral and emotional consequences. REBT attempts to change the clients basic value system with the goal to live a more rational life free from emotional disturbances and self-defeating behaviors that are based in irrational beliefs.

Strength-Focused Cognitive Behavioral Therapy

Strength-focused cognitive behavioral therapy (SF-CBT) is a variant of the cognitive therapy model developed with an emphasis on identifying and integrating the client's strengths at each stage of the therapy process. The premise of this approach is that clients will become more engaged and less discouraged in therapy if there is a focus on positive aspects of the client's world. Counselors help clients develop and construct new ways of interacting with the world that is more positive and focused on building resilience.

Cognitive Behavior Modification

Cognitive behavior modification (CBM) developed by Donald Meichenbaum (2017) stresses that clients must become aware of how they think, feel, and behave, and the impact they have on others. In keeping with CBT theory, CBM holds that distressing emotions are the result of maladaptive thoughts. But in CBM, behaviors are targeted for change first rather than thoughts. A three-phase process of change is employed in therapy that has clients (1) engage in becoming aware of their behaviors and internal dialogue, (2) change their maladaptive behaviors and start a new internal dialogue, and (3) learn new coping skills which are practiced in real life situations.

REALITY THERAPY/CHOICE THEORY

Reality therapy is based on choice theory, which rejects the medical model of mental illness and holds that people are responsible for what they choose to do. William Glasser, the key theorist of this model, maintains that we are internally motivated by needs and wants and have control over our behavioral choices (Corey, 2023). Taking responsibility for our choices leads to better mental health.

The counselor's job is to focus on the present rather than the past and help clients face reality to make more responsible choices. A key component of reality therapy is to plan for more responsible behavior that is reality-based. The plan is evaluated frequently and modified when needed. If successful, the client grows in moral responsibility and makes better behavior choices leading to a fuller and more enriching life.

MINDFULNESS- AND ACCEPTANCE-BASED CBT APPROACHES

As discussed in the behavioral therapy section, mindfulness and acceptance-based approaches are effective for substance use disorders when combined with cognitive therapy practices. **Mindfulness-based stress reduction therapy (MBSR)** is an 8-week program that applies mindfulness techniques such as meditation to promote physical and psychological health. **Mindfulness-based cognitive therapy (MBCT)** is another 8-week program that has been adapted from MBSR that incorporates teaching cognitive behavioral skills to help clients interrupt their automatic negative thought patterns. **Mindfulness-based relapse prevention (MBRP)** is designed as an aftercare program for clients who have been through substance use disorder treatment. It is intended to foster increased awareness of triggers, destructive habitual patterns, and "automatic" responses that can lead to relapse. MBRP uses mindfulness and acceptance-based practices to help client pause when becoming aware of relapse triggers so they can make choices that support a recovery lifestyle.

Dialectical Behavioral Therapy

Dialectical behavioral therapy (DBT) is a targeted therapy originally developed to treat suicidal individuals diagnosed with borderline personality disorder. This treatment modality has been expanded to include treating clients with substance use disorders and other mental health conditions. DBT teaches clients emotional regulation skills and how to embrace and accept the tension between two opposites, the dialect. DBT includes both acceptance-based strategies and change-oriented strategies to help clients learn mindfulness skills, distress tolerance skills, emotional regulation skills, and effective interpersonal skills to address the presenting problems that brought them into therapy.

Acceptance and Commitment Therapy

Acceptance and commitment therapy (ACT) is a cognitive behavioral approach that uses acceptance and mindfulness strategies, together with commitment and behavior change strategies, to increase psychological flexibility. The reduction of symptoms is not necessarily the primary goal of ACT as it is with most other therapies. Instead, the goal is to help clients accept and live in ways that are driven by their values rather than by avoiding unpleasant things.

▶ POSTMODERN AND SYSTEMS APPROACHES

Postmodern approaches to therapy include solution-focused, narrative, and feminist theories while family systems therapy understands problems within the structure of the family system (Table 7.7).

SOLUTION-FOCUSED THERAPY

Solution-focused therapy, developed by De Shazer and Berg (1997), is an evidence-based approach that is short term and strength-based. Solution-focused counselors focus on the individual's strengths and their ability to find solutions to their problems rather than the problem itself. This view is grounded in the philosophy that clients move toward health based on their strengths and experiences. These strengths can help them overcome their present challenges and change their behavior. The counselor is a part of a supportive environment that helps clients understand their experiences and create a different future. Solution-focused therapy is short term and time limited. The time in therapy is spent helping the client find solutions to their presenting concerns rather than on assessing the cause, the diagnosis, or the limitations of the client.

Fundamental to the solution-focused therapy approach is asking intentional and future-oriented questions such as the miracle question, scaling questions, and exception questions. The **miracle question** is used to help the client envision a future where the problem does not exist. An example of a

Table 7.7 Postmodern and Systems Approaches

Postmodern and Systems Approaches	Key Figures	Major Focus	Key Concepts	Techniques
Solution-focused therapy	• Insoo Kim Berg • Steven de Shazer	• Strengths and resiliencies of people • Focus on exceptions to problems • Antideterministic • Future oriented • Time limited, brief therapy	• Focus on present and future, what is working versus the problem • Clients have the solutions to their own problems • Language to reframe "problem-saturated" stories to solutions • Clients' strengths and competencies drive change	• Therapeutic alliance • Goal setting • Pretherapy change • Exception questions • Miracle question • Scaling questions • Formal first session task
Narrative therapy	• Michael White • David Epston	• Strength based • Problems are the stories we tell and that others tell us • Collaboration between client and therapist to "Re-story" • Empowerment versus labeling and diagnosis	• Therapeutic relationship • Listening to client's "story" nonjudgmentally • Separate client from the problem saturated stories • Deconstruct the judgements self and others make • Creative and imaginative thought	• Open and circular questions • Personify the problem • Externalizing • Deconstructing the story • Alternative stories and reauthoring • Therapist letters
Feminist therapy	• Jean Baker Miller • Laura Brown	• Social, cultural, and political context to personal problems • Addressing psychological oppression and constraints as an approach to therapy • Challenge male-oriented assumptions • Social change	• Gender-fair approach • Flexible-multicultural perspective • Interactionist view • Life-span perspective • Relational-cultural theory • The personal is political • Egalitarian counseling relationship • Focus on strengths	• Consciousness raising • Empowerment • Self-disclosure • Gender-role and social identity analysis • Power analysis • Bibliotherapy • Assertiveness training • Reframing-relabeling
Family systems therapy	• Salvador Minuchin • Murray Bowen • Virginia Satir	• Structural family therapy • Problems understood within the structure of the family system • Multilayered process of family therapy • Integrative model	• Reduce symptoms of dysfunction • Modify the family's transactional rules • Establish appropriate boundaries • Here and now family interactions • Collaborative stance, family as expert, therapist as "not-knowing"	• Joining-build relationship with family • Boundary setting • Unbalancing • Reframing • Paradoxical interventions • Enactments • Reflecting teams

miracle question would be "Imagine that a miracle occurred tonight and the problem that brought you into counseling did not exist. What would tomorrow look like?" The answers help guide treatment goals and shed light on solutions. The second type of question commonly used in solution focused therapy is the **exception question** which highlights times when the problem is *not* present and the reasons why. The answers to exception questions bring to the client's awareness the exceptions to the problem and the strengths to resolve the identified issues. Finally, **scaling questions** are used to measure progress on goals and client issues. Using a 10-point scale, the client is asked to rate how things are going in relation to their problem. A scaling question would be phrased as "On a scale of 1 to 10, with 1 being the problem is at its worst and 10 being the problem is resolved, rate where you are today." The counselor focuses on the parts of the answer that indicate progress and probes why the score is that high rather than how low it might be. The emphasis in solution-focused therapy is always on the positive and the exceptions to the identified problems. Incremental behavioral change is seen as the most effective way to measure progress and counseling is terminated when the client puts into action effective solutions.

NARRATIVE THERAPY

Narrative therapy is a strength-based approach that emphasizes collaboration between the counselor and the client to help clients view themselves in ways that are empowering. The counselor helps the client move toward the way they want to live by changing their life "story." The narrative approach directs counselors to see the client's life story in social, cultural, and political contexts. Themes in the story are identified and times when the client was challenging the social narrative are highlighted. Counselors focus on the capacity for creative and imaginative thought to change the "story." A key technique is helping the client externalize the problem to "re-story." This process separates the person from identification with the problem they bring to counseling. In substance use counseling, the substance use story is externalized from the client and the client is empowered to make changes that have them reconstruct their story without the problematic use of substances.

FEMINIST THERAPY

Feminist therapy is relatively new in the counseling field. Many theorists are contributing to this model; it has been a collective effort over time by several people with a focus on inclusion. Although not widely used in addiction counseling, the influence of feminist therapy is growing due in part to the focus on gender, multiculturalism, inclusivity, and more flexible approaches to psychological issues. The **flexible-multicultural perspective** in feminist therapy uses concepts and strategies that apply equally to individuals and groups regardless of age, race, culture, gender, ability, class, sexual orientation, or any other social positionality. There are seven overlapping and related foundations of feminist therapy: (1) the personal is political, meaning problems that people bring into counseling originate in political and social contexts, (2) counselors are committed to social change, (3) the voices of those who have been marginalized and oppressed are valued and honored, (4) the counseling relationship is egalitarian, (5) the focus in counseling is on strengths and the distress that is caused by an unjust system, (6) all types of oppression are recognized and connected, and (7) reflexivity and positionality are key practices for counselors. Counselors operating out of a feminist framework have responsibilities outside of the therapy room to advocate for those who are oppressed and to assist clients in viewing themselves as active agents on their own behalf and on behalf of others.

FAMILY SYSTEMS THERAPY

Family systems therapy holds the perspective that individuals are best understood in the context of the interactions between family members. Influential family systems theorists include Murray Bowen, Virginia Satir, Salvador Minuchin, and Jay Haley (Corey, 2023). These theorists developed a therapy approach that views the client's problems as a symptom of how the family system functions and not just how the individual thinks, feels, or behaves. Every individual in a family affects the family dynamic. Family systems are complex and include many interactions between different relationships. Family systems include families of origin, extended families, immediate family members, and combinations of individuals who may not be related but serve as family members in role and function. Family system therapy assumes that the client's problematic behavior may (a) serve a function or purpose for the family in which they are embedded, (b) be unintentionally maintained by family processes, (c) be a function of the family inability to operate productively, or (d) a symptom of dysfunctional patterns handed down through the generations. Because the family is an integral part of the client's issues, family systems therapists work with the whole family to resolve the client's presenting concerns. Addiction counselors must be knowledgeable about family systems therapy as addiction is defined as a family disease and counseling interventions must address the entire family system. Counseling with significant others and family members will be covered later in this chapter.

Unfolding Case Study

According to Jim's assessment and treatment plan, he will be attending outpatient counseling to increase the awareness of the impact his use of alcohol, gambling, and pornography has had on himself and others. He will also be working to develop alternate coping strategies and build informal supports to address his substance use disorder issues. Jim's goals will most effectively be treated using a **cognitive behavioral counseling approach** that will help him examine the thoughts, beliefs, behaviors, and emotions that have led to his difficulties and to change his behaviors. **Cognitive behavior modification** will help him become aware of how his thoughts, feelings, and behaviors have impacted others, and will also target change, helping Jim change his maladaptive behaviors and learn new coping skills which will be practiced in real life situations.

▶ STAGES OF COUNSELING

Individual counseling unfolds across time in a variety of stages. While each stage includes tasks to accomplish, it is not always a linear process. Clients often bring new issues to sessions that have not been explored previously along with some that had already moved through the stages to completion. All counselors should work from a framework that organizes the course of treatment process and helps clients resolve their presenting issues. Ivey et al. (2023) developed a five-stage counseling framework that can be used with multiple theories of counseling and with substance use disorder clients. Ivey's model highlights the interactive process between the client and the counselor by centering empathy and listening skills. From this center, the client's "story" unfolds through relationship building, information gathering about the client's concerns and strengths, goal setting, and "re-storying" to resolve the presenting issues through action. Many other models of counseling follow a similar pattern of stages:

- Stage 1: Developing the counselor/client therapeutic relationship
- Stage 2: Clarifying and assessing the presenting problem(s)
- Stage 3: Identifying and setting counseling/treatment goals
- Stage 4: Designing and implementing interventions
- Stage 5: Planning, termination, and follow-up

Substance use counselors include additional steps in the counseling process that are specific to gathering information related to the client's substance use. This involves evaluating the information regarding the severity and nature of the presenting symptoms based on the substance use and the level to which client's basic needs are being met, such as safety and physiological needs. Moving through the stages of counseling require that counselors use multiple methods of gathering information and techniques of counseling to help resolve the presenting issues.

▶ TECHNIQUES OF COUNSELING

Counseling as we have defined is an intensive personal process that requires the counselor to use **active listening skills**. Active listening requires that the counselor use the appropriate skills to be present and engaged in what the client is saying, both verbally and nonverbally, and then respond thoughtfully. The **techniques of counseling** encompass an active listening process to listen well and understand the client's personal issues, challenges, and opportunities helping them develop strategies for growth and change.

The microskills approach to counseling focuses the counselor on what the client is thinking, feeling, and doing regarding the issues that brought them into counseling and that encompass their "life story." The microskills are foundational for the development of the empathic therapeutic relationship. All counseling must occur in a safe and trusting environment. The microskills develop the empathy and safety that is needed.

Empathy is defined as experiencing the world of the client as if you were the client but keeping an awareness and performing actions that indicate you are separate from the client. An empathic relationship can be developed by listening carefully and communicating back to the client the things heard without adding your own thoughts, feelings, meanings, or stories. Empathy can be basic, additive, or subtractive. In **basic empathy** the counselor's responses are essentially the same as what the client has shared. **Additive empathy** focuses on enhancing and affirming the client's strengths and positives. This is a more skilled approach that requires careful listening and noticing and sharing the client's strengths amidst the difficulties. **Subtractive empathy**, on the other hand, occurs when the counselor distorts or misses the mark on what the client has shared. By using the microskills effectively, counselors ensure they are communicating basic and additive empathy, and limiting any subtractive empathy that may occur.

Using person-centered language is also important in developing empathy and building an empathic relationship especially in addiction counseling. **Person-centered language** is an approach to communication that puts people first, recognizing that they are more than their condition. Many clients experience the stigma of substance use disorders; using person-centered language breaks down stigma and communicates empathy, dignity, and respect (National Institute on Drug Abuse, 2021).

Many counselors come into the counseling room having experienced the stigma of substance use either professionally or personally. Some may be in recovery themselves. This is an issue to consider when developing an empathic relationship. Many counselors are tempted to share their own experiences and stories with clients to develop a therapeutic relationship and build empathy in the counseling relationship. **Counselor self-disclosure** refers to the counselor sharing personal information with the client regarding their own thoughts, feelings, ideas, and experiences. When used appropriately, this can be a powerful technique to enable the counseling relationship to move to deeper levels. This level of sharing occurs outside of the professional counseling experience all the time in day-to-day relationships. However, in the professional counseling setting, counselor self-disclosures must be limited and should only occur when it directly relates to the client's experience. Too much self-disclosure shifts the focus from the client to the counselor, while too little counselor sharing of self gives the appearance of disinterest in the client as a person worthy of being trusted.

MICROSKILLS

As noted earlier, communication in the counseling relationship based on microskills should be well integrated into the counselor's knowledge base and counseling practice. The microskills are separated into two categories: (1) **basic listening skills** and (2) **advanced counseling skills** (Table 7.8). The basic listening skills include attending, encouraging, paraphrasing, summarizing, client observation, and questions. The advanced counseling skills encompass reflection of feeling, focusing, empathic confrontation, reflection of meaning, and interpreting/reframing. These skills are used throughout the counseling encounter.

Basic Listening Skills

Attending skills are the key to building a working relationship with a client and are very important for building rapport. Attending behavior is referred to as the **3Vs + B: verbal tracking, visuals, vocal quality, and body language** (Ivey et al., 2023). Examples include:

- Maintaining good eye contact that is comfortable and culturally appropriate.
- Noting when a client breaks eye contact or looks away. This could indicate that the conversation is addressing important but potentially difficult topics for the client to discuss.
- Communicating warmth and interest in vocal tone and rate of speech. Verbally tracking with the client's story and not changing the subject or topic.
- Maintaining appropriate body language by being relaxed, sitting squarely facing the client, leaning in with an open body posture and conveying interest and warmth through smiling and facial expressions that are congruent to the topic being discussed.

Table 7.8 Microskills

Counseling Technique	Definition	Key Concepts	Purpose
Basic Counseling Microskills			
Attending	Demonstration of the counselor's care and support of the client by eye contact, vocal tone, verbal tracking, and body language	3 V's + B Verbal tracking Visual/eye contact Vocal qualities Body language	Develops the relationship Builds rapport and empathy
Encouraging	Verbal or nonverbal expressions used to prompt clients to keep talking	Head nods, hand gestures, facial expressions, one-word responses such as "mm," "uh-huh," "yes," "ok" Silence is used as an encourager for client to talk	To encourage the clients to keep talking Develop rapport and connection with client
Paraphrasing	Rephrasing the main concepts, key words, and phrases back to the client after listening to several sentences to reflect the client's view of the world	Accurate paraphrases help clients stop repeating the same story Use the client's key phrases and words to capture and distill the essence of what the client has shared	To clarify the client's story and facilitate client exploration of issues
Summarizing	Putting together and organizing many things the client has said over a longer period of conversation to capture the client's main concern, thoughts, feelings, and behaviors	Use at the beginning, middle, and end of sessions Include thoughts, feelings, and behaviors as well as the result or outcome	Puts together and organizes the client's concerns over many dimensions to help the client's executive functioning
Client observation	Observing the client's (and your own) verbal and nonverbal behavior to understand the discrepancies, mixed messages, and incongruities in the client's life and behavior	Conflict internal to the client and between the client and the external world Types of discrepancies: • Between two verbal statements • Between statements and nonverbal behavior • Between client and other people • Between client and a situation • Between goals • Between counselor and client	Provides guidance for which microskills and strategies to use Helps identify the major discrepancies to move client toward change
Questions	A counseling skill used to gather information, facilitate exploration of issues, and guide interventions based on theoretical orientation; can be open or closed	Open questions facilitate a deeper exploration of client issues when used correctly Closed questions help obtain specifics, use sparingly	Questions are used to start sessions, gather information, and guide the discussion when needed
Advanced Counseling Microskills			
Reflection of feeling	Statements made that highlight and reflect the feelings and emotions of the client that are implicitly shared or that are implied	Observe the emotion; identify the key emotions accurately and with the correct intensity and tone to clarify and process the feelings	Facilitates the client's awareness of their emotional world and the effect on their thoughts and behaviors

(continued)

Table 7.8 Microskills (*continued*)

Counseling Technique	Definition	Key Concepts	Purpose
Advanced Counseling Microskills			
Focusing	Enables multiple telling of the client's story from different frames of reference and the interconnected interpersonal and cultural/environmental relationships	Attend to broader dimensions of the client's issue using selective attention Focus on the client's individual issues first directing the client to talk about "self" and then the "self-in-relation" to others and the cultural/environmental context	Increases the client's awareness that the issues they present are not only about themselves Helps the client describe the issues from multiple points of reference
Empathic confrontation	A *gentle* skill that involves listening and observing the discrepancies presented and respectfully sharing them back to the client leading to creative new ways of thinking and behaving	A gentle skill, not a direct, hard challenge "Go with the client" and seek to clarify and highlight the discrepancies observed in the client observation skill Use only when a solid therapeutic relationship has been developed	Highlights the discrepancies observed, clarifying for the client the main issues to problem solve
Reflection of meaning	An influencing skill that helps clients find new or clearer ways to understand themselves and others, clarifying their purpose in life by examining values, meaning, and beliefs	Focus on the values and beliefs articulated by the client to help supply meaning; can be on the stated or implied level from the client	Helps clients find deeper meanings underlying their thoughts, feelings, and behaviors
Interpreting reframing	An influencing skill that is driven by theoretical orientation to arrive at new perspective The counselor supplies the client the new perspective and ideas to create new ways of thinking, feeling, and behaving	Counselor provides the new perspective, frame of reference, or way of thinking about the issues Counselor directed based on theoretical orientation	Provides a new way to understand thoughts, feelings, and behaviors for clients that shifts their perspective

Encouragers are verbal and nonverbal expressions used by the counselor to prompt the client to keep talking. They are things like head nods, hand gestures, facial expressions, and minimal encouraging words or sounds such as "yes" or "uh-huh" or "hmm" that let the client know the counselor is following them and wants them to continue. In contrast, **silence** is also an encourager as it lets the client know it's "still their turn" to talk. Silence can be uncomfortable but very effective if the counselor does not break the silence first. **Paraphrases** are short summaries that reflect to the client the content of what was shared. They are not meant to be word for word accounts of what was shared, but more of a shorter statement capturing the essence or meaning of what the client shared to show that the counselor was carefully listening and understands what the client is trying to communicate. Paraphrases help clarify the client's issues and provides movement to the session. **Summaries**, on the other hand, are longer, more comprehensive counselor responses that organize more of the information shared by the client. Counselors organize the information into the main points, identifying the main concern(s), what is known about it, and the thoughts, feelings, and actions that are creating and sustaining the client's issues. Summaries are used at the beginning, ending, and throughout the session to help with transitions and problem solving.

Another microskill is **client observation**. The counselor must observe the clients' verbal and nonverbal behavior and the discrepancies that often bring the client into counseling. The client observation skill is very important in building up to the more advanced skill of empathic confrontation. The counselor must first observe the discrepancy and when appropriate use the empathic confrontation skill to help the client resolve those discrepancies. There are many types of discrepancies that can be noted under two broad categories: (1) conflict that is internal to the client, and (2) conflict that is external. Conflict that is internal to the client includes discrepancies between two verbal statements (e.g., client says two different things that are incongruent); between statements the client makes, and the nonverbal behaviors displayed (e.g., client talks about how frustrated they are with the legal system but is smiling and laughing while talking about it); and between what the client says and does (e.g., client says they are going to talk to the boss about a raise, but does not initiate the conversation). Conflict between the client and the external world includes discrepancies between the client and other people (e.g., conflict between client and significant other); and discrepancy between a client and a situation (e.g., client wants to work as an accountant but did not finish high school), discrepancy between goals (i.e., client wants to stop drinking but wants to go to the bars with friends on weekends). By observing and noting these discrepancies, the counselor will be ready for the more advanced microskills.

Asking **questions** is the last basic counseling microskill. **Questions** are an essential component of the counseling process and are used in many ways according to a counselor's theoretical orientation. However questions can take away from the client's self-direction if not used properly or if used too frequently. **Open questions** are more facilitative in the counseling process. These are questions that cannot be answered in a few words and that require the client to give a more thorough answer. Questions that start with *who, what, when, where,* or *how* are considered open questions that elicit more information from the client. *Why* questions are also open questions but can come across as judgmental which runs the risk of the client becoming defensive. **Closed questions** are designed to gather very specific information and often start with *do, is,* or *are* (e.g., Are you married?). Closed questions are effective for gathering facts and information but should be used sparingly.

Advanced Counseling Skills

The **reflection of feeling skill** is an advanced counseling skill that facilitates the client's awareness of their own emotional world and its effect on thoughts and actions. Reflection of feelings are statements made by the counselor that emphasize the stated feelings shared by the client or that can be inferred from what the client is sharing. The reflection of feeling microskill is much like paraphrasing or summarizing but with an emphasis on the feeling content. The reflection of feeling involves observing or inferring the feelings, naming them, and sharing them back to the client in the proper context. Because many clients who come in for substance use counseling have difficulty with feelings and emotions, this is a very important microskill to use with them, especially on the implied level.

The advanced microskill of focusing enables the counselor to develop a more complete picture of the client and the complex set of issues they bring to the therapeutic environment. **Focusing** attends to the broader dimensions of the client's concerns and helps to clarify what is creating and sustaining the issues they are bringing into counseling. Counselors focus on the client's individual issues first, using selective attention and directing the client to talk about "self," and then move to "self-in-relation" to others and the cultural and environmental context. This encourages the counselor and client to think about alternative frames of reference, broader systems, and cultural issues that might affect the client.

Most clients come to counseling needing and wanting to change, however they face many challenges to get there. **Empathic confrontation** is an advanced counseling microskill that can promote change and activate a client to move beyond their challenges. Empathic confrontation is not a "harsh" skill but a "gentle" skill that relies on the power of the therapeutic relationship and the client observation microskill. Empathic confrontation goes "with" the client to clarify the problem and seek new resolutions. Empathic confrontation is done is three steps: (1) listen and observe the discrepancies the client presents, (2) label the incongruencies and reflect them back to the client in a nonjudgmental manner, and (3) observe the client's response and plan accordingly. If done correctly and with empathy, the client will have the chance to examine the situation and work through an opportunity to implement a change.

The final two advanced microskills are often thought to be the most important for long-lasting change: reflection of meaning and interpreting/reframing. The **reflection of meaning** microskill focuses beyond what the client says and goes to the deeper level of meaning and values. The reflection of meaning microskill involves observing, inferring, or drawing out the meanings, values, and beliefs of the client to connect them to the presenting issues with more clarity. The meanings and values explored come from within the client. **Interpretation**, or **reframing**, on the other hand, comes from the counselor's frame of reference in seeking to provide a new way of understanding the client's thoughts, feelings, and beliefs. Often this comes from the counselor's theoretical orientation and helps the client find new or clearer ways of understanding themselves and the world around them.

Using Microskills

Using the microskills in counseling is a very intentional process that is both a technique and an intervention using verbal and nonverbal communication skills. The microskills should be used with the learning style (visual, auditory, and kinetic) of the client in mind and within the cultural identity and differences that exist between the counselor and the client. The microskills are counseling techniques that are very effective. The microskills must be used with cultural intentionality. The microskills are based on seeking to understand the varied experiences of the client including the client's worldview and cultural experiences. We all exist in a cultural context that shapes us and how we experience the issues we face. The culturally intentional and culturally humble counselor focuses on the client's experiences while always watching closely for any presenting power imbalances and addressing those in the counseling process. Practicing cultural humility means that we bring a commitment to self-evaluation to move beyond our knowledge of differences and use active listening to empower and help others find the best ways to manage the issues that bring them to the counseling room.

Unfolding Case Study

During a session, Jim's counselor uses CBT to explore the goal of reducing the number of days he is drinking per month along with things he could do to increase his positive social interactions without drinking. The following exchange highlights the counselor's use of the counseling microskills.

Counselor (C):   Hello, Jim. Thank you for coming in today. How are you feeling? **(Open Ended question)**

Jim (J):   I'm okay, I guess. Just struggling with my drinking and feeling isolated.

C: I appreciate your honesty, Jim **(Affirmation of Strength)**. Let's focus on your goal of reducing the number of days you're drinking per month and finding positive social interactions without alcohol. To start, could you tell me more about the situations where you find yourself drinking excessively? **(Open-Ended Question)**

J: It's mostly when I'm stressed or feeling lonely. It's like a way to escape, you know?

C: I see, it seems like you're using alcohol when you are stressed or feeling lonely to escape your problems **(Reflection of Feeling)**. Recognizing these triggers and finding healthier ways to cope with your feelings such as reaching out to friends or doing something enjoyable might help **(Interpretation/Reframing)**.

J: I don't have many friends who don't drink, and I'm not sure what else to do, nothing is fun anymore.

C: It sounds like social interactions can be challenging because your friends who live here drink and you're not sure what else there is to do **(Paraphrase)**. You are also struggling with what to do because nothing seems fun, and you have lost your sense of purpose **(Reflection of Meaning)**. Sometimes engaging in hobbies or volunteering can be a great way to start working your way back to meeting new people and finding a sense of purpose **(Interpretation/Reframing)**. What are some things you used to enjoy before drinking became a problem? **(Open Ended Question)**

J: I used to play guitar and paint. I guess I could try picking those up again. I loved painting because I could get lost in the process and I wouldn't worry about my problems.

C: That sounds like a wonderful idea, Jim. Reconnecting with your hobbies can not only provide a positive way to "escape" from your concerns just as drinking did but could also potentially help you meet like-minded individuals who you could spend time with instead of the friends who drink **(Focusing)**.

J: I could try that I guess, it's usually the weekends when I drink too much, especially when I'm alone.

C: Got it. So, the weekends and being alone trigger the urge to drink. One strategy we can work on is creating a plan for the weekends. Maybe you can schedule activities or outings during that time to keep yourself occupied and reduce the temptation **(Interpretation)**.

J: I guess I could give it a try, but I know my wife will not approve of my going out on the weekends to do anything. She will nag at me and be suspicious. I know she will make it hard on me which stresses me out and makes me want to drink!

(continued)

(continued)

C:	She is worried you will drink if you leave the house and then nags at you creating more stress and tension in your relationship making you want to drink. We've discovered another trigger that makes you want to drink and that causes problems in your relationship **(Reflection of Meaning)**. On the one hand you want to try to do something different but are worried about your wife's reaction and how it will affect you and your relationship **(Empathic Confrontation)**.
J:	You nailed it! I am just so tired of the problems drinking causes [*client is smiling*].
C:	You sound very defeated and yet you are smiling **(Client Observation)**.
J:	I am defeated, I wish I could talk to her about how hard this is and could have her support.
C:	It sounds like you would like to have a heart-to-heart talk with her but are scared se wouldn't listen or be willing to help **(Reflection of feeling/Focusing)**. You could invite her into a counseling session to share the things you are worried about. Would you like to do that? **(Closed Question)**
J:	Yes, I would. I think that might be the best way to talk to her.

▶ GROUP COUNSELING

Group counseling is often suggested for clients seeking counseling for substance use issues because the collaborative group interactions that occur in the group combat the isolation that occurs in substance use disorders. **Group counseling** is defined as group sessions where group members can engage collaboratively in social skills practice, feedback, and behavioral modeling—all very important for those in treatment for substance use disorders. Groups can be **open**, where a member can join at any time during the group process, or **closed**, where members are selected at the same time and complete the group process together with no new members added after the group starts. For group counseling to be effective, counselors must create group environments that are empowering for members of the group. To do this, counselors must demonstrate both personal and professional skills. On the personal side, counselors must be willing to examine their own lives and engage in growth—promoting experiences. Group counselors' personal characteristics include the ability to be emotionally present in the moment and present for others. A group counselor should have self-confidence, an awareness of one's influence on others' courage, a willingness to challenge oneself, sincerity and authenticity, a sense of identity, a belief in the group process, enthusiasm, creativity, stamina, and a commitment to self-care.

LEADERSHIP STYLES

Along with possessing the previously mentioned characteristics, the group counselor must demonstrate appropriate leadership skills. The leader functions to provide the emotional stimulation needed to encourage members to confront their issues and to help make meaning from the group discussions. There are three general leadership styles that counselors typically use in group counseling. These styles are authoritarian, democratic, and laissez-faire. The **authoritarian leadership style** is characterized by an expert model where the leader is viewed as the expert and all communication is directed through the leader with no direct interaction with other members. The leader in this style is responsible for the success of the group. In the **democratic leadership style**, the leader is seen as a facilitator. Communication flows between the leader and members and among members. In this style, the success of the group is a shared responsibility. The leader is least active in the **laissez-faire leadership style** and essentially becomes a member of the group rather than its leader. Members take accountability for the group and communication flow among all members of the group with no leader. This style can be problematic as the group may become unproductive without anyone taking responsibility or leadership for the functions of the group.

GROUP CONTENT AND PROCCESSES

Group counseling involves both content and processes. The group is made up of many different dynamics with the group leader having the responsibility of setting the structure and processes, determining the content of the group, and fostering group cohesion. The group process is the continuing development of the individual members, and the group itself, to facilitate change. Group members go through the process of complying to the group, identifying with the group, and then internalizing the lessons learned in the group to the world outside of the group. Group cohesiveness is critically important to the group process and is just as important as the therapeutic relationship is in the individual counseling process. Group cohesion is defined as the level of trust, warmth, and belonging that exists in the group. Cohesion leads to group members feeling valued, respected, and supported by other members. The level of group cohesion impacts the group treatment outcomes. The more cohesive the group, the better the outcome for its members.

The foremost authority in group process, having developed universally accepted theory and practice, is Irvin Yalom. An important process in group therapy as described by Yalom and Leszcz (2020) is processing information in the "here- and -now." The here-and-now approach emphasizes processing the present feelings and interpersonal reactions in the group as they occur. It includes sharing honest thoughts and feelings about what is happening at the present moment. While this can be very difficult, it is very therapeutic.

Yalom categorized problematic group member behavior into different client types. These problematic client types will show up in substance use disorder groups and leaders must be ready to help them integrate into the group counseling experience by using open communication and working through these behaviors in the "here-and-now" to enhance group cohesion for better treatment outcomes. This modeling is necessary for group members to understand how to interact and intervene when problems in communication occur.

- The **silent client:** Does not engage or talk in group counseling, usually out of fear.
- The **boring client:** A frightened client who wants to be accepted and may speak but does not take risks to engage in the group in any meaningful ways.
- The **monopolizing client:** Takes up most of the attention of the group by excessively talking and focusing on self to the exclusion of letting others participate. This client is "hiding" by using compulsive talking to avoid delving into the group process with others.
- The **self-righteous client:** Insists they are right at all costs to cover up shame and fear of failure. Members often feel intimidated and, over time, resentful of this behavior and the division it causes.
- The **hostile client:** Uses anger to cover up their fear and to drive others away. This also leads to group division.

In addition to defining the different problematic client types, Yalom describes the group as developing through six phases (Table 7.9).

Table 7.9 Group Stages

Group Stage	Members Concerns	What is Seen	Leaders Tasks
Forming stage or Initial stage	Acceptance Identity Power Intimacy	Hesitant participation Superficial talk Giving and seeking advice	Model desired behavior; caring, genuineness, openness, acceptance, respect and listening
Storming stage or Transition stage	Dominance Control Power	Conflict arises Challenges to leadership; struggle for control Defensiveness, resistance, anxiety, fear, and anger Members become more committed to the group	Remain nondefensive, help the group see what is happening, encourage and model healthy behaviors such as response, feedback, healthy disagreement, and self-disclosure
Norming and Performing stage or Working stage	Resolving conflict Cohesiveness Encouragement Equality	Members taking risks to share More honesty Self-disclosure	Help members do more self-exploration Focus on here-and-now, model healthy confrontation Help shift learning from within the group to outside of the group
Adjourning stage or Final stage	Anxiety, worry, sadness, and fear Concerns about unfinished business and what comes next	Isolation, grief Members pulling away from group Processing thoughts, feelings, and reflections on group experience	Recognize and validate feelings Recognize and plan for unfinished business Identify and reinforce growth, changes, and achievements Reemphasize confidentiality

1. **Forming stage:** Group members come together and get acquainted with each other, the leader, and the group process.
2. **Storming stage:** Conflict often arises. Group members struggle to determine the issues of power and control. Negative comments, criticism, hostility toward the leader and others occurs. Leaders must be active in this stage to help the group work through these challenges in a healthy way to reach the norming stage.
3. **Norming stage:** Members start to acclimate to the norms of the group to begin group cohesion. This is the foundation of the safe environment needed to move forward.
4. **Performing stage:** The work of the group starts to pay off. Members are actively engaged in reflection, authenticity, and self-disclosure that lead to healing.
5. **Adjourning stage:** Termination of the counseling group begins.

Yalom's phases of group counseling follow a stage model of group development which is also conceptualized by other theorists as the initial, transition, working, and final stage of group therapy (Corey, 2023). Group stages are universal concepts that apply when working with all groups.

MODELS OF GROUP COUNSELING

There are models of group counseling that incorporate counseling theory and techniques. These groups can be structured using a set curriculum or can be more process oriented where the focus is on interpersonal development. According to the Center for Substance Abuse Treatment (2005), there are five models of group counseling that are commonly used in substance use disorder treatment.

Psychoeducational Groups

Psychoeducational groups typically have a set, structured curriculum that is designed to educate clients about substance use and related behaviors and consequences. The information presented is intended to have direct application to clients' lives, often targeted at self-awareness and taking action to treat their substance use disorder. They can also be used to help families understand the addiction process and how to support the family member who is in treatment. Psychoeducational groups are considered a useful and necessary component of treatment but not a sufficient component in and of itself. Psychoeducational groups often complement other group models in treatment.

Skills Development Groups

A primary goal of **skills development groups** is to build or strengthen the behavioral or cognitive skills needed for clients to cope with their environment and substance use disorder issues. The most common of these groups in addiction counseling are coping skills training groups. Clients are taught to build or relearn the coping skills necessary for achieving and maintaining recovery. Many of these are interpersonal skills which can be best learned and practiced in a group environment.

Cognitive Behavioral Groups

Cognitive behavioral groups are very common in substance use disorder treatment and encompass many different formats. Here, cognitive restructuring is used to change learned behavior. These types of groups are especially helpful for clients in early recovery when behavior change is necessary. In cognitive behavioral groups, behavior change is the result of changing thinking patterns, beliefs, and perceptions. In group therapy, the group leader provides a structured environment to challenge and examine behaviors, thoughts, and beliefs often using a treatment manual to guide the process. The power of the group is used to help members challenge each other to come to healthier ways of thinking and behaving.

Support Groups

Support groups are widely used in substance use recovery and originated out of the addiction field's self-help movement. The lifestyle changes that are needed in recovery are more easily undertaken when there is support for those changes. Support groups provide a nonjudgmental place to talk about current issues and situations that occur in the process of treatment. Unconditional acceptance, inward reflection, open and honest interactions, and commitment to change are the requirements for the group to build a safe place for change. Support group leaders model the desired behavior and facilitate the discussion but are not directive or active unless there is need to address negative behaviors and interactions.

Interpersonal Process Groups

The therapeutic approach to healing in **interpersonal process groups** is focused on changing the basic intrapsychic (within self) or interpersonal (between people) psychological dynamics. Interpersonal process groups use the knowledge of the way people function psychologically to promote change and healing. This includes attachment, social hierarchies, and cultural and spiritual concerns. Group leaders use the here-and-now process in the group and focus heavily on the interactions among members in the group to challenge and change the interpersonal patterns that occur to change relationships outside of the group.

ETHICS IN GROUP COUNSELING

Group leaders must be aware of and attend to many ethical issues in group counseling. The leader needs to address the rights and responsibilities of group members prior to starting the group. Group members must give their **informed consent** to participate in a group. This means that members are informed about the group process and what to expect during the group. Group members are also informed that they are free to leave the group at any time; however, they must also understand the consequences of leaving.

    Confidentiality is critically important to review at the beginning of group, throughout the group process, and must be reinforced at the end. Members must understand that they are expected and obliged to keep the confidences of the group members and the information shared in group must be held in confidence. They also must understand that absolute confidentiality in groups is very difficult and not necessarily guaranteed. Finally, group counseling is subject to federal law, 42 C.F.R. Part 2 (Center for Substance Abuse Treatment, 2005).

▶ FAMILY AND SIGNIFICANT OTHERS COUNSELING

Substance use disorder is often called a family disease because of the complex family dynamics that contribute to, and are often a result of, substance use. According to **family systems theory**, not only does the person with substance use disorder need counseling but their families and significant others should be involved and receive their own counseling as well for treatment to be effective (Lambert et al., 2018; SAMHSA, 2020a). Family counseling shifts the focus from the individual to the family structure and interactions that will help the whole system become well.

Tips From the Field

Regardless of your theoretical orientation, strive to use person-first language. For example, replace the term "addict" with "person with a substance use disorder." Person-first language puts people first, reduces stigma and negative bias when talking about substance use disorders, and has been shown to increase positive outcomes in therapy.

ROLES IN FAMILIES IMPACTED BY SUBSTANCE USE DISORDERS

To be effective, an addiction counselor must understand the common roles that a client's family members and significant other play (Table 7.10). Family systems theory proposes that the family system is a cohesive unit made up of the individuals in it and an environment that seeks homeostasis. Individuals in a system relate to and interact with each other through a feedback loop to maintain balance, stability, and order. The individual parts of the system change and adapt to maintain functioning, which can sometimes be unhealthy and maladaptive. This is often the case in families where a substance use disorder is present. The roles in family impacted by substance use disorders have been proposed and validated by many theorists and researchers over the years as a way to conceptualize and work with families and significant others impacted by addiction (Lambert et al., 2018; Wegscheider-Cruse, 1976). When working with families, it is very helpful to identify the role and provide psychoeducation as a treatment strategy.

Table 7.10 Family and Significant Others' Roles in Substance Use Disorders

Role	Function of the Role	Benefit for the System (The Payoff)
Person with a substance use disorder	Recovery is focused on the person with the substance use disorder; however the whole family needs to be involved in treatment.	Source of emotional pain
The caretaker (enabler/codependent)	Protects and keeps the balance in the family by being responsible for everything and everyone. Cares for everyone at the expense of self-care.	Peace, but only temporarily
The hero	Takes responsibility and is usually a high achiever. Job is to make the family look good; if they do the problem doesn't exist. Often the oldest child in the family unit.	Positive attention and achievement
The mascot	The jester or joker who provides laughter and fun, a distraction from family problems. Avoids conflict and is not taken seriously.	Fun and relief from fear
The lost child	This person doesn't cause any problems, avoids the family and interactions, and sacrifices self-needs for the family. Often the middle child in a family.	Escape
The scapegoat	Often rebellious, difficult, and in trouble. The family focuses all the problems onto the scapegoat to divert attention away from the person who has the substance use disorder.	Negative attention that is acceptable

INTERVENTION

When the family system has endured the disequilibrium and emotional pain for as long as can be tolerated, they may be ready for an intervention to move toward change. The **intervention** is a carefully crafted plan that gathers the whole family system together to intervene and "confront" the person with the substance use disorder with the effects their behavior and substance use has had on the family. Family members work with a counselor who helps them communicate how they have been harmed and what their "bottom line" will be if the person does not get help. The goal of the intervention is to get the person into treatment and, secondarily, to help the family and significant others in their own treatment process to heal and change the family dynamics.

FAMILY COUNSELING AND TREATMENT STRATEGIES

Once a client and their family members are ready, the individual and family treatment can occur in a parallel process, within an integrated framework, or sequentially. In the **parallel process**, the family and the person with the substance use disorder attend treatment independently but at the same time. In the **integrated framework**, family counseling is embedded in the substance use disorder treatment for the identified client. In the **sequential treatment** modality, the family-based treatment occurs after the person with the substance use disorder completes treatment and has maintained recovery. Each approach has benefits and challenges. The approach selected often depends on the resources and the philosophy of the treatment providers as well as the treatment strategy chosen.

There are many treatment strategies that can be used when providing family counseling. The treatment strategies described in the following are evidence-based practices that addiction counselors should familiarize themselves with. Each treatment is described by the major principles of the approach.

■ **Community reinforcement and family training (CRAFT):** A structured, family-focused, positive reinforcement model that teaches family members and significant others strategies for encouraging the family member with substance use disorder to change their behaviors and engage in treatment. The treatment is usually 4 to 6 sessions in length and helps the family members and significant others learn how to provide positive reinforcement for sobriety behaviors and how to avoid inadvertently reinforcing substance use. They are also taught how to recognize windows of opportunities that motivate the loved one to enter treatment and to act on it.

- **Behavioral couples therapy (BCT):** A structured treatment approach for people with substance use disorders and their intimate partners. BCT focuses on the partners ability to reward recovery efforts and aims to lessen relationship distress, improve partner interactions, and build a cohesive relationship. The therapy is typically between 12 and 20 sessions and covers two main treatment interventions: (1) substance-focused interventions to build support for abstinence, and (2) relationship-focused interventions that enhance caring behaviors, shared activities, and communication. BCT can also be adapted to work with family members and clients by adding interventions based on improving communications skills at home.
- **Functional family therapy:** Behaviorally based family counseling approach that is intended to change the family's dysfunctional behavioral and interactional patterns that maintain adolescent substance use along with reinforcing positive problem-solving approaches through three phases. The phases address all members of the family and include (1) engagement and motivation, (2) behavior change, and (3) generalization.
- **Brief strategic family therapy (BSFT):** A program designed for substance-using adolescents and their families where the adolescent is the identified client. Through problem solving and directive interventions targeting dysfunctional family interactions, BSFT aims to reduce or eliminate youth substance use and change family interactions that support drug misuse.
- **Multidimensional family therapy (MDFT):** Another type of treatment that targets adolescent substance use, MDFT is a flexible, family-based counseling approach that combines individual counseling, family counseling, and multisystem methods to elicit behavior change in many different contexts and pathways. MDFT is carried out in the home and in the community.

Family Systems Therapy Based on Theoretical Orientation

Many different counseling approaches can be adapted and used with families whose presenting concern is substance use disorder. These approaches are usually based on the counselor's theoretical orientation and include solution-focused brief therapy, cognitive behavioral family therapy, structural family counseling, and strategic family therapy. Modifying these approaches must consider the disease model of addiction and the interactional dynamics that exist in families impacted by substance use disorders.

SUPPORT FOR FAMILIES AND SIGNIFICANT OTHERS

Just as self-help groups are effective for people with substance use disorders, they are also very helpful for family members and significant others. Al-Anon, based on the 12-step model, is perhaps the most well-known self-help group for families and significant others of those with substance use disorders. There are also many other self-help support groups that provide support for many different types of loved ones based on the problems they are facing such as Alateen, Codependents Anonymous, Adult Children of Alcoholics, Nar-Anon (narcotics), Co-Anon (cocaine), Gam-Anon (gambling), and Families Anonymous. These groups provide education, support, and resources to help the family support recovery.

▶ CRISIS INTERVENTION CORE FUNCTION

The crisis intervention core function defines the services a counselor employs to respond to a client's needs during acute emotional or physical distress. Any significant event during treatment that threatens to jeopardize the treatment or recovery process can be defined as a crisis. Crises can include suicide ideation, suicide attempts, separation from loved ones, arrests, severe mental health episodes, overdose, relapse, or any other myriad of things that threaten the client's well-being. The crisis event must be recognized and therapeutically acted on as outlined in the global criteria of the core function. This includes using the crisis as a therapeutic opportunity to help the client move toward recovery.

In crisis intervention, the counselor needs to be able to recognize the crisis, implement a course of action to stabilize the client, and help resolve the crisis to move the client toward recovery. Implementing a course of action to respond to the crisis includes establishing rapport, gathering relevant data, assessing the client's ability to cope with the crisis, deescalating the situation, reframing the problem as solvable and taking realistic action to solve it. Contacting significant others with appropriate consent and following up with all parties involved are important parts of the crisis intervention plan (Box 7.2; Herdman, 2021).

Box 7.2 Core Function 8: Crisis Intervention

Definition: Those services which respond to an alcohol and/or other drug user's needs during acute emotional and/or physical distress.

Global Criteria:
30. **Recognize** the elements of client **crisis**.
31. Implement an **immediate** course of **action**.
32. **Enhance** overall **treatment** by utilizing crisis events.

Unfolding Case Study

In crisis, Jim calls his counselor in between counseling sessions. He had been in an accident after leaving a friend's birthday party. The party was held at a local brewery and Jim had several drinks. He thought he was sober enough to drive; however, he was breathalyzed after the accident and was over the legal limit for driving. He is now facing another legal charge and is distraught over the possibility that he will lose his driver's license, his job, and his marriage. Jim has never before been this scared about his drinking and admits to the counselor that he is having "dark thoughts." The counselor recognizes that Jim is in crisis and moves into implementing the **crisis intervention core function**. The counselor completes a safety assessment over the phone to determine the appropriate intervention with Jim. Jim does not think he should be alone with his thoughts and does not want to talk to his wife about the situation because he thinks she will be angry with him. Jim is concerned this will be "too much for him" right now.

Jim and the counselor review the social support list they previously developed in session and determine that Jim would reach out to his mother and his sponsor from the AA meetings he has been attending before he talks to his wife. He trusts his mother and sponsor and feels he can share his worries with them without judgment. The counselor gets Jim's assurance that he will utilize his support system and call the counselor's on-call number if his thoughts get worse throughout the evening. Jim also agrees to come in for a counseling session in the morning.

During the session the next day, the counselor engages the **client education core function** to give Jim information on available emergency services, legal resources, and groups he can attend to build his support system. To lay the foundation to work on how he will communicate his fears to his wife, the counselor also educates Jim on the impact of substance use on relationships.

▶ CLIENT EDUCATION CORE FUNCTION

The client education core function is defined as providing information to clients concerning substance use and the available services and resources. Information can be provided formally or informally to clients through a variety of ways such as formal courses, psychoeducational groups, and readings, or woven throughout individual counseling sessions or groups. Clients should be given information on self-help groups, community resources, and available services the client may qualify for as they move into recovery. An important consideration for sharing information with the client is the client's learning level and style, and making sure that the material can be fully understood by the client (Box 7.3; Herdman, 2021).

Box 7.3 Core Function 9: Client Education

Definition: Provision of information to individuals and groups concerning alcohol and other drug use and the available services and resources.

Global Criteria:
33. Present **relevant alcohol and other drug use information** to the client through formal and/or informal processes.
34. Present information about available alcohol and other drug **services and resources**.

▶ SPECIAL POPULATIONS

The term *special populations* is used to denote subgroups of people that have been historically underrepresented in substance use prevention and treatment. Special populations include racial and ethnically diverse groups of people such as Black/African Americans, Arab Americans, Native Americans, Latinx Americans, Asian Americans; culturally diverse populations such as youth, women, military members and veterans, older adults, justice-involved persons, the economically disadvantaged, and the LGBTQ+ community. This is by no means an exhaustive list; there are many different subgroups that need services. This list is intended to demonstrate that consideration must be given to assessing and modifying treatment approaches to meet the needs of those that have been underrepresented.

Counselors must give careful and thoughtful consideration to two areas of cultural awareness: (1) their client's cultural background, and (2) their own cultural background and identity. Counselors must assess each client and their identity to properly understand and conceptualize their issues from a holistic viewpoint. Counselors must understand how the various multicultural aspects of a person's identity impact their use of substances and how it corresponds with treatment barriers, counseling strategy adjustments, identifying risk factors, and treatment outcomes (SAMHSA, 2014). Counselors must also, and perhaps even more importantly, understand their own cultural development and background; examining their beliefs, biases, privilege, and attitudes toward people groups. This work can be difficult at times but it is the ethical responsibility of all counselors to continually engage in self-reflection and to practice cultural humility.

Cultural competence and cultural humility are the guiding principles for providers in the substance use field and throughout the helping professions. **Cultural competence** means attending to and learning the culturally diverse backgrounds of others and providing person-centered care based on cultural knowledge and respecting the differing beliefs, values, and communication preferences. It is the responsibility of the counselor to learn about cultural differences rather than relying on the client to provide the education. Cultural humility is a very important stance for every member of the helping profession to take. **Cultural humility** is the reflective process of understanding biases and privileges, knowing your own cultural identity, and being open to other people's identities and recognizing they are the experts on their own lives (Hook et al., 2017). Counselors must first have cultural self-knowledge and then a basic knowledge of other cultures, being careful not to overgeneralize to specific populations but using cultural humility to respectfully broach the topic of culture in session. In this way, counselors can deliver culturally responsive services.

Providing culturally responsive services is not just a goal for addiction counselors, it is an ethical mandate. The role of culture must be taken into consideration from intake to discharge. SAMHSA (2014) provides several steps for counselors to follow to incorporate culturally responsive evaluation and treatment planning into counseling care:

- Engage the client and establish rapport.
- Familiarize clients and family members with the evaluation process; do not assume they know how it works.
- Endorse a collaborative approach in the process and ask for feedback about the cultural relevance of the treatment plan.
- Obtain and integrate culturally relevant information and themes to better understand the client.
- With the client's permission, gather culturally relevant collateral information.
- Select culturally appropriate screening and assessment tools.
- Determine readiness and motivation for change using MI which is a more collaborative process that can help gather cultural information from the client in a respectful manner.
- Provide culturally responsive case management that includes cultural and community resources.
- Integrate cultural factors into treatment planning being flexible to meet the cultural needs of clients.

In addition to working on knowing your own cultural identity and practicing culturally responsive services, counseling should be knowledgeable about specific cultural groups and their needs related to addiction counseling. Counselors must be able to examine cultural factors with clients and how these factors may influence the presenting problems as well as how they play out in the session. This process is termed as **broaching**. Counselors must take the time to discuss culture and be sensitive to how they are impacting treatment to avoid cultural miscommunication and harm to clients.

It is beyond the scope of this text to review every cultural group and intersection of cultural identities that are possible. However, there are many resources listed in the "Study Resources" section at the end of this chapter that are good places to learn more about special populations encountered in addiction counseling and that may be on the exam.

▶ SPECIAL CONSIDERATIONS FOR ADDICTION COUNSELING

There are a few special considerations to know when working with substance use clients (and for the ADC exam) that have not been covered thus far. These include pathways of recovery, relapse prevention, co-occurring counseling, and the impact of trauma.

PATHWAYS OF RECOVERY

Recovery, defined by SAMHSA (2023) as a process of change through which individuals improve their health and wellness, live a self-directed life, and strive to reach their full potential, is a highly personal process. There are as many pathways to recovery as there are clients. This does not mean that there are no organized methods to recovery, it simply means that each client will find and use the tools to recovery that fit their unique life path. Counselors and clients have at their disposal many theories, techniques, and models of recovery that can be used in the counseling and treatment process. An important distinction to understand in the many different pathways to recovery are programs that are treatment-based and programs that are support group-based. Treatment programs offer structured treatment that is provided by licensed or credentialed clinical providers while support groups offer support and structure through a community or peer support system. Table 7.11 outlines many different recovery pathways categorized as clinical treatment programs provided by a healthcare provider, counselor, or other credentialed professional, or nonclinical community-based recovery programs utilizing peer support and support groups.

Table 7.11 Clinical and Nonclinical Recovery Pathways

Clinical Recovery Pathways	Nonclinical Recovery Pathways
• Counseling: Outpatient and residential programs • Pharmacology-medications for addiction treatment • Holistic-based recovery services • Acceptance and Commitment Therapy (ACT) • Community Reinforcement Approach (CRA)/ Adolescent Community Reinforcement Approach (ACRA) • Cognitive behavioral approaches/therapy • Contingency Management (CM) • Twelve-step facilitation therapy • Behavioral Couples Therapy (BCT) • Family therapy • Harm reduction • Relapse prevention	• Recovery residencies • Recovery community centers • Peer-based recovery services • Education-based recovery services • Employer-based recovery services • Faith-based recovery support (Celebrate Recovery 12-step program) • Community 12-step programs: Alcoholics Anonymous (AA), Narcotics Anonymous (NA), Cocaine Anonymous (CA), etc. • Self-Management and Recovery Training; SMART recovery • Women for sobriety • White Bison (Native American) • The Red Road (Native American) • Moderation management

12-Step and Other Support Groups

Self-help and other support groups are very important pathways for recovery that addiction counselors must be familiar with. There are many different support groups—Rational Recovery, Self-Management and Recovery Training (SMART) recovery, and Women for Sobriety are just a few but the most familiar and widely known. Twelve-step programs and support groups include Alcoholics Anonymous (AA), Narcotics Anonymous (NA), Cocaine Anonymous (CA), Al-Anon, Ala-Teen, and a variety of other "anonymous" groups. These groups operate worldwide, are free of charge, and provide a strong social support network. There is minimal formal structure for the groups and the only requirement for attendance is a desire to stop using substances. This makes the groups accessible and open to all. Membership in the support group is meant to be "anonymous" and of a voluntary nature, a key to the effectiveness of the group fellowship process. The groups operate out of the same principles that have guided the movement since the inception of the program in 1935. The "Big Book" (AA, 2021) outlines the principles along with stories of those who have been helped through the "fellowship" of the group. The Twelve Steps and Twelve Traditions (2002) outline and define the 12 steps and the traditions that define the internal operations of 12-step programs. It is important to understand that the 12-step programs are not meant as a formal treatment program but as a support for those seeking recovery in addition to treatment. There are, however, many treatment programs that use a 12-step facilitated model incorporating the principles of the steps into the treatment process. It is important for addiction counselors to understand and know each of 12 steps for the ADC examination (Box 7.4).

Twelve-step meetings are considered **open** or **closed**. Open meetings are open to anyone who chooses to attend, including the people with the desire to stop using substances, their family, friends, or support providers. Closed meetings are reserved for members of the fellowship who have or are

Box 7.4 12 Steps of Alcoholics Anonymous

1. We admitted we were powerless over alcohol—that our lives had become unmanageable.
2. Came to believe that a Power greater than ourselves could restore us to sanity.
3. Made a decision to turn our will and our lives over to the care of God *as we understood Him*.
4. Made a searching and fearless moral inventory of ourselves.
5. Admitted to God, to ourselves, and to another human being the exact nature of our wrongs.
6. Were entirely ready to have God remove all these defects of character.
7. Humbly asked Him to remove our shortcomings.
8. Made a list of all persons we had harmed, and became willing to make amends to them all.
9. Made direct amends to such people wherever possible, except when to do so would injure them or others.
10. Continued to take personal inventory and when we were wrong promptly admitted it.
11. Sought through prayer and meditation to improve our conscious contact with God *as we understood Him*, praying only for knowledge of His will for us and the power to carry that out.
12. Having had a spiritual awakening as the result of these steps, we tried to carry this message to alcoholics, and to practice these principles in all our affairs.

desiring to change their substance use. Visitors and others are not allowed to attend closed meetings, thereby protecting the anonymity of the membership of these meetings.

Meetings are typically organized around the substance of use or addictive processes (alcohol, illicit drugs, drugs of abuse, gambling, sex, etc.) or targeted at special populations affected by substance use such as family members (Al-Anon, Alateen). Meetings can be **discussion meetings**, where everyone has a chance to share, **speaker meetings** where a speaker shares their story of recovery, **step meetings**, where the focus is on working the 12-steps, or **chip-sobriety birthday meetings**, where sobriety dates are celebrated with presentation of chips or coins.

Sponsorship is a key concept in 12-step programs. Members are encouraged to find a **sponsor** in the program: someone who gives the support needed to stay on track in recovery and helps the member work through the 12 steps. Sponsors should be stable in their recovery and knowledgeable in the steps.

Anonymity is important and based on the members desire to either remain anonymous for confidentiality or safety reasons so that people are free to attend without pressure. The **spiritual experience** is a common misconception about the 12-step programs. Members are allowed to interrupt and define a higher power in any way they choose and are not forced to accept God as a religious or fixed concept based on traditional theological definitions. When members have a "spiritual awakening" they are not converting to a religion but instead are free from the hold the substances have had on them and are able to do, feel, and believe in a life of recovery.

RELAPSE PREVENTION

Historically, a return to substance use after a period of abstinence has been called **relapse** and the term **relapse prevention** has been used to define the work that counselors and clients do to prevent a relapse. In the case of substance use disorders, this implies that only two outcomes are possible for clients: success, defined as abstinence from substances; or failure, defined as a return to substance use categorized as relapse. This all-or-nothing thinking around recovery and relapse is problematic; the research is clear that relapse is a part of recovery (Miller et al., 2001). Given this, many have called for the term "relapse" to be defined as an interruption in one's attempt to change a behavior and to replace "relapse prevention" with "relapse management plans" with the goal to reduce the severity, length, and frequency of relapse (Miller & Rollnick, 2023; Roozen & van de Wetering, 2007).

Counselors must be prepared to work with clients to help them manage relapse and understand that it is a part of the recovery process. There are three models that are helpful for counselors to understand and use with clients during when addressing relapse during treatment: (1) relapse prevention model (RPM), (2) MBRP, and (3) Gorski's CENAPS model of relapse prevention. A common thread throughout all the models is the focus on identifying and managing relapse triggers and high-risk situations that lead to a relapse.

Relapse Prevention Model

The **relapse prevention model (RPM)**, developed in the mid-1980s, revolutionized the addiction treatment field by moving away from the dichotomous model of recovery—as complete abstinence or a return to using—to a continuous model of recovery that encompasses periods of return to use with longer durations of abstinence in between. In this model, clients are encouraged to make lifestyle changes and work to find joy and meaning in their sobriety. Counselors work with clients to monitor their obligations and incorporate healthy pleasurable activities in their daily routines, engage in self-awareness to identify interests and goals outside of substance use, and practice self-care activities. Clients are also taught to identify high-risk situations and triggers that may lead to relapse and intervene before a relapse occurs by using predetermined coping strategies. These high-risk situations are categorized into negative emotional states, interpersonal conflict, and social pressure. When clients are successful in managing these high-risk situations, their self-efficacy is increased. A lapse management plan is created to be used if a client does return to using. The lapse management plan includes agreed upon steps for the client to take such as calling the counselor or a sponsor, countering negative thoughts with positive ones, and removing oneself from high-risk environments or situations. The lapse is explored not as a failure but as an opportunity to learn and plan for continued recovery success (Marlatt & Gordon, 1985).

Mindfulness-Based Relapse Prevention

The integration of mindfulness with the more cognitive-based RPM already described has resulted in the **mindfulness-based relapse prevention (MBRP)** plan. Counselors using MBRP help clients become fully aware and present in their immediate experiences and learn to accept them without judgment, while continuing to help clients identify triggers and high-risk situations for relapse and prepare effective coping strategies. By incorporating mindfulness practices into relapse prevention, clients are better able to tolerate cravings and have more personal choice and self-compassion during the recovery process.

Gorski's CENAPS Model of Relapse Prevention

The CENAPS model of relapse prevention emerged in the 1970s and has continued to be used as a foundational approach to relapse. The CENAPS model is a biopsychosocial approach based in CBT. The model is structured into early, middle, and late recovery and several key components of intervention are addressed. These components are (a) conducting a thorough assessment of the client's substance use disorder and relapse history, (b) identifying the clients unique relapse warning signs and triggers for substance use, (c) developing coping strategies to manage each warning sign, (d) creating a structured recovery program based on a developmental model of recovery, and (e) constructing an early intervention plan for relapse (Gorski, 2000).

CO-OCCURRING DISORDERS

While mental health counseling is often out of the scope of practice for addiction counselors, it is critically important for an addiction counselor to understand how mental health and substance use disorders can co-occur. The term **co-occurring disorder (COD)** is defined as the occurrence of a substance use disorder and a mental health disorder where at least one disorder of each type can be established independently of the other and is not simply a cluster of symptoms resulting from the other disorder. Mental health issues that present in addiction counseling can be severe mental health disorders, such as schizophrenia, or mild to moderate mental health disorders, such as anxiety or attention deficit disorder. Common mental health disorders that co-occur with substance use disorders are mood disorders, anxiety disorders, schizophrenia and other psychotic disorders, and personality disorders (SAMHSA, 2020b). SAMHSA (2020b) suggests that addiction counselors assume all clients they encounter may have a COD. This approach means that addiction counselors must understand how to screen and assess for mental health disorders and know how to refer and coordinate with other treatment providers who provide mental health treatment.

There should be no "wrong door" for people who present to counseling with substance use and mental health symptoms to enter treatment for both conditions. Screening for mental health symptoms is the first step, followed by a referral for a full assessment by a qualified provider if the screening is positive for mental health issues. The screening should consist of more than just the counselor administering questionnaires related to mental health. It should also include exploring the client's risk of harm to self and others, trauma history, and functional impairments. The assessment should be a full biopsychosocial assessment that explores the client's physical health, and substance use along with psychiatric, social, educational, vocational, and family history. It must also include the appropriate questionnaires for diagnosis as well as risk of harm to self and others, trauma history, strengths and supports, cultural needs, readiness for change, and a determination of the **quadrant of care and locus of responsibility** (Figure 7.5) The quadrant of care and locus of responsibility refer to the conceptual framework that classifies clients into four groups based on the severity of their mental health and substance use symptoms and helps determine the most appropriate place for treatment to address the client's needs.

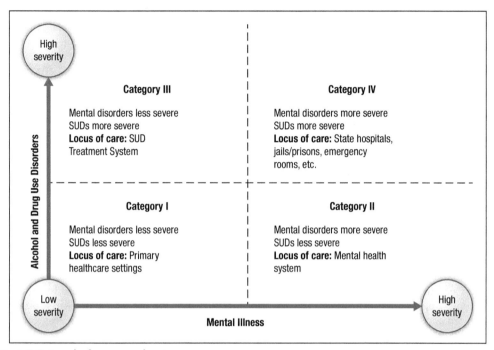

Figure 7.5 Level of care quadrants.

Source: From Substance Abuse and Mental Health Services Administration. (2020b). *Substance use disorder treatment and family therapy: Treatment improvement protocol (TIP) series No. 39. SAMHSA Publication No. PEP20-02-02-012.* Substance Abuse and Mental Health Services Administration.

When assessment is completed, the level of care and treatment plan is developed including all the appropriate providers in the provision of COD treatment. The services for clients with CODs must be person centered, trauma informed, culturally responsive, recovery oriented, comprehensive, inclusive of family and other support systems, and continuously offered across all levels of care. Treatment for people with CODs can be **sequential** (one treatment occurring after the other), **simultaneous but in parallel** (separate treatment providers and programs occurring at the same time), or **concurrent and integrated** (both disorders treatment simultaneously with one treatment team). Integrating the treatment services is the most effective way to provide the services and is the recommended best practice due to strong empirical support. Integrated treatment models include assertive community treatment, intensive case management (ICM), and mutual support and peer-based programming. Treatment settings include therapeutic communities (TC), outpatient and residential care, acute care, and other medical settings. Pharmacotherapy is another important aspect of treatment CODs and must be included in the treatment plan with the appropriate providers.

SUBSTANCE USE AND TRAUMA

Trauma, defined as exposure to an emotionally disturbing or life-threatening event with lasting adverse effects on an individual's functioning, plays a significant role in substance use and substance use disorders. Research has demonstrated a strong link between exposure to trauma and substance use that has a cyclical effect; trauma can lead to substance use disorders and substance use can lead to trauma. The interaction between trauma and substance use continues to be uncovered; however, trauma-related disorders and substance use disorders often co-occur. Trauma that occurred as far back as childhood can have a negative effect throughout the lifespan.

Childhood trauma, as measured and defined by a large-scale study known as the adverse childhood experiences (ACE) study (Felitti et al., 1998), has a negative impact on later adult life including substance use. Trauma early in life is particularly debilitating due to the impacts on the developing brain. The ACE study measured direct childhood trauma (physical abuse, neglect, sexual abuse, and emotional abuse) and indirect or family trauma (parental divorce, abandonment, domestic violence, substance use, and serious illness) and assigned a trauma "score," known as an **ACE score**, based on the number of traumatic events. They then examined the effect on later adult functioning. Findings on childhood trauma have been consistent, the higher an ACE score the more likely the person will engage in behaviors that lead to chronic health problems including problematic substance use.

Trauma is not only confined to childhood. Addiction counselors must assess for and address trauma that occurs throughout the lifespan. This is particularly true when clients are using substances as life can become chaotic and traumatic. Experiences that may be traumatic include physical, sexual, and emotional abuse; childhood neglect; living with someone who has a mental health or substance use problem; sudden or unexplained separation from loved ones; poverty; racism, discrimination, and oppression; violence in the community; war; terrorism; domestic violence; incarceration; car accidents; health problems—the list can go on and on. Trauma is an individual experience that must be clearly understood and accounted for in treatment using **trauma-informed practices**, defined as treating the whole person considering the past trauma and the resulting coping mechanisms.

Counselors are not immune to trauma and as an addiction counselor, the work itself can be traumatic. Day in and day out, counselors listen to traumatic stories that can impact emotional and mental well-being. Counselors can experience **vicarious trauma** due to the emotional residue from hearing and witnessing client's trauma, fear, pain, and terror. **Compassion fatigue**, a gradual lessening of compassion over time, can occur. The effect of vicarious trauma and compassion fatigue over time can lead to **burnout**, a long-term stress reaction and process that is characterized by emotional exhaustion, depersonalization, and reduced personal accomplishment or fulfillment. Counselors must guard against this by recognizing the warning signs of vicarious trauma and address it for their own emotion, mental, physical, and social well-being (Box 7.5).

Box 7.5 Vicarious Trauma Warning Signs for Counselors

- Free floating anger or irritation
- Difficulty sleeping
- Difficulty talking about own feelings
- Excessive worry about clients and whether they are doing enough to help them
- Taking responsibility for clients
- Dealing with intrusive thoughts about clients
- Diminished joy toward things that were once enjoyable
- Feeling trapped and hopeless by work
- Increase in work errors
- Blaming others
- Exhaustion
- Low motivation
- Withdrawal and isolation

▶ KEY POINTS

- This chapter highlights Domain 3: Evidence-Based Treatment, Counseling, and Referral and the Counseling, Crisis Intervention, and Client Education Core Functions.
- It is important to focus on these topics when studying because this area contains the highest percentage of questions on the exam.

- Special attention and focus should be paid to MI and the stages of change as they are frequently used when working in the substance use disorder field.
- Specialized evidence-based treatments associated with levels of care in treatment are covered in Chapter 4, "Engaging the Client," and should also be included in the study of this content area.
- The stages of counseling and counseling techniques include the important technical aspects of counseling in which the counselor should be proficient and know for the exam. Counseling with individuals, families, and groups are covered in detail, including the types of groups encountered in addiction counseling and group leader approaches.
- The crisis intervention and client education core function outline the key global criteria for each, which are critical to know for the exam.
- Recovery topics including pathways of recovery, self-help groups, and relapse prevention.
- Special populations and cultural diversity and co-occurring issues are also part of Domain 3. The reader is encouraged to seek out the study resources listed later to be fully prepared for the exam and to work with clients with intersecting identities.
- Finally, a counselor must understand trauma, both trauma the client may have experienced and the vicarious trauma that could occur for the counselor. This chapter should be reviewed carefully with extra attention to outside resources to feel confident on test day.

▶ STUDY RESOURCES

SAMHSA offers many free publications available for download that are key documents in the field for treatment of substance use disorders. The following study resources can be found on SAMHSA's webpage (https://store.samhsa.gov/).

TIP 26: Treating substance use disorders in older adults
TIP 33: Treatment for stimulant use disorder
TIP 34: Brief interventions and brief therapies for substance use disorders
TIP 35: Enhancing motivation for change in substance abuse treatment
TIP 36: Substance abuse treatment for persons with child abuse and neglect issues
TIP 37: Substance abuse treatment for persons with HIV/AIDS
TIP 39: Substance abuse treatment and family therapy
TIP 41: Substance abuse treatment: group therapy
TIP 42: Substance abuse treatment for people with CODs
TIP 48: Managing depressive symptoms in substance abuse clients during early recovery
TIP 50: Addressing suicidal thoughts and behaviors in substance abuse treatment
TIP 51: Substance abuse treatment: Addressing the specific needs of women
TIP 56: Addressing the specific behavioral health needs of men
TIP 57: Trauma informed care in behavioral health services
TIP 59: Improving cultural competence
TIP 61: Behavioral health services for American Indians and Alaska natives
TIP 63: Medications for opioid use disorder
TIP 64: Counseling approaches to promote recovery from problematic substance use and related issues

OTHER SPECIAL POPULATIONS STUDENT RESOURCES

Embracing Diversity: Treatment and Care in Addiction Counseling, Second Edition (2023)
   Author: Tiffany Lee
Multicultural Counseling: Responding with Cultural Humility, Empathy, and Advocacy (2022)
   Authors: LaTonya Summers and Lotes Nelson
Improving Cultural Competence, Tip 59 (2014)
   Author: SAMHSA
Counseling the Culturally Diverse: Theory and Practice, Ninth Edition (2022)
   Authors: Derald Sue, David Sue, Helen Neville, and Laura Smith
Multicultural Issues in Counseling: New Approaches to Diversity, Fifth Edition (2019)
   Author: Cortland Lee

▶ REFERENCES

Alcoholics Anonymous. (2021). *Alcoholics anonymous: The story of how many thousands of men and women have recovered from alcoholism* (4th ed.). Alcoholics Anonymous Worldwide Services.

Ardito, R. B., & Rabellino, D. (2011). Therapeutic alliance and outcome of psychotherapy: Historical excursus, measurements, and prospects for research. *Frontiers in Psychology, 2,* 270. https://doi.org/10.3389/fpsyg.2011.00270

Beck, J. (2010). *Cognitive therapy: The Corsini encyclopedia of psychology.* John Wiley & Sons. https://doi.org/10.1002/9780470479216.corpsy0198

Bordin, E. S. (1979). The generalizability of the psychoanalytic concept of the working alliance. *Psychotherapy (Chic.), 16,* 252–260.

Center for Substance Abuse Treatment. (2005). *Substance abuse treatment: Group therapy, treatment improvement protocol (TIP) series, No. 41. HHS Publication No. (SMA) 15-3991.* Substance Abuse and Mental Health Services Administration.

Corey, G. (2023). *Theory and practice of counseling and psychotherapy* (11th ed.). Cengage.

De Shazer, S., & Berg, I. K. (1997). "What works?" Remarks on research aspects of solution-focused brief therapy. *Journal of Family Therapy, 19,* 121–124. https://doi.org/10.1111/1467-6427.00043

Felitti, V. J., Anda, R. F., Nordenberg, D., Williamson, D. F., Spitz, A. M., Edwards, V., Koss, M. P., & Marks, J. S. (1998). Relationship of childhood abuse and household dysfunction to many leading causes of death in adults: The adverse childhood experiences (ACE) study. *American Journal of Preventive Medicine, 14*(4), 245–258. https://doi.org/10.1016/S0749-3797(98)00017-8

Gorski, T. T. (2000). The CENAPS model of relapse prevention therapy (CMRPT). In J. J. Boren, L. S. Onken, & K. M. Carroll (Eds.), *Approaches to drug abuse counseling* (pp. 23–38). National Institute on Drug Abuse. https://archives.nida.nih.gov/sites/default/files/approachestodacounseling.pdf

Herdman, J. W. (2021). *Global criteria: The 12 core functions of the substance abuse counselor* (8th ed.). John Herdman.

Hook, J. N., Davis, D., Owen, J., & DeBlaere, C. (2017). *Cultural humility: Engaging diverse identities in therapy.* American Psychological Association.

Horvath, A. O. (2001). The alliance. *Psychotherapy: Theory, Research, Practice, Training, 38*(4), 365–372. https://doi.org/10.1037/0033-3204.38.4.365

The International Certification and Reciprocity Consortium. (2022). *Candidate guide for the IC&RC alcohol and drug counselor examination.* International Certification and Reciprocity Consortium. https://internationalcredentialing.org/wp-content/uploads/2024/01/ADC-Candidate-Guide-09.2022_Final-Edit_10.31.22.pdf

Ivey, A. E., Ivey, M. B., & Zalaquett, C. P. (2023). *Intentional interviewing and counseling: Facilitating client development in a multicultural society* (10th ed.). Cengage Publishing.

Lambert, S. F., Unterberg, H., & Riggio, M. (2018). Family systems theory. In P. S. Lassiter, & J. R. Culbreth (Eds.), *Theory and practice of addiction counseling* (pp.177–198). SAGE Publications.

Marlatt, G. A., & Gordon, J. R. (1985). *Relapse prevention: Maintenance strategies in the treatment of addictive behaviors.* Guildford Press.

Maslow, A. (1943). A theory of human motivation. *Psychological Review, 50,* 370–396.

Miller, W. R., & Moyers, T. B. (2015). The forest and the trees: Relationship and specific factors in addiction treatment. *Addiction, 110*(3), 401–413.

Miller, W. R., & Rollnick, S. (2023). *Motivational interviewing: Helping people change and grow* (4th ed.). Guilford Press.

Miller, W. R., Walters, S. T., & Bennett, M. E. (2001). How effective is alcoholism treatment in the United States? *Journal of Studies on Alcohol, 62*(2), 211–220.

National Institute on Drug Abuse. (2021). *Words matter: Terms to use and avoid when talking about addiction.* National Institute on Drug Abuse. https://nida.nih.gov/nidamed-medical-health-professionals/health-professions-education/words-matter-terms-to-use-avoid-when-talking-about-addiction

Norcross, J. C., & Lambert, M. J. (2019). *Psychotherapy relationships that work, volume 1: Evidence based therapists contributions* (3rd ed.). Oxford University Press.

Padesky, C. A., & Mooney, K. A. (2012). Strengths-based cognitive-behavioral therapy: A four-step model to build resilience. *Clinical Psychology & Psychotherapy, 19*(4), 283–290. https://doi.org/10.1002/cpp.1795

Prochaska, J. O., Norcross, J. C., & DiClemente, C. C. (1994). *Changing for good*. Morrow.

Roozen, H. G., & van de Wetering, B. J. M. (2007). Neuropsychiatric insights in clinical practice: From relapse prevention toward relapse management. *American Journal of Addictions, 16,* 530–531.

Stubbe, D. (2018). The therapeutic alliance: The fundamental element of psychotherapy. *Focus: The Journal of Lifelong Learning in Psychiatry, 16*(4), 402–403. https://doi.org/10.1176/appi.focus .20180022

Substance Abuse and Mental Health Services Administration. (2014). *Improving cultural competence: Treatment improvement protocol (TIP) series No. 59. HHS Publication No. (SMA) 14-4849*. Substance Abuse and Mental Health Services Administration.

Substance Abuse and Mental Health Services Administration. (2019). *Enhancing motivation for change in substance use disorder treatment: Treatment improvement protocol (TIP) series No. 35. SAMHSA Publication No. PEP19-02-01-003*. Substance Abuse and Mental Health Services Administration.

Substance Abuse and Mental Health Services Administration. (2020a). *Substance use disorder treatment for people with co-occurring disorders: Treatment improvement protocol (TIP) series, No. 42. SAMHSA Publication No. PEP20-02-01-004*. Substance Abuse and Mental Health Services Administration.

Substance Abuse and Mental Health Services Administration. (2020b). *Substance Use disorder treatment and family therapy: Treatment improvement protocol (TIP) series, No. 39. SAMHSA Publication No. PEP20-02-02-012*. Substance Abuse and Mental Health Services Administration.

Substance Abuse and Mental Health Services Administration. (2023). *Recovery and recovery support*. https://www.samhsa.gov/find-help/recovery

Wegscheider-Cruse, S. (1976). *The family trap: No one escapes from a chemically dependent family*. Onsight Training & Consulting.

Yalom, I. D., & Leszcz, M. (2020). *The theory and practice of group psychotherapy* (6th ed.). Basic Books.

CASE STUDY 7.1

A 52-year-old cisgender female client who identifies as a lesbian comes to counseling and states that she has been drinking most of her adult life. She has lost her job, her relationship is failing, she is exhausted from parenting her 6-year-old daughter, and is facing the prospect of a liver transplant due to her poor health from years of heavy drinking. She is coming to counseling hopeful that she can change her life, repair her relationship, and watch her young daughter grow up. She is guardedly optimistic but overwhelmed and scared about her health. The counselor has had many experiences treating clients with alcohol use disorder but is not familiar with the LGBTQ+ population. The counselor reflects on theories, techniques, and training experiences while listening to the client's story. The counselor realizes they are not well prepared to address the issues that this client brings into counseling.

1. What issues might the counselor "not be prepared to address," given that she has a lot of experience treating clients with alcohol use disorder?

2. What steps should the counselor take to provide the best care for this client?

3. What things must the counselor consider when developing the treatment plan with this client?

(*See answers on the next page.*)

CASE STUDY 7.1 ANSWERS

1. The counselor has experience providing care to clients who are diagnosed with alcohol use disorder but seems to be having a difficult time with the diversity issues and cultural differences between herself and the client who identifies as a lesbian woman. The counselor needs to increase her cultural competency with this population by learning more about the LGBTQ+ community and the unique needs that present in treatment to provide the most ethical and effective care. The counselor must also self-examine regarding her own cultural identity.

2. The first step the counselor should take is to challenges her own beliefs, ideas, and preconceived notions about her own cultural identity and the differences between herself and the client and address any internalized heterosexism. She should also become more knowledgeable about the cultural identity of the client being careful not to overgeneralize but instead work with the client in the assessment process to broach the topic of cultural differences to build therapeutic rapport. The counselor must also understand the unique challenges this client brings into treatment related to her presenting issues and group identity.

3. Based on cultural factors, there are many things to consider when working with clients from the LGBTQ+ community. Factors related to this case study and the cultural implications for treatment include social support challenges due to possible rejection from family and others based on sexual orientation, age (lesbian women do not have the protective factor related to age that women in the majority population do), healthcare coverage issues (many marginalized populations do not have adequate healthcare coverage), and confidentiality issues related to the coming out process. The client may be uncomfortable with therapy modalities that require disclosing personal life details as is required in group therapy or sponsorship in 12-step support group meetings. The counselor should also carefully assess for any trauma or violence history based on discrimination related to sexual orientation. Assessing for co-occurring mental health issues which are historically much higher in marginalized groups due to the higher levels of stress and negative self and other messages is also a key factor to consider.

KNOWLEDGE CHECK: CHAPTER 7

1. In transactional analysis (TA), the _____ is the conscience concerned with moral behavior, while in psychoanalytic theory it is the _____.
   A) Adult, unconscious
   B) Parent, ego
   C) Parent, id
   D) Parent, superego

2. A client, Janet, shares in counseling that she hates her job and is depressed. She further shares that even though she is normally a rule follower, she drinks and uses marijuana on the job because none of her coworkers like her. Which counseling theory would best explain what Joan is expressing?
   A) Social learning theory
   B) Psychoanalytic theory
   C) Cognitive behavioral theory
   D) Transactional analysis

3. In counseling, Joan shares that she thinks the counselor doesn't like her because the counselor is the same age as Joan's mom who is very disapproving of Joan's behavior. The counselor is concerned about this and wants to address it in therapy. What is the most likely item to be on the treatment plan given this information?
   A) Joan will reduce her drinking by 4 drinks per day
   B) Joan and the counselor will work through the transference for insight into Joan's presenting issues
   C) Joan will write a letter to her mom sharing her thoughts, feelings, and actions that will be reviewed in session
   D) Joan will complete a depression inventory to determine if a referral to a medication provider should be made

4. A counselor is challenging a client who states that she can't make friends if she doesn't go to bars and that no one ever has fun at alcohol-free events. The counselor develops a targeted intervention to address these faulty beliefs. What type of therapy would the counselor most likely be using?
   A) Client-centered therapy
   B) Behavioral therapy
   C) Feminist therapy
   D) Rational emotive behavior therapy

5. A client with alcohol use disorder is struggling to stop drinking after several previous failed attempts. During therapy sessions, the client consistently makes statements such as "I can either drink or be miserable," "If I have one drink, I might as well have 10," and "I'm a total failure if I can't quit drinking completely." What is the best intervention to use with this client?
   A) Teach the client to identify and dispute the cognitive thought distortions they are engaged in and help them develop a rational rebuttal to be practiced frequently
   B) Review the stages of change to determine the client's level of motivation and develop an intervention based on the stage of change
   C) Work on mindfulness techniques with the client to help with the anxiety the client is experiencing
   D) Work with the client on keeping a drinking log to track how many drinks are consumed at a time to ensure an accurate count of drinks to be used to develop a treatment plan

(See answers on the next page.)

1. D) Parent, superego

Transactional analysis uses popular terminology—such as parent, child, and adult—when describing ego or personality traits. The parent state has been likened to Freud's superego personality state which also deals with the ethical component of personality and provides the moral standards out of which the ego operates. The parent ego state contains the values, morals, core beliefs, and behaviors copied from parental figures. If a child has nurturing caretakers, the child is said to develop nurturing "parent" qualities such as being nonjudgmental and empathic with others. If a child had critical or controlling caretakers, the child tends to act in harsh or intimidating ways.

2. B) Psychoanalytic theory

Janet's statement that she drinks and uses marijuana on the job because none of her coworkers like her is a psychoanalytic defense mechanism called rationalization. This defense mechanism is keeping Janet away from addressing the conflict between her desire to follow the rules (superego) and her wish to escape her loneliness at work by seeking gratification from using substances (id).

3. B) Joan and the counselor will work through the transference for insight into Joan's presenting issues

Joan's statement that she thinks the counselor does not like her because the counselor is the same age as Joan's mother is an example of transference. A psychoanalytic treatment technique is to uncover the past and work through the transference to reconstruct the client's basic personality to move toward health. A treatment plan objective that counts the number of drinks would be based in behavioral therapy and writing a letter to the client's mom regarding the client's thoughts, feelings, and actions would be appropriate in cognitive behavioral therapy. A treatment plan goal of completing a depression inventory for a medication referral is appropriate but does not address the transference issue that was raised in the question.

4. D) Rational emotive behavior therapy

While the counselor should be using the client-centered approach in all therapeutic interventions, the most likely and most effective therapy to use with faulty beliefs is rational emotive behavior therapy (REBT). REBT addresses faulty beliefs by helping the client develop more rational beliefs that are true, sensible, and constructive using the activating event, beliefs, consequences, dispute, and effective philosophy (ABC-DE) model. Behavioral therapy addresses behaviors and not beliefs and feminist therapy would be used to address social, cultural, and political problems the client is experiencing.

5. A) Teach the client to identify and dispute the cognitive thought distortions they are engaged in and help them develop a rational rebuttal to be practiced frequently

The client is engaging in all-or-nothing thinking, viewing events in black-and-white terms with no gray areas. This is a cognitive thought distortion. Cognitive therapy, developed by Beck, is the best intervention for thought distortions. In the cognitive restructuring process, counselors help clients identify thought distortions to identify their automatic problematic thoughts (cognitions), dispute the automatic thoughts, and develop a rational rebuttal that is practiced frequently to change the unhelpful thinking patterns. The other interventions may be helpful, but they do not address the thought distortions.

6. What is it called when reinforcement is withheld from a previously reinforced behavior in order to decrease the behavior?
   A) Unconditional response
   B) Law of effect
   C) Conditioned response
   D) Extinction

7. Thoughts, feelings, and behaviors characteristic of group members during the transition stage of group counseling include:
   A) Defensiveness, resistance, anxiety, fear, struggle for control, conflict, and confrontation
   B) Trust, cohesion, sense of inclusion, open communication, self-disclosure, shared leadership, giving feedback freely
   C) Defensiveness, resistance, anxiety, fear, giving feedback, and self-disclosure
   D) Anxiety, sadness, fear, concerns about unfinished business, and questioning next steps

8. In motivational interviewing (MI), what is the best description of the role of the counselor?
   A) An expert, providing unilateral direction and guidance
   B) A subordinate, primarily listening and reflecting
   C) A coach or consultant, asking key questions for learning
   D) An authority figure, creating a professional treatment plan

9. Working with clients who have substance use disorders can result in a counselor hearing many emotionally disturbing or life-threatening traumatic events that can have lasting adverse effects on the client. Which term best describes the impact this can have on counselors?
   A) Counselor burnout
   B) Vicarious trauma
   C) Counselor apathy
   D) Compassion overload

10. What is the best distinction between substance use treatment programs and peer-based support groups such as 12-step support groups?
    A) Treatment programs offer help and groups offer support
    B) Treatment programs are expensive; support groups are often free or low-cost treatment
    C) Treatment programs are run by paid professionals and support groups are run by lay people
    D) Treatment programs offer treatment led by licensed or credentialed providers and support groups are community based and led by peers offering support

11. Beyond the culture of the client, what is another key cultural issue that must be considered to provide culturally competent and sensitive care?
    A) The client's family's number of generations born in the United States
    B) Clients living in cultural groups
    C) Culture awareness of the client including beliefs, biases, and background
    D) Counselor's own cultural development, background, beliefs, biases, and privilege

12. There are five primary group models used in substance use treatment. Which model views problematic substance use as a learned behavior that can be modified?
    A) Psychoeducational groups
    B) Cognitive behavioral groups
    C) Skills groups
    D) Support groups

(See answers on the next page.)

6. D) Extinction
Extinction is the term that refers to the process of decreasing a behavior over time by withholding reinforcement for the behavior. An unconditional response is a behavior that occurs automatically without any previous learning, like salivating when biting into a lemon. The law of effect, coined by Thorndike (a behavior theorist), says that any behavior that is followed by positive outcomes is likely to be repeated and any behavior that brings unpleasant outcomes is likely to be avoided. A conditioned response happens when a reward or punishment for an involuntary response is changed to elicit a change in behavior. If you pair a bell with eating a lemon, over time you will salivate when the bell is rung even without the lemon, just like Pavlov's dogs!

7. A) Defensiveness, resistance, anxiety, fear, struggle for control, conflict, and confrontation
The transition stage, also known as the storming stage, elicits defensiveness, resistance, anxiety, fear, struggle for control, conflict, and confrontation from group members. Giving feedback and self-disclosure are part of the working stage of group counseling. Trust, cohesion, sense of inclusion, open communication, self-disclosure, shared leadership, and giving feedback freely are characteristic of the working stage of group counseling. Anxiety, sadness, fear, concerns about unfinished business, and questioning next steps are characteristic of the final stage of group counseling.

8. C) A coach or consultant, asking key questions for learning
MI utilizes techniques derived from numerous theoretical approaches that work in conjunction with the stages of change, with heavy emphasis on client-centered principles and client autonomy. MI is designed to explore the client's uncertainty about change using a client-centered directive approach. The counselor acts as a coach or consultant in this process using a nonjudgmental, collaborative style of counseling that uncovers the discrepancies between where the client is and where they would like to be. An expert style of counseling or positioning the counselor as authority figure does not honor the client's autonomy and undermines the exploration of the client's own reasons for change.

9. B) Vicarious trauma
Counselors who work with clients who are diagnosed with substance use disorders often hear traumatic stories from clients either prior to their substance use, often arising from adverse childhood events (ACEs), or because of their substance use. Hearing these narratives over time can result in counselors experiencing vicarious trauma, emotional residue from hearing and witnessing clients' trauma, fear, pain, and terror. Compassion fatigue and burnout can occur as a result of vicarious trauma if the vicarious trauma is not managed properly.

10. D) Treatment programs offer treatment led by licensed or credentialed providers and support groups are community based and led by peers offering support
Substance use treatment programs are organized and provided by licensed and credentialed entities that provide formalized treatment services. Mutual help support groups are often free of charge but are better described as being community-based, peer-led support groups that are an important part of recovery. Support groups are not considered "treatment" but an important part of overall recovery.

11. D) Counselor's own cultural development, background, beliefs, biases, and privilege
Not only do clients bring their own cultural background into the treatment experience so do counselors. Providing culturally competent care requires that counselors understand their own culture and that of the client. Counselors must understand their own cultural development, background, beliefs, and biases as well as understand the differences between themselves and their clients. It is an ethical duty for counselors to do ongoing self-exploration as well as learning about and understanding other cultural groups and the special issues that impact treatment.

12. B) Cognitive behavioral groups
The cognitive behavioral group model views problematic substance use as an issue of learned behavior that can be modified and changed through cognitive restructuring. Psychoeducational groups entail working through structured curricula to educate the client on substance use topics such as withdrawal and cravings. Skills groups are targeted at learning coping skills to maintain recovery, while support groups are about lifestyle change and unconditional acceptance. Interpersonal groups focus on the here-and-now experience of interpersonal processing to learn about self and interactions with other people.

13. Which counseling core function is focused on providing information to the client?
    A) Consultation
    B) Referral
    C) Client education
    D) Counseling

> Bill has been sober and in recovery from stimulant use disorder for 3 years. However, he has been struggling lately with many things at home, work, and in his social life. Bill and his partner, who is worried that he will start using methamphetamine again, has come to you for help. When you ask Bill's partner what concerns her, she shared several things. She has noticed that Bill has been coming home very late from work and has been hanging out with people she doesn't know who he says are "old" friends. She suspects he is going to the bar, but he denies it. He is "blowing up" at her in anger over the smallest things and cannot seem to control his temper. They are having money problems and she doesn't think that they can afford it if he needs to go back to treatment. Recently Bill's mother came to live with them to help with expenses, but this is also straining the family. The mother is very difficult to get along with and Bill has always blamed her for his substance use because she made his childhood "a living hell."

14. Which of the following would be the most concerning thing you heard regarding Bill's recovery?
    A) The buildup of anger that could signal a return to substance use
    B) The high-risk situations, people, places, thoughts, and activities that could trigger Bill
    C) Exposure to events that are the root cause of his substance use disorder
    D) The money difficulties and lack of financial means that are barriers to seeking treatment

15. Eleanor has been in recovery and abstinent from alcohol for 6 months. In order to reduce her temptation to drink, she is avoiding social situations which involve alcohol. Recently, she missed a work-related fundraiser that she was required to attend because there was alcohol available at the event. Eleanor is worried that she will be fired for not attending the event because she has been on probation in the past for missing work due to her substance use. She asks the counselor to help her figure out a way to let her boss know why she didn't attend the fund raiser. The counselor decides to
    A) Explore with the client her probation status and her feelings toward her boss
    B) Role-play with the client a conversation to have with her boss to explain the differences in her attendance problems and the workplace supports she needs for her recovery
    C) Develop a crisis intervention plan for the next work fundraiser
    D) Develop a plan to leave her job because there are too many triggers for her

16. The first step of the 12-steps requires
    A) A willingness to attend meetings
    B) A commitment to enter treatment
    C) An admission that you are not in control of your addiction
    D) Identifying a higher power

17. Sally is leading a skills development group for clients at a treatment center to help them develop better coping skills. Sally is having a lot of difficulty with group members staying on task as there are two group members who dominate the time. Sally asks her supervisor for help, and he observes the next group meeting. Two group members dominate the group, take leadership of the conversation, complain about the treatment center, and do not work on developing coping skills. In supervision, Sally is surprised when the supervisor confronts her about how poorly the group is going rather than talking about the two group members' behavior. Why is Sally surprised?
    A) Sally demonstrated a laissez-faire group leadership style
    B) Sally has poor boundaries and little insight and awareness of the group members
    C) The supervisor aligned with the group members
    D) Sally demonstrated an authoritarian leadership style

(*See answers on the next page.*)

13. C) Client education

The client education core function is defined as providing information to clients, either formally or informally, concerning substance use and the available services and resources. The information must be provided in ways that can be understood by the client, taking into account their learning style and level of understanding. The referral core function involves identifying the needs of the client that cannot be met through counseling and assisting the client to find ways to meet those needs. The counseling core function is the treatment provided to the client using counseling theory and techniques to resolve the client's presenting problems. The consultation core function is a counselor-based function that involves the counselor seeking out "in-house" or outside professional feedback to ensure they are providing quality care for the client. This must be done with the appropriate releases of information in place and following ethical and legal guidelines.

14. B) The high-risk situations, people, places, thoughts, and activities that could trigger Bill

Bill is experiencing many things that would be risk factors for relapse. A relapse is best defined as an interruption in one's attempt to change a behavior. Triggers for a return to use, or relapse, are defined as the high-risk situations, people, places, thoughts, and activities that the client experiences in the recovery process. In real-time monitoring, triggers are identified and a plan developed to replace these triggers with healthier coping mechanisms. A buildup of anger events can be a trigger for the client to return to substance use; however triggers are more than just emotions and they are not necessarily the root cause of the substance use disorder or a defining moment that indicates a client must return to treatment.

15. B) Role-play with the client a conversation to have with her boss to explain the differences in her attendance problems and the workplace supports she needs for her recovery

The client in early recovery would be in the relapse prevention stage of her treatment. In this stage, the counselor would work with the client on developing and implementing a relapse prevention plan to avoid high-risk situations and other triggers related to her past substance use. Role-playing the conversation with the boss and sharing about the triggers the event presented as well as requesting support for her recovery will help the client implement the relapse prevention plan and strengthen her recovery.

16. C) An admission that you are not in control of your addiction

The first step of the 12-steps is "We admitted we were powerless over alcohol (or our addiction) and our lives had become unmanageable." This first step is an admission of powerlessness over the effect of the substance and the consequences from using it; it is letting go and asking for help so healing can begin. People can attend 12-step support group meetings and not be in a treatment program. Identifying a higher power happens in step 2.

17. A) Sally demonstrated a laissez-faire group leadership style

In the laissez-faire group leadership style, the leader lets the group members take accountability for the group rather than the leader. Sally is demonstrating this style by not intervening with the group members or taking leadership of the process. In the authoritarian leadership style, the leader is seen as the expert and all communication is directed through the leader with no direct interaction with other members. This is clearly not the case. Sally does have awareness of what the group members are doing but has not changed her leadership style to intervene. The supervisor is not aligning with the members but rather is challenging Sally to grow and become a better leader.

A counselor receives a referral for Lorena, a 22-year-old, single, Latina female client who recently completed a residential treatment program for alcohol use disorder. She is ready to leave the treatment center. The referral states Lorena needs outpatient care to "develop a relapse prevention plan." During the first session, Lorena shares that knows she needs to develop a relapse prevention plan, but she thinks it's more important to talk about getting help from her family, finding a job, "hanging out with friends," and "staying out of trouble." She states she doesn't want to go to jail which will happen if she violates her probation again.

Lorena has been estranged from her family since entering treatment 3 months ago. Lorena was court ordered to treatment after violating her probation for the third time. Lorena had been living with her parents until she went to treatment. Her parents were embarrassed by Lorena's behavior and, after talking with a court advocate, decided that they would not let Lorena live with them once she completed treatment. Lorena's parents moved to the United States from Guatemala when Lorena was born. Lorena says her parents are "stuck in the old ways," don't understand American culture, and never understood the pressure she was under as a teenager or now as a young adult. Lorena shared that her father drinks a lot but "no one talks about that." Lorena has four siblings, one that is older and three that are younger. Her youngest brother still lives with her parents. She is worried about him because her dad gets very angry and has hurt him in the past. Lorena states, "I'm scared because he has been that way with me too." She did not want to elaborate and quickly changed the subject to talk about her sisters. Lorena doesn't get along with her oldest sister who she says is "perfect," however, she likes her two younger sisters who are "cool" and "fun." All her sisters have left the house and live on their own. They don't visit their parents much and prefer to stay in touch through social media. Lorena is frequently left out of those conversations which makes her angry.

Lorena is now living with a friend from high school who has been in trouble with the law for selling narcotics. Lorena is looking for a job to help pay the rent, but it has been difficult because she didn't finish high school. She used to make good money bartending; however, she is not allowed to do that while on probation. Lorena is sleeping a lot since moving in with her friend and she generally avoids everyone. She rarely goes out of the house unless it's for meetings with her probation officer or for counseling appointments. She states she doesn't feel safe leaving the house.

During the intake session Lorena states that she has been sober for 90 days and she is sure she won't drink again after what she has been through. She only wants to work on moving back into her parent's house. As the counselor you have many concerns about what Lorena shared and decide that you need to find out more information before a treatment plan can be developed.

18. Why is more information needed about this client even though she has been through treatment and comes to you for a relapse prevention plan?
   A) More information needs to be known about Lorena's trauma history and mental health symptoms to determine if she has unmet treatment needs
   B) Lorena has not been truthful in the past because of her substance use problems and may not be telling the truth about her sobriety
   C) More needs to be known about her employment history to determine if a referral to a vocational counselor is needed since this is a part of her probation
   D) It is unclear if Lorena is in the correct stage of change for outpatient therapy

19. Lorena shares a lot about her family and her wish to move back into their house. At this point in her treatment, the counselor does not recommend she moves home because
   A) The family is not willing right now to have her move in and this has not been addressed in family counseling
   B) The client doesn't understand her role in the family dynamics and wants only to rescue her brother
   C) The client would be at high risk for relapse if she moves back home without family counseling
   D) All of the above

18. A) More information needs to be known Lorena's trauma history and mental health symptoms to determine if she has unmet treatment needs

Lorena has shared many things that would indicate she has experienced trauma and adverse childhood events based on her comments about her father and living in a house where substance use was occurring. She also feels unsafe in her current living situation. More also needs to be known about her mental health symptoms to determine if co-occurring treatment is needed in addition to a relapse prevention plan. Truthfulness, employment, and stage of can be addressed in relapse prevention planning after determining the full extent of the issues she is presenting.

19. D) All of the above

The complicated family dynamics in this case call for an intervention with the family system to address the issues that have led to Lorena's substance use disorder and to address her risk of relapse. There are many models of family therapy that could be employed; however, the family first needs to be willing to engage in treatment which is the first step in helping Lorena toward her goal of moving back home. Educating Lorena on the family dynamics and her role in the family will be important in helping her understand the path forward with the family.

20. Lorena would like the family to be involved in her treatment in an attempt to protect her brother. What steps should you as the counselor take to help the family and Lorena address the family dynamics?
    A) Confront the family about the father's drinking to convince them to get the father to treatment
    B) Make a referral for abuse and neglect to the treatment center based on the information Lorena shared about her brother
    C) Discuss with Lorena the role of family dynamics in substance use disorders and ask for a release of information to discuss with the family their willingness to be involved in family counseling for Lorena's treatment
    D) Nothing, Lorena is your client and not the family

21. Lorena and the family have agreed to family counseling. The counselor has started brief solution family therapy. However, even though the counselor is following the counseling model precisely and everyone is attending and engaged, the sessions are not going well. The counselor notices that the father initiates most of the conversation and family members look to him for approval and guidance instead of examining their own roles in the family. What could be the problem?
    A) The family is not being honest in session because they are afraid of the father
    B) The family is not ready for family counseling. They have not worked through resentments and need to attend Al-Anon
    C) The treatment model does not fit the family. The counselor should change the treatment model to behavioral couples therapy
    D) The culture of the family is not being taken into consideration and has not been addressed. Furthermore, the counselor has not examined their own cultural identity in relation to the client and family and is not understanding the dynamics in the room based on culture

22. Lorena continues to have individual sessions with her counselor in addition to family sessions. She is making good progress on her goals, has been in recovery for 6 months (verified by negative drug screens), has a good job, and is meeting regularly with her probation officer. During the sessions, however, Lorena expresses many times that she is tired, irritated with everyone, does not want to leave the house, and is worried about her brother. She says she has thoughts that bother her, but she will not tell the counselor what those are, even though she says she trusts the counselor. The counselor is concerned Lorena may be having thoughts of self-harm. What is the best course of action to address these issues?
    A) Refer Lorena to another provider to assess her mental needs and include the recommendations into her relapse prevention plan to work on after her substance use counseling is complete
    B) Refer Lorena to another provider to assess her mental needs and develop a plan to treat both her substance use and mental health needs. Coordinating the care with other providers is indicated; include this in her relapse prevention plan
    C) Refer Lorena to another provider who can assess and treat her substance use and mental health symptoms, even if it means terminating care with this counselor
    D) Refer Lorena to another provider to assess her mental needs and incorporate the mental health treatment into the counselor's sessions even though they are not a qualified mental health provider; it's better to continue to provide the care to Lorena rather than switch providers since she trusts this counselor

23. During Lorena's last appointment, she states that while she has remained sober, she has been having a very hard time getting out of bed and has not been showering or eating. She called the crisis line last night worried that she will do something "stupid" because she was having "scary thoughts" and cannot get them to stop. The on-call counselor called Lorena's counselor while Lorena was on the line. What should Lorena's counselor do?
    A) Tell the on-call counselor to have Lorena call the office in the morning to schedule another appointment
    B) Review notes from the last appointment and have Lorena call 911
    C) Review notes from the last appointment and ask the on-call counselor to connect the counselor with Lorena to review the safety plan they put together in session. If Lorena cannot implement the safety plan, the counselor should arrange for law enforcement to intervene
    D) Ask the on-call counselor to remind Lorena about the safety plan and ask Lorena to follow up at the next appointment

(See answers on the next page.)

20. C) Discuss with Lorena the role of family dynamics in substance use disorders and ask for a release of information to discuss with the family their willingness to be involved in family counseling for Lorena's treatment

Lorena does not, at this point, appear to understand the family roles that emerge when a substance use disorder is impacting a family. She wants to rescue her brother who appears to be the lost child. Educating Lorena and getting permission to talk with the family about family counseling is the most appropriate course of action to help Lorena resolve the family conflict which will be an important relapse prevention goal. Confronting the father at this stage of change will only alienate the family as they have stated they do not want to be involved even though they have been in the past (contemplation stage of change). Reports of abuse or neglect do not go to treatment centers and it is unclear at this point if a report needs to be made based on the information presented and the brother's age.

21. D) The culture of the family is not being taken into consideration and has not been addressed. Furthermore, the counselor has not examined their own cultural identity in relation to the client and family and is not understanding the dynamics in the room based on culture

Culture is an important factor to address in every counseling encounter. There are important cultural factors to consider with this family. This includes learning more about the family's culture as they have immigrated from Guatemala, understanding the hierarchy in the family based on culture, the role of power and privilege, negotiating the treatment plan asking for feedback on cultural appropriateness, and adjusting treatment modalities when needed. A note on behavioral couples therapy: Although this modality can be modified to work with families, it is typically reserved for working with couples and intimate partners. In this case, it is not indicated based on the identified client being a child in the family.

22. B) Refer Lorena to another provider to assess her mental needs and develop a plan to treat both her substance use and mental health needs. Coordinating the care with other providers is indicated; include this in her relapse prevention plan

The mental health symptoms Lorena is reporting are a concern for her safety, recovery, and overall mental well-being. Lorena has been in recovery and sobriety long enough to determine that she is likely experience co-occurring disorders (CODs), defined as the occurrence of a substance use disorder and a mental health disorder when at least one disorder of each type can be established independently of the other and is not simply a cluster of symptoms resulting from the one disorder. Because Lorena has made good progress in her care and the therapeutic rapport is good, having Lorena assessed by an appropriate provider who is qualified to diagnosis mental health disorders and incorporating the recommendations into her care in a simultaneous and parallel treatment model for CODs (separate treatment providers and programs occurring at the same time) is the best treatment approach given how far she is into her substance use disorder treatment.

23. C) Review notes from the last appointment and ask the on-call counselor to connect the counselor with Lorena to review the safety plan they put together in session. If Lorena cannot implement the safety plan, the counselor should arrange for law enforcement to intervene

This is a crisis that requires the counselor to employ the crisis intervention core function. According to the crisis intervention core function, the counselor should respond to the client's acute emotional distress and implement an immediate course of action. The other options do not ensure the client's safety which is an ethical and legal concern.

24. Lorena was very angry during her last session after the counselor confronted her on choice of friends and her probation requirements. Lorena said "What do you know about it? You've probably never even smoked a joint! You don't know how hard it is to stay sober!" The counselor should
    A) Share their own substance use history to build rapport and defend themself
    B) Use silence to let the moment pass
    C) Say, "I understand that you are very upset with me and can't imagine that I would know what it's like to have these temptations and stay sober"
    D) Ask Lorena to work through her resentments with her sponsor

---

The following is an exchange that occurred during Lorena's session:

Lorena: "I really want to move back home with my family and get out of my friend's house. There is a lot of drug dealing going on in the neighborhood where I live now. I'm so tempted all the time and I'm worried I will be accused of using or selling if my probation office comes by unexpected."

Counselor: "You're scared because you are tempted by all the drug use around you and you might get busted for things you aren't doing. You want to get back to your parents' house."

Lorena: "Yes! I want out of here, but I don't want to be around my dad. He's such a jerk and it really sets me off; it makes me want to get high."

Counselor: "So you want to get out of the drug environment at your friend's house and move back home, but you don't really want to be around your dad because you're afraid you might want to get high."

Lorena: "Yes, does that make any sense? I'm so confused about what to do."

---

25. What should the counselors next response be?
    A) "Let's do a decisional balance activity to determine the best course of action; it will become clear what you should do"
    B) "You feel trapped and worry you might use; neither your current home nor your parent's house seems like the best place to be for your recovery"
    C) "You should definitely find your own place to live to remove all the temptations"
    D) Engage silence to let the client answer her own question

(See answers on the next page.)

24. C) Say, "I understand that you are very upset with me and can't imagine that I would know what it's like to have these temptations and stay sober"
Lorena is very upset and feels like the counselor doesn't understand her. In this case, a self-disclosure is inappropriate because it would be in response to the counselor feeling defensive and not to help the client. The counselor must acknowledge the client's feelings and build rapport by using the reflection of feeling skill to let the client know she has been heard and acknowledged. Ignoring the statement or asking someone else to work with the client on it will only increase the client's agitation with the counselor, rupturing the relationship.

25. B) "You feel trapped and worry you might use; neither your current home nor your parent's house seems like the best place to be for your recovery"
By examining the chain of responses, the counselor has used the empathic confrontation skill. The counselor has noticed a discrepancy in what the client is sharing—her desire to move out to live with her parents and her hesitation about living with her dad. The counselor reflects both sides of the client's discrepancy in a nonjudgmental manner leading the client to identify her confusion and the underlying issue: relapse. The counselor's next response should focus the identified discrepancy to the underlying issue that is creating and sustaining the client's problem—the potential of relapse.

Legal, Ethical, and Professional Issues

Becca Moore and Christine Tina Chasek

In this chapter, we cover the topics in the alcohol and drug counselor (ADC) exam under "Domain 4: Professional, Ethical, and Legal Responsibilities and the Report and Record Keeping and Consultation Core Functions." These core functions help in recognizing elements of discharge planning and when to terminate the counseling process. The professional, ethical, and legal responsibilities of an addiction counselor are critically important and, like all helping professions, ethical codes and legal statutes guide clinical practice. The important legal issues for addiction counselors are reviewed in this chapter. In addition, the ethical issues addressed in this chapter are drawn from the following ethical codes and sources applicable to addiction counselors—American Counseling Association (ACA, 2014); National Association for Alcoholism and Drug Abuse Counselors (NAADAC), the Association for Addiction Professionals (2021); Substance Abuse and Mental Health Services Administration (SAMHSA) TAP 21 competencies (Center for Substance Abuse Treatment [CSAT], 2015); and International Certification and Reciprocity Consortium (IC&RC) Code of Ethics—all of which can be adopted by members of the consortium.

LEGAL ISSUES

It is important to understand the laws that impact you in practice. As an addiction counselor, there are several laws and concepts that you need to understand. These include the Health Insurance Portability and Accountability Act (HIPAA), confidentiality, 42 CFR Part 2, scope of practice, and other federal, state, and local laws that apply to addiction counseling.

▶ HEALTH INSURANCE PORTABILITY AND ACCOUNTABILITY ACT

HIPAA is a guiding law for all medical, mental health, and substance use providers. Overall, there are two parts to HIPAA: the privacy rule, which guides the standards for protecting a person's personal health information, and the security rule which focuses on how to safeguard electronic records. Familiarity with the privacy rule is often because of one's own experience in the healthcare system. For example, if you have ever needed to share your medical information, you must sign a consent form to do so. This is because, due to HIPAA, your healthcare information is private. Your provider is not allowed to share your information without your written consent. Even then, what they share is often limited unless you specify otherwise. If you have been sick and need a note from your physician to excuse you from work, the note might say, "Patient was seen this week. Excused from work for the following dates." They do not tell your place of work what your diagnosis was or what symptoms you were treated for unless you specify that they can do so.

While you may be familiar with how HIPAA protects your medical records, it is important to be aware that those same laws apply to your counseling clients. If someone is or has been a client, it means all the information you have from treating them is private and confidential except under very specific circumstances, detailed later in the "Confidentiality" section.

In addition to giving you the right to privacy in your medical records, HIPAA also gives you the right to review your medical records and notes. Providers are required to provide you with your medical chart if you request that information. It is important to consider this when you do your documentation. Although not every client will request access to their information, all clients have the right to do so.

Parents also have the right to request information regarding their minor children, though it is important to note that what constitutes a minor child will vary by each state or governing body. According to the U.S. Department of Health and Human Services (DHHS, 2022), there are three situations when the parent would **not** be the minor's personal representative under HIPAA. These exceptions are:

1. The minor is the one who consents to care and the consent of the parent is not required under state or other applicable law.

2. The minor obtains care at the direction of the court, or a person appointed by the court.
3. The parent agrees that the minor and the healthcare provider may have a confidential relationship to an agreed-upon extent.

CONFIDENTIALITY

Confidentiality is a significant part of HIPAA and is also an important ethical issue. According to the code of ethics developed by the ACA (2014), **confidentiality** is the ethical duty of counselors to protect a client's identity, identifying characteristics, and private communications. Confidentiality in counseling includes many things such as privacy and trust, limits of confidentiality, informed consent, legal processes and terms, documentation and record-keeping, and technology.

Privacy and Trust

While there are limits to its scope, confidentiality itself is paramount to the therapeutic process. Clients are often hesitant to share their experiences with others. Assuring them that the information they share stays private helps them feel safe to share their stories and establishes trust.

Limits of Confidentiality

Addiction counselors must be aware of the limits to confidentiality. These limits generally fall into three categories: (1) danger to self or others, (2) abuse or neglect of minor children or vulnerable adults, and (3) and court orders or legal rulings.

Danger to Self

When working in the substance use field, you will almost certainly encounter clients who are struggling with serious concerns and suicidal ideation. Suicide can be an extremely complex issue as there are varying degrees of suicidal thought. Some clients may have thoughts like, "It would be easier if I just didn't wake up tomorrow" and with others may have a plan of how they are going to die, when they are going to die, along with other details that make it clear that suicide is a realistic possibility.

It is important for counselors to be aware of their responsibility to their clients in these situations. Although there are no specific laws regarding treatment protocols for suicidality, an addiction counselor has the legal and ethical right to break confidentiality if they believe their client is at risk. The important factor is having that right outlined in the informed consent (covered later) and by letting a client know at the outset of treatment that if they are suicidal, the counselor will break confidentiality if deemed necessary to keep them safe.

Harm to Others

If the client makes a credible threat of imminent harm to another person, you have a responsibility to your client and to the public to report the danger. This is known as the **duty to warn** (Gorshkalova & Munakomi, 2023). The duty to warn comes from the landmark Tarasoff court case. In the Tarasoff case, a client confided to his psychologist that he intended to harm his acquaintance, a woman named Tatiana Tarasoff. The psychologist did report the intended harm to law enforcement but failed to warn the intended victim or her family of the threat. After the client followed through on his threat and, tragically, murdered Tarasoff, her parents sued the psychologist and won.

The subsequent supreme court ruling in the Tarasoff case requires mental health and substance use counselors to break confidentiality when a client threatens bodily harm against a member of the public. However, each state has different requirements when it comes to the duty to warn. Some stipulate that, in order to break confidentiality, the client must mention a specific, named victim and imminent threat, while others require much less information to break confidentiality. In some states, a counselor can simply report threats to law enforcement, and in others, they must be able to prove that they made a conscious effort to contact the potential victim(s). It is also important to note that some states have statutes to protect the practitioner from breaching confidentiality if they report a threat. Because the guidelines vary so much by state, if you find yourself in a duty-to-warn situation, it is important to also seek legal advice as well as consultation from other seasoned practitioners.

Addiction counselors will likely work with clients who engage in behaviors that raise their risk of contracting infectious diseases (e.g., sharing needles). This is another instance where a duty to warn exists. For example, hepatitis, sexually transmitted infections (STIs), HIV, and other infectious diseases are common among people with substance use disorders. Rules and confidentiality guidelines set out by each state require the counselor to report HIV as appropriate (Centers for Disease Control and Prevention, n.d.). However, if a court requires information regarding client treatment, it is imperative to protect the client's HIV status. Some states require providers to break confidentiality to warn others if there is a known risk of imminent danger or serious bodily harm to another under the duty-to-warn guidelines.

Tips From the Field

You can find a map with more information about the duty to warn in each state at www.ncsl.org/health/mental-health-professionals-duty-to-warn (National Conference of State Legislatures, 2022).

Abuse or Neglect of Vulnerable Individuals

Counselors are **mandated reporters**, meaning that they have a legal obligation to break confidentiality and report suspected or known abuse or neglect of vulnerable individuals to the appropriate designated authorities in a timely manner. The designated authority can vary by state; however, the report is generally made to the child and adult protection authorities. If you suspect abuse or neglect of vulnerable individuals, you should gather as many details as possible to make a report so that authorities can make an informed decision regarding the safety of the individual.

A counselor must also keep in mind the potential abuse or neglect of vulnerable individuals when working with counseling records. According to the DHHS (2022), if a counselor deems that information in a client's chart could be harmful to the vulnerable individual (child or adult under guardianship), the information does not need to be released to the parent or guardian if requested. If you are working with a child who disclosed abuse and the parent subsequently requests access to the information in the child's chart, your primary role as a provider is to protect the best interests of the child and hold the information confidential, even though the parent or guardian may have a legal right to the information. This is to ensure safety and protection of the client.

INFORMED CONSENT

The ACA (2014) defines **informed consent** as a process of information sharing associated with possible actions clients may choose to take, aimed at assisting clients to understand the implications of a given action or actions. When a client starts the therapeutic process, part of the obligation of the counselor is to review informed consent with the client. Informed consent gives clients the information they need to determine whether the process is a good fit for them. In addition, informed consent helps them understand their rights and responsibilities as a client. According to Remley and Herlihy (2020), informed consent essentially tells a client what they are signing up for in the counseling process. Allowing clients to make an informed decision about their care empowers clients and helps them determine whether this is a good time for them to enter the therapeutic journey and if the counselor in question is a good fit for them (Remley & Herlihy, 2020).

Mandatory disclosure statements are usually included within the informed consent document. These disclosures give clients more information about their counselor's education, modes of service, fees, limitations of confidentiality, right to refuse services, roles of technology including telehealth services if offered, and electronic health record (EHR) systems. For a client to truly make an informed decision about whether the counselor or the counseling process is a good fit for them, they need to have as much information up front as possible.

While it is important for the informed consent to be thorough, it is also important for it to be concise and understandable by the client. The counselor should review the informed consent with the client and answer any questions they have. If the client is amenable to the services and the conditions in which they are offered, the client will sign the form showing they agree to these services.

Although there are many variations in the information covered by informed consent, the following are generally accepted universal concepts:

- The services provided and the benefits, drawbacks, and limitations of those services
- Client rights and responsibilities
- Counselor rights and responsibilities
- Confidentiality and the limits of confidentiality
- Right to refuse services
- Information regarding access to the client's information
- Modalities offered (e.g., in person, telehealth)

The informed consent can also have other important information regarding specific services or expected treatment experiences. Beyond having it in their records, it is also important for the counselor to review the paperwork with the client. Often, informed consent documents are written by lawyers. Because of this, the information and language in the documents can sometimes be overwhelming or confusing for clients to read. Some clients may just want to sign it without reading it; however, it is important for clients to understand what they are signing to avoid confusion and potential problems later on.

LEGAL PROCESSES AND TERMS

There are a few legal processes and terms that are important for addiction counselors to understand.

- **Privilege:** Counselors and clients have legal protection of communication. This means that clients have the right *not* to have their confidential information disclosed in court without their consent. Privilege can vary among different jurisdictions and there may be exceptions to the general rule of privilege, such as described in the limits of confidentiality and in the case of subpoenas and court orders.
- **Court order:** Broad legal directive issued by a judge or court that can cover a wide variety of actions or decisions that are legally binding.
- **Subpoena:** Narrow legal order for information, either as testimony or in documentation. It is extremely important to be aware that a subpoena can be issued by lawyers as well as judges. According to the American Psychological Association (2016), there are three different types of subpoenas: (1) a witness subpoena simply means that you must be in court to provide testimony. If you are not told to bring documents, do not do so; (2) a subpoena duces tecum for your counseling records; and (3) a deposition subpoena could request your records or require you to do a deposition (sworn evidence). Regardless of the type of subpoena you receive, it is important to be aware that these are matters of law and you can be charged with contempt of court if you do not comply. However, due to the sensitive nature and complexity of courts, it is recommended that if you receive a subpoena, you seek legal counsel to determine what you can do to protect yourself and your client's best interests.

As a counselor, you are legally required to document each session or significant interaction you have with your clients. Not only is it necessary if you are billing insurance, but it also helps you keep track of clients' information and guide your therapeutic process. One of the issues to keep in mind when you are writing therapy notes is to consider that your notes may be subject to release in the case of a subpoena or if your client requests to see their records. Although this is true in any domain of counseling, it is particularly relevant when we are working with clients who have a substance use disorder as there are more likely to be pending court cases, interactions with lawyers, and other professionals.

▶ SCOPE OF PRACTICE

Scope of practice is defined as the specific activities, procedures, and responsibilities you are legally allowed to do in your chosen line of work based on the education, training, licensure, and competencies areas. In the substance use field, the scope of practice is strictly related to diagnosing and treating substance use disorders. This can be complicated because clients often come to treatment with both physical and mental health symptoms. While a substance use counselor may recognize that a client is struggling with depression or health issues related to the use of substances, to diagnose or treat either would be completely outside the scope of substance use counseling. This is one of the many reasons why consultation, collaboration, and referral are integral parts of the field. Our clients often need mental health and physical health treatment.

The role of the substance use counselor is to treat the client's addiction and to make referrals to other professionals to ensure the client is getting the services they need to achieve sobriety. Throughout this book, we have detailed the 12 core functions of an addiction counselor. These core functions are a good indicator of the scope of practice for an addiction counselor. As with all things, however, you should check with your state licensure, certification, or credentialing department to completely understand the scope of practice for your specific credential.

▶ FEDERAL REGULATIONS: 42 CFR PART 2

42 CFR Part 2 regulations are related to the confidentiality of client records and client privacy for those who are being treated for substance use disorders and apply to programs that are federally assisted. According to Petrila and Fader-Towe (2010), there are three questions that can help in determining if 42 CFR Part 2 applies to the client:

1. Is the party _sharing_ the information a covered entity or a federally assisted program?
2. Is the party _requesting_ the information a covered entity or federally assisted program?
3. What purpose will the shared information serve?

The regulations in 42 CFR Part 2 are designed to further safeguard clients' confidentiality in substance use treatment. Those who are seeking treatment for substance use disorders can be assured that information they disclose will remain confidential under these circumstances. This includes any information regarding past crimes committed. 42 CFR Part 2 also prevents further redisclosure of records that might be shared with providers once treatment has concluded. As discussed later, the safekeeping of records is also addressed in 42 CFR Part 2.

There are special provisions for minors in the 42 CFR Part 2 regulations: Minors who are determined to have capacity to seek out their own treatment can do so without parental consent under 42 CFR Part 2 **if** state laws allow. For some states, minors can consent at age 16 for treatment without parental consent. In those states, a 16-year-old who is deemed to have the capacity to understand the implications of their choices can seek treatment without their parents' knowledge or consent. For states where minors are required to have parental consent, state laws take precedence over 42 CFR Part 2 regulations.

▶ DOCUMENTATION AND RECORDKEEPING

It is both a legal responsibility and your ethical duty to maintain complete records of your clients. This includes the assessment, results of screening instruments, any evaluations or reports you complete, treatment plans, progress notes, letters, and any other information generated or gathered during the counseling process. The tasks of reports and recordkeeping are covered by the core function reports and recordingkeeping (Box 8.1; Herdman, 2021).

Box 8.1 Core Function 11: Reports and Record Keeping

Definition: Charting the results of the assessment and treatment plan, writing reports, progress notes, discharge summaries, and other client-related data.

Global Criteria:
40. Prepare reports and relevant records integrating available information to facilitate the continuum of care.
41. Chart the ongoing information pertaining to the client.
42. Utilize relevant information from written documents for client care.

For each interaction you have with a client, you are required to keep notes in a confidential file. Many counselors use an electronic health record (**EHR**) rather than a paper file. In whatever manner you keep your files, you must ensure that you are keeping them safe and confidential. If you have paper files, the filing cabinet needs to be double locked (i.e., they need to be in a locked drawer, in a locked room). If you have an EHR, the records need to be kept electronically secure as indicated by HIPAA and 42 CFR Part 2. According to HIPAA and 42 CFR Part 2, you must limit access of your EHR to only authorized personnel and ensure that the EHRs are encrypted and securely transmitted if needed. You must have an audit trail indicating who has accessed the EHR, and you must have a business associate agreement if you are using a third-party service for your EHR. Your username and password should be protected, even if you are the only person who uses the device for the EHR. Your device should also have a locking mechanism that engages shortly after inactivity. When you are completing notes, you need to be in a private location where you do not run the risk of others seeing your documentation.

Beyond the logistics of privacy in notes, there are other details to consider. It is considered best practice to have your notes completed within 24 hours of the treatment activity to ensure they are accurate, that you have documentation of any information with legal repercussions, and that documentation can be sent to the client's insurance in a timely manner to prevent delays in payment.

As an addiction counselor, you will likely be doing much documentation, including writing many letters or reports. Prior to releasing any information about the client, it is essential to ensure the proper releases of information have been secured and the client understands what is being sent to whom and for what reason. When you are writing a letter or report, it is important to keep a few things in in mind.

- Who is the report for?
- What is the purpose of the report?
- What information needs to be in the report (and conversely, is there information that should not be in the report)?
- When does the report need to be completed?

Our professional responsibility is to be as accurate as possible and to keep in mind that the information may not stay confidential once it leaves our hands. Before releasing a report, it is important to discuss with your client what information will be in the report. Based on what you share, some clients may determine that they no longer want to have the report sent in. In these cases, it's important to educate your client on what the cost of moving forward with sending the report versus what the cost of not sending the report may be. If, for example, the report is ordered by their lawyer, it is up to the client to determine whether they want that information available to the lawyer and to understand the legal consequences if they do not comply. Outside of a court order or subpoena, it is important to remember that the decision to release information is always the client's.

▶ TECHNOLOGY

Prior to the COVID-19 pandemic, many states and regulating authorities had strict rules about utilizing telehealth. However, the pandemic necessitated the use of technology to connect with clients, supervisors, and others in the provision of services. **Telehealth**, defined as the use of technology and digital communication tools to provide counseling services remotely, has become commonplace in the counseling field. Telehealth includes videoconferencing with clients, phone counseling, messaging, and chatting through text-based platforms, and virtual reality–based therapy. While it is still essential to check with your state regarding specific telehealth laws and rules, many states have made it much easier to provide services through telehealth.

Another key consideration if you are utilizing telehealth services is ensuring HIPAA compliance. Data encryption, access control, informed consent, security measures, secure documentation, and business agreements with any third-party vendors are all required when providing telehealth that is HIPAA compliant. There may be other state specific laws that govern the use of telehealth as well. It is important to check to ensure your services that are legally compliant.

ETHICS

Ethics refer to the set of principles, values, and guidelines that govern and guide the behavior, actions, and decision-making of a particular profession, in this case addiction counseling. Corey et al. (2024) stress that while the law is a minimum standard of what is acceptable, professional ethics call counselors to a higher standard. We should not be focused only on following the law, but we should be guided by our professional ethics to do what is in the best interest of our clients.

Many ethical guidelines have been developed by different counseling organizations that can be used to guide clinical practice, such as the ACA (2014), the IC&RC Code of Ethics, the NAADAC, the Association for Addiction Professionals (2021), SAMHSA TAP 21 competencies (CSAT, 2015), or state adopted codes of ethics. Best practice indicates that you should follow the ethical code laid out and endorsed by your state or professional association. The code of ethics you adhere to will include the following basic ethical competencies in the following areas:

- Confidentiality
- The counseling relationship
- Communication and technology
- Ethical decision-making
- Grievances
- Supervision and consultation
- Professional development and licensure
- Diversity, equity, inclusion, and access
- Assessment, evaluation, and interpretation
- Referral
- Discharge planning and termination

▶ CONFIDENTIALITY

In addition to the legal issues described previously, confidentiality is a cornerstone of ethical practice. Confidentiality forms the basis of trust between clients and counselors and is critical for counseling to be effective. As an ethical issue, confidentiality build trust that forms the counseling relationship. All aspects of the legality of confidentiality also apply to the ethical aspects of confidentiality.

▶ THE COUNSELING RELATIONSHIP

To facilitate change, counselors must be competent in navigating an ethical relationship with their clients. This includes helping clients understand the limitations of confidentiality, informed consent, payment-related issues, treatment modalities, and a host of other important information about the counseling process. Corey and Schneider Corey (2020) assert that as counselors, we need to be able to put our views, values, and beliefs aside to meet the client where they are and build a counseling relationship that is healthy and therapeutic. In other words, we must work diligently to not let our own values and beliefs impact our work with clients.

Lambert (2013) suggests that there are four elements responsible for change to occur in treatment:

- The counseling relationship (accounts for 30% of change)
- Extra therapeutic factors that occur outside of counseling (40% of change)
- Expectancy and hope (15% of change)
- The model and techniques used (15% of change)

As you can see, the evidence suggests that the therapeutic relationship is essential in our work with clients. This means building trust, displaying empathy, and actively listening to our clients. How we present ourselves, our ability to connect with our clients, and our genuineness are all part of the key factors in creating a healing environment for our clients. While techniques can be powerful and theories can help formulate our process of therapy, it is important to remember that the therapeutic relationship is about developing an understanding of your client. Once you understand your client and their needs, you can use your therapeutic skills to help them make sense of their world.

BOUNDARIES

Boundaries help us understand the parameters of the therapeutic relationship. Boundaries set limits in the counseling relationship allowing for a safe connection between the client and counselor (Remley & Herlihy, 2020). In substance use counseling, the client gets to determine who can come into their world and where in their world that person can be. Conversely, the counselor also gets to determine what their role looks like. A client does not get to have unfettered access to the counselor. The counselor determines how often the client will be seen, what to do in case of emergency, and other parameters that need to be set for both the well-being of the client and the well-being of the counselor.

There are two types of boundary problems described by Remley and Herlihy (2020):

- **Boundary crossings:** Smaller and less obvious breaches that have *potential* to cause harm to the client and depart from an ethical relationship.
- **Boundary violations:** Serious breaches that cause harm to the client.

Understanding how fast "minor" boundary crossings can lead to boundary violations is integral to understanding how to maintain an ethically appropriate relationship. It is unlikely that those in a helping field set out to cause harm to the very people they are trying to help. Nonetheless, when they begin to cross boundaries, even with the best of intentions, harming clients can be the result.

Sexual Boundaries

Every counselor must understand that it is inappropriate to have a sexual relationship with a client or a family member of a client. In the counselor/client relationship, it is not uncommon to experience attraction from the client to the counselor, for the counselor to the client, or both. If attraction is expressed by the client, the counselor must initiate a discussion regarding boundaries and the professional nature of the counseling relationship. If the attraction is coming from the counselor, the counselor is responsible for seeking supervision to discuss those feelings and to have someone hold them accountable to their professional standards.

It is unlikely that a counseling relationship goes straight from appropriate to an intimate or sexual relationship. Like other intimate relationships, there are likely smaller signs and smaller boundary crossings that occur. Perhaps the client is sad and the counselor seeks to comfort them with physical touch. Perhaps the client is attracted to the counselor and actively fosters a deeper intimate relationship. It may start out innocently or not, but either way, clients who have a sexual relationship with their counselor are likely to have the same reactions as those who have been victims of rape, spouse battering, incest, and posttraumatic stress disorder (Remley & Herlihy, 2020). The client feels the need to flee but also to protect their abuser, leading to an increased risk of suicide.

SOCIAL RELATIONSHIPS

While we often understand a sexual relationship as a major boundary violation in the therapeutic relationship, it is also important to identify the other ways in which an unethical personal relationship can develop with clients. It is not uncommon to work with a client and realize you have things in common with them. Perhaps there is temptation to socialize with them outside of the therapeutic setting. Maybe you want to text or call them, especially if you know they have been struggling. While your motives might be good, and your client might even be fine with this, it is important to think about how this may impact your therapeutic relationship down the road. If, for example, you start texting your client, you need to ask yourself, "Would I do this for all clients? Am I doing this out of necessity? Is this in the best interest of my client or is this for me?" It is always a good idea to seek supervision or consultation to consider whether reaching out to your client outside of session is a good idea.

DUAL RELATIONSHIPS

A **dual relationship** is a relationship in which the client and the counselor have multiple roles in one another's lives. In general, the counselor should make efforts to avoid dual relationships as much as possible; however, it can be difficult at times to do that. For example, counselors interact with many people in their community in many ways. Perhaps the counselor sees a client who owns a business in the community where the counselor lives, and the counselor conducts business there. This would be considered a dual relationship. In the case where a dual relationship cannot be avoided, it is essential for the counselor to take steps to outline what the relationship will look like so that the client can be assured that boundaries exist to protect the therapeutic relationship and any possible implications or appearances of exploitation can be avoided.

Part of navigating dual relationships with clients is letting them know up front about the potential for the dual relationship and discussing what it will look like. For example, if the counselor sees the client in public, will the counselor avoid contact? Will they say hello? What are the implications of that if the counselor or client is not alone and someone asks, "How do you know that person?" Corey et al. (2024) lays out steps that counselors can take in the event of dual relationships.

- Obtain informed consent.
- Document thoroughly.
- Set clear boundaries and expectations, both for yourself and your clients.
- Pay attention to matters of confidentiality.
- Get involved in ongoing consultation or a peer supervision group.

In any therapeutic relationship, paying attention to matters of confidentiality is of utmost importance and when it comes to dual relationships, it is even more important. Other confidentiality and boundary issues arise if friends or relatives of clients are also clients in your practice. In these cases, a counselor may be tempted to reveal information they have learned from one client to help or facilitate the growth of another client. Regardless of how pure the counselor's motives are, they cannot breach confidentiality by sharing information between clients.

Finally, seeking supervision or consultation is always helpful when navigating dual relationship and boundary issues. Supervisors and other counselors can provide accountability that is sometimes helpful to keep us on track. It is also helpful to hear from others how they have handled similar situations or advice they may have about your situation.

CONFLICT OF INTEREST

A **conflict of interest** in counseling occurs when a counselor's personal, financial, or professional interests clash with their primary obligation to the client. The conflict of interest can compromise the integrity of the counseling relationship and interfere with the counselor's professional responsibility to hold the client's welfare and best interests in mind. Counselors are ethically bound to recognize and address any potential conflicts of interest. This can occur during the informed consent process or anytime it arises in the counseling process. Just as with dual relationships, supervision and consultation are good methods to manage and problem solve conflicts of interest as they happen.

SELF-DISCLOSURE

Self-disclosure occurs when you tell the client a little about yourself or your experiences. If done correctly, self-disclosure can be therapeutic, build rapport, and help your client to grow. However, anytime you utilize self-disclosure, the end goal always must be with your client's best interests in mind. If you are not sure your disclosure serves that purpose, then it is likely not a good idea to disclose. Johnson (2018) has a series of questions counselors can ask themselves to determine if self-disclosure is an appropriate intervention.

- **"Why?"** What is the purpose of your self-disclosure? If it is because the client says something that resonates with you or your experience, then the odds are this is not a good time to disclose because it's about you and not your client.
- **"What?"** What information are you going to share and what will it mean to your client? Self-disclosure runs the risk of your clients feeling like you are making the session about you. While some clients do like to know a little personal information about their counselor, others get angry because they are spending a lot of time and money on their treatment, and they do not want to spend it talking about their counselor. Depending on what you disclose, you run the risk of damaging the therapeutic relationship with your client. If your client is struggling with substance use and you disclose that you have been struggling with that yourself, your client may wonder if you have the capacity to help them. It is also important to consider the implications of sharing too much information and crossing boundaries. It may open the door for more personal disclosures, and later it may lead to blurry lines when it comes to professionalism.
- **"Is it acceptable to share this?"** While clients have confidentiality with you, the reverse is not true. Clients should not be expected to keep secrets for you. If you would be uncomfortable with the information getting out to others, then it is best to skip the disclosure.

If you are not sure how you would answer these questions, it is best to not disclose.

GIFTS

According to the ACA (2014), accepting gifts from clients needs to be well considered. What is the implication of accepting the gift? What is the implication of not accepting it? What is the motivation of the client and what is the motivation of the counselor in accepting or denying the gift? Is it going to harm your therapeutic relationship if you accept it or reject it?

Although there are not specific guidelines about what is acceptable and what is not acceptable, according to Nuekrug and Milliken (2011), most counselors agree that gifts of large monetary value are unethical to accept. Because there are no clear guidelines about accepting gifts, using your code of ethics standards regarding gifts can help you determine whether to accept gifts. Remley and Herlihy (2020) also point out that if you are not comfortable accepting gifts at all, then cover it in your informed consent and make it clear from the beginning that you have a no-gift policy.

Tips From the Field

When it comes to accepting gifts, it is important to consider the cultural background of your clients. Some cultures value gift giving. If you turn down a gift, you could be culturally insensitive to that client.

▶ COMMUNICATION AND TECHNOLOGY

In today's world, it is not uncommon for clients and counselors alike to use texting and e-mails to arrange meetings or to cancel sessions. While communicating with clients via text can be acceptable, there are several factors that need to be considered to ensure the legal and ethical implications of the communication are properly managed. The biggest priority in texting is making sure that any communication via text messages (or left on answering machines) is HIPAA compliant. The less information or details, the better. It is also a good idea to get permission from a client as to whether they agree with using texts and voice messages as a communication method. Some clients do not want information about their care in their texts or voice messages due to personal or confidentiality reasons.

Beyond privacy laws, it's also important to consider what is ethically appropriate when using technology to communicate with clients. If you use a cell phone to text with clients, clients need to know their expectations about this communication. If they are in crisis, can they call or text the number you shared with them? If not, they need to know an alternative method of contacting crisis support. If you have provided them with a cell phone contact but have not given them a specific plan of action for when they are in crisis, you can be held responsible if they leave a voice message on your cell phone indicating that they are in crisis and you do not reply. This is a very serious and critical topic to consider and cover with clients.

Counselors are not expected to be "on call" 24/7; however, your clients do need to know the expectations for communication after hours. This may entail a documented discussion with clients. It may also be a message on your voicemail that states who they should contact in case of emergencies. When you are on vacation or have other time away, it's important to communicate with your clients that you will be unavailable. They need to know where they can go if a crisis emerges and, for some clients, if there is a substitute counselor that can meet with them in your absence.

Another area of communication and technology to consider is the use of social media. The landscape of social media is ever evolving. It is helpful to think of social media existing in two arenas: professional and personal. When working with clients, the use of social media for professional reasons can seem clearer than the use of personal social media. Although there is no hard and fast "rule" about social media, it is helpful to consider it a type of "self-disclosure" or "dual relationship" in the ethics area.

If a client can see your information, is there a possibility that it could do harm to your therapeutic relationship? Some counselors use social media to post mental health content. The odds are, in those cases, that the content is not going to do harm to the client. But what if the counselor posts about their weekend drinking? That runs a great risk of doing harm to the therapeutic relationship. If you could see your client's information, what do you do with it and what are you responsible for? For example, if a client posts something like, "I might as well end it all" and you see it, what is your responsibility? If they do die by suicide and you saw the post but did not report it to law enforcement, can you be held liable? Or if you do say something, would it damage your therapeutic relationship if your client says they were just being dramatic? Or, if a client who is court ordered to not consume alcohol and they post pictures of themselves drinking, then what? Do you report it to their attorney?

While there is not a legal "right" answer for social media and counseling, the ethical answer is usually to avoid personal social media relationships on social media and use professional social media thoughtfully and carefully. If you do decide to utilize social media for professional purposes, you need to evaluate the specificities of the platform(s) you choose to utilize. Unfortunately, there are no clear cut guidelines about social media use other than that it needs to be carefully considered. The best recommendation is to consult with an attorney to consider all the potential legal ramifications of having a platform and allow the attorney to guide you.

▶ ETHICAL DECISION-MAKING

There are two processes that should be used when confronted with ethical dilemmas: the **moral principles of ethical decision-making** and the **framework for ethical decision-making**.

Corey et al. (2024) outlines six moral principles to ethical decision-making; autonomy, justice, beneficence, nonmaleficence, fidelity, and veracity. These moral principles as they apply to counseling are described as follows.

1. **Autonomy:** Clients have the right to make their own choices and decisions that they believe will benefit themselves.
2. **Justice:** Treat others justly or with fairness. "Fair" does not necessarily mean "equal." Justice entails making services accessible to our clients regardless of their backgrounds.
3. **Beneficence:** Beneficence means acting in the best interests of our clients and promoting their well-being. We must put our beliefs aside and work with clients to determine what is best for their unique situation considering their background and experiences.
4. **Nonmaleficence:** Counselors should take efforts to avoid doing harm. As counselors, not doing harm is of utmost importance. While this may seem easy enough, sometimes well-intended people do harm because they weren't considering things from their clients' points of view.
5. **Fidelity:** Make realistic commitments and keep promises. Essentially, you should avoid promising your clients something you cannot deliver, such as absolute confidentiality when there are times you may have to break it, or results after a certain number of sessions.
6. **Veracity:** Truthfulness and honesty in the client/counselor relationship defines veracity. Be honest with your clients about the therapeutic process, the ups and downs, and the time it can take to see results.

While these principles appear very straightforward, Corey et al. (2024) point out that we can never fully actualize these principles because our clients come from uniquely different backgrounds that cause us to assess these principles in different ways. It is not a "one and done" process, but rather a continual process with every client that we serve.

▶ FRAMEWORK FOR ETHICAL DECISION-MAKING

According to Corey and Schneider Corey (2020), there are eight steps to follow when making an ethical decision in counseling:

1. **Identify the problem:** To accurately identify the problem, gather data to determine what the problem is as well as what type of problem it is (ethical, legal, professional, or other type of problem).
2. **Identify the potential issues involved:** Perform a deeper exploration of the various factors, values, and stakeholders involved in the ethical dilemma to understand the problem in a broader context.
3. **Examine the relevant ethical codes:** Know what the appropriate credentialing or licensing body requires you to follow. After identifying the ethical code, match the problem and issues identified to the relevant individual ethical standards. This will help in developing a plan of action based on ethical guidelines.

4. **Consider the applicable laws and regulations:** Identify the relevant laws and regulations that pertain to the situation. Keep in mind HIPAA and 42 CFR Part 2 and ensure that compliance with each is being met. Match up any state laws, agency regulations, and other applicable regulations to the problem and the identified issues. This can help to develop a plan of action.

5. **Seek consultation:** Others in the field may have deeper insight based on their experiences. To make the best choices for clients, seeking consultation from others is not just a good idea, it is essential.

6. **Brainstorm possible courses of action:** Generate as many as possible potential solutions or actions that address the ethical problem. Requires creativity and opens many possibilities for resolving the issues.

7. **Detail the consequences of various decisions and reflect on the implications of each course of action for your client:** Analyze and evaluate the potential outcomes and consequences of each proposed course of action. Reflect on and get input into how each decision might impact the client, the therapeutic relationship, and others who may be involved in the ethical dilemma.

8. **Decide on the best course of action:** Based on the preceeding steps, make an informed decision on the course of action to take. The goal is to choose the option that upholds the welfare and rights of the client while aligning with ethical and legal standards.

Following these steps can help in navigating complex ethical issues. It is important to document the process and follow up with the action taken. The most important part of ethical decision-making is having a process and evaluating the outcome. This will go a long way to resolving ethical dilemmas and any further issues that may arise.

▶ GRIEVANCES

Grievances in counseling can arise when clients feel dissatisfied, misunderstood, or have complaints about the counselor or the treatment process. Handling the grievance effectively is crucial to maintain trust and ensure the therapeutic process remains supportive and effective. If you work for an agency, they likely have a path forward for grievances. But if you are establishing your practice, it is important that you detail how clients can handle their concerns and frustrations. Having a formal process in place for filing grievances is an asset. Having open communication, ensuring confidentiality, investigating the grievance, coming to consensus, reaching resolution, and documenting all steps of the grievance process is best practice. If a grievance filed against you may impact your counseling license or credential, consulting with a lawyer would be the best course of action to determine how to proceed.

▶ SUPERVISION AND CONSULTATION

Supervision occurs when a qualified and experienced counselor supervisor oversees and guides the work of the less experienced counselor to ensure ethical, effective, and competent practice. Key components in supervision are education and training, skill development, ethical guidance, reflective practice, case consultation, support and feedback, and evaluation. Supervisees meet with the supervisor to consult on specific clients, seek assistance related to client care, get help conceptualizing client cases, receive feedback about their performance, and discuss feelings that may arise from a variety of client situations. Supervision, if done correctly, should be a safe place for the counselor to navigate the therapeutic world. Ending the supervisory process is very similar to terminating the therapeutic relationship. It should not be done haphazardly, but rather with intention, planning, and foresight so that when the process is completed, the newly fully licensed and credentialed counselor feels competent in their knowledge and when difficult things arise, they know who to go to when asking for help.

Each state has their own guidance as to what supervision should look like and if it is required to be done face to face or if it can be done via telehealth or even telephone. It is important to note that when telehealth is used, the same guidelines that are required for client services are also required for counselor supervising, which means the platform utilized must be secure and HIPAA compliant.

Although those who have been practicing for any length of time may no longer have to have supervision, clinicians can always benefit from the knowledge of others. **Consultation** is an essential part of helping our clients and is a core function of an addiction counselor. Consultation with other professionals ensures quality care for the client by enabling the counselor to obtain new knowledge and skills when there are issues that are beyond the counselor's knowledge base (Box 8.2; Herdman, 2021).

Box 8.2 Core Function 12: Consultation With Other Professionals Regarding the Client's Treatment Services

Definition: Relating with in-house staff and/or outside professionals to ensure comprehensive quality care for client.

Global Criteria:
43. Recognize issues that are beyond the counselor's base of knowledge and/or skill.
44. Consult with appropriate resources to ensure the provision of effective treatment services.
45. Adhere to applicable laws, regulations, and agency policies governing the disclosure of client-identifying data.
46. Explain the rationale for the consultation to the client, if appropriate

Consultation can also be helpful in times when we need an outside perspective, such as in the case of countertransference. **Countertransference** occurs when your client is discussing something that stirs feelings within you of a previous event or is reminiscent of a person in your life. When you experience countertransference, being able to explore it with another professional in the field can help guide you so that you can do what is best for your client and not what may be based on your own needs.

▶ PROFESSIONAL DEVELOPMENT AND LICENSURE

Every state has its own guidelines for responsibility and workplace standards in professional development and licensure. It is important to check with your state to find out what specifically is required of you so that you can stay within legal and ethical expectations for practice. For example, your state will determine when you renew your license, what your scope of practice is, and what type of continuing education you need to maintain licensure, as well as how much and how often. When you are just starting out, most of these standards will be explained to you by your supervisor. However, when you become fully licensed in your state, it is your responsibility to adhere to these guidelines.

▶ DIVERSITY, EQUITY, INCLUSION, AND ACCESS

According to the ACA Code of Ethics multicultural/diversity standard (2014), counselors must maintain awareness and sensitivity regarding cultural meanings of confidentiality and privacy. Counselors must respect differing views toward disclosure of information and hold ongoing discussions with clients as to how, when, and with whom information is to be shared. Obviously, there is no possible way to understand every nuance of every client's culture, but it is the responsibility of the counselor to be as educated as possible and to understand the ways in which culture might impact your clients and their treatment issues.

Cultural competence, according to Sue et al. (2022), is the awareness, knowledge, and skills needed to function effectively with culturally diverse populations. Being a culturally competent counselor means we understand how culture impacts our client's view of the world and that it may be different than our view of the world. It also means the responsibility is on us to consider our client's perspective, not on them to understand ours.

When working with culturally diverse clients, it is important to understand your clients' beliefs, perspectives, and life experiences and not to make assumptions. An **etic** perspective is one in which we view the cultural experience from the outside. An **emic** perspective is one where we view the cultural experience from the inside. But as counselors, from different cultural backgrounds, how do we know the ins and outs of every cultural background of all our clients? According to Sue et al. (2022), there are three questions we can ask ourselves when working with culturally diverse clients:

1. What is universal in human behavior that is also relevant to counseling and therapy?
2. What is the relationship between cultural norms, values, and attitudes, on the one hand, and the manifestation of behavior disorders and their treatments, on the other?
3. Are there ways to both examine the universality of the human condition and acknowledge the role of culture in the manifestation of both the presenting concern and the treatment approach?

By asking these questions, we can better support our clients' needs by having greater insight into how culture impacts their beliefs about substance use as well as treatment. If we assume that our clients' cultural backgrounds and beliefs are not relevant in the treatment process, not only is it unlikely that we will be able to help them with their treatment, but it *is* likely that we will do harm, a clear ethical violation.

Being culturally competent also means practicing **cultural humility**, an approach that emphasizes openness, self-reflection, and a willingness to learn from and about individuals from diverse cultural backgrounds. According to Ivey et al. (2024), cultural humility addresses inequities in the healthcare field. It goes beyond the concept of cultural competence to include:

- A personal, lifelong commitment to reflexivity and self-evaluation
- A recognition of power dynamics and imbalances, and a desire to fix those power imbalances and to advocate for others
- An effort to hold institutions accountable and foster change

Practicing cultural humility means you are actively learning and reflecting, aware of your own potential for biases, understanding the microaggressions and injustices that your clients may face, advocating for change, and developing the knowledge to work competently with your clients.

Advocating for change means we must be willing to engage in social justice. **Social justice**, as described by Corey et al. (2024), encompasses providing fair opportunities and treatment to guarantee equal involvement in society, especially for individuals who have historically been marginalized due to factors such as race, gender, age, disabilities, education, sexual orientation, socioeconomic status, or other background characteristics or group affiliations. The counselor's job is to ensure that anyone who wants treatment can receive treatment regardless of their background, cultural identity, or abilities.

▶ ASSESSMENT, EVALUATION, AND INTERPRETATION

Chapter 5, "Assessing the Client" discusses the process of completing an assessment. We consider assessment again from the view of ethics. Clients will frequently come to treatment in search of a counselor who can provide an assessment, evaluate the results of the assessment, and interpret relevant screening instruments or reports from other providers. Regardless of why clients begin counseling, counselors need to be mindful of best practices and how to provide ethical services to their clients. It is important to understand that just because a client has a positive drug screen or was involved with illicit substances does not necessarily mean that they will meet criteria for a substance use disorder. Because it can be difficult to know what the client's relationship with substances is, completing an assessment is essential to understand the client's treatment needs.

ASSESSMENT

In completing an assessment, the counselor starts by considering the question they hope to answer by the end of the assessment with the client. Once this is clear, the counselor can intentionally choose the questions they will ask as well as the appropriate screening tools to gather the information needed. Counselors carefully consider if they have the adequate training and knowledge to utilize the chosen assessment method and if this assessment method is within their scope of practice. If the question posed for the assessment is not something within the counselor's competence, the counselor must make a referral to another provider. It is important to be mindful of what different screening tools and assessments may be. According to Doweiko and Evans (2024), by the end of the assessment process, the counselor should be able to make a diagnosis and proceed to the treatment planning phase of treatment.

EVALUATION AND INTERPRETATION

When a client presents for a substance use evaluation, they are requesting that you complete a bio-psycho-social assessment, utilize relevant screening instruments, gather relevant collateral information, and then make a conclusion or interpretation about this information in written form. To complete an assessment and evaluation in an ethical manner, it is important to be trained in all the assessment and screening instruments that you utilize.

▶ REFERRAL

A **referral** is the recommendation that a client see another clinician or provider. Sometimes, a client may be referred to another provider and still see the substance use counselor. Other times, the counselor may determine that the client's needs are outside of their scope of practice. In such cases, there may be a couple of ethical options. It would be possible for the counselor to continue to see the client if they are seeking supervision from someone who *is* within their scope, or it is also acceptable to refer the client in such cases where supervision is not an option. Sometimes counselors will give clients a choice between the two if both options are available. Either option is acceptable, but it is important to let clients know why a referral is being offered and the benefits and drawbacks of each situation so that they can make an informed decision about their care.

It is important to note that a referral must be in the client's best interest. Not liking a client or having an opposing world view is not an ethically appropriate reason for a referral. Clients come from many different backgrounds and there will be some who are easy to work with and others that pose a challenge. While that can be frustrating, it is our job to figure out how we can build a rapport to work effectively with each client. It is also a time when we need to seek supervision for our own feelings of dislike for clients or their worldviews. To do anything else would do harm, a clear ethical violation.

▶ DISCHARGE PLANNING AND TERMINATION

Discharge planning is a thoughtful process in which the counselor helps the client address possible issues that may arise in the future and work on strategies to address them as they arise. From the first session with a client, the counselor begins considering how the episode of care will end. Discharge planning is a task that begins during the assessment and continues throughout the counseling process. The counselor orients the client to understand that a counseling relationship is not a friendship and thus will not continue indefinitely. The counselor discusses with the client informal supports and how to connect to these supports, assists the client in gaining the skills to access resources in the community independently, helps the client develop skills to be successful beyond the counseling relationship, and creates a continued care plan which the client can reference later if they need to return to counseling for additional care.

CONTINUED CARE PLAN

A continued care plan is a document that helps the client reflect and summarize the changes they have made as well as identify signs and symptoms which may suggest a return to use, either as a lapse or possible relapse. Substance use disorders are not "cured" but rather go into remission. A substance use disorder is a chronic, life-threatening, relapsing condition; therefore, counselors assist clients in how to identify symptoms which suggest the disorder is becoming active again as well as steps the client can take to manage these symptoms.

Counselors may employ a variety of formats when completing a continued care plan. Often continued care plans are called relapse prevention plans. Though these terms are often used interchangeably, relapse prevention plans often focus on signs and symptoms of relapse; whereas a continued care plan focuses not only on the signs and symptoms of a relapse or return to use, it also focuses on what is going well now, the tasks that help the client continue to do well, the supports the client has, and specific actions the client can take if they see warning signs.

The steps for creating a plan of care are:

1. **A reflection on the client's current state:** The counselor and client discuss what is going well in life right now and how life is different than it was before counseling began.
2. **Client listing supportive people and resources they have in their life:** Having a written list of supports helps the client celebrate their connection with others as well as provides a starting point if the client needs to reach out during a difficult time. Writing a list of supports when life is going well is far easier than trying to remember who is supportive when a person is feeling down, alone, and wanting to drink or use substances.
3. **Identify what actions sustain the client's current recovery:** These often are daily actions that sustain or maintain the changes the client has made and provide a foundation for continued growth in recovery.

The next part of the continued care plan involves identifying early-, middle-, and late-stage warning signs of return to use, also known as warning signs of relapse. Though this is divided into three categories, it is viewed as a continuum of change whereas a person progresses through the stages and may experience some signs and symptoms of two stages at the same time (Gorski, 2016).

■ **Early-stage warnings signs:** Internal changes only the client may notice. Examples include changes in thinking pattern; increased difficulty with recognizing and naming feelings; stuffing and ignoring feelings; not dealing with grief, sadness, or anger; changes in appetite, sleep, and motivation; increased thoughts of using substances or engaging in other escape behaviors such as gambling, pornography, or getting lost in fantasy. During this stage, clients may begin to doubt why they need to keep engaging in recovery-based activities or begin to believe that they can "control" their use.

■ **Middle-stage warning signs:** Behavioral changes. Examples include becoming more irritable or withdrawn; reducing engagement in recovery-based activities; justifying to others as to why they are changing their behavior; verbalizing statements of blame and accusations that the behavior of others is "causing" their behavior change; changes in their sleep, appetite, motivation, and follow through; engaging in more avoidant or fantasy behaviors; "practicing" addictive behavior patterns by looking up old friends on social media, driving by places where they used to drink or use substances just to see "what's going on" or "who is still there"; or begin engaging in prior addictive behavior patterns but not actually using any substances. By this time, the client is often hearing complaints or concerns from others about their behavior. Friends may begin distancing themselves, family members start to revert to old patterns of behavior as if the client were using again, and the client's employer may begin expressing concern as well.

■ **Late-stage warning signs and symptoms:** The client's life is starting to become unmanageable once again. Typically, in this stage the client's thinking and behavior patterns have nearly fully reverted to how they were when the client was actively using. The client may have reinitiated contact with prior using associates, is beginning to go to high-risk places, is actively justifying why their behavior is not a concern, and believes that others should just "leave me alone." In the late stage, clients are either actively looking for an opportunity and a reason to resume substance use or are open to an opportunity presenting itself. Those around them when they were actively in recovery are frustrated with the client's behavior and may begin ending communication, thus further isolating the client. The client may return to substance use with attempts to control their use. This frequently results in a resumption of active addiction. Alternatively, some clients have become adept at hiding their behaviors from those close to them and the return to use is only discovered because of a crisis. This crisis often becomes a "crisis of use." This returns the client back to the pretreatment stage in Gorski and Miller's (1986) developmental model of recovery. The client often is also reverting to the precontemplation or contemplation stage of change.

For each of the warning sign stages, the client includes possible actions or interventions in their continuing care plan that can be taken to prevent the progression of the behavior. The client completes the care plan when they are doing well, so that if they begin to slide back toward substance use, they and their supports have options to intervene to prevent further progression. The question on the care plan regarding the biggest risk to recovery is meant to help the client look for blind spots, reservations about long-term behavior change, or justifications for when a resumption of substance use is acceptable. The counselor helps the client explore these areas during the completion of the continued care plan.

The final question on the care plan is designed to create a positive self-talk statement the client can use to help encourage them during difficult times. Actively practicing this statement assists the client in redirecting thoughts about use and builds hope when they begin to doubt. This utilizes the principles of cognitive behavior therapy that the client utilized during counseling.

Just as we are concluding this book, we also return to Jim, to conclude his story. Jim's completed continued care plan is described in the care plan.

Tips From the Field

Relapse is frustrating and disheartening for the client and the counselor. It is important to remember that your client's successes and failures are not yours. Clients have the autonomy to make their own choices and we must let them do so. However, we will be there when they need us.

Unfolding Case Study

JIM'S CONTINUED CARE PLAN
Date: 02/13/202X

Current state (what is going well and what is different than before?)
"My life is so much better than it was before. I am not anxious all the time, I don't feel like I have to drink to be around people, I am not lying to my wife, and I am doing well at work. I look back on how my life was before and it scares me to think how isolated and closed off I was. I don't know why my wife didn't leave me, but I am glad she stayed. I have a closer relationship with my children. I actually have friends now. Gambling was very difficult to stop, and I know this will continue to be a challenge. I haven't looked at any pornography in a year and my brain feels so much better."

Supportive people and resources:

- My wife
- My dad
- My friends from my church group
- My coworker, Jake
- The gambler anonymous (GA) group that meets on Friday nights

Actions that sustain recovery:

- Talk to my wife daily.
- Attend church support group and GA meeting each week.
- Take time to check in with myself each day to help manage the anxiety.
- Go to bed on time and get a good night's sleep.
- Exercise or be active at least twice a week.
- Say "yes" to invitations to social events.

Early-stage warning signs (thoughts)

- "Why did this happen to me? This isn't fair."
- "I should just stay home; there are going to be too many people there."
- "My (friends, kids, coworkers, and wife) don't really want to be around me."
- "No one really cares about me."
- "It is okay to look at the gambling or pornography site just to see if they have changed it (but not actually do anything)."
- "Having one beer after a stressful day would likely be okay."

Intervention/action

- Go to my church group and be honest with them.
- Talk to my wife or my dad.
- Identify why I am avoiding people or thinking that others don't like me. Talk to others about it.

Middle-stage warning signs (behaviors)

- Stop going to my support group.
- Stop talking to Jake.
- Avoid social events.
- Increased isolation.
- Increased irritability and anger.
- Hide my phone from my wife and change the password.
- Stay up late at night to have "alone time."

Intervention/action

- Listen to what others are telling me.
- Go to my support group meeting.

(continued)

(continued)

■ Get back into counseling to figure out what feelings I am not dealing with.
■ Get back into a consistent daily schedule.

Late-stage warning signs (life is becoming unmanageable)

■ Actively looking at pornography and gambling sites.
■ Stopping at the liquor store to see what new beers they have.
■ Drinking in secret/hiding alcohol use from others.
■ Actively lying about my behavior.
■ Avoid my wife and my friends.
■ Poor work performance.

Intervention/action

"If I am doing these things, I probably can't stop by myself. I give my wife permission to call my support group, my dad, and my counselor. I need her to confront me and not let me get away with these behaviors because the longer I do, the harder it will be to change."

Biggest risks to my recovery

■ If someone close to me dies.
■ If I lose my job.
■ If we get into debt for some reason and I feel we can't pay the bills or feel I failed my family.
■ If my wife left me, I would have no reason to be sober.

What can I say to myself when I don't think I can go on, when life gets hard, and I want to take a break from this journey

■ "I can do this. I am not alone. I am loved by my wife and kids."
■ "Remember how bad I felt when I was drinking."
■ "Gambling is not a way to pay the bills."
■ "I can't gamble, even just a little; I can't drink just a little; I can't watch porn just a little. It is all or nothing. And if I do them at all, I will have nothing!"

▶ TERMINATION

Termination is the discontinuation of counseling services and is the last piece of the treatment process. Termination occurs when the client has met their goals of counseling or discontinues care. Knowing how to terminate a client can be every bit as important as knowing how to do an intake and how to do treatment. Sometimes termination happens because a client stops attending sessions but ideally, termination is a process that the counselor and the client navigate together.

When preparing for termination, it is important to help clients understand their feelings about the process. Some clients discontinue services and feel like they are ready to tackle the world; others may be scared to go back out into the world because they have failed before, and they fear they may fail again. For both types of clients, and all the ones in between, a well-written continued care plan guides the conversation of discontinuing services. For the client that feels very confident, the plan assists in identifying warning signs "just in case." For the client that is fearful and doubts their ability, the continued care plan offers encouragement for the progress that has been made as well as a plan of action if they see concerning warning signs. The continued care plan also offers the encouragement to return to counseling if needed. It is unfortunate that many clients, and often counselors, feel shame if they need to return to counseling, seeing it as a failure in some way. It is up to the counselor, however, to dispel this feeling and focus on seeking counseling as a strength rather than a sign of weakness or failure.

The end of a counseling relationship can cause feelings of grief for clients. The therapeutic relationship may have been the best form of support they have ever had. The idea of leaving the safety of a therapeutic relationship may cause the client to seek reasons to stay in services or to discontinue services before the official termination has occurred. Counselors are aware of both possibilities and take steps to identify these risks and assist the client in navigating through the grief process.

Just as the end of a counseling relationship can cause feelings of grief for clients, it is important to understand that as the counselor, you also may have complicated emotions about your clients' leaving your care. We hope for the best for our clients, and we want them to succeed. We can be fearful if we think there may still be obstacles in their way, and we mourn when they leave, especially if they terminate early and we do not get to say goodbye. It's important to have a supervisor who can address these feelings with you as you navigate this process.

Tips From the Field

We celebrate when our clients are successful, but we might feel a sense of fear when they terminate. "What if they don't make it?" The end of a therapeutic relationship can be a loss just like the end of any relationship. If you are struggling, seek supervision.

The final step of termination is completing a **discharge summary**. The discharge summary is a document that summarizes the treatment the client received as well as recommendations for any next steps. The discharge summary serves as the ending document for the current episode of care. A discharge summary can be forwarded, with the appropriate consents, to individuals on the client's team such as primary care providers, probation or parole officers, or others who need to be aware that the client has completed counseling. If the client returns to counseling in the future, the discharge summary also provides a succinct understanding of the client's previous treatment and can be helpful to know where to begin the next episode of care. As we come to the end of our time with Jim, we write a discharge summary to close this episode of treatment with him.

JIM'S DISCHARGE SUMMARY
Name: Jim   **Date:** 02/15/202X
Date of admission: 08/15/202X
Date of discharge: 02/15/202X
Diagnosis at discharge:
F10.21 alcohol use disorder-moderate-in early remission
F63.0 gambling disorder
Services received: Outpatient individual and family counseling

Presenting problem:
Jim initially began counseling due to alcohol use causing problems for him with his employer. Jim also indicated possible concerns with gambling and pornography use.

Treatment summary:
Jim attended counseling for a total of 18 months. Jim attended weekly for the first 10 months, then every other week for 4 months and then once per month for the final 4 months. Jim's wife attended several sessions with Jim over the course of counseling. Jim also completed two family sessions which included his wife and their three children.
    At the time of the evaluation, Jim was uncertain if his alcohol use was as big of a concern as others were telling him. He hoped that he could find a way to manage his alcohol use and not have to quit drinking completely. Motivational interviewing was used to help Jim raise his awareness of the impact of his alcohol use as well as the impact of his gambling and pornography use. After Jim was arrested for driving under the influence (DUI), he and his wife, Samantha, began attending counseling together. Samantha shared her concerns about his alcohol use. Jim agreed to be honest with Samantha about how hard it was for him not to drink. He shared that he thought about drinking a lot more than he ever told her. He also shared with her how alcohol helped him when he felt anxious and uncomfortable in social situations. During these sessions, Jim and Samantha learned and practiced communication strategies and developed a new daily schedule whereas they prioritized time to talk every day and spend time together for just the two of them each week. Both have indicated this change has been essential to the improvement of their marriage and they must continue this after counseling ends.
    Jim attended Alcoholics Anonymous (AA) meetings weekly for 3 months as a part of a court diversion program related to the DUI conviction. He never felt he fit in at the meetings and began to seek other options. Jim was invited by a friend of the family to a men's group at a local church. The group focused on building trust and

(continued)

(*continued*)

communication with other men as well as sharing of the struggles of changing addictive behavior and learning to cope with life stresses in more effective ways. Jim reports this group has helped him feel less alone and reduced the shame he felt for not being able to cope with his stress and anxiety on his own. He feels the support of others allows him to accept help and to not feel drinking, gambling, or pornography are his only options when he feels overwhelmed. Jim plans to continue with this group indefinitely. Jim reports his last drink was 9 months ago.

Jim participated in cognitive behavior therapy with this counselor. Jim identified the thoughts and feelings that triggered his desire to drink. Jim also recognized that pornography and gambling had become substitutes for making connections with others or having a hobby. Jim indicated he could easily give up pornography use, especially once he was honest with his wife and they began talking more. Quitting gambling was much more difficult for him.

Jim was referred to a gambling counseling specialist for an assessment. Jim was diagnosed with compulsive gambling and attended five sessions with the gambling specialist to gain increased understanding of the thoughts and behaviors associated with gambling as well as new coping strategies and skills. Jim has reduced his gambling considerably over the past 18 months but admits to buying scratch tickets twice in the past month. Both times were when he was out of town for work. He feels that between the Gamblers Anonymous meetings, his church support group, and talking to his wife, he can continue to reduce this behavior. Jim identifies he is still looking for "some excitement" and needs to find a different way to manage these feelings when he is working out of town and frustrated with the monotony of his job.

Jim was referred for a medication assessment due to his reported discomfort and anxiety symptoms in social settings. The psychiatric nurse practitioner agreed that medication may be helpful for him, but Jim did not want to start taking medication. He decided he wants to continue to practice the new skills he has learned and continue to place himself in uncomfortable social situations in order to push himself to use the new skills. Jim is aware he can call and activate the prescription if he chooses.

Jim completed a continued care plan and reviewed this in session with his wife. Jim has also given a copy of the plan to his best friend and his dad. Jim and his wife agree to review the plan every 3 months and will return to counseling if they begin to see warning signs that are not resolved through their communication.

Reason for discharge/status upon discharge:
Jim has successfully met his goals of counseling. He has completed a continued care plan and feels he has adequate support in place to continue recovery without formal counseling services.

Prognosis:
Jim's prognosis is good. He acknowledges the difficulties that alcohol use, gambling, and pornography have had on his life, his marriage, and his employment. Jim has developed positive supports as well as friendships with people he feels he can trust. Jim and Samantha report their marriage is stronger than it has ever been and feel for the first time they can "actually talk to each other."

Recommendations:
There are no further counseling recommendations. Jim is encouraged to return to counseling as needed based on his continued care plan. Jim is encouraged to continue to attend his weekly church support group, attend Gamblers Anonymous meetings as needed, and review his continued care plan with his wife on a regular basis.

Counselor's signature_____   Date:_____

▶ KEY POINTS

- This chapter highlights the content on the ADC exam in Domain 4: Professional, Ethical, and Legal Responsibilities as well as the Report and Record Keeping and Consultation Core Functions. There are several legal, ethical, and practice issues to keep in mind as you study for the exam.
- On the legal side, HIPAA, 42 CFR Part 2, scope of practice, and other key legal terms are important to know. HIPAA is a guiding law for counselors that protects the privacy and security of the counseling process through the privacy rule and the security rule.
- HIPAA safeguards personal health information, requiring written consent for sharing, ensuring limited disclosure, and protecting client confidentiality barring certain circumstances under the limits of confidentiality such as the Duty to Warn Act and protecting the safety of clients or

others. 42 CFR Part 2 further safeguard client's confidentiality in substance use treatment from a federal perspective. Knowing the definition of basic legal terms such as privilege, court orders, subpoena, and scope of practice is important for the exam and for your counseling practice.

- Confidentiality is both a legal issue and ethical consideration in counseling. Confidentiality ensures protection for clients' identities, communications, and the counselor/client relationship. Understanding privacy and trust is vital, as it fosters an environment where clients feel safe to work through their issues. Informed consent is a cornerstone of ethical practice and entails informing clients about the counseling process, their rights and responsibilities, and the counselor's rights and responsibilities. The ethical issues of confidentiality include maintaining a professional counseling relationship by keeping good boundaries with clients.

- The counseling relationship is a key component of effective treatment and requires the counselor to set boundaries, avoid dual relationships whenever possible, manage conflicts of interest, and make good decisions about self-disclosure. Counselors must also manage communication with clients ethically when using technology and social media. In addition, counselors must also practice good documentation and record storage. This is a core function of an addiction counselor and an ethical mandate.

- Ethical decision-making in counseling involves navigating complete situations while upholding ethical principles and following a structured framework. Counselors should be familiar with the ethical principles of autonomy, justice, beneficence, nonmaleficence, fidelity, and veracity. Counselors also should be familiar with and be able to apply an ethical decision-making model to a case study as was outlined in the chapter as this is good clinical practice and will likely be on the exam. It is also important to note the concepts of cultural competency and cultural humility. Understanding clients' diverse backgrounds, beliefs, and experiences demands education and sensitivity, while cultural humility requires self-reflection and a commitment to learning from diverse cultural perspectives.

- Ethical assessment evaluation, and interpretation are vital counselor roles. Competence in utilizing screening instruments, conducting assessment within the scope of practice, and interpreting data ethically ensure appropriate client care. Referrals, while essential, demand careful consideration guided by the client's best interests rather than personal preference. Discharge planning, continued care plans, and termination are the final steps in the counseling process and must be done with intention.

- Supervision and consultation for counselors is another important part of ethical practice that guide the counselor in best practices. Supervision and consultation help counselors in their skill development, professional development, and in providing the best services to clients. In addition, consultation is a core function which must be understood for the exam.

▶ REFERENCES

American Counseling Association. (2014). *2014 ACA code of ethics*. https://www.counseling.org/docs/default-source/default-document-library/2014-code-of-ethics-finaladdress.pdf

American Psychological Association. (2016). *Protecting patient privacy when the court calls*. https://www.apa.org/monitor/2016/07-08/ce-corner

Centers for Disease Control and Prevention. (n.d.). *Duty to warn*. https://www.cdc.gov/std/treatment/duty-to-warn.htm

Center for Substance Abuse Treatment. (2015). *Addiction counseling competencies: The knowledge, skills, and attitudes of professional practice*. Technical assistance publication (TAP) Series 21. HHS Publication No. (SMA) 15-4171. Substance Abuse and Mental Health Services Administration. https://store.samhsa.gov/sites/default/files/sma12-4171.pdf

Corey, G., & Schneider Corey, M. (2020). *Becoming a helper* (8th ed.). Cengage Learning.

Corey, G., Corey, M. S., & Corey, C. (2024). *Issues & ethics in the helping professions* (11th ed.). Cengage Learning.

Doweiko, H., & Evans, A. (2024). *Concepts of chemical dependency* (11th ed.). Cengage Learning.

Gorshkalova, O., & Munakomi, S. (2023). *Duty to warn*. National Library of Medicine. https://www.ncbi.nlm.nih.gov/books/ NBK542236

Gorski, T. T. (2016). *Passages through recovery: An action plan for preventing relapse*. Hazelden Publishing.

Gorski, T. T., & Miller, M. (1986). *Staying sober: A guide for relapse prevention*. Independence Press.

Herdman, J. W. (2021). *Global criteria: The 12 core functions of the substance abuse counselor* (8th ed.).

Ivey, A. E., Zalaquett, C. P., & Ivey, M. B. (2024). *Essentials of intentional counseling and psychotherapy in a multicultural world* (4th ed.). Cengage Learning.

Johnson, M. (2018). Self disclosure: To Do or to Not Do? *Advances in Addiction Recovery, Fall*, 11. https://www.naadac.org/assets/2416/aa&r_fall2018_self-disclosure_to_do_or_not_to_do.pdf

Lambert, M. J. (2013). *Bergin and Garfield's handbook of psychotherapy and behavior change* (6th ed.). John Wiley & Sons.

NAADAC, the Association for Addiction Professionals. (2021). *Code of ethics*. https://www.naadac.org/assets/2416/naadac_code_of_ethics_112021.pdf

National Conference of State Legislatures. (2022). *Mental health professionals' duty to warn*. https://www.ncsl.org/health/mental-health-professionals-duty-to-warn

Nuekrug, E., & Milliken, T. (2011). Counselors' perceptions of ethical behaviors. *Journal of Counseling & Development*, 89(2), 206–216. https://doi.org/10.1002/j.1556-6678.2011.tb00079.x

Petrila, J., & Fader-Towe, H. (2010). *Information sharing in criminal justice-mental health collaborations: Working with HIPAA and other privacy laws*. Justice Center. https://csgjusticecenter.org/wp-content/uploads/2020/02/CSG_CJMH_Info_Sharing.pdf

Remley, T., Jr., & Herlihy, B. (2020). *Ethical, legal, and professional issues in counseling* (6th ed.). Pearson.

Sue, D. W., Sue, D., Neville, H., & Smith, L. (2022). *Counseling the culturally diverse: Theory and practice* (9th ed). Wiley.

U.S. Department of Health and Human Services. (2022). *227-Does the HIPAA privacy rule allow parents the right to see their children's medical records?* https://www.hhs.gov/hipaa/for-professionals/faq/227/can-i-access-medical-record-if-i-have-power-of-attorney/index.html

CASE STUDY 8.1

You are a recently licensed counselor. A friend, Alyona, who you went to school with, is also recently licensed and has begun working in a halfway house. She calls you with several questions about experiences she has recently encountered and would like your opinion.

1. What function of counseling is Alyona utilizing when she meets with you?
   A) Consultation
   B) Referral
   C) Case management
   D) Treatment planning

Alyona is concerned because she learned one of the other counselors is paying two of the clients to clean her house each week. She found out about it when the clients offered to come clean her house too. Alyona does not feel this is ethical but isn't sure what to do because the clients like the arrangement and she does not want to cause problems between her and her coworker after being on the job for only a week.

2. What would be the most appropriate advice to give Alyona?
   A) Take the clients up on the offer. Their rates are reasonable and if the other counselor trusts them, it is likely okay
   B) Decline the offer but do not say anything to anyone else since she just started the job and the clients do not seem to have a problem with it
   C) Start looking for another job; if this already happened in her first week, there are likely other problems too
   D) Contact her supervisor and share what the clients told her

Alyona wants to ask you questions about a new client she has been working with. She does not tell you the client's name, but you realize part way through the conversation that you know this client because you went to high school with them and are still connected on social media.

3. What is the appropriate next step?
   A) Report Alyona to her supervisor and the state licensing board because she broke confidentiality of the client
   B) Tell Alyona you think you know who the client is and that the two of you should not talk any further about this person
   C) Tell Alyona you think you know who the client is and look her up on your social media account, then share with Alyona what you remember about her and show her what is posted on the client's account
   D) Pretend you don't know who Alyona is talking about and continue with the conversation

(*See answers on the next page.*)

CASE STUDY 8.1 ANSWERS

1. A) Consultation

Consultation involves recognizing issues that are beyond the counselor's base of knowledge and/or skill and consulting with appropriate resources to ensure the provision of effective treatment services. Your friend is not making a referral to you for services nor is she coordinating services with you as would be done in case management. Though your friend may be gathering information for the client's treatment plan, her conversation with you meets the Core Function definition of Consultation.

2. D) Contact her supervisor and share what the clients told her

Having current clients clean a counselor's house is considered a dual relationship and is not ethical practice as there is risk of misunderstandings, unspoken expectations, or exploitation. Alyona should not just look the other way as this is a concern, and she definitely should not take the clients up on the offer. Alyona may decide to look for another job; however, starting with a conversation with her supervisor is the best initial course of action.

3. B) Tell Alyona you think you know who the client is and that the two of you should not talk any further about this person

Alyona did not share the client's name but gave enough identifying information that you concluded who the client was. This was not intentional on Alyona's part and there is no need to report her; however, it is your responsibility not to learn any additional information about the client. Further, it is unethical to talk more about the client and especially unethical to share other personal information you remember or look up the client online. Though it may seem pretending to not know the client and continuing with the conversation minimizes harm, this is also unethical as you are learning information you do not need to know, thereby still violating the client's confidentiality even if Alyona is not aware you know who the client is.

KNOWLEDGE CHECK: CHAPTER 8

1. A substance use counselor receives a call from a concerned family member seeking information about their adult child's progress in counseling. The client, who is over 18 years old, has not provided written consent for the release of information. Analyze the counselor's appropriate course of action in accordance with Health Insurance Portability and Accountability Act (HIPAA) regulations. What is the most ethically and legally compliant response?
   A) Politely share general information about the counseling process to alleviate the family member's concerns
   B) Request the family member to obtain written consent from the client before disclosing any information
   C) Share specific details about the client's progress, as family members are directly involved and have a right to know
   D) Politely tell the family that you cannot discuss any information with them

2. In substance use counseling, what is the primary focus of mandatory reporting requirements?
   A) Reporting any confidential information shared by clients during counseling sessions
   B) Reporting suspected abuse or neglect to children or vulnerable adults as required by law
   C) Reporting substance use patterns to law enforcement agencies
   D) Reporting any breach of client confidentiality to licensing boards

3. In a substance use counseling settings governed by 42 CFR Part 2, a counselor receives a request for confidential client information from a law enforcement officer. How should the counselor respond to ensure compliance with the regulations?
   A) Immediately provide the requested information to support law enforcement efforts
   B) Consult with the facility's legal team to determine the appropriate course of action
   C) Request a written consent form from the client before disclosing any information
   D) Share only nonidentifiable information to protect the client's confidentiality

4. A substance use counselor is treating a client for a substance use disorder. The client expresses a desire for their information to be shared with their primary care physician for holistic care. How should the counselor navigate this situation in compliance with Health Insurance Portability and Accountability Act (HIPAA) and 42 CFR Part 2?
   A) Share treatment information with the primary care physician, as it contributes to comprehensive care
   B) Obtain written consent from the client specifically allowing the sharing of information with the primary care physician
   C) Disclose only substance use treatment information to the primary care physician without obtaining consent, as it falls under 42 CFR Part 2
   D) Inform the client that treatment information cannot be shared with the primary care physician due to confidentiality laws

5. A substance use counselor is navigating the complexities of maintaining confidentiality under both Health Insurance Portability and Accountability Act (HIPAA) and 42 CFR Part 2 regulations. Which of the following scenarios best reflects an ethically sound approach to safeguarding client information while complying with both HIPAA and 42 CFR Part 2?
   A) Implementing strict measures to limit the disclosure of substance use treatment information only to those explicitly authorized by the client in writing
   B) Providing detailed client information to the primary care physician without written consent, as it contributes to comprehensive care
   C) Sharing substance use treatment information with a mental health professional within the same healthcare system without obtaining written consent
   D) Obtaining broad consent from the client to share information with any healthcare provider involved in their care to streamline communication

(See answers on the next page.)

1. D) Politely tell the family that they cannot discuss any information with them

Since the client has not provided written consent for the release of information, the counselor should inform the family member they cannot disclose any information. This option aligns with HIPAA regulations and emphasizes the importance of protecting the confidentiality of client information in substance use counseling. Providing general or specific information to the client would be against HIPAA regulations. The client, not the family member, would need to provide written consent. It is always good practice to check the client's file for a release of information before providing information to anyone.

2. B) Reporting suspected abuse or neglect to children or vulnerable adults as required by law

Mandatory reporting requirements in substance use counseling primarily focus on reporting suspected child abuse or neglect, or abuse or neglect of vulnerable adults. Counselors, like other mandated reporters in many jurisdictions, are legally obligated to report concerns of abuse or neglect to the appropriate authorities. This responsibility is in place to ensure the safety and well-being of vulnerable individuals, particularly children. A counselor should not report confidential information unless it is an instance where breaking confidentiality is required. Reporting substance use patterns to law enforcement agencies is not automatically appropriate. Reporting breaches of confidentiality to licensing boards is not the primary focus of mandatory reporting requirements.

3. B) Consult with the facility's legal team to determine the appropriate course of action

In a substance use counseling setting governed by 42 CFR Part 2, client confidentiality is highly protected. A counselor in this position should seek guidance from the facility's legal team. Confidentiality regulations, such as 42 CFR Part 2, require careful consideration and adherence to specific procedures when faced with requests for client information, especially from law enforcement.

4. B) Obtain written consent from the client specifically allowing the sharing of information with the primary care physician

In this scenario, the client expresses a desire for their information to be shared with their primary care physician. To navigate this situation in compliance with both HIPAA and 42 CFR Part 2, it is essential to respect the confidentiality requirements of both sets of regulations. Obtaining written consent from the client specifically for the sharing of treatment information ensures compliance with HIPAA, which governs the privacy and security of protected health information, and with 42 CFR Part 2, which specifically addresses the confidentiality of substance use disorder treatment records.

5. A) Implementing strict measures to limit the disclosure of substance use treatment information only to those explicitly authorized by the client in writing

Implementing strict measures to limit the disclosure of substance use treatment information only to those explicitly authorized by the client in writing is the only option that reflects a careful and compliant approach to confidentiality, considering the specific requirements of both HIPAA and 42 CFR Part 2 in substance use counseling. Providing information without a consent to release information as indicated in answer choice B and C is a violation of HIPPA and 42 CFR Part 2. Choice D is incorrect because the broad consent with ANY provider is not allowed. Consents must be written to a specific provider for specific information.

6. In the context of substance use counseling, the Tarasoff decision primarily addresses the counselor's duty to:
   A) Warn potential victims when a client poses a serious threat
   B) Maintain strict confidentiality of client information
   C) Report substance use issues to law enforcement
   D) Document client progress and treatment outcomes

7. A substance use counselor is working with a client who is struggling with trust issues and has difficulty forming therapeutic connections. Which of the following actions by the counselor best reflects an ethically sound approach to address the client's challenges?
   A) Sharing personal experiences to establish common ground and build rapport quickly
   B) Allowing the client to dictate the pace of the therapeutic relationship without offering any guidance
   C) Consistently demonstrating empathy, active listening, and unconditional positive regard to foster a safe and trusting environment
   D) Encouraging dependency on the counselor to create a sense of reliance for the client

8. A substance use counselor is working with a client who initially provided informed consent for counseling services that includes the treatment modalities the counselor provides. After a few sessions, the client expresses a desire to discontinue a specific treatment modality that was outlined in the original informed consent. What is the most appropriate course of action for the counselor regarding the client's request?
   A) Continue with the original treatment plan, emphasizing its importance for the client's progress
   B) Immediately modify the treatment plan based on the client's preference without further discussion
   C) Engage in a collaborative discussion with the client, reevaluating the treatment plan and obtaining updated informed consent
   D) Discontinue counseling services for the client, as their request deviates from the initially agreed-upon treatment

9. A former client who has successfully completed treatment approaches their previous counselor to become business partners in a venture unrelated to counseling. Which of the following options best reflects an ethically sound decision for the counselor?
   A) Accepting the business partnership since the client has successfully completed treatment, indicating a balanced and mutual relationship
   B) Politely declining the offer and maintaining clear professional boundaries to avoid potential conflicts of interest
   C) Accepting the offer but establishing clear ground rules to separate business activities from any potential counseling relationships
   D) Seeking guidance from colleagues about the decision, considering the potential benefits of the business partnership

10. A substance use counselor is tasked with maintaining progress notes for each client. Which of the following practices best reflects an ethically sound approach?
    A) Including highly detailed and personal information in progress notes to provide a comprehensive client profile
    B) Documenting only observable behaviors without delving into the client's emotions or subjective experiences
    C) Ensuring that progress notes contain relevant and objective information while respecting the client's privacy
    D) Sharing progress notes with other counselors in the same facility to facilitate information exchange without client consent

(*See answers on the next page.*)

6. A) Warn potential victims when a client poses a serious threat

The Tarasoff decision establishes a duty to warn or protect potential victims when a counselor becomes aware that a client presents a serious risk of harm to others. The other answer choices do not address the Tarasoff decision.

7. C) Consistently demonstrating empathy, active listening, and unconditional positive regard to foster a safe and trusting environment

This option reflects an ethically sound approach to building a therapeutic relationship by emphasizing foundational qualities that contribute to a safe and trusting counseling environment in substance use counseling. Self-disclosure can be a effective tool in counseling but must be used mindfully. A counselor should not put the burden of the therapeutic relationship on the client. Encouraging dependency on the counselor does not support a healthy therapeutic relationship.

8. C) Engage in a collaborative discussion with the client, reevaluating the treatment plan and obtaining updated informed consent

The counselor should encourage ongoing communication and collaboration, and obtain updated informed consent when there are changes to the treatment plan, aligning with ethical principles in substance use counseling. Continuing with a treatment plan the client wishes to discontinue is not ethical. Immediately making changes without client input or discontinuing all services are not helpful for the therapeutic relationship.

9. B) Politely declining the offer and maintaining clear professional boundaries to avoid potential conflicts of interest

Politely declining the offer and maintaining clear professional boundaries to avoid potential conflicts of interest reflects the ethical principle of avoiding dual relationships to protect the client's well-being and maintain the integrity of the therapeutic relationship established during counseling. Accepting or considering the partnership would lead to a conflict of interest for the counselor.

10. C) Ensuring that progress notes contain relevant and objective information while respecting the client's privacy

The counselor should prioritize the inclusion of pertinent information in progress notes while upholding the confidentiality and privacy of the client in substance use counseling. Including highly detailed personal information in progress notes does not uphold confidentiality and privacy. Documenting only observable behaviors is not effective record keeping. Sharing progress notes with other counselors without client consent is a violation of the client's confidentiality.

11. A substance use counselor is required to write a report detailing a client's progress for an external agency that requests specific personal information for research purposes. The client has not explicitly consented to the release of such detailed information. Which action by the counselor best aligns with ethical standards in substance use counseling?
    A) Fulfilling the external agency's request by providing all requested personal information to contribute to research
    B) Discuss the matter with the client and only proceed with written consent from the client before releasing any personal information to the external agency
    C) Redacting certain identifiable details from the report and submitting the remaining information to the external agency
    D) Decline the external agency's request, citing client confidentiality as the reason for nondisclosure

12. In substance use counseling, what is the primary ethical concern regarding sexual relationships between a counselor and a current client?
    A) The potential for harm to the counselor's professional reputation
    B) The risk of violating the client's right to confidentiality
    C) The impact on the therapeutic relationship and potential harm to the client
    D) The breach of professional standards related to counselor self-disclosure

13. A substance use counselor is working with a client who has a history of relapses and is struggling with maintaining sobriety. The counselor and client have previously discussed a crisis management plan where the client knows to call the counseling center's emergency line if they find themselves in crisis. One day, the client unexpectedly sends the counselor a text message outside of scheduled sessions, seeking immediate support during a challenging moment. The client makes it clear in their message that they are annoyed, not in crisis. What is the most appropriate course of action for the counselor, considering ethical boundaries in communication?
    A) Ignore the text message and address the client's concerns during the next scheduled session. Ensure that informed consent policy on after-hours requests is noted
    B) Respond promptly to the client's text message, providing reassurance and support
    C) Call the client immediately to discuss their challenges and provide real-time assistance
    D) Reply to the text message, expressing concern for the client's well-being, and arrange for an additional counseling session as soon as possible

14. In substance use counseling, how does the concept of privilege relate to the ethical principle of confidentiality?
    A) Privilege recognizes the counselor's responsibility to protect client information and maintain confidentiality
    B) Privilege emphasizes the counselor's right to withhold information from clients to maintain professional boundaries
    C) Privilege acknowledges the client's right to keep information confidential from the counselor
    D) Privilege implies that confidentiality is optional and can be waived based on the counselor's discretion

15. A substance use counselor is working with a diverse group of clients, each from different cultural backgrounds. Which of the following actions by the counselor best demonstrates an application of multicultural competence in substance use counseling?
    A) Utilizing standardized assessment tools that are designed without cultural considerations
    B) Applying a one-size-fits-all treatment approach to streamline counseling sessions
    C) Tailoring counseling interventions to consider the unique cultural backgrounds, values, and beliefs of each client
    D) Avoiding discussions about cultural differences to maintain a neutral and unbiased therapeutic environment

(*See answers on the next page.*)

11. B) Discuss the matter with the client and only proceed with written consent from the client before releasing any personal information to the external agency

Proceeding only with written consent from the client upholds ethical standards in substance use counseling by respecting the client's right to confidentiality and informed consent. In situations where the release of personal information is requested for research purposes, obtaining explicit written consent from the client is crucial. This ensures that the client is fully informed about the nature of the information being shared, the purpose of the disclosure, and has the opportunity to give or withhold consent. The counselor does not have to decline the request automatically but should discuss the request with the client.

12. C) The impact on the therapeutic relationship and potential harm to the client

Engaging in a sexual relationship with a current client can seriously compromise the therapeutic relationship and lead to potential harm for the client. Sexual relationships can introduce power imbalances, exploit vulnerabilities, and impede the counselor's ability to provide objective and client-centered care.

13. A) Ignore the text message and address the client's concerns during the next scheduled session. Ensure that informed consent policy on after-hours requests is noted

Ignoring the text message and addressing the client's concerns during the next scheduled session allows the counselor to maintain the structure of the therapeutic relationship, ensuring that support is provided within the established professional boundaries. The client is not currently in crisis and, if they were, they know to contact the counseling center's emergency line. Engaging with the client outside of the set boundaries of the therapeutic relationship is not appropriate.

14. A) Privilege recognizes the counselor's responsibility to protect client information and maintain confidentiality

This option accurately reflects the counselor's ethical obligation to uphold confidentiality and protect client information in the context of privilege in substance use counseling. All other choices are incorrect and do not accurately represent the concept of privilege as a legal concept.

15. C) Tailoring counseling interventions to consider the unique cultural backgrounds, values, and beliefs of each client

Tailoring counseling interventions to consider the unique cultural backgrounds, values, and beliefs of each client reflects the application of multicultural competence in substance use counseling by acknowledging and incorporating the diverse cultural aspects of clients into the counseling process, fostering a more effective and respectful therapeutic relationship. Avoiding or ignoring cultural considerations and adopting a "one-size-fits-all" approach does not demonstrate multicultural competence.

16. A substance use counselor is developing a treatment plan for a diverse group of clients. What action best demonstrates a commitment to fostering an inclusive and equitable therapeutic environment?
    A) Implementing the same treatment approach for all clients to maintain consistency
    B) Recognizing and addressing any cultural biases in the treatment plan and modifying interventions accordingly
    C) Prioritizing clients from certain cultural backgrounds over others based on perceived treatment success
    D) Avoiding discussions about cultural differences to prevent potential discomfort among clients

17. A substance use counselor is tasked with conducting assessments to evaluate a client's readiness for treatment and to inform the development of an appropriate intervention plan. Which of the following actions by the counselor best reflects an ethically sound approach?
    A) Administering assessments without explaining their purpose to the client to avoid potential resistance
    B) Utilizing a standardized assessment tool without considering the client's cultural background or language proficiency
    C) Tailoring the assessment process to respect the client's preferences, ensuring their understanding
    D) Selecting assessments solely based on personal familiarity, overlooking evidence-based practices in the field

18. A substance use counselor is active on social media platforms and notices that a current client has sent a friend request. Which of the following actions by the counselor best aligns with ethical standards in substance use counseling and social media use?
    A) Accept the friend request to maintain a friendly therapeutic relationship outside the counseling sessions
    B) Ignore the friend request and address the issue in the next counseling session, establishing clear boundaries regarding social media interactions. Ensure that informed consent policy covers social media
    C) Accept the friend request but limit access to personal information by adjusting privacy settings.
    D) Decline the friend request and provide the client with an explanation during the next counseling session

19. In the context of substance use counseling supervision, which of the following best defines the purpose of clinical supervision?
    A) Providing ongoing education and skill development for the counselor
    B) Evaluating the counselor's performance for employment decisions
    C) Offering therapy sessions to clients under the guidance of a supervisor
    D) Conducting research on the effectiveness of counseling interventions

20. In substance use counseling, what is the primary purpose of seeking consultation?
    A) Making employment decisions for the counselor
    B) Providing therapy sessions directly to clients
    C) Enhancing clinical skills and knowledge through expert advice
    D) Conducting research on substance use interventions

21. A substance use counselor is faced with a challenging ethical dilemma involving a client struggling with both substance use disorder and mental health issues. The counselor is unsure about the best course of action. Which step of the ethical decision-making model is the counselor most likely engaged in at this point?
    A) Identifying the problem and gathering relevant information
    B) Evaluating the potential courses of action based on ethical principles
    C) Consulting with colleagues or seeking supervision to gain different perspectives
    D) Making a decision and implementing the chosen course of action

(See answers on the next page.)

16. B) Recognizing and addressing any cultural biases in the treatment plan and modifying interventions accordingly

Engaging in ongoing self-reflection to identify and address personal biases that may impact counseling fosters a culturally competent and inclusive approach in substance use counseling. Implementing the same treatment approach for all clients, prioritizing clients from selected cultural backgrounds, and avoiding discussions of culture all together do not foster an inclusive and equitable therapeutic environment.

17. C) Tailoring the assessment process to respect the client's preferences, ensuring their understanding

Tailoring the assessment process to respect the client's preferences and ensuring their understanding reflects an ethically sound approach by considering the client's individual needs, preferences, and cultural background in the assessment process, fostering a more collaborative and client-centered approach in substance use counseling.

18. B) Ignore the friend request and address the issue in the next counseling session, establishing clear boundaries regarding social media interactions. Ensure that your informed consent policy covers social media

Ignoring the friend request temporarily allows the counselor to address the issue in a planned and professional manner during the next counseling session and promotes open communication and transparency, which enables the counselor to discuss the reasons for maintaining clear boundaries on social media. While declining the friend request and providing the client with an explanation during the next counseling may be acceptable, a client may feel rejection from the declined invitation. Ensuring that the informed consent covers social media policy also minimized the number of clients who add a counselor as a friend. Accepting the friend request can quickly lead to boundary violations.

19. A) Providing ongoing education and skill development for the counselor

Providing ongoing education and skill development for the counselor is the primary purpose of clinical supervision. Supervisors guide counselors in enhancing their clinical skills, staying current with evidence-based practices, and addressing any challenges they may encounter in their work.

20. C) Enhancing clinical skills and knowledge through expert advice

Enhancing clinical skills and knowledge through expert advice is the primary purpose of seeking consultation. Counselors may seek consultation to address challenging cases, gain insights into evidence-based practices, and receive guidance on effective interventions.

21. C) Consulting with colleagues or seeking supervision to gain different perspectives

When faced with a challenging ethical dilemma, it is common for counselors to seek input from colleagues or supervisors to gain different perspectives and insights. This aligns with the ethical decision-making model where collaboration and consultation are crucial in ensuring that the counselor considers various viewpoints and ethical principles before deciding. This step helps the counselor make a more informed and ethically sound choice, taking into account the complexities of the situation and the potential impact on the client.

22. In the context of substance use counseling, which statement best aligns with the ethical principle of nonmaleficence?
    A) Providing clients with challenging but effective therapeutic interventions, even if it may cause temporary discomfort
    B) Avoiding any discussions about the potential risks and negative consequences of substance use to prevent distressing clients
    C) Implementing treatment approaches that solely focus on short-term benefits without considering long-term consequences
    D) Withholding information about potential harmful effects of certain substances to maintain a positive therapeutic environment

23. In substance use counseling, what is a common ethical requirement related to client grievances?
    A) Encouraging clients to keep their concerns confidential to maintain a positive therapeutic environment
    B) Discouraging clients from expressing grievances to prevent potential conflicts within the counseling relationship
    C) Ignoring client grievances unless they directly impact the therapeutic process to maintain professional boundaries
    D) Providing clients with clear information about the process for expressing grievances and ensuring their right to voice concerns

24. In substance use counseling, what is the primary ethical consideration related to counselor self-disclosure?
    A) Encouraging self-disclosure to build a stronger therapeutic alliance
    B) Sharing personal experiences related to substance use to establish common ground
    C) Assessing the potential benefits and risks of self-disclosure on the client/counselor relationship
    D) Avoiding any form of self-disclosure to maintain a professional and distant demeanor

25. A substance use counselor is faced with a client who presents with both substance use issues and underlying mental health concerns. Which of the following actions best reflects an ethically sound approach to managing co-occurring symptomology, considering the counselor's expertise and limitations?
    A) Proceeding with counseling for both substance use and mental health issues, assuming that the counselor can address both effectively
    B) Collaborating with a mental health professional to provide comprehensive care, recognizing the need for specialized expertise
    C) Refusing to address the mental health concerns and focusing solely on substance use issues within the counselor's comfort zone
    D) Suggesting that the client seek mental health counseling independently to ensure appropriate and specialized care

26. A substance use counselor is working with a client who requires specialized services beyond the scope of the counselor's expertise. What is the most appropriate course of action for the counselor in facilitating a referral?
    A) Refer the client to a colleague within the same organization, assuming they have the necessary expertise
    B) Provide the client with a list of local service providers and allow them to choose based on personal preferences
    C) Conduct additional training to acquire the necessary expertise before continuing to work with the client
    D) Collaborate with the client to identify their specific needs and preferences before making a targeted referral to an appropriate external resource

(*See answers on the next page.*)

22. A) Providing clients with challenging but effective therapeutic interventions, even if it may cause temporary discomfort

Providing clients with challenging but effective therapeutic interventions, even if it may cause temporary discomfort aligns with the ethical principle of nonmaleficence by emphasizing the counselor's commitment to promoting the client's well-being through effective interventions, even if they involve temporary discomfort.

23. D) Providing clients with clear information about the process for expressing grievances and ensuring their right to voice concerns

This option aligns with the ethical principle of transparency and respects clients' rights in addressing grievances in substance use counseling. Ignoring or discouraging the client to take steps to address the grievance is unethical and detrimental to the counseling process.

24. C) Assessing the potential benefits and risks of self-disclosure on the client–counselor relationship

Assessing the potential benefits and risks of self-disclosure on the client/counselor relationship emphasizes the importance of careful consideration of the impact of counselor self-disclosure on the therapeutic alliance and the client's well-being in substance use counseling.

25. B) Collaborating with a mental health professional to provide comprehensive care, recognizing the need for specialized expertise

Collaborating with a mental health professional to provide comprehensive care, recognizing the need for specialized expertise reflects an ethically sound approach by acknowledging the counselor's scope of practice, collaborating with other professionals when needed, and ensuring the client receives comprehensive care for both substance use and mental health concerns. Suggesting the client seek mental health independently may be helpful to the client, but it is important to consider that because the client has already established rapport with the counselor, switching fully to another counselor could do harm.

26. D) Collaborate with the client to identify their specific needs and preferences before making a targeted referral to an appropriate external resource

Collaborating with a client is a client-centered and collaborative approach, ensuring that the referral is targeted to the client's specific needs and preferences. Referring the client without input, giving the client a list of local providers, and stopping treatment to conduct additional training are not appropriate courses of action.

27. A substance use counselor is developing a discharge plan for a client who has successfully completed an intensive outpatient treatment program. Which of the following components should be prioritized to ensure a smooth transition and ongoing support for the client?
    A) Providing the client with a list of local support groups and community resources
    B) Encouraging the client to maintain contact with the counselor for an extended period after discharge
    C) Sharing the client's treatment records with their primary care physician to facilitate coordinated care
    D) Discontinuing communication with the client after discharge to respect their privacy

28. A substance use counselor has been working with a client for several months, and the client has made significant progress in their recovery. Which of the following options best reflects an ethically sound approach to terminating the counseling relationship?
    A) Deciding unilaterally that the client is ready to end counseling, as significant progress has been made
    B) Collaboratively discussing the client's progress, goals, and readiness for termination, ensuring mutual agreement
    C) Extending the counseling relationship indefinitely to provide ongoing support, even if the client feels ready to end sessions
    D) Recommending termination abruptly to encourage the client to rely on their newfound coping skills

29. In substance use counseling, what is the primary ethical consideration regarding social relationships between a counselor and a current client?
    A) The potential impact on the counselor's personal life
    B) The risk of harm to the therapeutic alliance and the client's well-being
    C) The counselor's right to maintain personal friendships outside of the therapeutic setting
    D) The opportunity to enhance rapport and trust through shared social experiences

30. A substance use counselor is working with a client who has experienced multiple relapses while attempting to maintain sobriety. The client expresses frustration and disappointment. What is the most ethical and client-centered approach for the counselor in addressing the client's concerns about relapse?
    A) Collaboratively explore the factors contributing to relapse and develop a personalized relapse prevention plan
    B) Implement a more rigid and restrictive treatment plan to minimize the risk of relapse
    C) Share a personal experience of overcoming challenges and maintaining sobriety to inspire the client
    D) Suggest punitive measures to reinforce the consequences of relapse and discourage further substance use

(*See answers on the next page.*)

27. A) Providing the client with a list of local support groups and community resources

Providing the client with a list of local support groups and community resources prioritizes ongoing support for the client in their local community and encourages them to continue their recovery journey with available resources. It aligns with ethical considerations of promoting the well-being of the client after completing substance use counseling. The client should not be encouraged to maintain contact with the counselor for an extended period after discharge. However, discontinuing all contact is also inappropriate. Sharing the client's treatment records with another provider is not appropriate without written consent.

28. B) Collaboratively discussing the client's progress, goals, and readiness for termination, ensuring mutual agreement

Collaboratively discussing the client's progress, goals, and readiness for termination, ensuring mutual agreement reflects an ethical approach to termination, involving the client in the decision-making process and ensuring that the termination is a collaborative and agreed-upon decision, considering the client's progress and goals in substance use counseling.

29. B) The risk of harm to the therapeutic alliance and the client's well-being

Establishing social relationships with clients can pose a significant risk to the therapeutic alliance and the client's well-being. Mixing personal and professional boundaries can lead to power imbalances, loss of objectivity, and potential harm to the client. Maintaining clear professional boundaries is crucial for the effectiveness and integrity of the therapeutic relationship in substance use counseling.

30. A) Collaboratively explore the factors contributing to relapse and develop a personalized relapse prevention plan

Collaboratively explore the factors contributing to relapse and develop a personalized relapse prevention plan emphasizes a client-centered and collaborative approach to addressing relapse concerns. It also involves working closely with the client to identify specific triggers, challenges, and coping strategies. Developing a personalized relapse prevention plan tailors the approach to the client's unique needs, strengths, and circumstances.

PART III: PRACTICE TEST

Practice Exam

1. A substance use counselor is faced with a client who vehemently opposes any disclosure of their treatment information to external parties, even when there is a credible threat of harm to the client or others. Which of the following actions would best reflect an ethically sound decision-making process in this scenario?
   A) Respecting the client's wishes and maintaining strict confidentiality, even if there is a risk of harm
   B) Consulting with a supervisor to explore alternative approaches that respect the client's autonomy while addressing safety concerns
   C) Automatically disclosing all client information to relevant parties without the client's consent
   D) Terminating the counseling relationship to avoid ethical conflicts and potential legal ramifications

2. An adolescent shows signs of increased irritability, disturbed sleep, and persistent cravings after abruptly stopping heavy and chronic use of inhalants. Which aspect of substance misuse does this scenario primarily reflect?
   A) Tolerance development
   B) Reduced effectiveness of the drug due to frequent use
   C) Withdrawal effects of the substance use
   D) Long-term physical effects

3. Corroborative or collateral information is
   A) Unnecessary to complete an assessment unless the counselor thinks the client is not telling the truth
   B) Essential to a quality assessment
   C) Something that can be gathered without the client's consent if the client is completing an assessment
   D) Not permitted as this would violate the client's confidentiality

4. What is the relationship between the zone of proximal development (ZPD) and a learner's current developmental level?
   A) ZPD is always ahead of the learner's current abilities
   B) ZPD is equivalent to the learner's current abilities
   C) ZPD is behind the learner's current abilities
   D) ZPD is unrelated to the learner's current developmental level

5. Client-centered therapy is based on which of the following principles?
   A) Empathy, genuineness, and mirroring
   B) Unconditional positive regard, mirroring, and insight
   C) Congruence, unconditional positive regard, and empathy
   D) Genuineness, unconditional positive regard, and insight

6. A client is undergoing stimulant withdrawal. Which of the following symptoms would be expected in this client?
   A) Hypersomnia
   B) Increased motivation
   C) Irritability
   D) Increased energy

7. A client who has been sober from substances for several months attends 12-step meetings and participates in a fitness group as a coping mechanism for stress. Which stage of change is characterized by this client?
   A) Contemplation
   B) Action
   C) Maintenance
   D) Preparation

8. Which of the following occurs during the core function of screening?
   A) Conducting group counseling sessions
   B) Beginning to assess the client's readiness for change
   C) Providing immediate crisis intervention
   D) Collaborating with other professionals for consultation

9. A substance use counselor is considering incorporating telehealth services into their practice to better reach clients. Which of the following statements best reflects an ethically sound approach?
   A) Ensuring that the chosen technology complies with privacy and security standards to protect client confidentiality
   B) Utilizing video conferencing platforms without considering client preferences for communication
   C) Implementing electronic communication methods to share sensitive client information for efficiency
   D) Using social media platforms to connect with clients for informal check-ins outside of scheduled sessions

10. What is the primary purpose of ongoing assessment in the treatment planning function of substance use counseling?
    A) Avoid adapting the treatment plan
    B) Maintain a static approach to client needs
    C) Ensure the treatment plan remains relevant and responsive
    D) Limit collaboration with other professionals

11. Repeated legal charges are
    A) Sufficient symptoms for a diagnosis of a mild substance use disorder
    B) Sufficient symptoms for a diagnosis of a moderate substance use disorder
    C) Sufficient symptoms for a diagnosis of a severe substance use disorder
    D) Not sufficient symptoms for a diagnosis

12. Which strategy would be the most effective for managing nicotine withdrawal symptoms?
    A) Engaging in intense exercise to distract from withdrawal symptoms
    B) Using medications such as bupropion exclusively
    C) Combining nicotine replacement products with behavioral therapy
    D) Increasing caffeine intake to counteract the fatigue and symptoms of withdrawal

13. A counselor is conducting a mental health screening with a client who has a substance use disorder. Which of the following statements is true?
    A) Symptoms of some mental health disorders can be identical to those caused by substance use
    B) Chronic pain is the only medical condition that will impact mental health of those with a substance use disorder
    C) Substance use disorders don't affect mental health, only physical health
    D) Mental health disorders always precede substance use disorders

Annie shares with her counselor that she has been in and out of treatment for methamphetamine use disorder over the past 10 years. She has a great deal of difficulty staying sober after she leaves the structured environment of residential treatment. The first time she left treatment, she was sober for 5 days before using methamphetamine. The most recent time she left treatment, she was sober for 120 days before she started to drink alcohol. Currently she has maintained sobriety from alcohol for 5 months and methamphetamine for over a year but she is fearful she will drink again and go back to using methamphetamine. She has been able to use her supports to maintain sobriety. At this time, she is not able to go back to residential treatment because she cannot afford it. The counselor agrees to work with her on an income-based payment plan.

14. What is the first thing for the counselor to consider when working with Annie now that she has started therapy?
    A) Getting Annie into no-cost support groups
    B) Developing an agreement for abstinence
    C) Developing therapeutic rapport and the therapeutic relationship
    D) All the above

15. Annie states in session that she will never be able to be successful and get into recovery. The counselor can challenge this statement by mentioning that
    A) Annie is in recovery
    B) Annie can be successful without getting into recovery
    C) Annie has been abstinent before and can do it again
    D) None of the above

16. What is the primary effect of opioids on the brain's reward system, contributing to the development of dependence?
    A) Activation of the amygdala and prefrontal cortex
    B) Inhibition of the hippocampus
    C) Stimulation of the prefrontal cortex
    D) Activation of the mesolimbic dopamine system or reward pathway

17. A client comes into a counselor's office worried about their level of alcohol use and pending legal charge of driving under the influence. The client wants to quit "cold turkey" (abruptly stop using alcohol entirely) and has been encouraged to do so by their lawyer. How would the counselor determine if this is an appropriate course of action for the client?
    A) Conduct a simple medical exam to determine the client's health status
    B) Complete a mental health assessment to determine if the client has a co-occurring disorder that would be impacted by the withdrawal process
    C) Take a history of the client's alcohol use and administer the Clinical Institute Withdrawal Assessment Alcohol Scale Revised (CIWA-AR) to determine the potential severity of the alcohol withdrawal
    D) Get a release of information and talk to the lawyer

18. Which of the following might be a key aspect of enhancing the likelihood of a person being resilient to developing a substance use disorder?
    A) Both biological parents struggling with addiction
    B) A support social network and positive mentoring relationships
    C) Early exposure to alcohol leading to suspension from school
    D) A lack of community involvement and social connections

19. A specifier of severe is appropriate when there are
    A) Four to five diagnostic criteria met
    B) Two to three diagnostic criteria met
    C) One to two diagnostic criteria met
    D) Six or more diagnostic criteria met

20. A biopsychosocial assessment considers which of the following factors?
    A) Biological, psychological, and social factors
    B) Biological, psychiatric, and social factors
    C) Biological, physiological, and social factors
    D) Biological, psychosomatic, and social factors

21. In substance use counseling, which ethical principle emphasizes the importance of honesty and truthfulness in communication with clients?
    A) Veracity
    B) Fidelity
    C) Autonomy
    D) Nonmaleficence

22. Reinforcement and punishment are key components of which form of learning?
    A) Classical conditioning
    B) Modeling
    C) Operant conditioning
    D) Both classical conditioning and operant conditioning

23. A counselor is working with a client on their triggers for substance use after completing treatment. The counselor is in which stage of counseling?
    A) Stage 2: Clarifying and assessing the presenting problem
    B) Stage 3: Identifying and setting counseling/treatment goals
    C) Stage 4: Designing and implement interventions
    D) Stage 5: Planning, terminating, and follow up

24. A client states that they are an opioid user. What primary risk would be associated with this client?
    A) Increased heart rate
    B) Elevated blood pressure
    C) Central nervous system depression
    D) Enhanced lung function

25. Which of the following actions by a substance use counselor best demonstrates compliance with the confidentiality requirements outlined in 42 CFR Part 2?
    A) Sharing patient information with other healthcare providers involved in the individual's care without obtaining written consent
    B) Storing client records in an unlocked cabinet in the counselor's office for easy access during sessions
    C) Obtaining verbal consent from a client to share their substance use treatment information with a family member
    D) Providing a comprehensive explanation to a client about the limitations on the disclosure of their treatment information and obtaining written consent for any permitted disclosures

Jay is a 54-year-old Latino man who is married and has older teenage children. He has a history of heavy alcohol consumption. He started drinking regularly at age 17 and has been continually drinking since that time with periods of heavier alcohol use in his 20s and 40s. Recently, his doctor has recommended he slow down and gradually stop drinking entirely due to emerging health complications. Jay is agreeable to this and has been working on it. He is taking the medication the doctor prescribed and has not had anything to drink for 3.5 months. He comes to counseling at the insistence of his doctor and wife. He appears "edgy" and irritable, sometimes sad, and complains of insomnia, headaches, an upset stomach, heart pounding, and an inability to concentrate on anything. He tells the counselor he can barely stand not to drink: "I'm jumping out of my skin." The counselor asks Jay whether he has had these kinds of symptoms before he used alcohol. Jay says he has had trouble in the past with sleeping and having headaches, but it's never been this bad before and the edginess and irritability are new. When he was drinking, he reports he felt like he could never get enough alcohol to feel relaxed, he was spending too much money on alcohol, and he had a lot of trouble at work due to not being able to focus and making too many mistakes. He was fired for drinking on the job. He tried to stop drinking then but was not able to because he felt sick and had lots of cravings. Jay went to the doctor because he could feel his heart pounding out of his chest and missing beats which scared him. His doctor was very worried about his blood pressure, liver functioning, and ulcers in his stomach. His family is angry with him and very worried about his state of mind. They want to know what to do.

26. Based on the symptoms presented and Jay's history, what is the most likely substance use disorder diagnosis an alcohol and drug counselor would apply?
    A) Alcohol use disorder moderate
    B) Alcohol use disorder, cirrhosis of the liver
    C) Alcohol use disorder mild
    D) Alcohol use disorder, severe

27. Which medication could Jay have been prescribed to treat his alcohol use disorder symptoms?
    A) Methadone
    B) Lithium
    C) Naltrexone
    D) A selective serotonin reuptake inhibitor (SSRI)

28. Based on the symptoms Jay reports when he comes to counseling, what might be occurring?
    A) Jay is in the acute phase of alcohol withdrawal
    B) Jay is in the postacute phase of alcohol withdrawal
    C) Jay is still actively drinking
    D) Jay has an anxiety disorder and should be evaluated by a mental health counselor

29. Jay's doctor becomes increasingly worried about his health condition at his last checkup. Jay is not drinking anymore so he does not understand why the doctor is so concerned. The counselor notices that Jay's eyes do not look right, and he itches frequently in session. His wife reports that he has lost a lot of weight and has been very confused about things. What might be happening with Jay?
    A) Jay has a medical condition that the doctor will not share
    B) Jay has a co-occurring medical condition, mostly likely cirrhosis of the liver
    C) Jay is still actively drinking
    D) Jay is just going through extended withdrawal and will be better in a few months

30. After consulting with Jay's doctor, the counselor finds out that he indeed has a co-occurring medical condition, cirrhosis of the liver. The counselor tries to help Jay understand what is happening. Which statement below is the most accurate to aid in his understanding of his condition?
    A) "You are experiencing a liver disease called cirrhosis of the liver."
    B) "You are experiencing a liver disease, and you will make a full recovery if you stop drinking for good."
    C) "You are experiencing a liver disease diagnosed by your doctor called cirrhosis of the liver which occurs due to the liver being damaged by the lack of nutrients from long-term drinking."
    D) "You are experiencing a liver disease diagnosed by your doctor called cirrhosis of the liver due to the liver being damaged from metabolizing the alcohol you have been drinking over the years."

31. Jay is experiencing significant "craving" since he stopped drinking. What is happening in Jay's brain to cause this?
    A) Jay's brain reward pathway has been altered by his chronic alcohol use; he cannot help it
    B) Jay's brain reward pathway has been altered and he is in the withdrawal/negative effect stage of the addiction cycle involving the prefrontal cortex where environmental cues release dopamine and trigger the amygdala inducing a strong urge to use the substance
    C) Jay's brain reward pathway has been altered and he is in the preoccupation/anticipation stage of the addiction cycle involving the prefrontal cortex where environmental cues release dopamine and trigger the basal ganglia inducing a strong urge to use the substance
    D) Jay's brain reward pathway has been altered and he is in the binge/intoxication affect stage of the addiction cycle

32. A substance use counselor is faced with a dilemma involving the documentation of a client's noncompliance with the treatment plan. Which of the following actions by the counselor best reflects an ethically sound and effective approach to documenting noncompliance while maintaining the therapeutic relationship?
    A) Clearly documenting the instances of noncompliance with objective and nonjudgmental language to maintain transparency
    B) Omitting details about the client's noncompliance from the records to avoid potential confrontations during future sessions
    C) Exaggerating the client's noncompliance to ensure that the severity of the issue is accurately reflected in the records
    D) Avoiding any mention of noncompliance in the documentation to prioritize the positive aspects of the client's progress

33. A substance use counselor is working with a client who is hesitant to follow the recommended treatment plan, expressing a desire to explore alternative methods not aligned with evidence-based practices. Which of the following actions by the counselor best demonstrates a respect for the client's autonomy while maintaining ethical standards?
    A) Insisting on the recommended treatment plan without considering the client's preferences
    B) Collaboratively discussing the client's concerns, exploring alternative approaches, and adjusting the treatment plan accordingly
    C) Informing the client that alternative methods are not valid options for substance use counseling
    D) Ending treatment with this client

34. A person consumed a substance a few hours ago that made them feel relaxed and happy but now that the affects have worn off, they feel unpleasant emotions. What stage of the addiction cycle does this represent?
    A) Binge/intoxication
    B) Withdrawal/negative affect stage
    C) Preoccupation/anticipation stage
    D) All of the above

35. The first task of assessment is
    A) Gather relevant history from the client including but not limited to alcohol and other substance use using appropriate interviewing techniques
    B) Identify appropriate assessment tools
    C) Develop a diagnostic evaluation of the client
    D) Explain assessment results to the client in an understandable manner

36. During the intake process, the counselor gathers information about the client's
    A) Treatment progress and goals
    B) Eligibility
    C) Treatment plan
    D) Treatment modality preferences

37. In the context of the zone of proximal development (ZPD), what does "scaffolding" refer to?
    A) Assigning tasks beyond the client's current abilities
    B) Providing support and guidance to help a client succeed in a challenging task
    C) Allowing client's to work independently without assistance
    D) Assessing the client's current skill level

38. An instructor asks a student when it is appropriate to use empathic confrontation as a counseling technique. Which response by the student requires correction?
    A) Prior to establishing rapport with the client
    B) When directed at the client's strengths
    C) When addressed to specific aspects of a client's behavior
    D) When used to point out a discrepancy between a client's verbal statements and behavior

39. When is it appropriate for a substance use counselor to breach confidentiality?
    A) Whenever the counselor deems it necessary
    B) To protect the client's best interests
    C) Only with the client's written consent
    D) When discussing cases with colleagues

40. Orientation helps the client understand
    A) The counselor's personal experiences with substance use
    B) The consequences of continued substance use
    C) The rules, policies, and expectations of the treatment program
    D) The need for immediate crisis intervention

> Savannah, a 14-year-old female, presents at the request of her parents. She appears sober. She is opposed to attending the appointment but did come. Her parents report they have caught her multiple times in the past 6 months sneaking out of the house, coming home intoxicated with alcohol on her breath, getting high on marijuana at school, and hanging out with high-risk peers. The teen admits she is smoking marijuana every day and drinking to intoxication two to three times per week. Savannah and her parents deny any medical concerns and it has been more than 3 days since she drank. There is no history of depression or other major mental health symptoms. She denies any withdrawal history. She reports to you that marijuana is "not that big a deal" and that it is "way safer" than alcohol. She feels it helps her not be so worried all the time about what others think of her. She states that she would quit drinking, but never will give up marijuana. Her parents indicate they are looking for assistance and are not sure what to do next, but "want their daughter to get the help she needs."

41. Since Savannah does not believe she has a problem with marijuana use,
    A) The counselor should only focus on assessing the alcohol use to not lose rapport with Savannah
    B) The counselor should only focus on assessing the marijuana use because this is her main problem
    C) The counselor should use utilize motivational interviewing to gather as much information about all of Savannah's substance use
    D) The counselor should only interview her parents as Savannah is unlikely to be honest

42. Based on the information provided, what is the lowest risk American Society of Addiction Medicine dimension for Savannah?
    A) Dimension 3: Emotional, behavioral, or cognitive conditions and complications
    B) Dimension 4: Readiness to change
    C) Dimension 5: Relapse, continued use, or continued problem potential
    D) Dimension 6: Recovery/living environment

43. Given the information presented, what is the most likely level of care to be recommended for Savannah?
    A) Alcohol and drug early intervention (ASAM .5)
    B) Outpatient individual and family counseling (ASAM 1)
    C) Partial hospitalization services (ASAM 3.5)
    D) Medically managed intensive inpatient services (ASAM 4)

44. Informed consent is a crucial ethical consideration in substance use counseling. What does it primarily involve?
    A) Forcing clients into treatment
    B) Respecting clients' right to autonomy
    C) Concealing information from clients
    D) Ignoring clients' preferences

45. A substance use counselor is conducting an initial assessment with a new client. Which of the following actions by the counselor best reflects an ethically sound approach to assessment use?
    A) Administering a standardized assessment without considering the client's cultural background, assuming universality in the results
    B) Skipping the assessment phase to avoid discomfort for the client and diving directly into counseling sessions
    C) Sharing assessment results with other professionals without obtaining the client's explicit consent
    D) Utilizing multiple assessment tools to gather a comprehensive understanding of the client's unique needs and tailoring the treatment plan accordingly

46. A client shares that they inhale airplane glue. Which organ is particularly vulnerable in this client?
    A) Liver
    B) Brain
    C) Lungs
    D) Kidneys

47. A person consumes a substance and feels relaxed and happy. Which stage of the addiction cycle does this represent?
    A) Binge/intoxication
    B) Withdrawal/negative affect stage
    C) Preoccupation/anticipation stage
    D) All of the above

48. Based on the results of the Clinical Institute Withdrawal Assessment Alcohol Scale Revised (CIWA-AR) assessment, a counselor determines that it is not safe for a client to entirely stop alcohol use immediately. Where should the counselor refer the client for help?
    A) A medical detoxification facility
    B) A social detoxification facility
    C) Intensive counseling held three times a week
    D) An inpatient or residential treatment center

49. A client you are seeing is seeking relief from pain and is concerned about becoming addicted to opioids. They tell you they are using cannabis but are not getting high. How is that possible?
    A) They are using tetrahydrocannabinol (THC)
    B) They are using cannabidiol (CBD)
    C) They are using both THC and CBD
    D) They are not using THC or CBD

> Betty is a 43-year-old Black female who has been using heroin for 25 years. She is well known to the detoxification center, having been through the program there (which consists primarily of support and hydration) on many occasions over the years. Betty has overdosed on heroin many times but has been administered medication to "bring her back." Betty usually comes to the center after an overdose episode and though she looks gaunter and a bit more ill each time she arrives, her stay at the center is usually the same: 2 or 3 days of serious stomach cramps, nausea, and diarrhea, then a few days of feeling poorly, and then a return to the community where she continues to use heroin and has little support. This time, however, was different. Betty looked "sicker" than usual, was hostile and belligerent, yelling at staff that they were "bugs" and would eat her. This was very unusual for her. She was talking to herself, was not very alert, and was making no sense when she communicated with staff. On the third day of detoxification, Betty seemed acutely more ill. On the way to the bathroom, she was observed staggering, and then fell striking her head. She suffered a grand mal seizure and was taken to the hospital because the center did not have the resources to help her.

50. Betty has been coming to the detoxification center over several years and keeps returning to the community and relapsing. What might explain her failure to achieve recovery after coming to the center?
    A) Betty receives only social detoxification at the center without any medical intervention, follow-up care, or counseling to help her interrupt the addiction cycle
    B) Betty is caught in the addiction cycle; she can't get better because it has been too long
    C) Betty does not want to get better; she prefers her lifestyle and only occasionally talks about getting into recovery
    D) None of the above

51. After Betty fell, the staff wondered why this time at the center was so different. They wondered if something else was happening with her. Her drug of choice has always been heroin but occasionally she drank alcohol and at times overdrank to the point of blacking out. A toxicology screen was ordered at the hospital to determine the best course of action. What is the best explanation for why this was done?
    A) Because Betty's behavior was so different they thought she might have a mental health disorder
    B) Betty displayed symptoms that were very unusual for opioid withdrawal; medical personnel suspected drug interactions were occurring
    C) Betty needed medical attention rather than substance use treatment
    D) It is standard protocol for all patients in all hospitals to do a drug screen

52. At the hospital, Betty's toxicological screen showed the presence of phencyclidine (PCP), high levels of barbiturates, opioids, and trace amounts of benzodiazepines. How might this explain what happened at the detoxification center?
    A) Betty's incoherence and unusual behavior were not the result of being under the influence of the hallucinogen when she came in
    B) The PCP likely caused the grand mal seizure since she had never had one before
    C) The PCP and the benzodiazepines caused the grand mal seizures
    D) The PCP, barbiturates, benzodiazepines, and opioids interacted in a way that caused the grand mal seizure

53. What class of drugs showed up on Betty's toxicology screen?
    A) Stimulants, opioids, hallucinogens, and sedatives
    B) Depressants only
    C) Stimulants, depressants, opioids, sedatives, and hallucinogens
    D) Opioids only

54. After this experience, Betty is determined to get into treatment for her substance use. After the period of acute withdrawal, what might Betty be expected to experience?
    A) Increased energy, clear thinking, but some sleeping problems
    B) A period where it might be difficult to remember things and think clearly, emotional instability, problems sleeping, and sensitivity to stress
    C) Possible return to use and difficulty sleeping but no psychological problems
    D) Periods of relapse and sobriety with some coordination problems because of the seizure

55. Which of the following best describes the purpose of screening in substance use counseling?
    A) Identifying treatment goals for the client
    B) Conducting a comprehensive assessment of the client's substance use history
    C) Providing immediate support and intervention during emergencies
    D) Determining if an individual has a substance use problem and initially assessing its severity

56. What is the primary organ responsible for metabolizing alcohol in the human body?
    A) Kidneys
    B) Liver
    C) Stomach
    D) Pancreas

57. Which factor contributes significantly to the preference for inhalant misuse among adolescents?
    A) Affordability and accessibility
    B) Unique psychoactive effects
    C) Simplicity of administration
    D) Long-lasting euphoric effects

58. If a person reports a craving for a substance, it means that they
    A) Are about to return to active use
    B) Cannot be given a specifier of "in sustained remission" no matter how long they have been substance free
    C) Are experiencing a desire to use a substance
    D) Need to be referred to counseling immediately

59. An appropriate assessment tool for a 62-year-old male presenting for an assessment after being arrested for driving under the influence (DUI) a third time is
    A) SOGS
    B) AUDIT
    C) CRAFFT
    D) DAST-10

60. In the context of substance use counseling, what does the duty to warn generally refer to?
    A) Disclosing confidential client information to family members
    B) Informing the client about the potential risks of substance use
    C) Reporting imminent harm or danger to third parties when a client poses a serious threat
    D) Notifying law enforcement about any illicit substance use by the client

61. A substance use counselor is working with a client from a culturally diverse background who holds strong traditional beliefs regarding the treatment of substance use issues. Which of the following actions by the counselor best reflects an understanding of multiculturalism in substance use counseling?
    A) Encouraging the client to abandon traditional beliefs in favor of evidence-based Western treatment approaches
    B) Respectfully exploring the client's cultural beliefs around substance use and integrating them into the treatment plan
    C) Disregarding cultural considerations and applying a standardized treatment approach for all clients
    D) Referring the client to another counselor with similar cultural background for more appropriate treatment

62. According to 42 CFR Part 2, when can a substance use disorder treatment program disclose patient information without consent?
    A) For billing purposes
    B) In emergency situations
    C) To family members upon request
    D) As part of routine communication with other healthcare providers

63. In the context of specific, measurable, achievable, relevant, and time-bound (SMART) goals, what is the purpose of making goals "meaningful" and aligned with the individual's values and priorities in substance use counseling?
    A) Makes the goal easier to measure
    B) Makes the goal more specific
    C) Promotes accountability and commitment
    D) Reduces the importance of personal values

64. An example of a biological factor in a biopsychosocial assessment is
    A) Family history of mental illness
    B) Cultural history
    C) Physical health
    D) Spiritual history

65. A client shares that their place of employment tested them for drugs and discovered they used hallucinogens. Which physiological process mainly facilitated the detection of substances in this client?
    A) Activation of the liver enzymes
    B) Stimulation of the adrenal glands
    C) Modulation of the endocrine system
    D) Excretion through urine

66. A client has been misusing prescription opioids for a few years. What is the primary factor that contributes to the potential for overdose in this client?
    A) Increased tolerance
    B) Enhanced pain relief
    C) Reduced risk of respiratory depression
    D) Strict adherence to prescribed dosages

67. A counselor has several new clients on their caseload. Ashley is diagnosed with a cannabis use disorder; Jacob is diagnosed with an alcohol use disorder; Marshall is diagnosed with a sedative use disorder; and Jerry comes to session under the influence of a hallucinogen. Which client(s) should the counselor be most concerned about overdosing?
    A) Ashley
    B) Jacob and Marshall
    C) Jerry
    D) Marshall and Jerry

68. Which statement best describes the psychological effects of moderate caffeine intake?
    A) "When I drink a little bit of caffeine, I become less social and my mood is very negative."
    B) "When I keep my caffeine to a moderate level there is no impact on my mood or attention, but I do get a headache."
    C) "When I drink tea with caffeine, I feel great and have increased energy and can focus really well!"
    D) None of these statements describe the psychological effects of caffeine.

69. According to Vygotsky's theory, what is the primary role of a more knowledgeable person (MKO) in a client's development within the zone of proximal development?
    A) Completing tasks on behalf of the client
    B) Assessing the client's abilities
    C) Guiding and supporting the client in tasks just beyond their current ability
    D) Setting goals for the client

> Tanya is a 29-year-old woman who recently came to the United States from another country with her husband and young daughter. Tanya is referred to counseling for a substance use evaluation after a child abuse report was made to child protective services regarding her 3-year-old daughter. Two months ago, Tanya brought her daughter into the emergency department when the child was having trouble breathing. The child was lethargic, irritable, and having difficulty staying awake. Tanya's behavior in the emergency department was erratic and she was unable to concentrate or provide any information about what might have happened to her child. The doctor diagnosed the child as having opioid poisoning. There have been many calls to child protective services that the child is not well cared for, that she has been found wandering alone outside, and that the parents frequently argue loud enough for the neighbors to hear. The report also indicates Tanya "seems to be impaired" and "out of it" when she interacts with the child protective service workers.

70. During the interview with Tanya, the counselor notices that she is nervous and will not provide any information unless directly questioned and then will only give yes or no answers. What is most likely reason for Tanya's behavior?
    A) The counselor is not being attentive enough and Tanya feels interrogated
    B) Tanya is not ready to talk; she is in the contemplation stage of change
    C) The counselor is asking only closed-ended questions
    D) Tanya is uncomfortable in counseling but does not show any defensiveness and states she wants to get help

71. Tanya brought her husband, who is from the same country as she is, to the appointment. He wants to share information about his concerns. He states that he believes his wife takes too many pills for her "head pain" and this is why she does not take good care of their daughter. He shares openly but will not make eye contact with the counselor. What might this suggest?
    A) The husband is worried his wife will be upset with him for sharing this information with the counselor
    B) There could be cultural differences and expectations regarding eye contact between the client and the counselor
    C) The counselor has made the father uncomfortable by only looking at the wife to avoid cultural misunderstanding about who is the client
    D) This usually happens in family counseling

72. Which of the following would is the best way to address cultural differences in this scenario?
    A) The counselor should broach the topic of cultural differences and take time to learn about the client's cultural beliefs, values, and communication preferences; this will help the counselor understand how to help resolve concerns that have been raised in the referral
    B) Ask the husband what his cultural expectations are and ask the wife if she agrees, emphasizing the important cultural expectations of childcare in the United States that brought them into counseling
    C) Discuss the cultural differences and emphasize that the cultural norms regarding care of children in the United States should be followed since they are now living here and are subject to U.S. law
    D) Cultural difference should be discussed openly and nondefensively if the client brings it up; if they do not, the counselor should not address it

73. During the interview, the counselor verifies that Tanya is prescribed narcotics but has been overusing them. She becomes defensive and angry when this is brought up. The best course of action is for the counselor to
    A) Use the confrontation skill with Tanya about the overuse of medication and how it is harming her child
    B) Ask the husband to leave the session so Tanya can talk freely
    C) Share with Tanya that she is in the denial stage and educate her on the dangers of overusing narcotics
    D) Use open-ended questions, reflections, affirmations, and summaries to explore her fears with Tanya

74. During the evaluation, Tanya shared that she had been seeing doctors in her home country because she had been "hearing things in her head" and was losing track of time. Since coming to the United States, she has not been able to find a doctor to help her, so she is taking more of her medication to block out the "noise" in her head and alleviate her "head pain." The counselor is concerned about this and should
    A) Complete the evaluation focusing on the overuse of medication and neglect of the child as was indicated in the referral
    B) Complete the interview, gather information on the substance use, history of medical and psychiatric problems, and coordinate care to address all these issues
    C) Halt the interview and tell her they are not able to help; she needs to go back to social services and ask about a referral to see a medical doctor
    D) Halt the interview and tell her they are not able to help and that she needs to go back to social services to ask about a referral for a psychiatric evaluation

75. Which of the following is a reason a counselor might tell a client that they should avoid going to bars?
    A) The counselor operates out of a behavioral theoretical orientation
    B) The counselor operates out of a cognitive theoretical orientation
    C) The counselor is engaging in motivational interviewing with the client
    D) The counseling is using a family systems approach

76. A substance use counselor is treating a client with a co-occurring mental health condition and needs to collaborate with a mental health professional. How should the counselor navigate the requirements of Health Insurance Portability and Accountability Act (HIPAA) and 42 CFR Part 2 to ensure compliance and provide effective care?
    A) Share the client's complete medical history, including substance use and mental health information, with the mental health professional to ensure comprehensive care coordination
    B) Obtain written consent from the client to share specific information related to their substance use and mental health treatment with the mental health professional involved in their care
    C) Share only general information about the client's substance use treatment without seeking consent, as mental health information is exempt from confidentiality regulations
    D) Communicate with the mental health professional without disclosing any specifics about the client's substance use or mental health treatment to maintain confidentiality

77. What foundational principle is emphasized in ethical guidelines for substance use counselors, particularly regarding confidentiality?
    A) The right to autonomy
    B) Informed consent
    C) Duty to warn
    D) Duty to report

78. A substance use counselor learns that their client is engaging in illegal activities. What is the appropriate course of action?
    A) Report the client to law enforcement
    B) Ignore the information to maintain trust
    C) Address the issue in therapy
    D) Terminate the counseling relationship immediately

79. Which of the following is an example of a structured interview format?
    A) Addiction Severity Index (ASI)
    B) Alcohol Use Disorder Identification Test (AUDIT)
    C) Substance Abuse Subtle Screening Inventory (SASSI-4)
    D) Adverse childhood experiences (ACEs) scales

80. A substance use counselor is conducting a therapy session with a client who is struggling with opioid addiction. The client asks the counselor about their personal experience with substance use. How should the counselor approach the ethical considerations of self-disclosure in this situation?
    A) Share personal experiences to create a sense of camaraderie and understanding
    B) Provide a general acknowledgment of having personal experiences with substance use without disclosing specific details
    C) Avoid any mention of personal experiences to maintain professional boundaries and focus on the client's needs
    D) Share detailed personal experiences to illustrate the challenges and potential outcomes of substance use

81. A substance use counselor is working with a client who expresses romantic feelings toward the counselor. How should the counselor navigate this situation while considering ethical considerations of boundaries?
    A) Acknowledge the client's feelings, set clear boundaries, and seek supervision
    B) Politely reject the client's advances and terminate the client
    C) Consider reciprocating romantic feelings if it seems beneficial to the therapeutic process
    D) Temporarily suspend the counseling relationship to allow both parties to reassess their feelings before continuing

82. A substance use counselor is preparing to obtain informed consent from a client before initiating counseling services. Which of the following elements is crucial to address during this process for ethical and legal reasons?
    A) Explaining the counselor's personal background and qualifications
    B) Clearly outlining the specific treatment techniques that will be used during counseling
    C) Discussing potential risks, benefits, and alternatives to the proposed treatment
    D) Obtaining the client's consent to share their treatment progress in a group therapy setting

83. A substance use counselor in a rural community is facing a situation where they may have a dual relationship with a client due to the close-knit nature of the community. Which of the following actions by the counselor best demonstrates an ethically sound approach by the counselor?
    A) Maintaining professional boundaries by avoiding any interaction with clients outside of scheduled counseling sessions
    B) Acknowledging the potential for dual relationships and discussing it openly with the client, seeking their input and consent
    C) Actively participating in community events and gatherings to build a stronger rapport with clients, considering it a normal practice in rural settings
    D) Providing extra favors or services to clients in the community to enhance their therapeutic experience and strengthen the counselor/client relationship

84. Which ethical standard emphasizes the counselor's responsibility to avoid harming clients?
    A) Autonomy
    B) Beneficence
    C) Nonmaleficence
    D) Fidelity

85. In substance use counseling, what is the primary goal of incorporating multicultural competence into the therapeutic process?
    A) Eliminating cultural diversity to create a standardized treatment approach
    B) Respecting and integrating clients' diverse cultural backgrounds into the treatment plan
    C) Avoiding clients from different cultural backgrounds to prevent potential conflicts
    D) Prioritizing one specific cultural approach over others for simplicity in treatment

86. How does the referral function in substance use counseling contribute to client empowerment?
    A) Reduces the work the counselor must do on their own
    B) Allows the counselor to direct treatment
    C) Provides clients with options and choices for additional support
    D) Avoids collaboration with external service providers

87. A client states that when they use opioids, their back pain goes away. How does this client's substance of choice exert its pain-relieving effects in their body?
    A) By increasing pain sensitivity
    B) By inhibiting pain receptors in the spinal cord
    C) By promoting inflammation
    D) By binding to specific receptors in the central nervous system

88. The primary goal of the intake process is to
    A) Provide education about substance use disorders
    B) Complete initial agency paperwork
    C) Assess the client's level of motivation for change
    D) Establish rapport and build a therapeutic relationship

89. A specifier of moderate is appropriate when there are
    A) Four to five diagnostic criteria met
    B) Two to three diagnostic criteria met
    C) Six to seven diagnostic criteria met
    D) Seven or more diagnostic criteria met

90. Why is the prefrontal cortex considered significant in the context of substance use disorders?
    A) It triggers the rewarding effects of substances during the binge/intoxication stage
    B) It maintains habit circuitry in the basal ganglia, reinforcing cravings
    C) It functions as the executive center and controls decision-making
    D) It induces negative emotions during the withdrawal/negative effect stage

91. In substance use counseling, what is the primary purpose of obtaining informed consent from clients?
    A) To ensure the counselor has legal protection in case of a dispute
    B) To guarantee the client's attendance at scheduled counseling sessions
    C) To provide clients with information about the nature of counseling and the potential risks, benefits, and alternatives
    D) To obtain permission to share the client's treatment progress with other healthcare professionals

92. In the context of substance use counseling, what does the ethical principle of beneficence primarily emphasize?
    A) Respecting the client's autonomy in decision-making
    B) Ensuring fair and equal treatment of all clients
    C) Promoting the well-being and welfare of the client
    D) Maintaining strict confidentiality of client information at all times

93. What ethical principle emphasizes the importance of making services accessible to all clients regardless of background?
    A) Autonomy
    B) Veracity
    C) Fidelity
    D) Justice

94. When faced with a conflict of interest in substance use counseling, what should a counselor prioritize?
    A) Personal interests
    B) Financial gain
    C) Client welfare
    D) Career advancement

95. What does the duty to refer in substance use counseling emphasize regarding the client's best interests?
    A) Encouraging the client to self-refer
    B) Ignoring the need for specialized care
    C) Prioritizing the counselor's convenience
    D) Ensuring the client receives appropriate and specialized care

96. A substance use counselor is committed to enhancing their cultural competence to better serve a diverse group of clients. Which of the following actions best reflects an ethically sound and effective strategy for improving cultural competence?
    A) Collaborating with colleagues from diverse backgrounds to share insights on cultural perspectives
    B) Assuming cultural knowledge based on personal experiences without seeking additional training
    C) Avoiding discussions about cultural differences to prevent potential discomfort among clients
    D) Implementing a standardized treatment approach for all clients to ensure consistency

97. What ethical principle emphasizes the importance of being honest and trustworthy in the counseling relationship?
    A) Autonomy
    B) Veracity
    C) Fidelity
    D) Justice

98. What is a potential consequence of a substance use counselor engaging in a dual relationship with a client?
    A) Improved therapeutic alliance
    B) Enhanced trust
    C) Impaired objectivity and professional judgment
    D) Increased client autonomy

99. Which of the following best describes the zone of proximal development (ZPD)?
    A) Tasks a client can do independently
    B) Tasks that are too difficult for the client
    C) The gap between what a client can do without assistance and what they can do with assistance
    D) The curriculum's core content

100. How does specific, measurable, achievable, relevant, and time-bound (SMART) goal-setting impact the client–counselor relationship in substance use counseling?
    A) It increases the likelihood of conflict
    B) It reduces the likelihood the counselor will have a bad audit review
    C) It fosters collaboration and shared understanding of treatment objectives
    D) It is irrelevant to the therapeutic relationship as it is just a process

> Susan presents for an assessment because she feels she is addicted to clonazepam (Klonopin). She tells you that she is prescribed .5 mg of clonazepam twice a day. She takes it every day as directed and never asks for a refill early. She is concerned because when she went on vacation with a friend, she forgot to bring her medication with her. After 2 days, she began to think a lot about her medication, began to feel physically uncomfortable and more anxious than usual, and had a hard time getting to sleep.

101. The most likely explanation for Susan's symptoms are that she
    A) Is reliant on her prescription medication
    B) Has a mild substance use disorder
    C) Has actually been taking more than prescribed and is now having withdrawal
    D) Is about to ask the counselor to advocate to her doctor for an increase in her dosage

102. Rick is pulled over while driving by a police officer for crossing the center line and driving erratically. When the officer does field sobriety tests, they suspect Rick might be over the legal blood alcohol concentration for driving and take him to the hospital for a blood test. Why would the officer suspect Rick is over the legal limit?
    A) Rick reaction time is very slow and he cannot walk a straight line when required
    B) Rick is relaxed but refuses to do some of the field tests
    C) Rick's speech is slurred and he fell when he tried to do the final field test
    D) Rick's reaction time is very slow and he cannot walk a straight line when required. In addition, his speech is slurred and he fell when he tried to do the final field test

103. A client is engaging in problem-solving and acquiring the necessary skills to overcome substance use challenges. Which stage of change applies to this client?
    A) Contemplation
    B) Maintenance
    C) Preparation
    D) Action

104. The advantage of a standardized screening tool such as the Alcohol Use Disorders Identification Test (AUDIT) or Substance Abuse Subtle Screening Inventory (SASSI) is that it
    A) Provides a way for the counselor to compare the current client to clients with similar concerns
    B) Provides a way for the counselor to spend less time interviewing the client
    C) Provides a way for the counselor to measure the impact of a client's substance use on their family
    D) There is no advantage

105. Orientation in substance use counseling involves
    A) Developing a treatment plan
    B) Identifying triggers and coping skills
    C) Providing information about the treatment program
    D) Evaluating treatment progress

106. Which of the following is a common medical condition that often co-occurs with substance use disorders?
    A) Depression
    B) Schizophrenia
    C) Chronic pain
    D) Attention deficit/hyperactivity disorder (ADHD)

107. What does the term "cross tolerance" refer to in the context of substance use?
    A) Increased sensitivity to various drugs
    B) Reduced effectiveness of a drug due to frequent use
    C) The body's adaptation to one substance affecting another in the same class
    D) The development of multiple drug dependencies simultaneously

108. A client is undergoing opioid withdrawal. Which of the following symptoms would be expected in this client?
    A) Increased heart rate
    B) Elevated blood pressure
    C) Nausea and vomiting
    D) Increased energy

109. Motivational interviewing utilizes
    A) Open-ended and close-ended questions
    B) Open-ended questions only
    C) Close-ended questions only
    D) Motivational interviewing is not used during the assessment process

110. During which stage of change might an individual experience setbacks but remains committed to overcoming them and continuing with the behavior change process?
   A) Relapse
   B) Maintenance
   C) Action
   D) Preparation

111. Paulo has been seeing a counselor for several weeks and has made good progress on counseling goals. Recently, however, he has started missing sessions and becoming very argumentative when in session. When the counselor address this in session, Paulo said "You treat me just like my mom use to!" The best response to this statement would be for the counselor to
   A) Ignore it and confront the client on his anger
   B) Address it using the reflection of feeling skill
   C) Highlight the irresponsibility of missing sessions using empathic confrontation
   D) Remind the client of boundaries as an example of how to keep feelings for others separate from the counselor

112. What is the significance of addressing co-occurring disorders in the treatment planning process?
   A) It reduces the likelihood of relapse
   B) It promotes overall well-being and increases the likelihood of sustained recovery
   C) Co-occurring disorders impact all stages of recovery
   D) All of the above

113. The AUDIT is
   A) Primarily used for adolescents with substance use concerns
   B) Expensive and requires extensive training to successfully utilize
   C) Available in multiple languages
   D) A valid measure of cannabis use

114. Which of the following statements regarding the interaction of nicotine and other substances is accurate?
   A) Nicotine interacts with caffeine, reducing its stimulant effects and lowering the heart rate
   B) Nicotine intensifies the effects of antidepressants and antipsychotic medications
   C) Nicotine increases the rate of alcohol metabolism, potentially leading to increased alcohol consumption to achieve the same effects
   D) Nicotine primarily affects the brain's opioid receptors, leading to cross tolerance with opioids

115. A client is determined to be in the late recovery stage of the developmental model of recovery. What is one of the primary foci at this time?
   A) Establishing a sense of purpose and meaning
   B) Rebuilding relationships with peers
   C) Maintaining abstinence and preventing relapse
   D) Achieving financial stability

116. The most appropriate specifier for a client who has a substance use disorder and who has spent the past 6 months in a treatment center is
   A) In sustained full remission
   B) In a controlled environment
   C) No specifier
   D) Mild

Autumn has been attending counseling for 3 months. She and her counselor are reviewing her treatment plan. Autumn has been attending individual and group counseling as well as a women's Alcoholics Anonymous (AA) meeting each week. She has a sponsor and meets with her on a weekly basis.

Autumn reports she has been alcohol free for the past 4 month since she was released from jail after being arrested for driving under the influence (DUI). Autumn has been identifying high-risk people and places, working on improving her support system, developing and using refusal skills when friends and family offer her alcohol, and building an understanding of the reward she gained from alcohol use. Autumn reports success in improving her support system, developing and using refusal skills, and understanding the reward she gained from alcohol use. She has struggled with not associating with high-risk people as her family continues to drink and her coworkers go out to the bar each night at the end of the shift. Autumn reports that though she has not drunk for the past 4 months, she is not sure she really needs to remain fully abstinent as she feels she can likely not have problems if she only drinks 2 drinks when she goes out.

117. For Autumn, who is considered a more knowledgeable other?
    A) Coworker who goes to the bar nightly and goes home after drinking two drinks
    B) The bartender at her favorite bar
    C) A friend who drinks to intoxication nightly but says she is considering cutting back
    D) Coworker who goes to the bar once per week and drinks to intoxication

118. The counselor expresses concern that Autumn wants to go to the bar after work with her coworkers. Autumn feels she will be fine. Which of these is a harm reduction treatment objective?
    A) Autumn will tell her sponsor about her belief that she will be fine to go to the bar
    B) Autumn will stop going to Alcoholics Anonymous meetings because she is not serious about recovery
    C) Autumn will arrange a ride home prior to going to the bar to prevent driving after drinking
    D) Autumn will contract with the therapist to not go to the bar

119. According to Gorski and Miller's Developmental Model of Recovery, what stage of recovery is Autumn in?
    A) Stabilization
    B) Action
    C) Maintenance
    D) Preparation

Darin has been struggling with maintaining sobriety the past 6 months. He desires to be sober given his wife is pregnant and she has told him she is not "going to raise this baby with an alcoholic." He shares with you that this statement really affected him because this is the same thing his mother said to his father when she was pregnant with Darin's little sister. His dad walked out the front door that day and never came back. He has not seen his dad since. Darin tearfully confides that he never wants to be like his dad, but now understands how hard it must have been for his father to stop drinking. Darin reports that, before he cut back 6 months ago, he was drinking 12 to 15 beers per night, but over the past 6 months he has cut back to 12 beers every other night or so. He has tried to quit completely, but by the third day of abstinence he finds he cannot sleep, he is irritable and feels too miserable to even go to work unless he has a couple of beers. Darin completed an assessment last week which recommended withdrawal management services followed by outpatient counseling. Darin reported he is ready for his life to be different and reports he now realizes he cannot just quit on his own. Darin has been in contact with his primary care doctor who stated he is willing to admit him to the local hospital to facilitate safe detoxification from alcohol.

120. What is Darin's stage of change?
    A) Contemplation
    B) Preparation
    C) Action
    D) Precontemplation

121. Darin asks his counselor why he needs to continue with outpatient counseling after he completes detoxification from alcohol in the hospital. What information should the counselor include in the response?
    A) Darin does not likely need to follow up with outpatient counseling due to his willingness for sobriety
    B) It will make his wife happy
    C) Because he needs to follow the recommendation of the evaluation
    D) Withdrawal management by itself is not an effective treatment for any substance use disorder

122. The counselor coordinating care with Darin's primary care doctor is an example of
    A) Treatment planning
    B) Referral
    C) Case management
    D) Assessment

123. After Darin returns to his counselor for outpatient counseling, what referrals would be most appropriate to consider to aid in his stabilization?
    A) Housing assistance, money management classes, and parenting classes
    B) Self-help meetings, marital counseling, and housing assistance
    C) Marital counseling, self-help meetings, and medication assessment for medication-assisted treatment
    D) Pastor, personal trainer, and self-help meetings

124. Darin's initial treatment plan goal is: "I want my life to be better before my child is born." How could this goal be improved?
    A) There is no reason to improve this goal because it is in Darin's own words
    B) Make it specific and measurable
    C) Make it relevant to his sobriety
    D) Make it more time bound

125. Explaining to the client the rationale for the use of assessment techniques
    A) Reduces the client's defensiveness
    B) Increases the client's defensiveness
    C) Permits the client to "trick" the evaluator more easily
    D) Only occurs with noncriminal justice-involved clients

126. The central focus of the 12th step of Alcoholics Anonymous (AA) is
    A) Service to others
    B) Reflecting on the people harmed
    C) Identifying a higher power
    D) Entering treatment

127. Which of the following is a reason a counselor might use progressive muscle relaxation in session?
    A) The counselor operates out of a behavioral theoretical orientation
    B) The counselor is working on a relapse prevention plan with the client
    C) The counselor operates out of both a behavioral theoretical orientation and is working on a relapse prevention plan with the client
    D) None of the above

Jane has recently been hired as a counselor at a long-term, co-occurring residential treatment program. Her first client is Sylvester. He tells Jane in the first session that he has struggled with connecting to any counselor, feeling that no one really understands him because they have not "been through what I have been through." He also tells Jane he has been talking to a recently hired part-time overnight treatment staff for the past month. He further tells Jane this staff has been sitting in Sylvester's room by his bed each night until he falls asleep, so he does not feel so alone. Sylvester tells Jane he finally feels someone "gets it" and now he can start "making progress because I have someone on my side who is willing to do what I need."

128. Sylvester asks Jane to share her history so he can decide if he can trust her as his counselor. What ethical tenet provides the best justification for her decision?
    A) Beneficence: For the benefit of Sylvester, Jane should share a detailed history of her experiences. Otherwise, Sylvester may not connect with her as a counselor
    B) Dual-relationships: If Jane shares her full history with Sylvester, it may create a more peer-to-peer relationship rather than a counselor/client relationship
    C) Personal disclosure: Sharing her history with Sylvester will help him connect with Jane and build rapport
    D) Confidentiality: It is okay for Jane to share her history with Sylvester because he is bound by confidentiality guidelines not to share your story with anyone else

129. The staff that is sitting by Sylvester's bed at night until he falls asleep is engaging in
    A) A boundary crossing
    B) A boundary violation
    C) A helpful behavior for Sylvester
    D) A law violation

130. After Jane refuses to share her full history with Sylvester, he storms out of the office saying, "You are just like all the others." Jane then informs her supervisor about her concerns about the staff that is sitting by Sylvester's bed at night. The supervisor shares Jane's worries that the staff is engaging in a boundary crossing by sitting in Sylvester's room. The supervisor tells the staff to cease this behavior immediately. The next day when Jane comes to work, Sylvester is waiting for her. He screams that she violated his confidentiality by talking about something he said in his counseling session and that he is going to "get you." Which of the following is the most appropriate analysis of this scenario?
    A) Jane needed written consent to talk to her supervisor about what Sylvester said in session
    B) Jane should have asked Sylvester if it was okay to talk to her supervisor about her concerns
    C) Jane should report Sylvester's threat to law enforcement because she does not know what he meant when he said he was going to "get you."
    D) Restrictions on disclosure do not extend to staff within the treatment program

131. In the context of the referral function, why is it important for substance use counselors to maintain a network of community resources?
    A) To maintain the counselor's referral base
    B) To reduce competition among external providers
    C) To prevent counselor burnout
    D) To provide clients with diverse and appropriate support options

132. A client shares that their substances of choice are hallucinogens. Which neurotransmitter system is primarily influenced in this client?
    A) Glutamate
    B) Serotonin
    C) Gamma-aminobutyric acid (GABA)
    D) Acetylcholine

133. When conducting an assessment to determine potential withdrawal complications in clients with substance use disorders, which of the following addresses preventing hazardous consequences resulting from sudden substance discontinuation?
    A) The assessment of co-occurring conditions and medical conditions
    B) The diagnosis of the substance use disorder
    C) The history of psychosocial factors influencing substance use
    D) Assessing acute intoxication, substance use history, and withdrawal potential

134. A counselor determines their client is in the contemplation stage. What should the primary goal in counseling be at this time?
    A) Developing coping strategies
    B) Building awareness of the issue
    C) Taking concrete steps toward change
    D) Enhancing readiness for change

135. During screening, a potential client who has been using methamphetamines shares that they experience intermittent suicidal thinking. A counselor's next step should be to
    A) Refer the client to another facility as they are not eligible for services with recurrent suicidal thinking
    B) Ignore this information because the suicidal thinking is likely a psychological symptom of methamphetamine use and will remit once the client is sober
    C) Be aware of the services the counselor's facility can offer and determine if the potential client is appropriate for services
    D) Call emergency services to complete a safety check at the client's home

136. A counselor explores irrational thinking with their client. The counselor is utilizing which counseling theory?
    A) Rational-emotive behavior therapy
    B) Existential theory
    C) Behaviorism
    D) Client-centered

137. The conceptualization of addiction as a disease influenced by biological, psychological, and sociocultural factors and involving complex interactions among brain circuits, genetics, the environment, and life experiences is best captured by which addiction model?
    A) Biopsychosocial
    B) Disease
    C) Sociocultural
    D) Biological

138. A specifier of mild is appropriate when there are
    A) One diagnostic criteria met
    B) Two to three diagnostic criteria met
    C) Six to seven diagnostic criteria met
    D) Four to five diagnostic criteria met

139. A counselor determines their client is in the preparation stage. What process is important during this time for the client?
    A) Developing awareness of the issue
    B) Seeking social support
    C) Taking concrete steps toward change
    D) Exploring pros and cons of change

140. An instructor asks a student to name techniques used in solution focused therapy. Which response by the student needs correction by the counselor?
    A) Miracle question
    B) WDEP
    C) Scaling questions
    D) Pretherapy change

141. Christine is a client who has been gaining weight steadily since entering treatment. She has been snacking often and has been sedentary since entering treatment. When this is brought up in counseling, the counselor notices her response is a defense mechanism. Based on this information what did the client say?
    A) "Why do you want to talk about this?"
    B) "I deserve to relax and have my favorite snacks; it helps me keep my mind off drugs."
    C) "I know I shouldn't eat so much and should be more active; I would feel better."
    D) None of the above

142. In group therapy, Beth has been very angry and often makes statements that are hurtful and spiteful to other group members. Other group members are complaining about it and are threatening to kick Beth out of the group. The group leader also joins in the threat to kick Beth out of the group. What is the most likely leadership style of the group counselor?
    A) Laissez-faire
    B) Democratic
    C) Authoritarian
    D) Authoritative

143. In session, a counselor asks the client to talk to his estranged father about their anger as if the father were in the room. The counselor is operating out of which theoretical orientation?
    A) Cognitive behavioral therapy
    B) Gestalt therapy
    C) Client-centered theory
    D) Psychodynamic therapy

144. Which counseling theory emphasizes the importance of understanding an individual's unconscious conflicts and childhood experiences to address current psychological problems?
    A) Person-centered therapy
    B) Cognitive behavioral therapy
    C) Gestalt therapy
    D) Psychoanalytic therapy

145. Jack is recently discharged from the Air Force after serving in Afghanistan. He has been diagnosed with posttraumatic stress disorder (PTSD) and alcohol use disorder. His substance use counselor at Verteran Affairs (VA) arranged for Jack to attend a support group for veterans who have been deployed while he is in treatment for his alcohol use. The counselor also has arranged for him to go to a mental health treatment program for PTSD after he completes his alcohol use disorder treatment. Which of the following statement is true?
    A) The counselor recognized that Jack has a co-occurring disorder and is providing simultaneous treatment
    B) The counselor recognized that Jack has a co-occurring disorder and is providing parallel treatment
    C) The counselor recognized that Jack needs support and friends and is providing integrated treatment
    D) The counselor recognized that Jack has a co-occurring disorder and has arranged for sequential treatment

146. The ABC-DE model is used in which type of therapy?
    A) Motivational interviewing
    B) Adlerian therapy
    C) Rational emotive behavior therapy
    D) Cognitive behavior therapy

147. How does effective communication contribute to successful referral and case management in substance use counseling?
    A) Requires monthly team meetings to exchange information without the client present
    B) Limits information exchange with other professionals to only what they need to know
    C) Fosters collaboration and ensures a seamless process for clients
    D) Fosters competition between providers to serve the client the best

Tim, a 20-year-old sophomore in college, presents to a counselor after he and two female friends are caught in his residence hall room with a bottle of tequila and a bottle of gin. He and his friends did not leave his room during a fire alarm at 2 a.m. because they were drunk and did not want to get in trouble. He indicates he has not drunk alcohol since this incident which was 2 weeks ago. Prior to this, he was drinking each Friday and Saturday night to intoxication and would occasionally black out. He reported this pattern has been consistent throughout his freshman year and the beginning of his sophomore year of college. He indicated he drank off and on during high school with friends, usually two to three Saturday nights per month. He denies any cravings for alcohol. He reports he is physically healthy. He denies any other substance use.

    Tim stated that he likes drinking because it helps him be more social and less anxious around women. He is not sure if he wants to stay sober as he feels he cannot talk very well to women without drinking. He denies ever having any school problems or that anyone has complained about his drinking. This is the first time he has had any consequences related to his alcohol use. He does not want his parents to know that he was caught drinking as he worries what they will do. He does express some concern that once he starts drinking, he has a hard time predicting how much he will drink that night. He feels this contributes to the blackouts he has. He endorses that he needs to drink more than he used to in order to get the same effect. Due to being caught with alcohol in his residence hall room, he can only continue to live on campus if he follows your recommendations. Several of Tim's friends drink, but he has not felt any pressure from them to drink lately as they know that he is in trouble with the university due to getting caught in his room drinking.

148. Based on the information provided, what is the most likely diagnosis for Tim?
    A) No diagnosis
    B) Alcohol use disorder, mild
    C) Alcohol use disorder, moderate
    D) Alcohol intoxication

149. Tim does not consent to have his parents contacted to provide collateral information due to his concerns about their response if they discover what has happened. Given his refusal, what are the counselor's options to gain collateral information?
    A) Contact Tim's parents anyway; since he is in trouble with the university, it is okay even if he does not consent
    B) Tell Tim that he must allow the counselor to talk to his parents or he will get kicked off campus
    C) Have Tim complete a release of information so the counselor can check Tim's grades and if Tim has any other behavioral infractions on campus
    D) Complete the assessment without any collateral information

150. An example of a psychological factor for Tim is
    A) His friends continue to drink alcohol even though he is not
    B) He is anxious when he talks to women
    C) He experiences blackouts and drinks larger amounts and for longer amounts of time than intended
    D) He did not leave his room during a fire alarm due to fear of getting in trouble

Practice Exam: Answers

1. B) Consulting with a supervisor to explore alternative approaches that respect the client's autonomy while addressing safety concerns
Consulting with a supervisor to explore alternative approaches that respect the client's autonomy while addressing safety concerns reflects a commitment to both the duty to warn and the principle of confidentiality. By consulting with a supervisor, the counselor seeks guidance and explores alternative approaches to address safety concerns while respecting the client's autonomy. This approach allows for a thorough consideration of the ethical dilemma, drawing on the expertise and guidance of a supervisor to make a well-informed decision. Maintaining confidentiality even if there is a risk of harm is both unethical and illegal. Disclosing all client information to relevant parties automatically is a violation of confidentiality. Terminating the relationship does not address the issue at hand.

2. C) Withdrawal effects of the substance use
People who abruptly stop heavy and chronic use of inhalants may experience mild withdrawal symptoms such as outlined in the question. Tolerance and long-term physical effects may occur; however, they don't produce the symptoms identified and the symptoms described are mostly psychological. Read the question and answers carefully and critically evaluate what is being asked.

3. B) Essential to a quality assessment
Clients are informed that gathering collateral information is a part of the assessment process. Consents to disclose to the collateral contact that the client is completing an assessment are secured prior to contacting any collateral contacts to protect the client's confidentiality.

4. A) ZPD is always ahead of the learner's current abilities
The ZPD represents tasks that are just beyond the learner's current abilities, providing a zone for potential learning and development.

5. C) Congruence, unconditional positive regard, and empathy
Using the mnemonic technique as described in the Tips From the Field section, you can remember that client-centered therapy is built on congruence, unconditional positive regard, and empathy: CUE!

6. C) Irritability
The withdrawal symptoms of stimulants fall under the category of irritability, fatigue, trouble sleeping, depression, and lack of motivation.

7. C) Maintenance
Maintenance involves the sustained effort to maintain behavior change and prevent relapse over the long term. Contemplation is the stage characterized by an awareness of the problem and the consideration of change, but no commitment to action has occurred. The action stage is where individuals are engaged in efforts to modify their behavior and environment to overcome substance use. In the preparation stage, individuals start taking specific actions to address their substance use, such as setting a quit date or seeking support.

8. B) Beginning to assess the client's readiness for change
Beginning to assess the client's readiness for change occurs during screening. Conducting group counseling, providing crisis intervention, and collaborating with other professionals are not part of the screening process.

9. A) Ensuring that the chosen technology complies with privacy and security standards to protect client confidentiality
Ensuring that the chosen technology complies with privacy and security standards is crucial for maintaining client confidentiality, which is a fundamental ethical principle in counseling. It aligns with legal requirements and standards related to the protection of sensitive client information, such as the Health Insurance Portability and Accountability Act (HIPAA) in the United States. Using technology that prioritizes privacy and security helps mitigate the risk of unauthorized access to client information, contributing to a safe and secure therapeutic environment. Not seeking client input does not promote client-centered care. Electronic communication methods should not prioritize efficiency over security. Using social media to communicate with clients can lead to boundary violations.

10. C) Ensure the treatment plan remains relevant and responsive
Ongoing assessment in treatment planning ensures that the treatment plan is adjusted as needed to meet the evolving needs of the client. The treatment plan should be regularly reviewed and updated. It is not a "fixed" document as the other choices suggest.

11. D) Not sufficient symptoms for a diagnosis
Repeated legal charges are not one of the diagnostic criteria for a substance use disorder. All the other choices would indicate that it is a diagnostic criteria.

12. C) Combining nicotine replacement products with behavioral therapy
Combining behavioral therapy with the effectiveness of nicotine replacement products such as gums or patches is an evidence-based treatment that works better than medications alone.

13. A) Symptoms of some mental health disorders can be identical to those caused by substance use
Mental health symptoms can mirror substance use disorder symptoms making it critical to screen for and address both when there are co-occurring disorders suspected.

14. C) Developing therapeutic rapport and the therapeutic relationship
The first step in any therapeutic encounter is to build rapport and establish a solid therapeutic relationship. Developing a good rapport and relationship must be done before moving forward to other referrals. Developing an agreement for abstinence is not appropriate at this time.

15. A) Annie is in recovery
Historically, only two outcomes have been seen as possible substance use disorders: abstinence or a return to substance use. The all-or-nothing thinking around recovery and relapse is problematic. The research is clear that relapse is a part of recovery; therefore, Annie is in recovery but has had a relapse.

16. D) Activation of the mesolimbic dopamine system or reward pathway
Opioids activate the brain's reward pathway or mesolimbic dopamine system, commonly referred to as the reward pathway, reinforcing drug-seeking behavior and contributing to the development of dependence.

17. C) Take a history of the client's alcohol use and administer the Clinical Institute Withdrawal Assessment Alcohol Scale Revised (CIWA-AR) to determine the potential severity of the alcohol withdrawal

Alcohol withdrawal can be dangerous if the client has developed tolerance and dependence on the substance. As an alcohol and drug counselor you cannot do a medical exam or a mental health assessment. These would need to be done by the appropriately licensed and credentialed professional. The client's lawyer also has no knowledge regarding the safety of withdrawal. The counselor should take a history of the client's substance use and administer an assessment such as the CIWA-AR to determine the potential severity of withdrawal and then make the appropriate referrals for care.

18. B) A support social network and positive mentoring relationships

This question asks for the protective factors for substance use. Reading carefully the question asks for a protective factor because it asks for the likelihood of a person being resilient to developing a substance use disorder. A supportive social network and positive mentoring relationships are protective factors. Answer B is the only protective factor in the choices.

19. D) Six or more diagnostic criteria met

A severe specifier requires six or more diagnostic criteria to be met. Less than six criteria indicate a diagnosis with a specifier of moderate or mild depending on the number of criteria met.

20. A) Biological, psychological, and social factors

A biopsychosocial assessment considers biological, psychological, and social factors that contribute to potential substance use disorders.

21. A) Veracity

The ethical principle of veracity pertains to truthfulness and honesty in communication. In substance use counseling, it underscores the counselor's obligation to provide accurate and transparent information to clients. This involves being truthful about the nature of the counseling process, potential risks and benefits of treatment, and any other relevant information that can contribute to the client's understanding and decision-making. Fidelity refers to making realistic commitments and keeping promises. Autonomy refers to having the right to their own person, desires, and to make choices that they believe will benefit themselves. Nonmaleficence refers to the avoidance of causing harm.

22. C) Operant conditioning

Operant conditioning is learning that occurs when consequences, either reinforcement or punishment, follow a behavior, while classical conditioning is learning that occurs when two things are repeatedly paired together. Modeling is a behavioral technique that involves the learning of skills through imitating another person.

23. D) Stage 5: Planning, terminating, and follow up

Working with clients on triggers after treatment indicates that the counselor is in Stage 5 of the process; more specifically, following up.

24. C) Central nervous system depression

Opioids can depress the central nervous system, leading to slowed breathing and, in extreme cases, fatal respiratory depression. This is a significant risk, especially in cases of opioid overdose.

25. D) Providing a comprehensive explanation to a client about the limitations on the disclosure of their treatment information and obtaining written consent for any permitted disclosures

42 CFR Part 2 is a federal regulation that mandates the confidentiality of substance use disorder client records. The regulation requires written consent from the client before their substance use treatment information can be disclosed, even to other healthcare providers. It is necessary to obtain written consent for any permitted disclosures and provide a comprehensive explanation to the client about the limitations on the disclosure of their treatment information. This approach ensures that the client is informed and consents to the specific disclosures outlined in the written consent. All other options involve potential breaches of confidentiality or insufficient consent processes, which could violate the requirements of 42 CFR Part 2.

26. D) Alcohol use disorder, severe
Jay presents with symptoms of alcohol use disorder, severe based on the amount and frequency of alcohol use and the number of symptoms reported (more than six: financial problems, health problems, sleep problems, failure to keep a job, craving, withdrawal symptoms, and family problems). Cirrhosis of the liver is not a diagnosis an alcohol and drug counselor can make based on the medical specifier. This diagnosis is outside the scope of practice for an alcohol and drug counselor.

27. C) Naltrexone
Medications are prescribed by doctors to treat alcohol use disorders and other symptoms caused by the withdrawal process or co-occurring disorders. In this case the question asks for medication to treat the alcohol use disorder and not the co-occurring mental health disorders or withdrawal symptoms. Naltrexone is the correct medication from the choices that treat alcohol use disorders. Lithium and an SSRI are used to treat co-occurring mental health disorders and methadone is a medication used to treat opioid use disorder.

28. B) Jay is in the postacute phase of alcohol withdrawal
Jay presents with symptoms of postacute alcohol withdrawal or extended withdrawal. There is no indication of current alcohol use; he has been sober for 3.5 months. Postacute withdrawal syndrome (PAWS) typically starts 3 months after the last drink and can last up to 18 months or even longer. Symptoms Jay reports are consistent with PAWS; that is, headaches, irritability, sadness, craving, cognitive issues, physical discomfort, and sleep problems.

29. B) Jay has a co-occurring medical condition, mostly likely cirrhosis of the liver
Based on the symptoms presented and Jay's history of heavy alcohol use, the doctor is likely concerned about cirrhosis of the liver. Confusion, itching, yellowing of the eyes, and losing weight are all indicators of concern. In this case, coordinating care with the doctor would be indicated to help Jay understand what is happening with his health.

30. D) "You are experiencing a liver disease diagnosed by your doctor called cirrhosis of the liver due to the liver being damaged from metabolizing the alcohol you have been drinking over the years."
While telling Jay "You are experiencing a liver disease called cirrhosis of the liver" is technically correct, it is not the MOST correct. The counselor should provide the correct diagnosis and an explanation to help Jay understand what is occurring and why. The liver metabolizes alcohol which causes scarring and the inability to filter toxins from the body. The buildup of toxins results in many of the symptoms Jay is experiencing. Mentioning that the disease has been diagnosed by Jay's doctor also attributes the diagnosis to the correct medical professional which is important in the scope of practice and in helping the counselor "stay in their professional lane."

31. C) Jay's brain reward pathway has been altered and he is in the preoccupation/anticipation stage of the addiction cycle involving the prefrontal cortex where environmental cues release dopamine and trigger the basal ganglia inducing a strong urge to use the substance
Jay is in the preoccupation/anticipation stage of the addiction cycle involving the prefrontal cortex. Jay is not currently drinking so he is not in the binge/intoxication stage. "Jay's brain reward pathway has been altered by his chronic alcohol use; he cannot help it" could be correct; however, there is more to explain as in the other choices. The withdrawal/negative effect stage is most closely connected to the amygdala and the prefrontal cortex is most closely connected to the preoccupation/anticipation stage.

32. A) Clearly documenting the instances of noncompliance with objective and nonjudgmental language to maintain transparency
Clear documentation with objective and nonjudgmental language maintains transparency in the therapeutic relationship. This is essential for trust between the counselor and the client. Documenting instances of noncompliance accurately reflects the client's progress, ensuring that the treatment plan can be adjusted as needed. Objective and nonjudgmental language demonstrates professionalism and adherence to ethical standards, promoting a collaborative and respectful approach.

33. B) Collaboratively discussing the client's concerns, exploring alternative approaches, and adjusting the treatment plan accordingly

Collaboratively discussing the client's concerns, exploring alternative approaches, and adjusting the treatment plan accordingly reflects a client-centered and collaborative approach. Respecting client autonomy involves acknowledging and exploring the client's concerns and preferences. The counselor can engage in open communication, discuss the reasons behind the recommended treatment plan, and explore alternative approaches that align with evidence-based practices. Adjusting the treatment plan based on mutual agreement and understanding respects the client's autonomy while maintaining ethical standards. Insisting on continuing the current plan, telling the client that alternative methods are invalid, or terminating treatment do not promote client-centered care.

34. B) Withdrawal/negative affect stage

The withdrawal/negative affect stage involves a decrease in dopamine release and an increase in stress related neurochemicals contributing to negative emotions and withdrawal symptoms.

35. A) Gather relevant history from the client including but not limited to alcohol and other substance use using appropriate interviewing techniques

The first task of assessment is to gather relevant history. Identifying assessment tools, developing a diagnostic evaluation, and explaining assessment results occur after the gathering of relevant history from the client.

36. B) Eligibility

The counselor is confirming the information gathered during the screening process and documenting the client's eligibility to attend treatment at this specific agency. Treatment progress and goals, treatment plans, and treatment modality preferences are not addressed in the intake process.

37. B) Providing support and guidance to help a client succeed in a challenging task

Scaffolding involves giving structured support to a learner as they work on tasks within their ZPD, gradually reducing support as they gain proficiency.

38. A) Prior to establishing rapport with the client

Empathic confrontation is a "gentle" skill that relies on the power of the therapeutic relationship to promote change. Using confrontation before rapport is built with a client can have the effect of weakening the therapeutic relationship.

39. C) Only with the client's written consent

Confidentiality is crucial, and counselors can breach it only with explicit, written consent from the client or when mandated by law in specific situations.

40. C) The rules, policies, and expectations of the treatment program

The primary task of orientation is to help the client understand what is expected of them and what they can expect from the program. The counselor's personal experiences with substance use are not relevant at orientation. Consequences of continued substance use is addressed during counseling. Crisis intervention is not a target during orientation.

41. C) The counselor should use utilize motivational interviewing to gather as much information about all of Savannah's substance use

Both Savannah and her parents should be interviewed as part of the assessment. Only focusing on one substance misses the rest of the picture. Using a motivational interviewing approach will help build rapport and help the counselor gather relevant information.

42. D) Dimension 6: Recovery/living environment

Savannah's parents appear supportive of her not using substances. Savannah mentions worry; therefore, there appear to be emotional conditions present (Dimension 3), she has little interest in changing (Dimension 4), and it is highly likely she will return to use in the short term (Dimension 5).

43. B) Outpatient individual and family counseling (ASAM 1)

Savannah was willing to come with her parents to an outpatient assessment. Her parents appear willing to be involved in her care and Savannah is still maintaining in her home, attending school and living in her community. Savannah is using substances on a regular basis; therefore, early intervention is not appropriate. Because she is able to maintain in her home and community, other interventions can be tried before partial hospitalization. Savannah is not exhibiting medical concerns that would require a medically managed intensive inpatient service.

44. B) Respecting clients' right to autonomy

Informed consent involves respecting clients' autonomy by ensuring they have sufficient information to make decisions about their treatment, fostering transparency and respecting their right to choose.

45. D) Utilizing multiple assessment tools to gather a comprehensive understanding of the client's unique needs and tailoring the treatment plan accordingly

Utilizing multiple assessment tools to gather a comprehensive understanding of the client's unique needs and tailoring the treatment plan accordingly demonstrate an ethically sound approach to assessment by emphasizing the use of multiple tools to gather comprehensive information about the client. Tailoring the treatment plan based on a thorough understanding of the client's unique needs ensures that interventions are relevant and effective. Assuming universality in results does not demonstrate multicultural competence. Sharing results with other professionals without consent is a violation of confidentiality. Skipping the assessment phase is not conducive for effective therapy.

46. C) Lungs

Misuse of inhalants, solvents, and aerosols has detrimental effect on several organs; however, among the options, the organ most vulnerable to the toxic effects is the lungs. Inhalants, when misused, can cause serious harm to the respiratory system leading to complications and potential damage to the lungs.

47. A) Binge/intoxication

The Binge/intoxication stage of the addiction cycle involves the consumption of intoxicating substances, activating the brain's reward pathway causing a person to experience the pleasurable effects and rewards from substance use.

48. A) A medical detoxification facility

Alcohol withdrawal can be life-threatening if the client has developed tolerance and dependence on the substance. Referring to a facility that can medically monitor and detoxify the client is the safest course of action.

49. B) They are using cannabidiol (CBD)

THC is the compound that is psychoactive in cannabis. CBD is known for its analgesic pain-relieving properties and does not create the euphoric effects of THC.

50. A) Betty receives only social detoxification at the center without any medical intervention, follow-up care, or counseling to help her interrupt the addiction cycle

It appears that Betty has not been able to go through a medical withdrawal to receive intervention to help her address the biopsychosocial issues of her disease. There are many medications that can help with withdrawal and treatment for opioid use disorder. Follow-up care and counseling are indicated when in recovery from opioid use disorder.

51. B) Betty displayed symptoms that were very unusual for opioid withdrawal; medical personnel suspected drug interactions were occurring

The usual symptoms for opioid withdrawal are flu-like symptoms such as joint pain, muscle aches, mood swings, runny nose, increased heart rate, stomach distress, and heightened reflexes. The other symptoms such as confusion, decreased alertness, and seizures are clues something else may be happening. Even though there may be a co-occurring mental health issue, drug screens cannot detect mental health issues. It is clear Betty needs substance use treatment. It is not true that every hospital screens all clients for drugs.

52. D) The PCP, barbiturates, benzodiazepines, and opioids interacted in a way that caused the grand mal seizure

This is the most comprehensive and accurate explanation as the combined effects of multiple substances can often lead to unpredictable reactions or complications, and potentially inducing seizures. The interaction among all the substances could have significantly contributed to the occurrence of the grand mal seizure due to their combined effects on the central nervous system and their potential to amplify the substance effects.

53. C) Stimulants, depressants, opioids, sedatives, and hallucinogens

Phencyclidine (PCP) is a hallucinogen, barbiturates are sedatives, opioids are opioids, and benzodiazepines are depressants.

54. B) A period where it might be difficult to remember things and think clearly, emotional instability, problems sleeping, and sensitivity to stress

The question highlights the postacute withdrawal syndrome that happens after the acute phase of withdrawal and recovery. Difficulty with memory, emotional instability, problems sleeping, and sensitivity to stress are common symptoms that can occur up to 12 to 18 months after sobriety is achieved. Difficulty with coordination and sensitivity to stress can also occur.

55. D) Determining if an individual has a substance use problem and initially assessing its severity

Screening involves determining if the person needs counseling and if this agency is the most appropriate for the person to receive services. This assessment of severity is not a comprehensive assessment, but rather an initial screening of the person's concerns. This initial screening helps route a potential client to the appropriate level of care. Though intervention in the case of an emergency may occur, this is not the purpose of screening. Treatment goals are identified later in the counseling process.

56. B) Liver

The liver is the main organ responsible for metabolizing alcohol. It processes alcohol into less harmful substances, including acetaldehyde and acetate.

57. A) Affordability and accessibility

The most significant factor from the choices is affordability and accessibility. Inhalants are readily available as common household substances and are relatively inexpensive and easy to buy making them appealing to adolescent.

58. C) Are experiencing a desire to use a substance

A desire to use a substance does not mean a person is going to use the substance nor necessarily need to be referred to treatment. Further, craving is not considered for a specifier of "in sustained remission." Counselors should recognize that craving is a common experience for those in recovery from substance use and may continue for much of their life due to the physiological changes within the person's brain.

59. B) AUDIT

The Alcohol Use Disorder Identification Test (AUDIT) is used to assess risk related to alcohol use. The South Oaks Gambling Screen (SOGS) is used to assess gambling. (car, relax, alone, forget, family or friends, trouble) is used for adolescents. And the drug abuse screening test (DAST-10) assesses drug use.

60. C) Reporting imminent harm or danger to third parties when a client poses a serious threat

The duty to warn is a legal and ethical obligation that arises when a counselor becomes aware that a client poses a serious and imminent risk of harm to themselves or others. In such situations, the counselor may have a duty to disclose information to protect potential victims from harm, even if it involves breaching confidentiality. This duty is in place to prioritize the safety of individuals who might be at risk due to a client's behavior.

61. B) Respectfully exploring the client's cultural beliefs around substance use and integrating them into the treatment plan

Acknowledging and respecting the client's cultural beliefs demonstrate multicultural competence. Multicultural competence in counseling involves recognizing and valuing diverse cultural perspectives. Instead of dismissing the client's traditional beliefs or referring them to another counselor entirely, the counselor explores them with respect and integrates them into the treatment plan, fostering a collaborative and culturally sensitive therapeutic relationship.

62. B) In emergency situations

According to 42 CFR Part 2, disclosure of client information without consent is allowed in emergency situations to prevent serious harm or danger to the client or others. In emergency situations, when there is an immediate threat to the health or safety of an individual, confidentiality rules may be relaxed to the extent necessary to address the emergency. This exception is in place to prioritize the well-being and safety of individuals in critical situations.

63. C) Promotes accountability and commitment

Making goals meaningful and aligned with personal values promotes a sense of accountability and commitment, increasing motivation and the likelihood of successful goal attainment.

64. C) Physical health

Physical health is an example of a biological factor. Family history of mental illness is part of behavioral health. Cultural history and spiritual history are part of biopsychosocial assessment.

65. D) Excretion through urine

Hallucinogens undergo metabolism primarily in the liver before being excreted from the body. This metabolic process results in detection in the urine through drug tests.

66. A) Increased tolerance

Misuse of prescription opioids, such as taking higher doses than prescribed, can lead to increased tolerance and increased risk of overdose as individuals may take larger amounts to achieve the desired effects.

67. B) Jacob and Marshall

In this scenario, the risks of overdose are most concerning with the clients who are using alcohol and sedatives. Both can be life-threatening; alcohol poisoning can occur if too much alcohol is consumed at once and sedatives can depress the central nervous system and cause respiratory depression, coma, or death if too much is in the system. The risks of overdose on cannabis and hallucinogens are very low in general and are not life-threatening.

68. C) "When I drink tea with caffeine, I feel great and have increased energy and can focus really well!"

Moderate caffeine use typically results in positive psychological effects including increased energy, alertness, heightened sense of well-being, and enhanced cognitive skills. Choice B includes physical effects and is not true regarding the known psychological effects.

69. C) Guiding and supporting the client in tasks just beyond their current ability

The MKO's role is to assist and guide the client in tasks that are challenging but achievable with support.

70. C) The counselor is asking only closed-ended questions

The counselor is most likely asking closed-ended questions because it is the most common type of interviewing technique that elicits yes or no answers. There is not enough information to know how attentive the counselor is being, what stage of change Tanya might be in, or how uncomfortable she is.

71. B) There could be cultural differences and expectations regarding eye contact between the client and the counselor

Eye contact is a common behavior that differs among cultures. In the dominate culture of the United States, eye contact is a sign of engagement and respect. In other cultures, direct eye contact is seen as disrespectful or challenging. The eye contact pattern of the husband combined with the statement that he shares with the counselor openly suggests a cultural difference between the counselor's U.S. culture and the client's culture.

72. A) The counselor should broach the topic of cultural differences and take time to learn about the client's cultural beliefs, values, and communication preferences; this will help the counselor understand how to help resolve concerns that have been raised in the referral

Counselors must be able to examine cultural factors with clients and how these factors may be influencing the presenting problems as well as how they are playing out in the session. This process is termed as broaching. Counselors must take the time to discuss culture and be sensitive to how they are impacting treatment to avoid cultural miscommunication and harm to clients.

73. D) Use open-ended questions, reflections, affirmations, and summaries to explore her fears with Tanya

Open-ended questions, reflections, affirmations, and summaries are counseling techniques that are designed to help lower client defensiveness and help the client feel heard. Confrontation will increase a client's defensiveness as will educating a client before they are ready to listen.

74. B) Complete the interview, gather information on the substance use, history of medical and psychiatric problems, and coordinate care to address all these issues

The information indicates that Tanya may be experiencing a psychiatric disorder as well as a substance use disorder. For people who present to counseling with substance use and mental health symptoms, there should be no "wrong door" for them to enter. Treatment for both conditions and both issues should be addressed through coordinating care.

75. A) The counselor operates out of a behavioral theoretical orientation

Going to bars is an action or "behavior" that can lead to relapse. Addressing behaviors and coping skills is a common technique used by counselors who operate out of a behavioral theoretical orientation.

76. B) Obtain written consent from the client to share specific information related to their substance use and mental health treatment with the mental health professional involved in their care

HIPAA and 42 CFR Part 2 both mandate the confidentiality of client information, including substance use and mental health treatment records. To comply with these regulations and ensure effective care coordination, obtaining written consent from the client is necessary. All other options do not use the appropriate approach of respecting the client's privacy and obtaining explicit permission to share specific information with the mental health professional. This written consent should specify the type of information to be shared and the individuals or entities with whom the information will be shared.

77. B) Informed consent

Informed consent is a foundational principle in ethical guidelines for substance use counselors, particularly regarding confidentiality, because it reflects the respect for the client's autonomy and the right to make informed decisions about their treatment. When it comes to confidentiality, informed consent involves providing clients with clear and comprehensive information about the limits of confidentiality, potential exceptions (such as duty to report or duty to warn), and the purpose of collecting and disclosing information.

78. C) Address the issue in therapy

Counselors should address such issues within the therapeutic context, working collaboratively with the client to explore and address concerns without automatically resorting to legal intervention. Confidentiality laws also prevent counselors from reporting illegal activity unless it is occurring on the counselor's premises, or the behavior is a threat to the client or an identified other.

79. A) Addiction Severity Index (ASI)

The ASI uses a structured interview format to assess an adult's condition in areas that are typically affected by substance use, including medical status, employment, family/social functioning, behavioral health, legal status. The AUDIT, SASSI-4, and ACE are client-completed questionnaires.

80. B) Provide a general acknowledgment of having personal experiences with substance use without disclosing specific details

Provide a general acknowledgment of having personal experiences with substance use without disclosing specific details is the most appropriate because it acknowledges the counselor's personal experiences with substance use in a general manner without divulging specific details. This approach allows the counselor to maintain professional boundaries while providing a level of relatability and understanding. It helps address the client's curiosity without compromising the therapeutic relationship or shifting the focus away from the client's needs. Self-disclosure can be a powerful tool in therapy. While it should not be avoided entirely, it must be done mindfully.

81. A) Acknowledge the client's feelings, set clear boundaries, and seek supervision

Seeking supervision will help guide and navigate the situation while providing accountability and protection for the clinician. It is common for clients to experience attraction to their substance use counselor, and it is important to acknowledge it, setting clear boundaries as outlined in the informed consent. Exploring those feelings can be helpful to clients. Terminating or suspending the client is not conductive for the therapeutic relationship. Reciprocating romantic feelings is a violation of boundaries and can harm the client.

82. C) Discussing potential risks, benefits, and alternatives to the proposed treatment

Informed consent is a critical ethical and legal requirement in counseling, and it involves providing clients with clear and comprehensive information about various aspects of the counseling process.

83. B) Acknowledging the potential for dual relationships and discussing it openly with the client, seeking their input and consent

Openly discussing the potential for dual relationships and seeking the client's input and consent demonstrates respect for their autonomy and provides them with the information needed to make an informed decision. Acknowledging the possibility of dual relationships fosters transparency in the therapeutic relationship, which is essential for maintaining trust. In rural communities where dual relationships may be more common, discussing these possibilities allows for a client-centered approach that considers the unique dynamics of the community. Avoiding all interactions outside of scheduled sessions is not realistic in this community. Actively engaging clients in the counselor's social life is a violation of boundaries.

84. C) Nonmaleficence

Nonmaleficence underscores the duty to do no harm. Substance use counselors must prioritize interventions that minimize the risk of harm to clients. Autonomy refers to having the right to their own person, desires, and to make choices that they believe will benefit themselves. Fidelity refers to making realistic commitments and keeping promises. Beneficence means acting in the best interests of clients and promoting their well-being.

85. B) Respecting and integrating clients' diverse cultural backgrounds into the treatment plan

Multicultural competence in counseling involves acknowledging, respecting, and integrating clients' diverse cultural backgrounds into the therapeutic process. The goal is to ensure that counseling practices are sensitive to and inclusive of various cultural perspectives, fostering a more effective and relevant treatment approach for individuals from different cultural backgrounds. It emphasizes cultural humility, understanding, and adaptation to the unique needs and values of each client.

86. C) Provides clients with options and choices for additional support
Referral empowers clients by offering them choices and options for additional support, allowing them to actively participate in their treatment.

87. D) By binding to specific receptors in the central nervous system
Opioids exert their analgesic effects by binding to opioid receptors in the central nervous system, modulating pain perception and response.

88. B) Complete initial agency paperwork
The completion of initial paperwork is the primary goal of the intake process. Providing education about substance use disorders, assessing the client's readiness for change, and establishing rapport are part of the assessment process.

89. A) Four to five diagnostic criteria met
Less than four criteria indicate a specifier of mild or no diagnosis and six or more criteria indicate a specifier of severe.

90. C) It functions as the executive center and controls decision-making
The prefrontal cortex plays a crucial role in decision-making, impulse control, and emotional regulation. In the context of substance use disorders it is involved in regulating substance-seeking behavior and decision-making processes.

91. C) To provide clients with information about the nature of counseling and the potential risks, benefits, and alternatives
Obtaining informed consent is a fundamental ethical practice that ensures clients are fully informed about the nature of counseling, the goals of treatment, potential risks and benefits, and any alternatives available to them. It empowers clients to make informed decisions about their participation in counseling and establishes a foundation of transparency and collaboration between the counselor and the client. It is not primarily about legal protection, ensuring attendance, or obtaining permission to share treatment progress, although those aspects may be included as part of the informed consent process.

92. C) Promoting the well-being and welfare of the client
The principle of beneficence highlights the counselor's ethical responsibility to act in ways that promote the well-being, welfare, and positive outcomes for the client. It involves actively working toward the best interests of the client, fostering their growth, and ensuring that counseling interventions contribute to their overall well-being. This may involve implementing evidence-based practices, providing appropriate interventions, and considering the client's best interests in decision-making. Autonomy refers to having the right to their own person, desires, and to make choices that they believe will benefit themselves. Justice means making services accessible to all clients regardless of background. While confidentiality is essential to the therapeutic relationship, there are times when the counselor is legally and ethically mandated to break confidentiality.

93. D) Justice
Justice means making services accessible to all clients regardless of background. Veracity involves truthfulness and honesty. Autonomy refers to having the right to their own person, desires, and to make choices that they believe will benefit themselves. Fidelity refers to making realistic commitments and keeping promises.

94. C) Client welfare
Counselors must prioritize the best interests and welfare of their clients over any personal, financial, or professional considerations to maintain ethical integrity.

95. D) Ensuring the client receives appropriate and specialized care
The duty to refer emphasizes ensuring the client's best interests by directing them to professionals who can provide appropriate and specialized care when needed.

96. A) Collaborating with colleagues from diverse backgrounds to share insights on cultural perspectives

Collaborating with colleagues from diverse backgrounds allows the counselor to gain insights and perspectives from individuals with different cultural experiences, enhancing cultural competence. Engaging in discussions and sharing insights creates a mutual exchange of cultural knowledge, contributing to a more inclusive and culturally sensitive practice. Seeking input from diverse colleagues demonstrates a commitment to ongoing professional growth and development, aligning with ethical standards in the counseling profession. The counselor should never assume cultural knowledge based on personal experience alone. Avoiding discussions about cultural differences and utilizing standardized treatment approaches do not represent multicultural competency.

97. B) Veracity

Veracity involves truthfulness and honesty. Counselors must provide accurate information and foster trust within the counseling relationship. Autonomy refers to having the right to their own person, desires, and to make choices that they believe will benefit themselves. Fidelity refers to making realistic commitments and keeping promises. Justice means making services accessible to all clients regardless of background.

98. C) Impaired objectivity and professional judgment

Dual relationships can compromise the counselor's ability to maintain objectivity and professional boundaries, potentially leading to ethical violations. They are not likely to improve the therapeutic alliance, enhance trust, or increase client autonomy.

99. C) The gap between what a client can do without assistance and what they can do with assistance

The ZPD represents the zone where learning occurs, as it is the range of tasks that a client cannot yet do independently but can do with guidance.

100. C) It fosters collaboration and shared understanding of treatment objectives

SMART goal setting promotes collaboration between the client and therapist, enhancing shared understanding and engagement in the recovery process.

101. A) Is reliant on her prescription medication

Taking a medication such as clonazepam and then abruptly stopping can result in withdrawal symptoms. If Susan is taking the medication as directed, withdrawal symptoms do not mean she has a substance use disorder; rather, her brain has become "reliant" on having the medication in regular dosages. When taken as prescribed by her doctor, the medication will affect her symptoms in an expected and controlled manner.

102. D) Rick's reaction time is very slow and he cannot walk a straight line when required. In addition, his speech is slurred and he fell when he tried to do the final field test

The legal blood alcohol concentration limit for driving in most regions is .08. At that level, impaired speech, reaction time, and balance occur. At lower levels relaxation occurs and refusing to do some of the tests is merely a choice rather than evidence of impairment.

103. D) Action

Action involves actively engaging in problem-solving and acquiring skills to overcome challenges related to substance use. Maintenance involves the sustained effort to maintain behavior change and prevent relapse over the long term. Contemplation is the stage characterized by an awareness of the problem and the consideration of change, but no commitment to action has occurred. In the preparation stage, individuals start taking specific actions to address their substance use, such as setting a quit date or seeking support.

104. A) Provides a way for the counselor to compare the current client to clients with similar concerns

By comparing the client's results to the cutoff scores provided by the standardized screening tool, a counselor is able to gather additional information to make an accurate diagnosis. Screening tools are not solely utilized to reduce the time spent interviewing a client, but rather to augment the information gathered during the interview. The screening tool's focus is not typically assessing the impact of the client's substance use on their family.

105. C) Providing information about the treatment program

During orientation the counselor provides information about the treatment program. Developing a treatment plan, identifying triggers and coping skills, and evaluating treatment progress are not a part of the orientation process.

106. C) Chronic pain

The only correct choice is chronic pain; depression, schizophrenia, and ADHD are mental health disorders. Chronic pain is a serious medical issue that often co-occurs with substance use disorders.

107. C) The body's adaptation to one substance affecting another in the same class

Cross tolerance pertains to the phenomenon where tolerance to one substance in a certain drug class can influence or affect the body's response or tolerance level to another substance with the same class of drugs.

108. C) Nausea and vomiting

Nausea and vomiting are common symptoms of opioid withdrawal. Withdrawal occurs when a person dependent on opioids abruptly reduces or stops opioid use.

109. A) Open-ended and close-ended questions

Both open- and close-ended questions are used during the motivational interviewing process. The counselor is intentional in choosing what type of question to ask based on the information desired from the question.

110. C) Action

Action involves dealing with setbacks and continuing the commitment to behavior change. Relapse refers to the return to substance use after a period of abstinence or successful behavior change. Maintenance involves efforts to prevent relapse and consolidate the gains made during the action stage. In the preparation stage, individuals start taking specific actions to address their substance use, such as setting a quit date or seeking support.

111. B) Address it using the reflection of feeling skill

The client is displacing (a defense mechanism) his anger toward his mom on the counselor. The reflection of feeling skill can be effectively used to appropriately identify who the client is angry at and "work through" the transference.

112. D) All of the above

Failure to identify and address co-occurring disorders increases the likelihood of relapse, whereas addressing co-occurring disorders promotes overall well-being and increases the likelihood of sustained recovery. Further, co-occurring disorders impact all stages of recovery and thus must be addressed in the treatment planning process.

113. C) Is available in multiple languages

The AUDIT is available in multiple languages and is used with adults. It is free of charge and a counselor can become competent in the use of the AUDIT with little training. It measures alcohol use only; it does not measure cannabis use.

114. C) Nicotine increases the rate of alcohol metabolism, potentially leading to increased alcohol consumption to achieve the same effects

Nicotine increases the stimulant effects of caffeine; it doesn't reduce it. Nicotine reduces the effects of antidepressants and antipsychotics. Nicotine effects receptors in the brain that are very specific to the effects of nicotine, so it is difficult to say if any cross tolerance with other substances occurs. Nicotine does increase the rate of alcohol metabolism which can lead to using more alcohol to feel the effects desired.

115. A) Establishing a sense of purpose and meaning

Advanced recovery involves finding purpose and meaning in life beyond overcoming substance use. Rebuilding relationships with peers is a focus of early and middle recovery. Maintaining abstinence and preventing relapse is a focus of the maintenance stage.

116. B) In a controlled environment

The client does not meet a specifier of in full remission based on 6 months of sobriety. A client would not be referred to a 6-month treatment program if the specifier for their diagnosis is mild.

117. A) Coworker who goes to the bar nightly and goes home after drinking two drinks

The coworker who goes to the bar nightly and drinking two drinks appears to have knowledge as to how to be in a high-risk place and not drink more than intended. The coworkers and friends who currently drink to intoxication each time they are at the bar do not seem to have knowledge that could be useful to Autumn. There is not enough information provided about the bartender to consider them a more knowledgeable other.

118. C) Autumn will arrange a ride home prior to going to the bar to prevent driving after drinking

Arranging a ride home will reduce the risk of Autumn receiving another DUI or injuring herself or someone else due to driving while impaired. This is a harm reduction strategy. The other objectives are attempts for the counselor to convince Autumn to remain abstinent. Though each of the other choices are reasonable objectives, they are not in line with a harm reduction plan. Autumn is not committing to sobriety and desires to experiment regarding her ability to manage her alcohol use. The counselor must work with Autumn to minimize her risk as she engages in this experiment.

119. A) Stabilization

The stabilization stage focuses on stabilizing one's life including the people she associates with and the behavioral choices she is making. Action involves actively engaging in problem-solving and acquiring skills to overcome challenges related to substance use. Maintenance involves the sustained effort to maintain behavior change and prevent relapse over the long term. In the preparation stage, individuals start taking specific actions to address their substance use, such as setting a quit date or seeking support.

120. B) Preparation

Darin has made the decision that he is ready and willing to make a change in his life. He is currently making plans of how he will do this.

121. D) Withdrawal management by itself is not an effective treatment for any substance use disorder

Darin ultimately has a choice if he follows the recommendation of the evaluation. Therefore, he needs information on what effective treatment looks like. Ongoing counseling may make his wife happy; but this is not a clinical rationale for ongoing counseling.

122. C) Case management

Darin has already reached out to his doctor and set into motion his admission to the hospital; therefore, a referral is not necessary. The action of coordinating Darin's care after his discharge from the hospital is a function of case management.

123. C) Marital counseling, self-help meetings, medication assessment for medication-assisted treatment
If Darin consents, he will benefit from these additional services. There is no indication in the information that he needs housing assistance or a personal trainer at this time.

124. B) Make it specific and measurable
Darin can choose for this to be his goal. It is relevant to his sobriety as this is a primary reason he wants to be sober and is time bound because his wife is currently pregnant. However, we do not know what Darin specifically means by this goal or how it can be measured.

125. A) Reduces the client's defensiveness
Explaining to a client what to expect and why a certain technique is going to be used is advised for all clients because it increases the client's engagement, is honest, and lowers their defenses.

126. A) Service to others
Step 12 of AA is as follows: Having had a spiritual awakening as the result of these steps, we tried to carry this message to alcoholics, and to practice these principles in all our affairs. Carrying the message to others is considered service and giving back.

127. C) The counselor operates out of both a behavioral theoretical orientation and is working on a relapse prevention plan with the client
Progressive muscle relaxation is a behavioral counseling technique that is used effectively in relapse prevention.

128. B) Dual-relationships: If Jane shares her full history with Sylvester, it may create a more peer-to-peer relationship rather than a counselor/client relationship
If Jane shares her full history with Sylvester, it may create a more peer-to-peer relationship rather than a counselor/client relationship. Counselors must be cautious with self-disclosure and always consider how the disclosure may impact the counselor/client relationship. Sylvester is not bound by confidentiality guidelines as a client, only you are as the counselor.

129. A) A boundary crossing
Based on the information we currently have, this staff is engaging in behavior that is not typical for a staff member. This is not a behavior that the staff is engaging in with other clients. It is not a boundary violation, as the behavior has not resulted in harm to the Slyvester. However, when the staff is asked to cease sitting in his room, this will likely create a treatment disruption for Sylvester. Boundary crossings create an increased risk for future boundary violations.

130. D) Restrictions on disclosure do not extend to staff within the treatment program
42 CFR Part 2 states that the restrictions on disclosure do not apply to communications of information between or among personnel having a need for the information in connection with their duties that arise out of the provision of diagnosis, treatment, or referral for treatment of clients with substance use disorders if the communications are within the treatment program.

131. D) To provide clients with diverse and appropriate support options
Maintaining a network of community resources allows substance use counselors to offer clients a diverse range of appropriate support options.

132. B) Serotonin
Hallucinogens predominantly affect the brain's neurotransmitter system. Among the options presented, the neurotransmitter system primarily impacted is serotonin. Activation of serotonin receptors leads to alteration in sensory perception, mood regulation, and cognition, aligning with changes in perception, mood, and cognitive processes induced by hallucinogens.

133. D) Assessing acute intoxication, substance use history, and withdrawal potential
Some substances are hazardous to withdraw, making it very important to assess the withdrawal potential of the substance to make appropriate recommendations for treatment.

134. D) Enhancing readiness for change
Contemplation involves assessing and enhancing the individual's readiness and commitment to change. Building awareness of the issue is the goal during the precontemplation stage. Taking concrete steps toward change is a goal of the preparation stage. Developing coping strategies is a goal of the action stage.

135. C) Be aware of the services your facility can offer and determine if the potential client is appropriate for services
Some facilities have the capacity to treat and/or monitor mental health symptoms such as suicidal thinking whereas others do not. It is essential that a counselor is aware of their facility's ability to serve this client. Suicidal thinking is an appropriateness criteria not an eligibility criteria. Ignoring the information and making assumptions is not effective screening. The counselor should not call emergency services as there is no evidence that the client is in imminent danger.

136. A) Rational-emotive behavior therapy
Irrational thinking is a concept used most often in rational-emotive behavior therapy (REBT). While other theories may reference it, such as cognitive therapy, REBT relies on irrational thinking as a key target of change.

137. A) Biopsychosocial
The most comprehensive model of substance use is the biopsychosocial model of addiction which combines the disease model with the psychological and social/cultural models of substance use disorders to arrive at a comprehensive conceptualization of addiction; and the one that is the most well accepted in the treatment field. This is clearly seen in the definition of addiction as put forth by the American Society of Addiction Medicine.

138. B) Two to three diagnostic criteria met
One criteria is insufficient for a diagnosis, more than three criteria indicate a moderate or severe specifier depending on how many criteria are met.

139. C) Taking concrete steps toward change
In preparation, individuals take specific actions to prepare for behavior change. Building awareness of the issue is the goal during the precontemplation stage. Building social support is a goal of the contemplation stage. Taking concrete steps toward change is a goal of the preparation stage. Examining pros and cons of change is part of the contemplation stage.

140. B) WDEP
WDEP is an acronym that refers to the structure used in reality therapy; it stands for wants, doing, evaluation, and planning. Solution focused therapy is a brief model of therapy that is built on the client's strengths and problem-solving abilities. In solution focused therapy, the miracle question is used to help clients envision a future where the problem does not exist, and scaling questions are used to measure client progress. Pretherapy change in solution focused therapy is the change that occurs from the time the client made the counseling appointment to the first session. This focuses the client on the reality that change does and can occur.

141. B) "I deserve to relax and have my favorite snacks; it helps me keep my mind off drugs."
The rationalization defense mechanism is finding a satisfactory way to do something unacceptable, such as eating too much because it will help relieve the urge to use substances. Asking a question and admitting that she would feel better if she was more active is not a defense mechanism.

142. A) Laissez-faire
The group leader has become a part of the group indicating that the style of leadership is laissez-faire, allowing the group members to take accountability for the group. In the democratic style of leadership, the leader would be sharing the communication but not taking a "side" and the authoritarian group leader would make all the decisions. There is no category of group leadership labeled authoritative.

143. B) Gestalt therapy
Gestalt therapy uses many experiential techniques to bring client's issues into the here and now in the counseling session. A client talking to their estranged father as if he were in the room is an empty chair technique which is used frequently in Gestalt therapy.

144. D) Psychoanalytic therapy
Psychoanalytic therapy is based on Freud's theories of unconscious conflicts, drives, and personality structures that are set in early childhood resulting from the child's experiences. Person-centered therapy was developed by Carl Rogers based in a humanistic approach of unconditional positive regard and empathy. Cognitive behavioral therapy is the most researched approach that emphasizes thoughts and behaviors as mechanism of change, while Gestalt therapy is a process-based therapy where the individual is understood in relation to the environment and things around them.

145. D) The counselor recognized that Jack has a co-occurring disorder and has arranged for sequential treatment
The counselor did recognize that Jack has a co-occurring disorder and the arrangements he made for treatment are sequential. That is, Jack is first being treated for the substance use disorder and then will be treated for the mental health disorder after the substance use disorder treatment is completed.

146. C) Rational emotive behavior therapy
Rational emotive behavior therapy is a structured therapy process with the steps described by the acronym ABC-DE where *A* is the activating event, *B* is the belief about the event, and *C* is the consequences, both emotional and behavioral, of holding on to the irrational beliefs. It is the irrational beliefs in *B* that are targeted in counseling. Counselors have the client dispute (*D*) the irrational beliefs and work toward embracing more rational beliefs which leads to a new effective philosophy (*E*) that has healthier behavioral and emotional consequences.

147. C) Fosters collaboration and ensure a seamless process for clients
Effective communication enhances collaboration among professionals, leading to a seamless process for clients and improving the overall effectiveness of referral and case management.

148. B) Alcohol use disorder, mild
Tim identifies two symptoms of an alcohol use disorder: drinking more than intended and tolerance. A specifier of mild is appropriate as two to three symptoms are endorsed by the client. Tim was intoxicated the night he was discovered in his residence hall room; however, he is not intoxicated now, thus a diagnosis of alcohol intoxication is not appropriate.

149. C) Have Tim complete a release of information so the counselor can check Tim's grades and if Tim has any other behavioral infractions on campus
Tim indicated his alcohol use has not caused any other problems, including any other campus infractions or grade concerns. Verifying this information is an important part of the assessment and will offer valuable information whether Tim's alcohol use is impacting him more than he acknowledges. Completing the assessment without collateral information is not best practice. Contacting Tim's parents without a release of information is a violation of confidentiality and demanding Tim do so by issuing a threat damages the therapeutic relationship and violates Tim's right to confidentiality.

150. B) He is anxious when he talks to women
Anxiety when talking to women is a significant psychological factor and appears to be his main motivation to drink. Tim's friends continuing to drink is a social factor while blackouts and drinking more than intended is a physiological factor. Tim not leaving his room due to fear of getting in trouble is not an ongoing factor in his alcohol use.

Index

ACA. *See* American Counseling Association
acceptance and commitment therapy (ACT), 169
accurate empathic understanding, 159
ACT. *See* acceptance and commitment therapy
active listening skills, 172–173
actualizing tendency, 159–160
addiction
    binge/intoxication stage, 25, 26
    biological model, 23
    biopsychosocial model, 23
    definition of, 23
    disease model, substance use, 23
    preoccupation/anticipation stage, 25, 26
    psychological model, 23
    sociocultural model, 23
    withdrawal/negative affect stage, 25, 26
addiction counseling exam
    alcohol and drug counselor (ADC) exam (*see* alcohol
        and drug counselor (ADC) exam)
    credentialing basics, 2–3
    history of, 1–2
Addiction Severity Index (ASI), 90
ADHD. *See* attention deficit hyperactivity disorder
Adlerian therapy, 157
advanced counseling skills, 176–177
adverse childhood experiences (ACE), 190
alcohol
    drug interactions and cross tolerance, 32
    pharmacological actions of, 30–31
    psychological and social effects, 31–32
    short- and long-term effects, 32
    withdrawal effects, 32–33
alcohol and drug counselor (ADC) exam, 1, 153, 209
    12 core functions, 3, 4, 7–9
    client assessment, 89–112
    client counseling, 153–190
    client engagement, 71–81
    co-occurring disorders, 188–190
    pathways of recovery, 186–187
    performance domains, 3, 6–7
    physiology and psychopharmacology, 23–52
    professional, ethical, and legal responsibilities,
        209–228
    scoring guidelines for, 4–5
    testing logistics for, 5
    test-taking strategies and tips, 13–18
    treatment planning, 123–142
alcohol and drug screening, 98
alcohol withdrawal syndrome, 32
American Counseling Association (ACA), 209

American Society of Addiction Medicine (ASAM), 124
    continuum of care, 102–104
    dimensions, 100, 101
    risk rating, 100–102
analytical psychology, 157
ASAM. *See* American Society of Addiction Medicine
ASI. *See* Addiction Severity Index
assertive community treatment, 189
association for addiction professionals, 214
attention deficit hyperactivity disorder (ADHD), 34
authoritarian leadership style, 178
aversion therapy, 167

BAC. *See* blood alcohol concentration
basic listening skills
    asking questions, 175, 176
    attending, 173–175
    client observation, 174–176
    encouragers, 174, 175
    paraphrases, 174, 175
    summaries, 174, 175
BCT. *See* behavioral couples therapy
behavior theory
    aversion therapy, 167
    behavior modification, 166
    biofeedback treatment, 167
    in classical conditioning, 164
    exposure therapies, 166
    extinction, 164
    mindfulness and acceptance, 167
    operant conditioning, 164
    progressive muscle relaxation, 166
    social skills training, 167
    systematic desensitization, 166
behavioral couples therapy (BCT), 183
biofeedback treatment, 167
biopsychosocial assessment, 89
blood alcohol concentration (BAC), 30, 31
boundaries, 215–216
brief strategic family therapy (BSFT), 183
BSFT. *See* brief strategic family therapy
burnout, 190

caffeine, 33–34
cannabis, 34–35
CBM. *See* cognitive behavior modification
Center for Substance Abuse Treatment (CSAT), 1, 209
client assessment
    Addiction Severity Index (ASI), 90
    alcohol/other drug history, 95–96

client assessment (*cont.*)
  behavioral health history, 97–98
  biopsychosocial assessment, 89
  biopsychosocial history, 91
  clinical impression, 102–107
  cognitive behavioral assessment, 90
  collateral information, 90, 98–99
  co-occurring assessment, 90
  definition, 89
  demographics, 92
  diagnosis/screening instruments, 99–102
  evidence-based screening and assessment, 90
  family/social/peer history, 97
  gathering relevant history, 90–91
  legal history, 96
  limits of confidentiality, 91
  medical history, 92, 94–95
  motivational interviewing (MI), 90
  observation and clinical interviews, 90
  open-ended *versus* close-ended questions, 91
  presenting problem/primary complaint, 92
  school/work/military history, 95
  standardized screening tools, 90
  substance use assessment, 92–94
client engagement
  definition, 71, 72
  intake process, 76–78
  orientation, 78–81
  screening, 72–76
clinical impression
  DSM-5-TR diagnostic criteria for diagnosing and
    classifying substance use disorders, 103–106
  gambling behaviors, 105
  length of time, 105
  recommendations, 107
cognitive behavior modification (CBM), 168
cognitive behavioral approaches
  cognitive behavioral therapy, 168
  cognitive therapy, 167
  mindfulness- and acceptance-based cbt approaches, 169
  reality therapy/choice theory, 168–169
cognitive behavioral groups, 180
cognitive behavioral therapy (CBT)
  behaviorism, 164, 166–167
  cognitive behavior modification, 168
  cognitive therapy, 167
  rational emotive behavior therapy, 168
  strength-focused cognitive behavioral therapy, 168
community reinforcement and family training (CRAFT),
  182
compassion fatigue, 190
confidentiality
  limits of confidentiality, 210–211
  privacy and trust, 210
conflict of interest, 217
congruence/genuineness, 159
co-occurring disorders (CODs), 153, 188–189
coping skills, 90, 168, 180
counseling
  client education core function, 184
  cognitive behavioral approaches, 164–169
  core function and global criteria, 153–154
  crisis intervention core function, 183, 184

family and significant others, 181–183
group counseling, 178–181
humanistic- and relationship-oriented approaches,
  158–164
postmodern and systems approaches, 169–172
psychodynamic approaches, 154–158
special considerations for addiction, 185–190
special populations, 184–185
stages of counseling, 172
study resources, 191
techniques, 172–178
theories and evidence-based treatments, 154
counseling relationship
  boundaries, 215–216
  conflict of interest, 217
  dual relationships, 216–217
  gifts, 218
  self-disclosure, 218
  social relationships, 216
counselor self-disclosure, 173
countertransference, 155–156
CRAFT. *See* community reinforcement and family training
craving, 26, 28, 32, 35, 38, 40, 42, 43, 47, 48, 53, 90, 96,
  105, 106, 126, 131, 188
credentialing process
  International Certification and Reciprocity
    Consortium, 2
  job analysis, 2
CSAT. *See* Center for Substance Abuse Treatment
cultural competence, 185, 221, 222

DBT. *See* dialectical behavioral therapy
defense mechanisms, 155, 156
democratic leadership style, 178
Department of Health and Human Services (DHHS),
  125, 209
DHHS. *See* Department of Health and Human Services
dialectical behavioral therapy (DBT), 169
discharge planning
  continued care plan, 223–224
documentation and record keeping, 213–214
dual relationships, 216–217

ego, 155
EHR. *See* electronic health record
electronic health record (EHR), 211
EMDR. *See* eye movement desensitization and
  reprocessing
empathy, 173
engagement process, 71
ethical decision-making, 219
ethics
  assessment, evaluation, and interpretation, 222–223
  communication and technology, 218–219
  confidentiality, 215
  counseling relationship, 215–218
  discharge planning and termination, 223–226
  diversity, equity, inclusion, and access, 221–222
  ethical decision-making, 219
  framework for ethical decision-making, 219–220
  grievances, 220
  professional development and licensure, 220–221
  referral, 223

supervision and consultation, 220–221
termination, 226–228
existential therapy, 160
exposure therapies, 166
eye movement desensitization and reprocessing
(EMDR), 166

family counseling
intervention, 182
self-help group, 183
substance use disorders roles in, 181, 182
treatment strategies, 182–183
family systems therapy, 171–172
feminist therapy, 171
flooding, 166
functional family therapy, 183

Gestalt, 160
Gorski's CENAPS model, 188
grievances, 220
group counseling
content and processes, 178–180
ethics in, 181
leadership styles, 178
models of, 180–181

hallucinogens, 35–37
harm reduction, 127
Health Insurance Portability and Accountability Act
(HIPAA), 209
confidentiality, 210–211
informed consent, 211–212
legal processes and terms, 212
HIPAA. *See* Health Insurance Portability and
Accountability Act
humanistic- and relationship-oriented approaches
existential therapy, 160
gestalt, 160
Maslow's hierarchy of needs, 158–159
motivational enhancement therapy, 164
motivational interviewing, 160–161
person-centered therapy, 159–160
hyperalgesia, 38

IC&RC. *See* International Certification and Reciprocity
Consortium
id, 154
individuation, 157
inhalants, solvents, and aerosols, 37–38
intake process
complete required documents for admission, 77
documentation of eligibility and appropriateness, 77
signed consents, 77–78
intensive case management (ICM), 189
interpersonal process groups, 181
International Certification and Reciprocity Consortium
(IC&RC), 1, 2, 153, 209

job analysis, 2

laissez-faire leadership style, 178
legal issues
documentation and record keeping, 213–214

federal regulations: 42 CFR part 2, 213
HIPAA, 209–212
scope of practice, 212–213
technology, 214
limits of confidentiality
abuse or neglect of vulnerable individuals, 211
danger to self, 210
harm to others, 210–211

Maslow's hierarchy of needs, 158–159
MBCT. *See* mindfulness-based cognitive therapy
MBRP. *See* mindfulness-based relapse prevention
MBSR. *See* mindfulness-based stress reduction therapy
MDFT. *See* multidimensional family therapy
MET. *See* motivational enhancement therapy
MI. *See* motivational interviewing
microskills
advanced counseling skills, 176–177
basic listening skills, 173–176
using verbal and nonverbal communication skills,
177–178
mild substance use disorder, 28, 29
mindfulness- and acceptance-based CBT approaches
acceptance and commitment therapy, 169
dialectical behavioral therapy, 169
mindfulness-based cognitive therapy (MBCT), 169
mindfulness-based relapse prevention (MBRP),
169, 188
mindfulness-based stress reduction therapy (MBSR), 169
moderate substance use disorder, 28
motivational enhancement therapy (MET), 164
motivational interviewing (MI)
action, 161
ambivalence to change, 161
change talk, 162
confidence ruler, 163
contemplation, 160
importance ruler, 163
maintenance, 161
motivational interviewing pyramid, 161
open ended questions, affirmations, reflective
listening, and summarizations (OARS), 162
precontemplation, 160
preparation, 161
principles of, 161, 162
sustain talk, 162
multidimensional family therapy (MDFT), 183

NAADAC. *See* National Association for Alcoholism
and Drug Abuse Counselors
narcotics. *See* opioids
National Association for Alcoholism and Drug Abuse
Counselors (NAADAC), 209

OARS. *See* open ended questions, affirmations,
reflective listening, and summarizations
open ended questions, affirmations, reflective
listening, and summarizations (OARS), 162
opioid neurotransmitters, 24
opioids
drug interactions and cross tolerance, 39
medications for, 33, 40
natural, 38

opioids (*cont.*)
  psychological and social effects, 39
  semisynthetic, 38
  short- and long-term effects, 39, 40
  synthetic, 38
  withdrawal effects, 39–40
orientation
  client obligations and rights, 79–80
  goals and objectives, 78–79
  program operations, 80–81
  program rules, 79

person-centered language, 173
post acute withdrawal syndrome, 47–49
postmodern and systems approaches
  family system structure, 169, 170
  family systems therapy, 171–172
  feminist therapy, 171
  narrative therapy, 171
  solution-focused therapy, 169, 171
psychoanalytic theory, 154–157
  Carl Jung theory, 157
  countertransference, 155–156
  defense mechanisms, 155, 156
  ego, 155
  Erikson psychosocial stages, 156, 157
  id, 154
  psychosexual stages, 155–156
  superego, 155
  transference, 155–156
psychodynamic approaches, counseling
  adlerian therapy, 157
  psychoanalytic theory, 154–157
  transactional analysis, 157–158
psychoeducational groups, 180

rational emotive behavior therapy (REBT), 168
reality therapy/choice theory, 168–169
REBT. *See* rational emotive behavior therapy
recovery
  clinical and nonclinical recovery pathways, 186
  crisis of identity, 128
  developmental model of recovery, 127–130
  goal and objective development, 134–137
  Gorski's developmental model of recovery, 126
  harm reduction, 127
  meetings, 187
  motivational crisis, 128
  relapse prevention, 187–188
  stage-based treatment planning, 130–133
  12-step and other support groups, 186–187
  zone of proximal development (ZPD), 133–134
referral, 223
relapse prevention
  Gorski's CENAPS model, 188
  mindfulness-based, 188
  relapse prevention model, 187–188
relapse prevention model (RPM), 187–188
reward pathway, 24
RPM. *See* relapse prevention model

SAMHSA. *See* Substance Abuse and Mental Health
  Services Administration

scope of practice, 212–213
screening
  admission or referral eligibility, 75–76
  appropriateness for admission or referral, 74–75
  identifying coexisting conditions, 76
  laws, regulations, and agency policies, 76
  psychological, social, and physiological symptoms
    of, 72–74
sedatives, hypnotics, and anxiolytics, 40–41
self-disclosure, 218
severe substance use disorder, 28
sexual boundaries, 216
sexually transmitted infections (STIs), 211
SF-CBT. *See* strength-focused cognitive behavioral
  therapy
skills development groups, 180
SMEs. *See* subject matter experts
social detoxification programs, 33
social relationships, 216
social skills training, 167
solution-focused therapy, 169, 171
stage-based treatment planning
  catalysts for change, 131, 132
  environmental reevaluation strategies, 131
  homework assignments, 130–131
  level of awareness and acceptance, 130
  social liberation, 132
  stages of change, 130, 131
  stimulus control and reinforcement management, 133
stimulants, 41–42
STIs. *See* sexually transmitted infections
strength-focused cognitive behavioral therapy
  (SF-CBT), 168
subject matter experts (SMEs), 2
Substance Abuse and Mental Health Services
  Administration (SAMHSA), 130, 162
substance use disorders
  addiction cycle, 25–26
  alcohol, 30–33
  brain structures involved in, 24–25
  caffeine, 33–34
  cannabis, 34–35
  clinical impression, 102–107
  common substances of misuse, 44–46
  co-occurring medical and mental health conditions,
    49–52
  cross tolerance, 30
  *Diagnostic and Statistical Manual of Mental Disorders
    (DSM)* criteria, 28–29
  hallucinogens, 35–37
  inhalants, solvents, and aerosols, 37–38
  medications and medication-assisted treatment, 47
  models and scientific principles, 23
  neurobiology of, 24
  opioids, 38–40
  post acute withdrawal syndrome, 47–49
  principles for effective treatment, 126, 127
  progression of, 28
  risk and protective factors for, 26–27
  roles in families impacted by, 181, 182
  sedatives, hypnotics, and anxiolytics, 40–41
  stimulants, 41–42
  substances of misuse by drug class, 44

tobacco/nicotine, 43–44
trauma, 189–190
withdrawal assessments, 47, 48
withdrawal effects, 30
superego, 155
synesthesia, 36
systematic desensitization, 166

TA. *See* transactional analysis
telehealth, 214
termination, 226–228
test-taking strategies and tips
accommodations, 15
brain's role in testing anxiety, 13
counseling, 16
positive self-talk, 18
practice tests, 14
reschedule, 16
schedule your exam, 14

tolerance, 28, 30, 32-36, 38-41, 96, 105
transactional analysis (TA), 154, 157–158
transference, 155–156
treatment planning
case management, 138–139
creating a recovery pathway, 126–137
plan development, 125–126
referral, 137
resistant or ambivalent, 124
treatment plan reviews, 139–142

unconditional positive regard, 159

vicarious trauma, 190

Wernicke–Korsakoff's disease, 32

zone of proximal development (ZPD), 133–134
ZPD. *See* zone of proximal development